Understanding
Mutual
Funds
Your No-Nonsense
Everyday Guide

STEVEN G. KELMAN

THE GLOBE AND MAIL

Penguin Books

PENGUIN BOOKS
Published by the Penguin Group
Penguin Books Canada Ltd., 10 Alcorn Avenue, Suite 300, Toronto, Canada, M4V 3B2
Penguin Books Ltd., 27 Wrights Lane, London W8 5TZ, England
Viking Penguin Inc., 40 West 23rd Street, New York, New York 10010, USA
Penguin Books Australia Ltd., Ringwood, Victoria, Australia
Penguin Books (NZ) Ltd., 182-190 Wairau Road, Auckland 10, New Zealand
Penguin Books Ltd., Registered Offices: Harmondsworth, Middlesex, England

Published in Penguin Books, 1996

10 9 8 7 6 5 4 3 2 1

Copyright © Steven G. Kelman, 1996. Tabular and graphic materials in Chapters 11, 12, 13 and 14 and Appendixes 2, 3 and 4 © Portfolio Analytics Limited, 1996.
All queries should be addressed to Globe Information Services, 444 Front Street West, Toronto, Ontario M5V 2S9; (416) 585-5250

Canadian Cataloguing in Publication Data
The National Library of Canada has catalogued this publication as follows:

Kelman, Steven G. (Steven Gershon), 1945 –
 Understanding mutual funds
(Financial times personal finance library)
Annual.
Description based on: 1993
At head of title: Financial Times, 1989-1995; The Globe and Mail, 1996-
Issues for 1996-... published in the series: The Globe and Mail personal finance library.
Continues: Kelman, Steven G. (Steven Gershon), 1945- , Mutual fund advisor.
ISSN 1193-8994
ISBN 0-14-026256-3 (1996)
1. Mutual funds – Canada – Periodicals. I. Title. II. Title: Financial Times. III. Title: Globe and Mail. IV. Series: The Globe and Mail Personal Finance Library.
HG5154.5.K45   332.63'27   C93-030705-4

Cover design by: Creative Network
Cover illustration by: Peter Yundt

CONTENTS

Tables and Illustrations

Charts

Tables

Introduction

READERS OF THE PREVIOUS nine editions will notice a major change in the current edition of *Understanding Mutual Funds*. Rather than abandon readers to wallow through the 1,300 or so funds offered in Canda to make their choices, I decided to take a more aggressive stance and recommend some funds by name. The recommendations are tied to certain scenarios. You should think of them as guidelines to consider against your own specific needs and analysis, or the recommendations of your financial adviser.

I decided against using any sort of historical ranking as the sole means of choosing funds. While past performance is important, especially when fund managers' contributions are separated from market performance, historical rankings are generally poor indicators of future performance.

More important are a fund's current holdings when examined against possible market scenarios. That is the direction I have taken in constructing my lists of recommended funds. These lists include those funds whose managers have demonstrated an ability to provide superior performance usually without excessive risk and which, in my opinion, would most likely meet investors' particular needs, market views and objectives as certain market scenarios unfold.

I was able to do this because of the collaboration of Portfolio Analytics Inc. and specifically Scott Mackenzie. Portfolio Analytics is in the business of supplying fund information to the mutual fund industry. Portfolio Analytics is best known among mutual fund professionals as the provider of the PALtrak mutual fund disk which many use for their analysis of funds.

Portfolio Analytics has a superb data base of mutual fund holdings which are key to many of my recommendations. It created the unique Appendix 3 which provides mammoth amounts of information about specific groups of funds in an easy-to-comprehend format. Portfolio Analytics also provides the ratings which I use as my initial screen in selecting funds.

I should note at this point that Portfolio Analytics' chairman, Dr. William R. Waters, designed the first monthly Canadian mutual fund tables which categorized equity funds by risk. They first appeared in *Financial Times of Canada* in January, 1978, and covered the fund universe of a couple of hundred funds with total assets of $1.5 billion — less than 1 per cent of the industry asset base today.

As everyone who follows fund performance quickly learns, the best performing funds in any given period aren't necessarily the best performers in the subsequent period. Indeed, securities regulations require fund companies and anyone who distributes fund sales material to include in the small print a notice to the effect that past performance may not be indicative of future performance.

Nevertheless, past performance of course is an important consideration in choosing mutual funds. But it should not be viewed in isolation. Rather it should be viewed in terms of its components and risk. For my purposes, risk or volatility measure the magnitude of the variation in a fund's monthly rate of return. Risk generally reflects a fund's objectives and management style is fairly constant over time.

As I previously noted, in building the lists I asked Portfolio Analytics to screen for funds which have provided superior performance which cannot be explained by market movements alone. In other words, I searched for those funds whose superior performance reflects the decisions of their managers as well as the moves of markets in which they invest.

My analysis went one step further by considering the holdings of a specific fund against a market scenario. For example, I believe that the Canadian stock market will be a world leader over the next several years as global economic expansion buoys commodity prices and sales values and volumes. That bodes well for Canadian equity funds as well as resource funds. On page 121 you will find a table listing those equity funds which have hefty weightings of resources and a superior track record. These are the funds I recommend you choose from if you agree with the scenario. A similar analysis of portfolio holdings results in the list on page 111 of bond funds which will likely do well if interest rates decline from current levels over the short term.

In total, I make recommendations covering about 30 scenarios.

Diversification among mutual funds is an important means of moderating risk. Portfolio Analytics prepared lists of funds whose monthly returns are highly correlated. Investors seeking diversification among fund managers will be able to use these lists to build portfolios whose risk will probably be less than each of the component funds taken separately.

In addition, Portfolio Analytics has prepared what are the most comprehensive and most useful fund tables available in Canada. At a glance readers will be able to determine the key elements of a fund's portfolio as well as its relative performance and risk.

Readers should realize that there are always unpredictable elements which can affect the performance of a fund. Consequently, they should consider my recommendations as opinions based on the data available at the time the recommendations were made, adapted to my views on the outlook for the various markets. Despite the shortcomings inherent in these recommendations, the methodology seems to work better than systems which simply take a medium— or long-term performace figure as the basis for purchase.

We've had a bull market in equities since October, 1990, (some people use 1987 as their starting point). However, markets move in cycles and at some point prices will move sharply lower. To put expected returns in context of what has happened in the past, I asked Portfolio Analytics to include best-case and worst-case performance figures for holding funds for various time periods. I strongly recommend that newcomers to the markets acquaint themselves with these figures.

Since the last edition of *Understanding Mutual Funds* there have been two major developments which will have significant impact on mutual fund investors and the industry.

The first is the development of a draft Code of Sales Practices by the mutual fund industry. The second is the establishment of the Financial Planners Standards Council of Canada.

The draft Code of Sales Practices will probably be adapted (possibly with minor variations) by securities regulators in 1996 and will apply to fund managers and fund distributors. The development of the code was spurred in part by the 256-page report

Regulatory Strategies for the Mid-'90s: Recommendations for Regulating Investment Funds in Canada which was released by OSC Commissioner Glorianne Stromberg in January, 1995.

If implemented, the code will prohibit sales practices which could result in conflicts between the interests of an investor and the fund manager, fund distributor and salesperson. The major area covered is distributor compensation. Some of the recommendations simply implement what most people would consider good business practices and internal control. For instance, the code requires that all compensation be payable to the distributor rather than its officers, directors, salespeople, or employees and that no officer, director, salesperson or employee accept compensation tied to mutual fund sales except from the distributor firm — his or her employer.

All compensation payable to a fund distributor must be disclosed clearly and completely in a fund prospectus.

The code prohibits specific practices which might lead to conflicts. For instance, the payment of bonus commissions based on sales or asset levels could give rise to conflict. Similarly, tying the rate paid on trailer commissions to sales volumes or assets is also prohibited (trailer commissions are deferred commissions paid to a salesperson generally quarterly for servicing an account).

Fund salespeople are generally paid a portion of the commission received by the distributor. Some distributors, to encourage sales of one fund group over another, would apply different payout ratios to different fund groups. The code prohibits discrimination among mutual fund companies through such payout variations.

The code also puts restrictions on cooperative marketing practices in which a fund company finances a portion of the expenses pertaining to an investment seminar, newsletter or advertisement. The new rules require that all parties contributing to the funding or the cooperative effort be clearly identified and the amount of reimbursement be restricted to 50 per cent of the costs. Previously, a dealer might approach several fund companies asking each to pick up a portion and recoup all of its costs

Another area covered is what is known as reciprocal commissions. In the past, it was not uncommon for a mutual fund manager to direct that a portion of the portfolio commissions be allocated to certain brokers as a reward for selling units of the fund. As there is absolutely no benefit to the unitholders and major potential for conflict of interest, this practice has been banned (commissions can continue to be allocated to certain firms for payment of research and certain other services which benefit the investors in a fund).

In the area of education, fund managers may sponsor conferences, seminars and reimburse distributor firms for the cost of fees of third party educational courses taken by salespersons. The managers are prohibited from paying sales or subsidizing travel and hotel expenses. As to conferences sponsored by fund distributors, no fund manager may pay more than 10 per cent of the total conference costs, and total subsidies provided by all fund managers may not exceed two-thirds of the total costs.

Some distributors had lists of recommended funds which it encouraged its salespeople to promote. The criteria for getting on such a list was a payment to a marketing incentive program. Payment of cash marketing allowances or other marketing incentive is prohibited. The exceptions are the normal tickets and trinkets companies in every industry use to promote their products and services to independent sales forces.

Switching investors from one fund to another has always been an area of potential conflict. However, there has been some specific concern about a practice in which a fund manager sets up a program to reimburse investors for redemption fees payable if investors redeem a fund and buy units of the manager's fund. This encourages switching, which may or may not benefit investors and generally leads to a new redemption schedule. Fund managers are prohibited from participating in such programs except when one mutual fund company is acquired by another fund company or where the transfers are within the same company and there is no change to the investor's original redemption schedule.

Distributors are given more leeway. A distributor can rebate commissions to a client provided the client is provided with written disclosure of any applicable changes in the redemption schedule and costs and the trade complies with the suitability rules.

The code also prohibits a fund manager providing loans or guarantees to a fund distributor or salesperson. Similarly, it prohibits payment of commissions in advance. The prohibition doesn't apply to financial assistance among affiliated companies. However, a fund manager must fully disclose any such arrangement in its prospectus where it has an equity interest in the distributor that may sell the manager's funds.

While investment counsellor or investment adviser are terms defined in securities legislation, anyone (outside Quebec) can call himself or herself a financial planner whether or not he or she has any qualifications. Moreover, there are a number of organizations which have been offering programs which led to various financial planning designations.

This appears to be changing. The Financial Planners Standards Council of Canada includes eight associations whose members deal with the personal finances of individuals — the Canadian Association of Financial Planners, the Canadian Institute of Chartered Accountants, the Canadian Institute of Financial Planning, the Canadian Securities Institute, the Certified General Accountants Association of Canada, the Credit Union Institute of Canada, the Life Underwriters Association of Canada and the Society of Management Accountants of Canada. At time of writing the Institute of Canadian Bankers had not joined.

Prior to its joining the Standards Council, the Canadian Institute of Financial Planning offered an educational program which led to the Chartered Financial Planner designation. The CIFP was embroiled in litigation with the Denver-based Certified Financial Planner Board of Standards over the use of the CFP designation. This had ended and the Standards Council has joined the U.S. organization and will offer the Certified Financial Planner designation. It will replace the designations Chartered Financial Planner, Registered Financial Planner and Chartered Financial Consultant.

Candidates for the CFP designation must complete an approved educational program and pass a standardized examination as well as satisfy a work experience requirement. Moreover, it appears that CFPs will have to meet a continuing educational requirement each year to maintain their designation. CFPs must also agree to comply with a code of professional conduct and the continuing education requirement.

Steven G. Kelman
October, 1996

About the author

Steven G. Kelman is an investment counsellor and president of Steven G. Kelman & Associates Limited. His company provides specialty communication, analysis, publications and training for the mutual funds industry. He is consulting editor with the *Mutual Fund Sourcebook*, the mutual fund information guide used by fund professionals in Canada, and an adviser on the *Mutual Fund Sourcedisk*. Mr. Kelman is the author of *RRSPs 1997*, co-author of *Investment Strategies* (both published as part of The Globe and Mail Personal Finance Library) and co-author of *Investing in Gold*. His articles have appeared in *The Globe and Mail*, *Financial Times of Canada*, *Investors Digest*, in magazines and on the pages of daily newspapers from coast to coast.

He has lectured on financial planning, RRSPs and mutual funds across the country and is co-author and co-instructor of a proficiency course in Labour Sponsored Investment Funds recognized by securities commissions in four provinces. For several years, he taught a course in applied investments to MBA students at the Faculty of Administrative Studies at Toronto's York University. He has served as chair of the education committee of the Investment Funds Institute of Canada and his contributions included writing several sections of the revised Canadian Investment Funds Course.

Mr. Kelman is a Chartered Financial Analyst and a member of the Toronto Society of Financial Analysts. He received his B.Sc. in 1967 from McMaster University, after graduating with his MBA in 1969 from York University. Mr. Kelman worked as an analyst, then portfolio manager, for a major insurance company before becoming a senior analyst with an investment dealer. In 1975, he joined the *Financial Times* as a staff writer; he became investment editor in 1977. He joined Dynamic Fund Management Ltd. in 1985 and held a number of positions within Dynamic and affiliated companies until the end of 1994 when he left to establish Steven G. Kelman & Associates.

CHAPTER 1

How It Started

NINETEEN-THIRTY-TWO WAS an unlikely time to establish Canada's first open-end mutual fund. Unemployment in the depression-ravaged economy was running at about 40 per cent. Canadian share prices, as measured by the *Financial Times of Canada,* were off about 80 per cent from their 1929 highs. Yet it was in 1932 that 31-year-old Alan Chippindale of the New York-based Calvin Bullock organization travelled to Montreal. His assignment: to start and manage Canada's first open-end mutual fund, the Canadian Investment Fund (CIF).

It was not an easy task. First, tax regulations had to be changed to accommodate the mutual fund corporation concept. Second, he faced the problem of selling a new investment concept to a public that was gun-shy, to say the least.

The only experience most people had with funds of any type involved investment trust shares. These were closed-end funds whose shares were bought and sold on stock exchanges. Most had leveraged, unpublished portfolios and there were few restrictions on what they could buy and hold in their portfolios. Chippindale's open-end fund was different in that the fund issued and redeemed shares on an ongoing basis at a price reflecting the full value of the assets the fund held.

The closed-end investment pools had performed exceedingly well during the Roaring Twenties. But when the market crashed, the value of their underlying assets plunged as well. Those investors who wanted to sell couldn't because the market for the shares had dried up.

CIF offered shares through dealers and brokers in the United States and Britain as well as in Canada. Chippindale spent $50,000 on newspaper advertising in Canada in the three months after launching the fund in December, 1932. Gross sales during that period were disappointing — only about $50,000. It was years before the fund turned a profit. But Chippindale had pioneered the concepts that mutual fund investors today take for granted: regular reports to investors, redemptions at net asset value, diversification, no borrowing, and no conflicts of interest.

The concept of open-end funds caught on slowly. In 1934, Commonwealth International (now Laurentian Commonwealth Fund Ltd.) changed to an open-end fund from a closed-end fund. In the same year, a new fund, United Gold Equities, was established. (It later was wound up as investor interest in gold declined.) In 1938, Corporate Investors Ltd. converted to an open-end fund from a closed-end fund.

But funds really didn't take off until the 1950s. It was at this time that Investors Syndicate of Canada formed Investors Mutual of Canada. This group, with an expanding sales force, increased investor awareness in funds by selling through instalment accumulation plans.

Statistics on mutual funds covering that period are sketchy. The Investment Funds Institute of Canada (IFIC) — the umbrella organization of the Canadian mutual fund industry — estimates that the market value of funds offered by its members in 1951 was about $57 million held in 22,000 accounts. But through the 1950s the industry grew quickly. By 1960, IFIC members had assets of about $540 million in 179,000 accounts. In 1963, the figure broke $1 billion in 324,000 accounts.

It was during 1962 that IFIC's predecessor organization, the Canadian Mutual Fund Association, was founded, with the objective of becoming a self-governing and self-disciplining association of mutual fund companies. The name was changed to the Investment Funds Institute of Canada in 1976.

IFIC membership includes funds representing more than 80 per cent of fund assets held by Canadians. (Representation increases to almost 100 per cent if the segregated funds of insurance companies and other near-fund products are excluded.) Its Canadian Investment Funds Course is recognized by provincial regulators as a requirement for registration of mutual fund salespeople. Its views are sought by provincial securities commissions. Its various committees — which consider everything from advertising ethics to education — have a major influence on the funds business in Canada.

As the stock market soared in the 1960s, the industry expanded. A number of "private" funds were established during this period. Tradex Investment Fund Ltd. was set up for federal government employees posted overseas. MD Growth Investments was established by the Canadian Medical Association for its members.

At the end of 1968, IFIC-member funds controlled $2.8 billion in assets in 702,000 shareholder accounts. Sales continued at a hefty pace until 1969. But the stock market peaked in May and prices began to fall. By year-end, total assets for the industry were down marginally. More importantly, redemptions began to exceed sales.

For the next nine years, the industry's shareholder base shrunk as redemptions outpaced sales. Several U.S.-based fund companies left Canada because of declining sales as well as new regulations that required Canadian ownership of investment companies. Many fund salespeople who jumped in during the boom years also left the industry, leaving their clients to fend for themselves.

Most importantly, it was in the early 1970s that the mutual fund business suffered through a scandal that shattered investor confidence. In the late 1950s, Bernard Cornfeld, an American, established Investors Overseas Services (IOS) to manage and distribute mutual funds. By the late 1960s, he was the undisputed king of the fund business with more than one million investors and more than $2 billion in assets under management. His organization, which was registered in Panama, operated primarily in Europe, Central and South America and the Middle East. It was not registered with the U.S. Securities and Exchange Commission (SEC) so it could not operate in the U.S. Similarly, these offshore funds were not cleared in Canada. IOS, however, did purchase a Canadian group of funds. These were operated under Canadian law and were not involved in the subsequent IOS offshore funds scandal and the collapse of IOS.

Cornfeld and his colleagues, as controlling shareholders of IOS, were paper multimillionaires. To convert some of this paper wealth to cash they decided to go public. Their first step was to change IOS from a Panamanian company to a Canadian one, registering the head office in Saint John, N.B. Its base of operations, however, was Switzerland. The share issue in 1969 was a roaring success, with the opening price more than double the $10 issue price.

But when IOS released its annual report in April, 1970, its financial results were dismal. Moreover, its auditors questioned the value of some of the company's assets, including 22 million acres of Arctic oil leases. By the summer, IOS shares were trading at $2.

Concerns about IOS caused massive redemptions of its fund shares and, as a result, bailout proposals were made by a number of parties. In the summer of 1970, control of IOS passed to Robert Vesco, an American financier. Vesco obtained control as part of a deal that included a $5 million rescue loan to IOS. He then allegedly diverted assets of the offshore IOS funds into investments which provided indirect benefits to him. In November, 1972, the SEC and other regulators in Canada, Luxembourg, the Netherlands Antilles and the United Kingdom forced IOS and its related funds into liquidation.

When the Canadian operations of IOS were liquidated by a trustee, the Eaton group of funds bought the contracts to manage the Canadian IOS funds and integrated them into the Eaton group — now the Laurentian group.

It took a long time for the industry to recover. By 1978, fund sales began to exceed redemptions once again and the industry began its major growth from a base of about 150 funds and an asset base of about $2 billion. By 1985, there were about 200 funds with assets exceeding $10 billion. Two years later, there were more than 350 funds with assets exceeding $35 billion.

The surge reflected the growing recognition by both investors and the investment industry that funds are the best way for many people to participate in the stock and bond markets. Billions of dollars of RRSP money flows into mutual funds each year from people seeking better long-term returns than are available from guaranteed plans. And many stockbrokers who previously ignored funds or discouraged their clients from investing in funds now see them as an important source of business. Indeed, a number of investment dealers offer their own families of funds or funds managed by their chartered bank parents. Similarly, many insurance companies are offering mutual funds to their clients. Banks and trust companies have also expanded their fund operations. These newcomers have increased general investor awareness about mutual funds.

As well, the industry has expanded its product line to include a wider range of funds. Besides the traditional stock and bond funds, investors have a choice of ethical funds, precious metals funds, and funds that specialize in foreign government bonds, technology companies and investments in telecommunications.

The October, 1987, crash had a short-term negative impact on fund sales, which plunged in the months following the crash. However, sales growth returned, reflecting the variety of funds available to meet investor needs and expectations of high returns. The slide in interest rates over the past few years brought the investment of billions of dollars into mutual funds by people who had never previously invested in anything other than guaranteed investments.

At midyear, industry assets totalled about $180 billion, a record level. The mutual fund industry is undoubtedly profitable but its profits are largely due to aging baby boomers and falling interest rates rather than the astuteness of its executives.

At some point, growth will level and assets could even decline. That is normal in any cyclical industry or business and will happen if interest rates move significantly higher making fixed-income investments more attractive than equity funds. Alternatively, a sharp decline in the stock market will push many investors into a more conservative stance.

Some commentators have made reference to a mutual fund bubble. As they see it, a drop in share prices would panic investors and trigger massive redemptions which in turn would push prices even lower. All things are possible. But the billions of dollars that have poured into mutual funds are spread among many different types of funds: Canadian equity, foreign equity, bond, mortgage, foreign currency bonds, and money market. Moreover, many investors hold more than one type of fund. They are less vulnerable to a market correction than investors who hold only one type of fund.

Companies continue to introduce new funds to meet investor needs, real or perceived. The banking and trust industries have trained individuals to sell their funds through their branch networks. The credit unions are becoming more of a force in fund marketing. The banks continue to expand their market share through their discount brokerage arms which sell funds of many management companies. The independent dealers continue to compete on service.

There are some trends apparent. Service has become more of an issue than in the past and all participants in the industry recognize its importance. Education has become a major issue in the industry and it will almost certainly develop more consumer educational materials at the same time as it requires higher professional standards from its participants.

Fund investors are becoming more sophisticated and are likely to demand more for the money they pay for service directly or indirectly. At some point, management expense ratio will become an issue and a selling point to consumers.

CHAPTER 2

What Is a Mutual Fund?

A MUTUAL FUND IS A POOL of savings that belongs to many investors. This pool is invested by a professional manager or a team of managers in a broad portfolio of investments. Depending on the objectives of the fund, these can be Canadian common stocks, foreign common stocks, bonds, mortgages, preferred shares, precious metals, specialty investments, treasury bills or combinations of several groups. Some funds are designed for specific purposes, such as RRSPs, others are multipurpose.

Funds that issue and redeem shares or units on a continuous basis are called open-end funds. There are more than 1,200 open-end funds offered in Canada. The value of their shares or units changes with the underlying value of the securities in the fund. But each share or unit represents a portion of the underlying portfolio. Most funds are valued daily, although some are valued weekly and a few monthly or quarterly. The fund company determines the value of the underlying portfolio at the close of the stock and bond markets, then divides that value by the number of shares or units outstanding to determine the net asset value of each share or unit. The number of shares or units outstanding varies on a day-to-day basis, depending on sales and redemptions.

C.I. Canadian Growth Fund is a typical open-end fund that invests primarily in Canadian common stocks. Its portfolio, as of June 30, 1996, was valued at $1.06 billion. At that date it had about 153 million units outstanding. So the value per unit was $6.93. That is the amount you would pay for a share on June 30. It is also the price you would have received for your shares if you redeemed them on that date. (Both purchase and sale prices would be adjusted by any transaction fees you might pay.)

In addition to open-end funds, there are a handful of closed-end funds. Unlike open-end funds, closed-end funds have a fixed number of shares. These are traded on stock exchanges. The market value of their shares may be greater or less than the underlying value of their securities. For example, BGR Precious Metals shares trade on the Toronto Stock Exchange. On Oct. 3, 1995, BGR shares closed at $18.70. But the underlying value was $24.15 a share. Closed-end funds can be useful for some investors and will be discussed in detail in Chapter 6.

The majority of investors in funds hold open-end funds. With the exception of the chapter on closed-end funds, all examples and comments in this book refer to open-end funds.

The advantages of funds

A mutual fund offers several important advantages to you as an investor which you might have difficulty achieving on your own:

1. Diversification

Funds generally hold a large number of securities. It is common for a fund invested in Canadian common stocks to hold shares of 40 or more companies. By holding such a large number of securities your risk is spread — if one company flounders, it will have little impact on the performance of the overall portfolio. Few individuals have enough assets to build a diversified portfolio on their own. With a mutual fund you can get diversification with a small amount of money.

How small? The minimum contribution allowed to most funds is between $500 and $1,000. However, most funds also have monthly contribution plans that allow you to start with as little as $50 or $100 a month. According to the Investment Funds Institute of Canada, the average investment by individuals in a fund in mid-1996 was about $9,000. But many investors hold several funds and the holdings of mutual fund investors range from a few hundred dollars to $1 million or more.

2. Liquidity

A key benefit of mutual funds is that they are liquid. You can purchase or redeem shares and units on short notice, generally locking in a purchase or sale price on the day you make your decision to buy or redeem (in the case of funds valued daily). This is an advantage to individuals who want to be able to cash in their investments at any time. In this way, holding a mutual fund can be more advantageous than holding stocks, particularly if the stocks held rarely trade in large volumes and may be harder to sell at any one time at a good price.

Orders to buy mutual fund shares or units received by the fund before the close of business on a day when shares are valued will be purchased at that price, less any sales fee if applicable. Orders received to redeem shares will be redeemed at that price, less any redemption fee if applicable, and your money will be available within a few days, generally in three. Virtually all major fund groups now price daily. (In the U.S., some funds are priced hourly.)

A handful of funds, mainly real estate funds, are valued monthly and as a result are somewhat less liquid.

3. Professional management

Mutual fund investors benefit from having investment professionals decide what securities should be held and at what prices they should be bought or sold. Most fund managers have substantial experience in the investment field and have taken specialized investment courses leading to the designation of chartered financial analyst. The cost of professional management is low to mutual fund holders because the cost is spread so widely. Generally, you can expect to pay about 2 to 3 per cent a year for portfolio management and other fund expenses, excluding the costs of trading the underlying securities. This management fee is generally charged to the fund rather than to your account.

Mutual funds are the only cost-effective way for individuals with limited funds to get a diversified, professionally managed portfolio. No stockbroker or other investment professional can afford to service a small account, except through mutual funds. Unless you are able to generate several thousands of dollars of trading commissions a year, you are unlikely to get timely advice and top-quality service on a stock portfolio from a stockbroker.

But small investors aren't the only investors who use mutual funds. Many wealthy individuals who don't want to be bothered making decisions about the stock market also use funds. Similarly, some people use funds for specific purposes in their investment portfolios. For instance, if you decide you want to invest part of your assets in Japanese securities, the easiest way is through a fund that specializes in this market.

The funds in Canada can be divided into two broad categories: those that invest in growth securities such as common stocks and whose objective is to provide long-term growth, and those that invest in income securities and whose objective is to provide current income or stable growth. Balanced, or asset-allocation, funds combine growth and income securities to provide growth, income and, in theory at least, superior long-term returns.

Types of funds

Growth funds historically give the highest rates of return measured over most long periods of time, say, 10 years. While the returns of all mutual funds are a combination of capital gain and income, the major portion of return from growth funds is from capital appreciation. It is impossible to predict what a growth fund's future rate of return will be. The assumption is that it will be higher than the rate of return of a fund that invests for income. That has been the case historically. But annual rates of return for growth funds vary widely. In some years, the returns will be large; in other years, the returns will be mediocre. There will be years when fund values drop.

Fixed-income funds give somewhat lower long-term rates of return than growth funds, but their annual returns are generally more stable since the major portion is income. There are sometimes exceptions — sharp declines in interest rates in the early 1980s are reflected in long-term bond fund returns. These returns exceed 15-year returns on Canadian equity funds. Income comes in the form of interest in the case of bond and mortgage funds, and dividends in the case of preferred-dividend income funds.

Growth funds

Growth funds include common stock and real estate funds as well as balanced funds whose portfolios may include both stocks and bonds to provide more stable growth than pure growth funds.

The largest group of growth funds — more than 200 funds — is Canadian common stock funds. Because they concentrate in the Canadian market, holding no more than 20 per cent of their assets in foreign securities, they can be registered as RRSPs.

Most Canadian common stock funds invest across the spectrum of the market, generally sticking to issues traded on the Toronto Stock Exchange and the Montreal Exchange. A few funds, however, specialize in specific segments of the market. For example, Altamira Resource Fund invests in Canadian resource issues; Dynamic Precious Metals Fund invests in shares of precious metals producers and precious metals.

There are about 100 growth funds that invest in American stock markets. While most of these funds stick to senior blue-chip issues, others such as Zweig Strategic Growth Fund concentrate on specific areas, in this case, small company stocks.

If international diversification interests you, there are more than 200 funds that invest outside North America. Some, such as AGF Japan Fund or Dynamic Europe Fund, concentrate on specific markets. Others, such as BPI International Equity Fund, invest in a variety of overseas markets. A few funds, such as Trimark Fund, will invest in whatever markets, including Canada and the U.S., are perceived to offer the best values. There are also about a dozen international bond funds which may provide growth through changes in currency values as well as shifts in interest rates.

Mutual funds that invest primarily outside Canada are considered "foreign property" by the federal government for purposes of the Income Tax Act and cannot be registered as RRSPs. However, they can be held in self-directed RRSPs as part of the foreign property component, provided the total foreign property holding does not exceed 20 per cent of the plan.

Balanced funds

More than 180 funds call themselves balanced or asset-allocation funds. Historically, a balanced fund was one that invested a portion of its assets in bonds and a portion in stocks. Such funds aimed to have long-term rates of return that were larger than those offered by pure bond funds and more stable than pure stock funds.

The term "balanced" has been used by a number of funds which have the traditional balanced fund objectives but whose portfolios are primarily equities. Depending on their holdings, some balanced funds are eligible for RRSPs, while others are not. As a group, balanced funds are significantly less volatile than pure equity funds.

Real estate funds

There are a few funds that invest in real estate. These differ from other mutual funds in several major respects. First, they use borrowed capital in addition to shareholder capital; virtually all other funds use just shareholder capital.

Second, their unit or share values are based on appraisals rather than actual market transactions. The net asset value per unit or share in an equity fund is determined by the value of the portfolio as measured by the closing trades in each stock divided by the number of shares outstanding. With a real estate fund, the value of the fund is based on annual appraisals of each property the fund owns. An appraisal is simply the opinion of a real estate expert of the market value of a particular property.

Third, real estate funds are less liquid than other funds and, in fact, over the years several funds have suspended redemptions because of liquidity problems. During the first quarter of 1993, four of the seven real estate funds suspended redemptions.

It is unlikely that the regulators will allow any new real estate funds to be established. Given the problems of liquidity, real estate is best suited for closed-end funds rather than open-end funds.

One specialty fund, Dynamic Real Estate Equity Fund, holds shares of real estate companies rather than real estate directly.

Income funds

The second major category of funds is income funds which aim to produce a predictable and relatively stable flow of income. Also, the rates of return on income funds are less uncertain than the rates of return from growth funds, albeit slightly lower.

Income funds can be divided into two broad categories: those that invest in bonds, mortgages or both, and those that invest primarily in preferred shares of Canadian corporations. In mid 1996, there were about 136 funds which invested in Canadian bonds, 30 mortgage funds, 74 funds which invested in foreign-currency bonds and 39 funds which invested primarily in preferred shares of Canadian companies or common shares for dividend income. In addition, there were about 115 money market funds which invested primarily in treasury bills, top quality commercial paper and bank deposits, and about 20 U.S. and international money market funds.

To understand the differences between the two broad categories, you have to consider how the federal government taxes individuals on the interest and dividends they receive from Canadian corporations. Interest is taxable at the marginal tax rate — the rate of tax paid on an individual's last dollar of income earned. A person with taxable income of $40,000 could have a marginal tax rate of about 41 per cent, depending on the province and ignoring surtaxes. So, on $1,000 in interest income, this person would have to pay $410 in taxes.

To encourage Canadians to invest in dividend-producing shares, the government devised the federal dividend tax credit. It works like this: Instead of simply adding dividend income to other sources of income, dividends are grossed up by 125 per cent. Then, after you have determined how much tax you owe, you can subtract a tax credit equal to 13.33 per cent of 125 per cent of your dividends. In the end, you pay less tax than if you'd simply added the dividends to income in the normal way.

For example, let's say you have $1,000 of dividend income. For tax-calculation purposes this would be grossed up to $1,250. Assuming your federal tax rate is 26 per cent, the federal tax payable on the dividend would be $325. From this, subtract the dividend tax credit of 13.33 per cent of $1,250, or $167. The net federal tax payable on the dividend would be $158. Add the provincial tax at 54 per cent of federal tax ($85) and the total tax bill on $1,000 in dividends ends up being $243, or about 24 per cent of the actual dividend received. That would compare with $410, or 41 per cent, on interest received by the same person. The rule of thumb is that on an after-tax basis, $1 of dividend income has the same after-tax value as $1.26 of interest income. So a 6 per cent dividend yield is about equal to a 7.5 per cent interest yield.

Now, back to the two categories of income funds. Funds that invest primarily in preferred shares are usually called preferred-dividend income funds. Their purpose is to maximize after-tax income. They are popular with people who want current income and the highest after-tax return possible without taking significant risk.

Bond and mortgage funds may have slightly lower after-tax rates of return than preferred-dividend income funds. But many people prefer the security of having debt instruments and are willing to give up some income as a trade-off for more security.

When an income fund is to be registered as an RRSP, bond and mortgage funds make more sense. All income is untaxed inside an RRSP and RRSP investors cannot take advantage of the tax break that comes with the preferred-dividend income.

There are several different types of non-dividend fixed-income funds. There are funds that invest only in bonds, those that invest only in mortgages, funds that mix bonds and mortgages and, finally, there are money market funds and savings funds.

Bond funds generally invest in government or government-guaranteed bonds and bonds and debentures issued by the strongest banks and corporations. Besides quality of underlying bonds and general interest rate levels there are other factors that can affect performance, such as the maturities of the various bonds held and whether a major portion of the fund is invested in bonds that are denominated in currencies other than the Canadian dollar.

Mortgage funds are designed to provide maximum current income to investors by investing in mortgages. Mortgage rates are generally at least a point higher than bond yields. They are less likely to provide capital appreciation than bond funds because mortgage funds rarely trade their mortgages.

Money market funds have similar objectives: to provide current income with no fluctuation in the value of an investor's capital. Money market funds invest in short-term debt securities with maturities of less than a year. In fact a fund can be called a money market fund only if the average term to maturity of its holdings is 180 days or less. Typically, a money market fund's portfolio will be concentrated in treasury bills, bank-guaranteed debt and short-term issues of strong corporations. Many invest only in treasury bills.

The unit value of most money market funds is fixed at either $10 or $1, so the unit value of the fund is always constant. Income earned on capital accrues to your account daily, weekly or monthly, depending on how often the fund is valued, and is generally used to purchase additional units of the fund. Money market funds are by far the least risky of mutual funds.

How funds can be used

Mutual funds can be used for virtually any type of savings or investment program. The fund or funds you use should be matched to your specific investment objective. You should also develop an understanding of what is called fund volatility or rate-of-return variability.

Unlike a guaranteed investment, you do not know what your rate of return will be from a mutual fund because the rate you earn will depend on the rates of return of the underlying investments. You expect to get back substantially more than you put in — that's the reason you would buy a fund rather than purchase a guaranteed investment certificate or hold money in the bank. However, the rates of return from some types of mutual funds are a lot more stable than rates of return of some other types of funds.

Since money market funds invest only in short-term securities, you can predict fairly accurately your rate of return over a relatively short period of time. In contrast, there are some funds whose rates of return over short periods are virtually impossible to predict. These funds may give very high rates of return over long periods but over the short term their rates will vary widely.

For example, funds that invest in the Japanese stock market are very volatile. Much of this volatility is caused by the exchange rate of the Canadian dollar against the Japanese yen. Exchange rate fluctuations can be as much as several percentage points up or down in a month. Similarly, funds that invest in gold and other precious metals have historically been volatile.

Money market funds as a group are the least volatile, followed by mortgage funds, bond funds and preferred-dividend income funds. Common stock funds are more volatile than fixed-income funds. Equity funds that invest in senior stocks and balanced funds are generally much less volatile than equity funds that concentrate on specific groups of stocks such as energy, junior companies or gold.

Stocks vs. T-Bills

Total returns
for periods ending June 30

Year	TSE total return	T-bills
1975	10.0	7.5
1976	4.8	8.5
1977	3.1	8.2
1978	14.7	7.5
1979	50.4	10.2
1980	33.0	12.9
1981	19.0	14.8
1982	-39.2	16.5
1983	86.9	10.7
1984	-5.7	10.0
1985	26.7	10.7
1986	17.4	9.3
1987	24.6	8.0
1988	-5.2	8.7
1989	13.5	11.1
1990	-2.4	12.8
1991	1.9	10.9
1992	1.1	7.3
1993	20.8	6.5
1994	3.9	4.8
1995	15.2	6.0
1996	13.9	5.6

TABLE 1

So if your savings objective is short term, like saving for a vacation or a down payment on a home, the fund that would best suit your needs is a money market fund. Your money would not be at risk and you would likely earn a rate of return that is a couple of points above what you would get in a bank account.

If you don't need your money for a couple of years, a mortgage or bond fund might suffice. Similarly, you could consider a preferred-dividend income fund. In this case you would have to consider the individual portfolios of the funds and your tax situation. Fixed-income funds with securities maturing in a few years are likely to be less volatile than fixed-income funds whose portfolios have securities that mature in 15 to 20 years.

If you are saving for the long term, you would likely consider funds invested primarily in equities. But on a month-to-month or year-to-year basis such growth funds would have more volatile rates of return than fixed-income funds. Historically, investors who are willing to accept some fluctuation in their rates of return have done better over the long haul than investors who want guaranteed returns.

On a 10-year basis to June 30, 1996, funds that invested primarily in Canadian equities had annual average returns of 7.7 per cent. Bond funds had returns averaging 9.2 per cent, while money market funds had returns averaging 7.6 per cent.

In Table I you can see the dramatic difference between the year-by-year performance of the Toronto Stock Exchange total return index and the rate of return you would have earned if you held treasury bills. The TSE index is a good representation of what an "average" mutual fund investing in Canadian stocks earned. On average, you can expect a good return. However, the returns from year to year vary dramatically. The average annual returns of Canadian equity funds for the one-year, three-year, five-year and 10-year periods ending June 30, 1996, are 13.4 per cent, 12.6 per cent 10.4 per cent and 7.7 per cent. The returns for money market funds for the same time periods are 5.2 per cent, 4.9 per cent, 5.5 per cent and 7.6 per cent. The picture is quite different if you choose a different ending date: the returns for the one, three, five and 10 years ending June 30, 1989, are 13.5 per cent, 10.3 per cent, 14.8 per cent and 13.0 per cent for equities and 11.1 per cent, 9.3 per cent, 9.5 per cent and 11.2 per cent for T-bills.

This narrow spread between equity and T-bill returns in 1989 is not an endorsement of treasury bills over equities. Rather, it means that returns from equities have been below expectations in some years in that particular time period.

CHAPTER 3

The Impact of the Changing Environment

SINCE THE LAST EDITION OF *Understanding Mutual Funds*, industry assets have grown by about $20 billion to $180 billion. In the previous 12 months, they grew about $10 billion. Few, if any, other industries have increased their assets by 20 per cent in two years. In fact, this recent growth is a pittance compared to the tripling of assets over the previous three years.

Much of the increase came from the "GIC refugees" who, faced with the lowest GIC rates in a generation, turned to mutual funds in the hope of maintaining the returns they had previously enjoyed from guaranteed investments.

Given the rapid growth in the industry, a number of investors in mutual funds and sellers of mutual funds are relative newcomers to these investment alternatives. Importantly, the stock market has been rising for more than five years without a significant decline. Consequently, many of these new investors and the people who advise them have never experienced a bear market. This begs the question about whether a mutual fund bubble will form, a question sometimes asked by the media. The question itself seems to reflect a flawed understanding of mutual funds. They are not a homogeneous product, such as GICs which are basically the same no matter which of the top six banks issue them.

There are various types of mutual funds to meet different investor needs. In mid-1996, Canadian equity funds made up about 27 per cent of industry assets, U.S. equity funds were 4 per cent, foreign equity funds were about 22 per cent, while balanced funds represented 14 per cent of the market. Canadian bond and income funds made up 8 per cent of the market, mortgage funds 7 per cent, and money market funds 15 per cent.

Each type of fund performs in a distinct manner under specific market conditions. A sharp decline in the Canadian stock market would undoubtedly trigger some redemptions of equity funds. Much of the proceeds, however, would almost certainly move into other types of mutual funds. Similarly, a sharp rise in interest rates would trigger some redemptions of fixed-income funds.

That is just what happened during part of 1994 and 1995 when interest rates rose to levels traditionally representative of GIC rates. Mortgage funds are good examples of how the mutual fund market works. These funds were valued at $13 billion at the end of December, 1994, down from $15 billion a year earlier. The decline primarily reflected transfers from mortgage funds into other segments. In fact, new sales of mortgage funds were just under $1 billion as some investors bought these funds to benefit from higher rates. Even during December, mortgage fund net redemptions and transfers totalled only about $200 million. In contrast, net sales of equity funds were much higher: foreign common share mutual funds were $603 million, Canadian common share funds $528 million, balanced funds $350 million, and bond and income funds $75 million.

Mutual funds are, of course, a major sector of the capital markets and the growth reflects growing sophistication among investors, an aging population and a desire to diversify investments away from traditional guaranteed portfolios. Pension funds, deposits, real estate and direct investments in the market are also significant investments for individuals.

The stock market cycles

At the end of 1993, many fund companies reported double-digit one-year returns for their Canadian equity funds. In fact, returns of 30 per cent and more were common. Unfortunately, some of the investors who moved from GICs to equity funds failed to comprehend that such high returns were not a guarantee and that it was unreasonable to expect annual returns of 20 or 30 per cent or more to continue indefinitely — just as it was unreasonable to have feared that the poor returns of the previous few years would continue indefinitely. In the last rising, or bull, market, which lasted from July, 1982, to August, 1987, the Toronto Stock Exchange 300 index climbed 202 per cent over 60 months. That bull market was also helped by falling interest rates which made equities and equity funds attractive alternative investments.

While the bull market ended in August, 1987, it was the October, 1987, crash that demonstrated the obvious cyclical nature of the markets. The stock market slide in October, 1987, was not a surprise to most professional investors. In fact, most fund managers had been building cash positions in the months prior to the decline because they felt that stocks were expensive or that the market was ahead of itself. As well, the markets had become exceptionally volatile, with the major indexes moving sharply up and down on a day-to-day basis as investor confidence rose and fell.

What caught virtually every manager off-guard was the magnitude of the decline. In the six sessions to Oct. 23, the Toronto Stock Exchange 300 composite index — a widely used measure of stock market performance — fell about 16 per cent.

The biggest drop was on Black Monday, Oct. 19, when the TSE 300 fell 407 points, losing 11 per cent of its value. However, the blood bath really began on the previous Friday when the TSE 300, taking its lead from the New York market, fell 76 points, or 2 per cent. By the time the month ended, the TSE was more than 22 per cent below its September closing level. Investors who bought near the top of the market in August saw the value of their investment, assuming they had a broadly based portfolio, plunge by one-quarter. If they bought the day the market peaked and sold the day the market bottomed, they would have lost about 31 per cent of their capital before commissions.

While some investors bought at the peak, hundreds of thousands of investors had been in funds for years, holding them as long-term investments. These investors saw the crash eliminate most of the gains they had made over the previous 12 months. Even then, many funds tied to the stock market showed significant gains in 1987 despite October. Several funds tied to natural resource stocks had gains of more than 25 per cent. Some funds with substantial cash positions and broadly based portfolios showed small but positive returns.

Surprisingly, the industry was not hit with a flood of redemptions. While there was a substantial amount of switching from growth funds to more stable bond and money market funds, few fund companies reported a mass exodus from funds. In total, about 2 per cent of mutual fund assets were redeemed the week of the crash.

There are several explanations for this. Many fund salespeople claim that most of their clients are long-term investors and decided to continue holding. Indeed, with 10-year rates of return for many funds in excess of 16 per cent, long-term investors could still smile. But the lack of redemptions might also reflect the fact that many investors got busy signals when they tried to call their brokers to redeem. By the time they got through, the market had levelled and they decided to hold, particularly when they realized that the damage wasn't as great as they thought.

There was concern in the industry that some investors who bought their holdings partly with borrowed money would be forced to sell by banks and trust companies which had financed the purchases. However, this did not become a major problem because the crash only trimmed profits and did not eliminate them, at least for investors who had held funds for some time.

As to the cause of the crash, a simple explanation is that the number of people who wanted to sell exceeded the number of people who wanted to buy. There are many more complex explanations. One points to sales of stocks by major U.S. fund companies. Mutual fund investors can redeem at any time. Apparently, on Friday, Oct. 16, fund companies were hit by an extraordinary number of redemptions when the New York Stock Exchange fell 108 points as measured by the Dow Jones industrial average. To raise cash to meet these redemptions, some funds became major sellers of stocks on Oct. 19. This helped drive the market down further because many potential buyers were on the sidelines.

Those investors who bought stocks or funds which invest in stocks on Oct. 19 did quite well. By the end of June, 1989, they were showing gains of about 40 per cent, using the Toronto index as a benchmark.

The crash has had some major effects on fund investing. For one thing, many investors started taking a more cautious approach. Rather than putting everything in funds that invest in growth stocks, more and more investors are taking a balanced approach, spreading their money among different classes of assets such as bond funds, precious metals funds and money market funds.

However, new sales dried up and the incomes of people who sold funds plunged. The drop in sales hurt fund sales organizations, which quickly discovered that revenues were not enough to cover overheads. Several firms decided to close their doors. Salespeople at various firms jockeyed for position within their own firms or with other firms that offered them a better deal.

The drop in interest rates over the past few years has had a major influence on the funds industry, particularly on banks and trust companies. As rates declined they were faced with the prospect of losing deposits to mutual fund management companies which offered money market funds. In response they offered their own money market funds. Indeed, much of the growth in mutual funds in the past few years has been the movement of money from savings accounts and deposits into bank and trust company money market funds.

Many people also moved out of maturing GICs into bond and mortgage funds, unaware that these fund unit values would decline if interest rates moved higher. When rates did rise during the first half of 1992 some people were shocked by the decline in value of their funds. They redeemed their units and moved back into guaranteed investments, which raises questions about their knowledge of the market. Although deposit-taking institutions had added a statement to their literature that mutual funds were not covered under deposit insurance, the quick retreat also raises doubts about the quality of advice that investors were given by the people selling the funds.

Finally, the cost of distributing funds has been rising, which is reflected in higher management fees and fund expenses charged to investors. The increased cost is a result of the shift from front-end loads, which are paid by the investor, to declining redemption fees, which are paid by the fund company out of management fees. During 1992, many fund companies raised sales commissions from 4 to 5 per cent, a 20 per cent increase in the income to the salesperson. However, to finance this increase some funds have had to ask their investors for permission to raise their management fees, which has led to embarrassing confrontations at annual meetings. Other fund companies have simply launched new rear-end load funds with higher management fees. A couple of fund companies simply tacked on an additional fee for clients who, when they bought a mutual fund with load options, chose the declining redemption fee rather than the front-end load. This has created confusion among clients and some administrative difficulties for the companies themselves.

Virtually all fund companies which sell their funds through dealers pay a portion of their management fee to the salesperson as a "trailer fee" for providing ongoing service to the client after the initial sales commission has been paid. This trailer, or servicing fee, is a deferred commission and is generally one-quarter of the management fee for funds sold on a declining-redemption fee basis. So, if a fund has a 2 per cent management fee, 0.25 per cent of the value of the client's holding will be paid to the broker every year for as long as the client holds the fund and the broker remains the client's broker.

A new twist developed in early 1993 involving funds sold on an acquisition-fee basis. Acquisition fees are negotiable. To compete with banks and trust companies, some financial planners do not charge a commission on the load funds they sell, receiving their compensation from the fee charged the client for advice instead. Many fund companies raised the trailer fee paid on funds sold with acquisition fees to one-half of the management fee. Some funds moved to a level load, which involves charging a 1 per cent front-end commission to the client and the payment of half the management fee as a trailer to the dealer or broker. If a client redeems within one year, a redemption fee of 1 per cent is charged.

Several fund companies introduced series of the same fund with different management fees to reflect different structures of dealer compensation. This new twist can be confusing to both investors and dealers. For example, AGF Management Limited series A securities are sold with a negotiable acquisition fee of zero to 6 per cent. The management fees on a series A equity fund are 2 per cent; series B securities are sold with a deferred declining redemption which is 5.5 per cent in the first two years and declines to zero after eight years. The management fee is 2.5 per cent. However, after nine years an investor's B shares will be reclassified as A shares giving the investor the lower fee. The third class, series C, is sold at no charge and the management fee is 2.5 per cent, although there is a minimum purchase level for this series of the fund. By mid-1996, AGF was streamlining its commission and fee structure, apparently realizing investors and dealers prefer simplicity. Sales commissions and fees will be explained in detail in Chapter 10.

CHAPTER 4

All About Growth Funds

IF YOUR INVESTMENT GOAL IS long-term capital growth, consider equity funds, which invest primarily in common stocks. This is the most popular type of fund and there are about 600 available.

There are several major groups of equity funds that are designed to meet particular objectives by investing in specific markets or certain areas of specific markets. Regardless of their type, all equity funds have the common thread of a diversified portfolio of shares, and performance that reflects individual funds' objectives and the skills of their managers.

Many people buy equity funds the same way they buy GICs. They look at rates of return and buy the one with the highest rate. This is a mistake. An equity fund's long-term rate of return indicates how that fund has performed in the past. It is not a guarantee, or even a strong indicator, of future performance. Performance is a single indicator which is best used combined with another indicator, volatility. Both must be viewed against the outlook for the market and the holdings of a specific fund.

In fact, it is very important to consider a fund's volatility, the stability of its monthly rate of return, when choosing an equity fund. The *Report on Business* monthly performance tables, as well as the tables of other newspapers and computer disk fund measurement products, provide information on a fund's volatility. While the method of showing volatility differs among products, they all seek to provide information about the variation in a fund's monthly rate of return using a statistical measure called standard deviation.

Volatility is useful in comparing two funds with similar rates of return. For investors who buy and hold for the long term, a fund with a high historical return and a low volatility ranking would be preferable to a fund with the same return but a high volatility. On the other hand, if you're trying to catch the swings in a market cycle, you might want to choose a fund with a high volatility rating over one with a low rating.

For example, Guardian Canadian Balanced and Maxxum Canadian Equity Growth Fund have average annual returns of about 9.6 per cent over the 10 years ended June 30, 1996. However, the stock fund is much more volatile than the balanced fund. A fund's volatility will change from time to time. But usually the changes are not significant because the fund objectives and investment philosophy are generally stable.

Certain groups of funds tend to be more volatile than others. Gold funds, for instance, are among the most volatile, reflecting the volatility of precious metals prices and gold mining stocks. Similarly, Japanese funds are fairly volatile as a result of swings in the exchange rates of the Japanese yen and Canadian dollar. Generally, funds that invest in a narrow segment of the market are more volatile than funds that draw their portfolios from a broad spectrum of industries. Equity funds that have relatively low volatility tend to invest in securities that are more stable in price than the general market. For example, a fund holding stocks with substantial dividend yields would have below-average volatility. One such fund is Corporate Investors Ltd., which invests in shares that pay, or are expected to pay, above-average dividends. Here is a summary of the major types of growth funds:

1. Canadian equity funds
The largest group of investment funds are those that invest primarily in Canadian stocks and are eligible for RRSPs. Most invest in a broad spectrum of industries and have rates of return that are similar to that of the Toronto Stock Exchange total return index. Others, however, have somewhat different objectives. For instance, several invest primarily in dividend-paying common shares of mature companies giving rates of return that are somewhat more stable than the market. Others specialize in specific areas of the market such as natural resources.

2. U.S. equity funds
Funds that invest in the U.S. are also very popular among Canadian investors. These funds appeal to individuals who expect the U.S. markets to outperform their Canadian counterparts or who want a hedge against the Canadian dollar. Within this group there is a wide

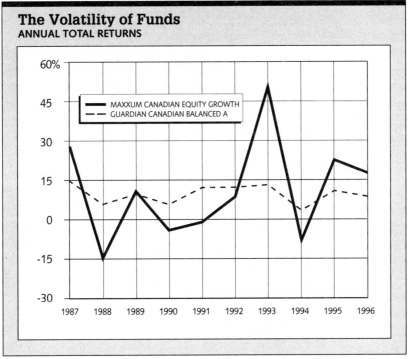

The Volatility of Funds
ANNUAL TOTAL RETURNS

MAXXUM CANADIAN EQUITY GROWTH
GUARDIAN CANADIAN BALANCED A

CHART I

variety of choices. Some invest primarily in blue chips. Others base their portfolios on companies that offer above-average growth potential or are in specialty areas of the marketplace.

3. International funds
International funds take advantage of investment opportunities in different countries. Some will invest in any country, including Canada. Others will exclude Canada or concentrate on overseas markets. International funds performed quite well until recently as the Canadian dollar fell against overseas currencies. In the past year or so, Canadian funds had the performance edge as the Canadian dollar moved higher against most other currencies.

4. Specialty equity funds
A number of funds specialize in specific industries, specific markets or follow hedged investment strategies. For instance, Royal Trust Energy Fund invests in energy stocks. Several funds specialize in Japanese securities, while a number concentrate on precious

metals. In addition, some funds attempt to give their investors stable rates of return through hedging strategies such as writing call options against positions. This involves buying a stock then selling a call option which gives the buyer the right to buy that stock at a set price up until a specific date.

5. Balanced or asset-allocation funds

Balanced or asset-allocation funds try to stabilize returns by combining equities with fixed-income securities and varying the mix to reflect the outlook for the markets.

Canadian equity funds

Lured by promises of returns far above those available from guaranteed investments, individuals poured billions of dollars in recent years into mutual funds that invest primarily in Canadian equities. Indeed, many funds have given their holders rates of return far in excess of the rates that could be earned by holding guaranteed investments.

But it's important to realize that year-to-year rates vary widely. Over the 16 years ended June, 30, 1996, the annual returns of the Toronto Stock Exchange total return index ranged from a low of -39.1 per cent to a high of 86.6 per cent.

And because stock markets move in cycles, annual rates don't tell the whole story. The returns depend on when stocks are bought and when they are sold. Over the past 60 years, the Toronto market has gone through 11 cycles consisting of declining markets followed by rising markets.

Toronto statistician Richard Anstett has compiled some of the most comprehensive statistics available on the performance of the TSE. Looking at some of the more recent cycles, Anstett notes that the Toronto market rose 193 per cent in the 72 months ended November, 1980, then proceeded to slide 44 per cent over the next 20 months to June 1982. Between June, 1982, and August, 1987, the market rose 202 per cent. Then it started its slide, which ended in late October, down 31 per cent from its peak. From October, 1987, to October, 1989, it rose about 42 per cent before pulling back 25 per cent over the following 12 months. In each of these cycles, day-to-day swings varied widely. For example, the June 30, 1994, level of the TSE index was about 12 per cent below its level of Jan. 31, 1994.

Market Cycles Since 1921
on the Toronto Stock Exchange

Bull markets	No. of months	% Gain	Bear markets	No. of months	% Loss
August 1921 to September 1929	97	300	September 1929 to June 1932	33	80
June 1932 to March 1937	57	201	March 1937 to April 1942	61	56
April 1942 to May 1946	49	159	May 1946 to February 1948	21	25
February 1948 to July 1956	101	273	July 1956 to December 1957	17	30
December 1957 to May 1969	137	162	May 1969 to June 1970	13	28
June 1970 to October 1973	40	64	October 1973 to December 1974	14	38
December 1974 to November 1980	72	193	November 1980 to July 1982	20	44
July 1982 to August 1987	61	202	August 1987 to October 1987	2	31
October 1987 to October 1989	24	42	October 1989 to October 1990	12	25

Note: Changes in market sentiment reflect gains or declines of 20 per cent or more. The stock market began climbing in October, 1995, gaining more than 68 per cent in the 69 months to June, 1996.

TABLE II

The return that a broadly based fund earns in any period or cycle depends on what happens in the market and on the skills of the fund's investment adviser. But it is difficult for a fund manager to consistently outperform the market. Superior returns do occur but usually only for short periods of time or with smaller funds. Such performance is generally due to the decisions of a single manager or a handful of individuals working together. But most managers parrot the general market or follow the crowd. As a result, on a long-term basis it is unrealistic to expect mutual funds as a whole to generate returns significantly greater than the general market.

To understand why, you have to look at the environment in which managers of broadly based Canadian equity funds have to work. You also have to consider a fund manager's objectives and management style.

Most fund managers try to outperform the market. So a manager of a broadly based Canadian equity fund would gauge his or her performance against the TSE 300 composite index, the index which includes the 300 stocks with the largest market capitalizations traded on the exchange, or against the TSE total return index, which includes dividends paid by the stocks included in the TSE 300.

There are several ways fund managers can construct portfolios. One way is to structure portfolios along the lines of the general index, overweighting or underweighting specific industry groups. In fact, there are funds such as First Canadian Equity Index Fund which invest in each industry group in the same proportion as the index.

As Table III shows, the index is divided into 14 major industry groups: metals and minerals, gold and silver, oil and gas, paper and forest, consumer products, industrial products, real estate and construction, transportation and environmental services, pipelines, utilities, communications and media, merchandising, financial services and conglomerates. At the end of June, 1996, metals and minerals were 9.3 per cent of the index, while financial services were 15.4 per cent. A portfolio manager who is positive on the outlook for metals and minerals but negative on banks might put a heavier weighting than 9.3 per cent in metals shares and a lower weighting in financial services.

A variation of this is to adjust the cash component of the portfolio. All mutual funds hold cash. But the percentage held in cash reflects the fund manager's view on the direction of the market. A manager who expects a sharp rise in the market soon might hold only enough cash to cover normal redemptions. A manager who expects the market to pull back or who believes that prices of individual stocks are expensive might have 30 per cent or more of the fund's assets in cash. Alternatively, fund managers can build portfolios choosing individual securities while ignoring what is in the general index. Many fund managers, however, end up with portfolios that are similar to the general index.

The major problem they face is finding stocks that can be bought and sold in volume. There are several thousand public companies listed on Canadian exchanges. But only a relatively small number trade in large enough volume or have enough shares outstanding to be considered by fund managers. A fund with assets of $5 million could have a portfolio of smaller companies. But a fund of $500 mil-

Toronto Stock Exchange Subindex Weights

As a percentage of the TSE 300

Metals and minerals	9.26	**Real estate**	0.27
Integrated mines	6.51		
Mining	2.74	**Transportation and environmental**	
		services	1.53
Gold and precious metals	11.00		
		Pipelines	2.33
Oil and gas	12.26		
Integrated oils	3.02	**Utilities**	9.03
Oil and gas producers	9.13	Telephone utilities	7.25
Oil and gas services	0.11	Gas and electric utilities	1.78
Paper and forest	4.16	**Communications and media**	3.27
		Broadcasting	0.37
Consumer products	6.84	Cable and entertainment	0.82
Food processing	0.13	Publishing and printing	2.08
Tobacco	1.12		
Distilleries	3.15	**Merchandising**	3.53
Breweries and beverages	0.53	Wholesale distributors	0.42
Household goods	0.51	Food stores	1.03
Biotechnology/		Department stores	0.35
pharmaceuticals	1.40	Specialty stores	0.59
		Hospitality	1.14
Industrial products	16.96		
Steel	1.13	**Financial services**	15.41
Fabrication and engineering	0.95	Banks and trusts	12.80
Transportation equipment	1.58	Investment companies	1.06
Technology - hardware	5.92	Insurance	0.71
Building materials	0.54	Financial management	0.84
Chemicals and fertilizers	4.39		
Technology - software	0.94		
Autos and parts	1.51	**Conglomerates**	4.14

June 30, 1996   SOURCE: TORONTO STOCK EXCHANGE

TABLE III

lion would have to have the bulk of its assets in larger companies. Otherwise its manager would be faced with a portfolio containing too many companies to be manageable.

You can figure out a stock's capitalization by multiplying its share price by the number of shares outstanding. A company with 10 million shares outstanding and a stock price of $25 would have a market capitalization of $250 million.

The heaviest weighting among the 300 stocks in the TSE composite index belongs to BCE Inc., with 4.8 per cent of the index on June 30, 1996. Next is Barrick Gold with 3.2 per cent, followed by Seagram Co. with 3.1 per cent and Royal Bank with 2.9 per cent. These four stocks represent about 14 per cent of the total value of the TSE 300. The top 10 stocks in the index represent 29 per cent of the index; the top 100 represent 81 per cent; the top 200 represent 95 per cent. In contrast, the smallest 50 stocks in the index represent less than 2 per cent of the index; the largest of that 50 is 0.05 per cent of the total.

Virtually all funds have rules that limit their holdings of individual stocks. For example, concerns about liquidity would prevent a fund, along with any other funds managed by the same adviser, from holding more than 5 per cent of the outstanding shares of a specific stock.

Consequently, Canadian equity funds, particularly medium and larger funds, almost always end up having larger companies as a major portion of their portfolios, and these are generally the stocks that are found in the TSE 300.

Since the federal government allows RRSP-eligible mutual funds to hold up to 20 per cent of their assets in foreign stocks, many Canadian equity funds have a U.S. or overseas component that may contribute to results that differ from the Canadian market.

Some managers try to beat the market by catching the swings. They build up cash when they believe the market is near the top and they spend their cash when the market is near the bottom. These managers are called market timers and they often base their decisions on technical analysis — the analysis of market cycles and graphs. Market timers face some major difficulties.

First, it is very difficult to call a market top or bottom. Second, it is even more difficult to move out of or into a stock if you have a large portfolio. The manager will simply be unable to sell as much as he or she wants at peak prices, or buy at the bottom. The third problem faced by market timers is that if they are wrong in their timing, they will drastically underperform their competitors.

The funds that do seem to outperform the market have three things in common: the decisions are made by a single person or a small group of individuals, the decisions are made quickly, and the decision-makers are not afraid to act differently from the crowd.

Moreover, their methods of choosing stocks are based on finding undervalued situations. They seek out companies whose shares trade in the market at levels below the values of the assets, less liabilities, and which offer good potential for earnings growth. Such managers will spend cash when they find plenty of stocks that meet their criteria and will build cash when shares become overvalued and they cannot find undervalued stocks to purchase.

Alternatively, some fund managers have had superior performance by aiming at companies with above-average growth rates or by moving from sector to sector in anticipation of price movements.

In most cases the stocks held may not represent the largest companies. Moreover, such funds' monthly performance may differ from the general market's performance.

In contrast, many funds have their decisions made by ponderous committees that are unable to act quickly. By the time they act on the data available — which is most likely the same information available to other institutional investors — the information has been fully reflected in share prices. Consequently, such funds are unlikely to do better than the market, nor much worse.

U.S. equity funds

If you're interested in investing in U.S. markets, you can choose from among almost 90 U.S. equity funds. These are very popular among investors who believe that the U.S. market offers investment opportunities not available in Canada and who expect the U.S. economy to outperform Canada's.

Since most U.S. funds accept subscriptions in either Canadian or U.S. dollars, these funds also appeal to people who have U.S. dollar savings and want to keep this money in U.S. dollar-denominated growth securities. Similarly, individuals who plan to retire in the U.S. often invest a portion of their assets in U.S. securities.

U.S. equity funds should be considered as an alternative to U.S. stock portfolios in estate planning. If you own substantial U.S. assets, such as stocks, and you die, your estate could be subject to

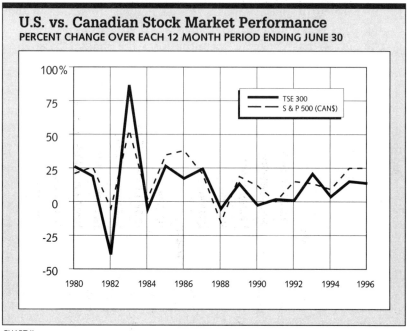

U.S. vs. Canadian Stock Market Performance
PERCENT CHANGE OVER EACH 12 MONTH PERIOD ENDING JUNE 30

CHART II

U.S. probate. However, holding mutual funds invested in U.S. assets avoids this potential problem because the funds are a Canadian asset.

Like Canadian equity funds, there is a wide variety of funds that invest in the U.S. Many try to parrot the major U.S. stock market indexes. For example, Atlas American Large-Cap Growth Fund invests primarily in companies included in the Standard & Poor's 500 composite stock index and which "best represent the investment characteristics of blue-chip securities." Similarly, Green Line U.S. Index Fund tracks the performance of the S&P 500.

Other funds have investment policies that are a variation of this theme. Century DJ Fund seeks above-average rates of return by investing in major blue-chip companies with above-average earnings and dividend records.

Others attempt to beat the averages by choosing investments from a broader range of stocks. AGF Special Fund Ltd. looks for companies that are expected to grow at above-average rates of return. AGF American Growth Fund Ltd. has a similar objective but puts the greatest portion of its assets in stocks listed on the New York Stock

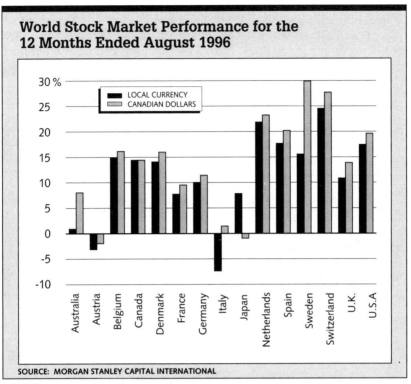

World Stock Market Performance for the 12 Months Ended August 1996

LOCAL CURRENCY
CANADIAN DOLLARS

SOURCE: MORGAN STANLEY CAPITAL INTERNATIONAL

CHART III

Exchange. United American Fund seeks long-term capital growth by investing its assets in U.S. common stocks that its managers consider undervalued in relation to earnings, dividends and assets.

The relative performance of Canadian and U.S. funds is mixed and depends on the period measured. U.S funds did much better as a group in the 12 months ended June 30, 1995, a reflection of a falling Canadian dollar and, more importantly, a stronger U.S. economy. Different measurement dates, however, will provide different results and in the 12 months ended June 30, 1993, Canadian equity funds beat their U.S. counterparts.

International equity funds

Virtually every industrialized country and many Third World nations have stock markets that trade shares of local companies. The performance of any given market reflects local and international economic conditions. And while all important markets move somewhat in concert because of the shrinking global marketplace, there can be large differences in performance. This reflects the fact that at any given time certain markets might be in an earlier or later stage of the economic cycle than North American markets. A nimble portfolio manager can take advantage of these differences. The result is that an international fund might show gains in a year in which U.S. and Canadian markets head lower.

The performance also reflects the fact that some markets perform better than others. For example, in the 12 months ended June 30, 1996, virtually all major world stock markets had positive returns. These ranged from Japan, with an increase of 55 per cent, to 8 per cent for Italy. Canada was at the low-middle of the range with an 11.4 per cent gain for the TSE 300.

While there are several dozen countries with stock markets, most international funds stick with the major European, Far East and Australian markets as well as Canadian and U.S. markets. A typical fund might restrict the bulk of its portfolio to shares traded in the United Kingdom, Germany, France, Switzerland, Australia, Japan, Canada and the U.S.

Occasionally, it will invest in shares traded in other markets such as Italy, Austria, Singapore, Hong Kong or the Scandinavian countries. But equity investments in these markets usually reflect a view of the outlook for a specific company rather than an economy or currency. Trading volumes in many overseas markets are simply too light to allow a portfolio manager to invest with reasonable diversification. So while a specific overseas market may rise 32 per cent, as Sweden's did, it is unrealistic to expect a fund manager to have a heavy position of Swedish stocks in a portfolio.

Managers of international funds must consider the relative values of assets in different countries, currency trends and, of course, stock market movements.

Managing an international fund can be more complicated than managing a single-market fund. Some firms have developed the expertise and have Canadian managers who base their decisions on their own research or on information supplied from abroad. Others retain overseas advisers to make recommendations. For instance, Global Strategy uses N. M. Rothschild International Asset Management Ltd. of London for the Global Strategy Fund, as well as a number of other managers for various funds. Several funds formerly used Baring International Investment Limited which collapsed in scandal. No Canadian assets were affected. In contrast, Dynamic

Europe Fund uses the expertise of its Toronto-based manager, Goodman & Company. The rates of return of the top-performing international funds suggest that location of the manager should not be a concern for investors.

Equity funds which invest in specific markets include some of the best and worst performers in different periods of time. For example, in the 12 months ended June 30, 1994, some of the top performers were funds which invested in certain segments of the Far East (month-to-month performance during the period, however, was exceptionally volatile). For the 12 months ended June 30, 1995, Japanese funds were among the poorest performers; however, Japanese funds and those funds which invested in Japan in the past have had some of the highest 10-year returns, ranging from 15 to 20 per cent.

However, the long-term returns mask year-to-year volatility. In 1986, for instance, the four top-performing mutual funds in Canada were Universal Sector Pacific, formerly Universal Savings Japan (up 68 per cent); Royal Trust Japanese Stock Fund (up 63.5 per cent); Investors Japanese Growth Fund (up 61.2 per cent); and AGF Japan Fund Ltd. (up 54.7 per cent). In the 12 months ending June 30, 1992, their returns in Canadian dollars were dismal. In the subsequent 24 months, performance was very good.

The 10-year average annual compound rates of return for Japanese funds are superior to the rates for Canadian funds over the same period. However, to understand these rates you have to look at year-by-year performance. An investment made in the Japanese market in 1976 and held until 1983 or 1984 would have performed about the same as an investment in the Canadian market, although year-by-year performance would have varied widely. But 1985 and 1986 were banner years for Japanese funds because stock prices and the yen soared.

Emerging market funds

During the past few years, several companies have launched funds which invest in Latin America. Others are investing in those countries which are referred to as emerging countries economies or emerging markets — countries whose economies are moving toward capitalism. There are funds which specialize in specific emerging markets such as India and China, and funds which may place a portion of their assets in Eastern Europe. There is even one fund,

GlobeInvest Emerging Markets Country Fund, whose portfolio includes closed-end country funds which in turn invest in emerging markets.

The attraction of emerging market funds is their potential for growth. An economy that is moving toward capitalism is likely to have a much higher growth rate than Canada or other already industrialized nations. The trade-off for this rapid growth is the volatility that a developing market is likely to exhibit over time. These markets are usually thin with relatively few stocks and small capitalizations; consequently, relatively small flows of capital in or out of such a market can have substantial effects on prices.

Emerging market funds are best left for the speculative segment of an investor's portfolio. They are risky and some of the risk elements are rarely faced by investors in Canada, the U.S. or Europe. For example, many of the areas considered emerging markets may be areas of political unrest. It is unlikely that regulation of trading and other issues related to securities will be stringently enforced in regions where government itself is unstable.

Specialty funds

For investors who want a hefty weighting in a specific industry sector there are a number of specialty funds. These can be useful for investors who want to speculate in one industry or who want a heavier weighting in their portfolio of a specific type of investment than they can get by holding a broadly based fund.

Specialty funds can be roughly divided into several categories: precious metals funds, energy funds, natural resource funds, technology funds, small company funds, real estate funds, and health funds. Because these funds concentrate in specific market areas, they are often much more volatile than equity funds which invest in many industries. Precious metals funds have been among the best performers over the past several years as gold share prices rose dramatically. But the area is volatile. For example, in 1979, Goldfund jumped 161.5 per cent; in 1980, it added 89.7 per cent. The following year it was off 38.7 per cent.

Energy funds have also had their ups and downs. They rose spectacularly during the late 1970s as world energy prices soared. But the federal government's national energy program and the oil glut made them dismal performers from 1981 to 1986, underperforming the general market. In 1987, they did well because of rising energy prices and increased investor interest in energy-related stocks. Their fortunes reversed again in 1988, but during the first part of 1989 they had mixed results. In August, 1990, when Iraq invaded Kuwait, energy funds were indeed the market leaders.

The specialty group includes what are called "small-cap" funds. These invest in companies with smaller capitalizations. Small can mean capitalizations of less than $150 million or less than $50 million, depending on the fund.

Several studies of market performance suggest that small-cap companies outperform the general market during bull markets and don't fall as much as the general market during bear markets. The theory is that smaller companies have a better growth rate than large, mature companies. Consequently, portfolios holding small-cap companies would have, over time, superior performance. In fact, the performance of small-cap funds reflects this.

Labour-sponsored investment funds

While labour-sponsored investment funds are included as specialty mutual funds in some mutual fund tables, they are not mutual funds. They are driven by tax legislation and are riskier than most mutual funds and a lot less liquid. Labour-sponsored funds invest in venture situations and hold the risk of failure inherent in a start-up situation. Although labour-sponsored funds may be redeemed, there are conditions. For instance, investors who redeem within eight years face repayment of government credits. Investors who cash in within the first eight years also face redemption charges. In addition, the funds are required to invest a specific portion of their assets in qualified companies within a specified number of years; failing to do so may result in government penalties to the fund.

Balanced funds and asset-allocation funds

Balanced, or asset-allocation, funds have as their objective maximizing growth and income while preserving capital. They do this by changing the asset mix ratio of stocks to bonds to reflect anticipated market conditions. Some funds restrict their investments to Canadian stocks and debt securities. Others will include a wider range of instruments.

The funds that are truly balanced should be less volatile than pure equity funds because of the revenue from the fixed-income portion of the portfolio or because of the types of stocks held, and indeed, the majority of balanced funds are less volatile than equity funds. Some balanced funds, however, have investment policies that allow them to hold any proportion of fixed-income securities and equities so from time to time the fund could be 100 per cent equities. Because they do not have to be diversified among asset classes, they may prove more volatile than funds that always have some stocks and some bonds. The vast majority, however, have both equities and fixed-income securities at all times, varying the proportions according to market conditions.

While equity funds are the largest group, balanced funds have been attracting new investors at a faster pace. The toughest investment decision for many people centres upon asset mix — the percentage they should hold in Canadian stocks, bonds, short-term deposits, foreign securities and gold. For investors who don't want to get involved in this type of investment decision, a good balanced fund might make the most sense.

The latest wrinkle in this area is the asset-allocation service. These are essentially market-timing services. The fund management company (or broker) advises you when to switch from one type of fund to another — to adjust your asset mix. In theory, such a service should provide top returns. However, you should consider all the costs involved in switching. You might also question whether it is in your best interests to be in a fund that is part of an asset allocation service. If you want to remain in equities, yet the management company recommends a switch into cash, the equity fund manager might face substantial redemptions which could result in the sale of fund assets and a change in the portfolio mix. This change might not suit your objectives.

Any mixture of funds with different management styles or asset classes or currencies is likely to produce returns which are more stable than the individual components. Mackenzie Financial has an asset allocation service that uses its funds. Called STAR Strategic Asset Allocation, Mackenzie's Star portfolios blend seven mutual funds in proportions to meet specific investor needs.

A variation of an asset-allocation service is the mutual fund "wrap" account in which a broker offers a portfolio of house funds, each managed by one or more fund managers chosen by the brokerage house. The client's money is invested in a variety of these pooled funds and managed for a flat fee based on the assets being managed. A typical minimum investment is $50,000 and the annual fee is about 2.5 per cent, although limits and fee depend on the firm. There are no acquisition or redemption fees.

The brokerage house retains a number of managers who have different management styles. Each fund may have more than one manager. To take advantage of different management styles, a fund might be managed in part by a company that seeks out growth situations, while another part is managed by a firm that bases its decisions on value. Your portfolio is tailored from these funds to suit your specific needs and investor profile. As a result, you get a customized asset mix which can be better monitored than mutual funds. A disadvantage for some investors, however, is the inability to move one's holdings to another broker if desired.

Wrap accounts in the U.S. are run somewhat differently. Rather than owning units in a pool, investors hold the specific securities individually. This allows more control over individual holdings. For instance, an investor may choose to avoid, say, tobacco stocks in his or her account. This kind of selectivity would be harder when holding units in a pool of securities.

Real estate funds

At one point in time real estate mutual funds were quite popular with investors. Today only three remain, the rest forced to liquidate or convert into closed-end funds. These generally trade at discounts to the underlying asset values. Unlike other mutual funds which hold marketable securities, real estate funds hold commercial buildings which in some cases might have been purchased in part with borrowed money. Moreover, the values placed on real estate funds were based on appraised values rather than market values. When real estate prices started their decline several years ago, astute investors in these funds redeemed. Once cash reserves were exhausted, the funds could meet no more redemptions. Regulators have changed the rules and it is unlikely that the authorities will allow the establishment of new real estate funds as open-ended funds.

It is fair to say that many investors who bought real estate funds failed to read the fine print of the prospectuses which noted that there could be delays in meeting redemptions and that if there wasn't enough cash on hand to meet redemptions, the fund would redeem on a pro rata or proportional basis.

There is at least one specialty fund, Dynamic Real Estate Equity Fund, which invests in shares of publicly traded real estate companies.

Non-Policy 39 funds

Mutual funds are regulated under what is called National Policy 39. There are a number of funds which at first glance look like mutual funds but are far riskier and which do not have to comply with NP 39. These include hedge funds which may use leverage or futures and options to enhance returns. While these offer the potential for extremely high returns, they can also result in huge capital losses. They are suitable only for those investors who can afford to lose the capital they invest in these.

Commodity funds

It's even possible to have a mutual fund that speculates in the futures markets. Futures are contracts calling for the delivery of a specified commodity, security or currency at a specific price on a specific date. Futures contracts cover major food commodities, precious metals, trading currencies, bonds and even the stock market. Trading in futures is very risky because investors have to put up only a fraction of the value of the underlying contract as a "down payment." Because of this enormous leverage, investors either make a lot or lose a lot.

Because of the risks involved in futures trading, anyone who wants to offer a mutual fund that invests in commodity futures must meet some stringent criteria. And while commodity funds have been brought to market from time to time in Canada, they have failed to generate lasting investor interest. Currently, it appears that none is being offered nationally, although several funds are available in British Columbia and Alberta. At least one fund is especially unique since its manager earns an incentive fee based on profits.

The lack of interest in commodity funds largely reflects the regulatory environment. First, the provincial securities regulators, whose rules must be followed by anyone who wants to sell securities to the public, must be satisfied that an investor's liability is limited to the amount invested. If you speculate in commodities on your own, your liability is unlimited.

Second, the people selling such a fund generally have to be registered under the Commodity Futures Act as well as the Securities

Act. This dual registration reflects the regulators' recognition that someone selling a commodities fund should have expertise both in trading commodities futures and mutual funds.

Third, to be a potential investor, you have to be wealthier and more experienced in investing than the average person. The rules demand that dealers offering such an investment must determine that the potential investor understands the nature of the investment through work experience, education, independent advice or prior experience.

As well, there are minimum suitability standards based on income and assets:

- Investors must have a minimum annual gross income of $30,000 and a net worth of $30,000. Alternatively, a net worth of $75,000 is required.
- The maximum annual management fee can't exceed 6 per cent of net assets of the fund. Incentive fees can't exceed 25 per cent of the profits calculated no more frequently than quarterly.
- The minimum capital for a commodity fund is $500,000.
- The prospectus must state on the front page that a participant in the fund must be able and prepared to lose his or her entire investment, that the fund is highly speculative, and that there are substantial management and advisory fees and brokerage commissions before an investor is entitled to a return on investment.
- Investors in a commodity fund must be notified within seven days of any decline in net asset value of 50 per cent or more from the beginning of the year or the last valuation date.
- Potential investors must be informed in the prospectus whether the fund will wind up automatically if the fund's net asset value per share falls below a certain level. As well, the manager of the fund must disclose his or her track record in managing comparable pools.

Because of the volatile nature of commodities futures, disclosure requirements are more stringent than for other mutual funds. Investors get monthly reports on performance, commissions paid, and the like.

CHAPTER 5

All About Income Funds

FIXED-INCOME MUTUAL FUNDS are primarily designed to provide maximum income rather than growth, while preserving capital. These types of funds invest in income-producing securities — bonds, mortgages, treasury bills, and in some cases common stocks and preferred shares that have high yields. By investing for income rather than growth, fixed-income fund returns are more stable than equity fund returns. Some fixed-income funds, specifically bond funds, can be used as growth funds in periods of falling interest rates.

Managers of fixed-income funds are concerned primarily with the quality of the issuers of the securities they purchase, interest-rate trends and, depending on the fund, currency exchange rates.

Because preservation of capital is a primary objective, most fixed-income funds have similar policies regarding the quality of the investments they make. All mortgage funds invest primarily in first mortgages, the most secure type of mortgage. If a borrower defaults, the holder of the first mortgage has first call on the assets. Similarly, most bond funds have a major portion of their assets in government bonds and government-guaranteed obligations. Any debentures in fixed-income portfolios are usually of large companies whose assets are significantly greater than their debt loads and whose earnings have historically exceeded interest expense by a broad margin.

Preferred-income funds generally have the vast majority of their assets invested in preferred shares of blue-chip Canadian companies whose securities are rated highly by the widely used rating services, Canadian Bond Rating Service Ltd. and Dominion Bond Rating Service, or in securities which the manager's analysis indicates are secure. In order to assign ratings, the rating services examine the income statements and balance sheets of major companies that issue preferred shares, and consider industry trends. Most preferred-income funds have some common shares but the portion is generally limited to a maximum of 20 to 25 per cent.

Returns from fixed-income funds have two components. First, of course, there is the income which reflects interest and dividends paid by the underlying securities. Second is capital appreciation, which reflects the impact of the market on the value of the underlying securities. Although it is a secondary objective for most bond, mortgage and preferred-dividend funds, capital appreciation or depreciation can be a significant portion of total return, particularly during periods of volatile interest rates.

During 1992 and 1993, interest rates declined dramatically in Canada to their lowest levels in a generation. Bond and mortgage funds produced double-digit rates of return, attracting new investors to mutual funds. Many GIC investors facing renewal rates as low as 5 per cent for a five-year term jumped into bond and mortgage funds unaware of the potential volatility.

In January, 1994, the U.S. Federal Reserve Board decided to raise interest rates to slow economic growth and cool inflation. Other countries did so as well. Canada, faced with international concern about its deficit and the forthcoming Quebec election had to raise rates even more than other countries to attract and maintain investment capital in Canadian bonds. As a result, interest rates soared over a short period of time. Government of Canada bonds with 8 per cent coupons and due June 1, 2023, fell from $1,111 at the end of January, 1994, to $859.50 by the end of June, 1994. This was a decline of almost 23 per cent. If a bond mutual fund had been completely invested in bonds of similar maturities over that period, it would have had a similar decline. However, most bond fund managers have a mix of maturities to hedge against the impact of an unexpected surge in rates.

This is an extreme example because the shift in interest rates over that time was exceptional. By June, 1995, the bond in our example had recovered to $967. The volatility of a specific bond depends on the number of years to maturity — the date when the issuer will redeem the bond at face value. Bonds with only a few years to maturity are much less volatile than bonds that won't mature for decades. This is why bond funds with heavy positions in shorter-term bonds perform better than funds emphasizing long-term bonds in periods of rising interest rates.

Bond fund and preferred-share fund managers can control the performance of their funds through the structure of their portfolios. Managers who expect a jump in rates sell their longer-term securities and move into shorter-term securities. Mortgage fund managers have less control because they have few, if any, opportunities to trade their portfolio to shorten or lengthen the terms of mortgages they hold. Also, the terms of the mortgages which they hold largely reflect what was available in the marketplace at the time they made their purchases. More on this later.

Some fixed-income fund managers try to increase their returns by holding debt instruments issued in foreign currencies. Several provinces, some Crown corporations and many major banks and corporations borrow abroad by issuing bonds and debentures denominated in U.S. dollars, Japanese yen, Australian dollars and European currencies. Funds that hold these securities will benefit if the foreign currencies appreciate against the Canadian dollar. However, performance suffers if the Canadian dollar does better.

Preferred-dividend income funds

If your investment objective is current income, and the capital you want to invest is outside your RRSP, consider a preferred-dividend income fund. Your after-tax rate of return will generally be higher than the after-tax return from an interest-income mutual fund.

The federal government taxes various types of investment income differently. Interest income is fully taxed. In contrast, the first $100,000 of capital gains is tax-free, as a lifetime exemption, subject to certain adjustments. Dividend income from Canadian corporations is treated in yet another way. To encourage Canadians to invest in shares and to help companies raise capital, the government invented the federal dividend tax credit to reduce the effective tax rate on dividend income from Canadian corporations. Your after-tax rate of return from investing for dividends should exceed the after-tax return from interest vehicles. Table IV compares the taxation of interest and dividends and shows that you would pay just under $30 tax on $100 of dividend income compared with just over $44 tax on $100 of interest income. However, pretax yields on dividends are generally lower than interest yields. But market spreads on an after-tax basis generally mean you get a higher return from dividends.

Taxation of Interest and Dividends

	Interest	Dividend
Interest received	$100.00	–
Dividend received	–	$100.00
Dividend "gross up"	–	$25.00
Taxable dividend	–	$125.00
Federal tax (29%)	$29.00	$36.25
Less dividend tax credit	–	$16.67
Net federal tax + surtax	$29.87	$20.17
Add provincial tax*	$15.66	$10.57
Total tax paid	$44.66	$30.74
NET RETURN	**$55.34**	**$69.26**

NOTE: *54% of basic federal tax. Provincial tax rates vary from province to province.

TABLE IV

The impact of the dividend tax credit is to reduce the tax you pay on dividends from Canadian corporations so that, for most income levels, on a pretax basis $1 of dividends is equal to about $1.26 of interest. On an after-tax basis a 6.4 per cent dividend yield is equal to 8 per cent interest, an 8 per cent dividend yield is equal to 10 per cent interest, and a 12 per cent dividend yield is equal to a 15 per cent interest.

Quebec sets its own tax rates independent of federal rates. A Quebec resident paying the top federal and provincial tax rates would net about $47 after tax on $100 of interest income and about $61 on $100 of dividend income.

Managing a preferred-share fund is a complicated task. First, there are several different types of preferred shares. Straight preferred shares pay a fixed dividend in perpetuity. They can be very volatile in periods of rapidly changing interest rates and, as a result, many investors are reluctant to buy them. So the investment community has developed other types of preferred shares in response to changing market conditions.

Floating-rate preferred shares, for instance, offer a dividend rate that is a certain percentage of the prime rate, say, 70 per cent. And there are floating-rate preferreds that have a fixed-minimum dividend rate. Retractable preferreds give investors the right to return their shares to the issuer at full face value at a specific date. Sinking-fund preferreds require the issuer to purchase or redeem a specific number of shares each year so that the total issue is retired after a certain number of years. Convertible preferred shares give the holder the right to convert the shares into common stock. Investors buy convertible preferred shares because they provide more income than common shares. If the common dividend grows to a point where it exceeds the preferred they can convert the preferred share to a common.

A few companies have issued preferred shares denominated in U.S. dollars. A fund manager might also hold some common shares in a preferred fund if the yield on the shares was attractive.

Most fund managers use a similar universe of preferred shares, basing their investment decisions on quality, yield, liquidity and specific features of a preferred share, such as whether it is floating or retractable. Quality considerations don't vary much from fund to fund. All invest the majority of their assets in high-quality preferred shares. By high quality, most Canadian fund managers mean preferred shares that carry P1 and P2 ratings issued by the Canadian Bond Rating Service and Dominion Bond Rating Service. A portion of a fund may be invested in preferred shares that aren't rated or that have a lower rating if the expected returns are superior, provided the manager is satisfied with the safety of the dividend and the return is superior. Similarly, a portion of the portfolio may be invested in high-yielding common shares.

Depending on interest rate spreads, a portion of the fund might also be invested in treasury bills. Because fund expenses, such as the management fee, can be charged against interest income, a fund manager will include some interest-paying investments such as treasury bills if the interest rate is higher than the rate available from preferreds.

Interest income funds

If interest income or a stable return is your major investment objective, as it is for many investors in RRSPs or registered retirement income funds, you have your choice of four different types of mutual funds: bond funds, mortgage funds, funds that invest in both bonds and mortgages, and money market and savings funds. Savings funds, which hold wholesale bank deposits, have virtually disappeared from the marketplace.

All four are backed by assets that carry little or no risk. Bond funds, for example, include bonds and debentures that are guaranteed by governments, Crown corporations, major banks or the creditworthiness of major corporations. Mortgage funds have as their underlying securities mortgages that are secured by specific properties. In some cases these mortgages are insured against default, guaranteed by a government agency or guaranteed by the manager of the fund. Money market funds generally hold treasury bills that are guaranteed by the federal government, provincial treasury bills that are guaranteed by the issuing province, securities issued or guaranteed by major financial institutions and sometimes top-quality short-term notes issued by major corporations.

As a result, with an interest-income mutual fund you don't have to worry much about losing your money. On rare occasions, bond funds suffer defaults, but the quality of the overall portfolios as well as the various guarantees make the impact of any losses insignificant to the value of an interest-income fund.

There are, however, some differences among the four different types of income-interest funds, and these affect the returns you may receive. These differences reflect the types of securities they hold. To understand how this works you have to look at the underlying securities in which such funds invest.

Let's assume you have a choice of three funds. The first invests only in Government of Canada treasury bills, the second in Government of Canada bonds and the third in mortgages guaranteed by the federal government under the National Housing Act. In all three cases we have Ottawa guaranteeing the underlying securities.

Even so, the returns you can earn from these funds may differ widely. For instance, during the 12 months ended June 30, 1995, the top 10 bond funds (excluding specialty bond funds) had rates of return that ranged from 24.8 per cent to 17.5 per cent; the top 10 mortgage funds had returns between 14.3 per cent and 12.5 per cent; and money market funds had returns clustered around 6.7 per cent. The high returns of bond and mortgage funds during the year reflect the sharp declines in bond yields and mortgage rates during that year.

Of course, that is only one period. Looking at the six months ended June 30, 1994, when interest rates surged, bond fund returns ranged from -14.9 per cent to 2.8 per cent; mortgage fund returns ranged from -10.2 per cent to 2.9 per cent while money market fund returns were clustered around 1.8 per cent.

Money market and savings funds have the most stable rates of return. That's because the securities they hold are very short term and will be redeemed at full face value by the issuer within one year. So the rates of return on money market funds are almost entirely income, with little that can be attributed to changing market values of the underlying securities.

A mortgage fund is more volatile than a money market fund. A mortgage fund holds securities that may mature in as little as six months or as long as five years. Its rate of return includes the interest paid on the mortgages it holds, plus or minus an adjustment to the market value of the mortgages in its portfolio. The market values change with changes in mortgage rates. If rates go up, the values of mortgages in the portfolio decline, with longer-term mortgages declining more than shorter-term mortgages.

A $50,000 five-year mortgage issued at 9 per cent, for example, would have a higher market value if new five-year mortgages were available at 8 per cent. But mortgage funds are not as volatile as this example seems to indicate because fund holdings include both short- and long-term mortgages. Also, new money coming into the fund or mortgages coming up for renewal will enter at prevailing rates. This serves to stabilize returns. In addition, when rates fall dramatically, as they did in 1992 and 1993, some borrowers would pay interest penalties to switch to lower rates.

Bond funds are generally more volatile than mortgage funds because they hold securities that may not mature for 20 years or more. A manager expecting rates to fall will increase the percentage of bonds which mature in, say, 20 years. This way the portfolio locks in a high rate of return. Conversely, a manager expecting higher rates will move into the shorter end of the market.

To sum up, money market and savings funds have the most stable rates of return. But over the long haul that stability has a cost. The cost comes in the lower rates of return that money market funds earn over the longer term compared with bond or mortgage funds. Bond funds have given higher long-term total returns than mortgage funds. But they have been more volatile and in some years have underperformed mortgage funds. For current income, however, mortgage funds often have an edge over bond funds because mortgage rates are generally higher than bond yields. Funds that invest in bonds and mortgages combine the characteristics of both types of funds.

Bond funds

The primary objective of most bond funds is to earn the maximum interest income possible without taking significant risk. But an important part of a bond fund's total return can include capital gains that stem from trading. Still, earning income is more important. The fund manager meets this objective by investing in quality bonds. Virtually all bond funds offered in Canada hold a major portion of their assets in government and government-guaranteed bonds, issues guaranteed by the major chartered banks and high-quality corporate debt. Some, such as AGF Canadian Bond Fund, restrict their holdings to Government of Canada bonds.

The investment policies of bond funds generally reflect the investment objectives of the conservative investors who use them for their RRSPs, RRIFs and for income. Even though virtually all funds invest in the same quality of issuers, performance can vary widely. These variations reflect the expertise of the fund manager as well as the fund's investment policy.

There are many ways that bond fund managers can increase returns. Most involve structuring a portfolio to reflect anticipated moves in interest rates. A fund manager who expects long-term rates to fall might increase the fund's holdings of long-term bonds. This would lock in high-yielding coupons of bonds which mature in, say, 20 years. Conversely, a manager who expects interest rates to rise will move into shorter-term bonds. A manager who expects rates to rise then decline might hold a mixture of long and short bonds with few medium-term holdings.

The actual management of the bond portfolio can be quite complicated. Not only does the manager have to consider the direction of interest rates, but also the relative yields of short-term and long-term bonds. In some periods long-term bonds yield significantly more than short-term bonds. At other times their yields will be about the same. There have been some occasions, such as 1989, the first half of 1990, and early 1995, when short-term rates have actually been higher than long-term rates.

Managers will trade bonds to improve yields. Each trade may improve the yield of a small portion of the portfolio by only a fraction of a percentage point. But done often enough, this can have a significant impact on overall performance.

Bond funds can also generate significant capital gains. This can happen when a manager sells bonds at a profit. For instance, a fund manager expecting an imminent drop in rates might buy discount bonds — bonds that sell at a discount to their face value because their coupons offer lower yields than new bonds.

Fund managers can also boost yields by increasing the portion of their portfolios invested in corporate bonds. Corporate bonds generally have higher coupon rates than government bonds of the same maturity. The higher yields, of course, reflect the fact that corporate bonds don't have the backing of a government. In addition, corporate bonds aren't as liquid as government bonds so the spread between the buy and sell prices can be significantly wider. As a result, the trading costs of a fund that has a heavy corporate component may be higher.

Another way of potentially boosting return is to invest in bonds denominated in foreign currencies. Crown corporations, provinces, banks and companies sometimes raise money outside Canada by issuing bonds and debentures in foreign currencies. The U.S. dollar is the most common currency used but Canadian governments and companies also commonly raise money in French francs, Australian dollars, New Zealand dollars, Japanese yen, Swiss francs and German marks.

Even though these bonds are denominated in foreign currencies, their issuers are Canadian so they are eligible for inclusion in RRSPs and pension funds. A fund manager might hold foreign currency bonds if the interest rate paid were substantially higher than the rate paid on Canadian dollar bonds of the same issuer and same maturity and there appeared to be no foreign exchange risk. Or, the manager might want to hold foreign currency bonds because he or she expected a sharp decline in the value of the Canadian dollar.

Specialty bond funds

Most of the bond funds offered by investment counsellors, investment dealers, banks and trust and insurance companies are designed to appeal to investors seeking income rather than capital appreciation. These funds are eligible for RRSPs and pension funds.

There are several exceptions, such as AGF Global Government Bond Fund. It invests in bonds issued by central governments of countries with developed capital markets. Its objective is high income and capital appreciation. Dynamic Global Bond Fund invests primarily in foreign currency bonds issued by Canadian governments, agencies and corporations, and by organizations such as the World Bank. Consequently, the fund is RRSP-eligible.

Some years ago, one company launched a "junk-bond" fund that invested in lower-quality bonds of U.S. corporate issuers. The fund provided a yield much higher than other bond funds offered in Canada. The fund failed to attract investor attention and was dropped. Apparently, few investors understood how the manager selected securities for the portfolio.

Mortgage funds

Mortgage funds are designed to provide maximum interest income for investors. Because mortgage rates are generally at least a point higher than bond yields, mortgage funds pay more current income per dollar invested than bond funds. Unlike bond funds, mortgage funds rarely trade what they buy. Consequently, capital gains are unlikely to be part of a mortgage fund investor's income — unless he or she redeems fund units when interest rates are relatively low at a value in excess of average cost. And because few mortgages are available with interest rates fixed beyond five years, mortgage funds as a group are less volatile than bond funds.

A mortgage is a loan secured by property. A residential mortgage is on a home; a commercial or industrial loan is on a commercial or industrial property. Commercial and industrial loans often have longer terms than residential mortgages and higher yields. A property can have several mortgages on it representing several loans. A second mortgage is less secure than a first mortgage; a third mortgage is less secure than a second mortgage. Virtually all the major bank, trust company, investment counsellor and insurance company mortgage funds hold first mortgages only. The amount of the loan is generally no more than 75 per cent of the value of the property (in some markets a lower ratio will be used). Lenders can go higher than the 75 per cent ceiling but in these cases they usually insure the mortgage against default.

Some funds, such as London Life Mortgage Fund, invest in residential, commercial and industrial mortgages. But most restrict their investments to residential mortgages.

Because the funds invest in first mortgages, investors needn't worry much about losses. For example, First Canadian Mortgage Fund, offered by the Bank of Montreal, invests only in mortgages that amount to no more than 75 per cent of the value of the property or are guaranteed under the National Housing Act or insured by the Mortgage Insurance Co. of Canada. If a mortgage goes into default, the bank guarantees to buy it at no penalty to the fund.

As part of its marketing strategy, the bank has had its fund reviewed by the Canadian Bond Rating Service and Dominion Bond Rating Service, the first fund to be rated by the two agencies. Both gave it an "AAA" rating, which demonstrates minimum risk and good returns. Generally, ratings are used for institutional investment products rather than investments aimed primarily at smaller investors.

Unlike bonds, mortgages — especially residential mortgages — are not traded actively. Consequently, mortgage fund managers are somewhat restricted in their ability to change the structure of their portfolios in anticipation of changes in interest rates. Mortgage fund managers, particularly of bank and trust company funds, have little choice in the terms of mortgages purchased by the funds. The mix of six-month, one-year, three-year and five-year mortgages is dependent largely on market conditions rather than on what the managers want. For instance, if most mortgage customers of the sponsoring bank or trust company choose four- and five-year terms — as happens in periods of rising interest rates — then that's where new money in the fund will be invested. Conversely, in periods of falling rates, when managers would like to increase the portion of four- and five-year mortgages, more borrowers will opt for shorter-term mortgages.

How this affects a fund depends on the portion of mortgages up for renewal in a given period and the growth rate of fund sales. Of course, if demand for longer-term mortgages drops drastically, then the spread between longer-term and shorter-term mortgages will narrow, shifting some of the demand.

The difference in the rate of return between two mortgage funds reflects the manager's ability to keep the portfolio balanced to minimize interest rate risk and keep the unit value relatively steady. Funds offered by the larger financial institutions probably have more flexibility because the funds are often a small fraction of the total mortgage portfolio offered by the institution, in some cases less than 1 per cent of the total. This gives fund managers some discretion over mortgages that will be acquired by the fund.

Short-term bond and mortgage funds

There are a number of funds that invest in both bonds and mortgages. Some have rigid asset-mix ratios. Others don't follow fixed ratios. Several may include common and preferred shares with attractive yields and the opportunity for capital appreciation. Rates of return of these funds, as a group, are more volatile than simple mortgage funds but less volatile than pure bond funds.

A number of these funds hold mortgage-backed securities. These securities are backed by a pool of residential mortgages with both principal and interest guaranteed by Canada Mortgage and Housing Corporation. Most issues have two- to five-year terms and, on the 15th of each month, a portion of the principal is repaid as well as interest. The yields on mortgage-backed securities are generally the highest available among AAA-rated fixed-income investments.

Mortgage-backed securities are more liquid than mortgages so funds holding these instruments may allow a manager more trading opportunities than a fund holding mortgages. However, the cost structure of a fund holding mortgage-backed securities is generally higher since the costs built into holding mortgage-backed securities are added to the fund's management fees.

Money market funds

Money market funds provide interest income with virtually no risk to capital. In fact, most money market and savings funds price their units at a constant value — $1 and $10 are the most common. However, these values are not guaranteed and the fund company is required to make this known in the prospectus and in advertising. Yields on these funds move in concert with short-term yields such as on treasury bills. Interest earned on the fund is used to purchase additional units on investors' behalf. Income is credited to clients' accounts daily in the case of funds that price their units daily and weekly in the case of funds that price weekly. Depending on the fund, interest compounds weekly or monthly.

Money market funds invest in a portfolio of highly liquid short-term debt instruments which generally mature within one year and have an average maturity of less than 90 days. These include federal and provincial government treasury bills, chartered bank certificates of deposit and instruments guaranteed by chartered banks, such as banker's acceptances, and short-term notes issued by the most creditworthy major corporations. Changes in the yields on money market funds may lag or precede changes in the prime rate, depending on the holdings of the portfolio and the moves in the "short end" of the market, say, T-bills maturing in less than 30 days. Therefore, in periods of volatile interest rates, the yield a buyer gets on a fund reflects the yield generated by the portfolio and may not match current yields. In fact, in July, 1992, many money market funds were providing yields that exceeded T-bill rates by a percentage point.

In times of high short-term rates, most fund management companies disclosed two rates of return or yields for their money market funds in their advertisements. The first was the indicated yield; the second was the effective yield. The indicated yield is more accurate. Generally, it is the yield earned by the fund in the latest seven-day period and calculated on income accrued or paid during the seven days. It's shown on an annualized basis. The effective yield is based on the compounding of the indicated yield; it assumes that the fund will continue to yield this amount every week — which is not likely.

Fund companies are required to show the indicated yield in any advertising that includes yields. They have the option of showing the effective yield but do not have to do so. The effective yield, however, could mislead an investor into expecting a higher return than will actually be earned, especially if rates are declining.

It would be more accurate for a fund company to show its indicated yield and the period or average term to maturity over which investors could expect to continue to earn that yield. Both the indicated yield and average term to maturity will change as new units are sold or investors redeem.

Returns vary moderately among money market funds, with the differences reflecting the aggressiveness of the manager. Some funds will restrict their holdings to instruments that mature within 90 days and keep them until maturity. Even a sharp jump in interest rates would have only a moderate impact on such funds' performance. Other funds might hold instruments with longer maturities to pick up a slightly higher return or because they expect rates to fall. Managers of these funds would trade their holdings to increase yields, too. Rates will also reflect management fees which vary from 0.5 per cent to 1 per cent or more.

Income payments

Before buying an income fund, find out how often you will receive your income payments. Bond funds usually distribute income quarterly or monthly, mortgage funds distribute income quarterly, preferred-share funds distribute income monthly, and money market funds usually distribute income weekly, or monthly. Realized capital gains for bond funds and preferred-share funds are generally distributed at year end.

Knowing the payment dates may have a bearing on the timing of your purchase. For instance, don't buy a bond fund the day before the dividend date because you'll be responsible for paying taxes on the interest paid, if the holding is outside your RRSP, even though you held the fund for only a day before the payment date. You will receive the interest but you will have converted a portion of your capital into taxable income.

CHAPTER 6

All About Closed-End Funds

NOT ALL FUNDS ISSUE NEW shares automatically when investors want to buy. A handful of funds called closed-end funds have a fixed number of shares or units. These are traded on a stock exchange such as the Toronto Stock Exchange. Closed-end precious metals funds even have their own TSE subindex. If you want to own shares of a closed-end fund, you have to buy them from someone who already owns them by placing an order with your stockbroker.

Closed-end funds, like other funds, invest in a portfolio of investments. Most closed-end funds are specialty funds that invest in particular areas such as precious metals, global investments or bonds. These funds are closed-end investment holding companies.

There is also a small group of funds called income trusts. These use investors' and borrowed capital to invest in a portfolio of fixed-income investments that pass on the interest income to investors.

Some closed-end investment holding companies that invest in gold and in international portfolios are corporations, just like other companies listed on stock exchanges. But instead of making or selling something, they invest capital. They have the same powers and responsibilities as other corporations. In fact, they can have much more leeway in their investment policies than open-end funds.

In addition, their profits are taxable like those of other corporations. Any income earned or capital gains realized by a closed-end fund are taxable at corporate rates. This differs from open-end funds where income and gains generally flow through to the individual investor. Since corporations aren't eligible for the lifetime capital gains exemption, the rate of return to an investor holding a closed-end fund might be lower than the rate of return earned on an open-end fund with a similar investment program.

Closed-end funds have been around for more than half a century, but their numbers increased in the early 1980s. The surge in popu-

A Survey of Closed-End Funds

Fund	TSE share price	Net asset value
BGR Precious Metals Inc.	$18.70	$24.15
Central Fund of Canada	6.50	6.30
Economic Investment Trust	73.00	106.76
First Australia Prime Income	13.90	14.45
United Corporations Ltd.	38.00	28.44

Oct. 3, 1996

TABLE V

larity of closed-end funds coincided with the push by brokerage houses to promote self-directed RRSPs. At the time, shares listed on Canadian stock exchanges could be held in self-directed RRSPs without restrictions. Closed-end funds qualified, even if their portfolios held investments, such as gold bullion, that would be ineligible if held directly in an RRSP or if their portfolios exceeded the 10 per cent limit on foreign property in RRSPs.

Therefore, closed-end funds were promoted by investment dealers as a way of getting around the intent of the rules restricting RRSP investments. During this period, Central Fund of Canada Ltd., one of the older closed-end funds, became a gold fund and had a share issue. Three new closed-end gold funds — Goldcorp Investments Ltd., Guardian-Morton Shulman Precious Metals Inc. and BGR Precious Metals Inc. — were also established. Shortly after, several global funds were underwritten — Guardian Pacific Rim, Guardian International Income and Worldwide Equities.

Ottawa revised its rules in 1986 so that closed-end funds that were primarily invested in foreign securities would be considered foreign property and, at that time, limited to 10 per cent of an RRSP. Closed-end funds that were already primarily invested in foreign property were "grandfathered" provided they did not arrange to issue additional shares after Dec. 4, 1985.

In the past few years several real estate open-ended mutual funds suffered from liquidity problems when the market for commercial real estate plunged in many areas of the country. To provide liquidity to their unitholders when they could not redeem their units, several converted to closed-end funds which were listed for trading on the Toronto Stock Exchange. More recently, several companies have established closed-end "country" funds, allowing investors access to markets whose trading levels may not support conventional open-ended mutual funds.

Closed-end funds have a limited following compared with open-end funds. That's largely because closed-end funds have tended to trade at a significant discount to the value of their underlying assets. The discounts apparently reflect the relative lack of liquidity of closed-end funds. Shareholders of open-end funds can redeem their shares at full net asset value on any valuation day. But holders of closed-end funds can sell their investments only if other investors are buyers. In a falling market, potential buyers of a closed-end fund might be scarce. The discount from underlying asset value will increase accordingly, reducing the market value of the fund units.

In a rising market the discount may shrink or even disappear. If, for instance, foreign investors become heavy buyers of closed-end gold funds as a way of buying a portfolio of Canadian gold shares, their prices might rise sharply.

The discount might also shrink on speculation that a closed-end fund might convert to an open-end fund.

Although there can be disadvantages to the fact that the shares of a closed-end fund cannot be redeemed on demand, there are also advantages. For instance, managers have more leeway in making investments. Because shareholders can't redeem shares on demand, the manager of a closed-end fund might decide to invest more heavily in shares with restricted marketability than would the manager of an open-end fund. About 90 per cent of the portfolio of open-end funds must be in liquid investments.

Also, a closed-end fund might invest in part with borrowed funds. For investment income trusts, the Ontario Securities Commission restricts debt to a maximum of 25 per cent of the assets of the fund. In contrast, open-end funds may not borrow other than temporarily to meet redemptions — even then only up to 5 per cent of assets.

The minimum equity capital for an investment income trust closed-end fund is $1 million. The minimum for an equity mutual fund is $100,000. The investment policies of closed-ends funds are generally included in their annual reports.

CHAPTER 7

What to Do First

MUTUAL FUNDS CAN BE USED successfully to meet both your short-term and long-term objectives, either inside RRSPs or outside of them. The trick, of course, is to make sure the funds you choose meet your objectives and are compatible with your financial picture.

Assuming you've taken care of the basics, such as making sure you have adequate life and disability insurance, an up-to-date will and a cash cushion equivalent to several months' salary, the first thing you should do is make a list of your investments, including your home, and your debts.

Interest paid on personal debts such as outstanding credit card balances and mortgages is generally not deductible from income for tax purposes. The cardinal rule to follow is to pay off all personal debt before starting any long-term investment program outside your RRSP.

Look at it this way. Paying off your debt is like making a risk-free investment that pays premium rates of return. Bank credit card charges are around 18 per cent, higher in some cases. And while some mutual funds have given moderately higher long-term rates of return, you wouldn't run out to borrow money at 18 per cent in the hope of earning 20 per cent, particularly if the 20 per cent rate wasn't guaranteed and the 18 per cent wasn't deductible from tax. Yet that is exactly what you would be doing if you invested in mutual funds while carrying unpaid balances on your credit cards.

Paying off your mortgage isn't as cut-and-dried as paying off your credit card debts because mortgage rates are generally a lot lower than the historical rates earned on equity-based mutual funds. Even so, you should still pay off your mortgage as quickly as possible. You always have the option of borrowing against the equity in your home and using the proceeds to buy mutual funds. You'll still owe money on your home. But this way the interest on the loan will be tax-deductible. Whether you should borrow against your home is another story. More on this later.

Once you've got your balance sheet in order, you should develop a basic understanding of how the federal government taxes different types of investment income. Knowing this will help you structure your portfolio so that you'll pay the least amount of income tax possible on your investment income.

There are four basic types of investment income to consider: interest from Canadian sources, dividends from Canadian corporations, interest and dividends from foreign sources and capital gains.

Interest income from Canadian sources, such as interest earned on bank and trust company deposits, Canada Savings Bonds and mortgages, is fully taxable at marginal tax rates. (Remember, your marginal tax rate is the rate of tax you pay on the last dollar you earn. As income increases, so does your tax rate in most cases. So your marginal rate is the highest rate of tax you pay.)

Interest income and dividends from foreign corporations are fully taxable at your marginal tax rate. This includes interest earned on foreign bank deposits, such as a trust company account in Florida, income from a U.S.-based money market fund or from one of several Canadian money market funds which hold U.S. dollar short-term investments. It also includes dividends from U.S. corporations such as General Motors Corp. and International Business Machines Corp., even if the shares are listed on Canadian exchanges or flowed through to you through a Canadian mutual fund.

Dividends from Canadian corporations, whether paid directly or flowed to you through a mutual fund, are eligible for the dividend tax credit which effectively reduces the rate of tax paid.

Capital gains are the gains made on the sale of capital property. This includes real estate, stocks, mutual funds and precious metals. The property can be Canadian or foreign. Gains on the sale of your principal residence are tax-free and excluded from capital gains, but gains on the sale of a second property, such as a cottage, are considered capital gains for tax purposes.

In its Feb. 22, 1994, budget, the federal government ended the lifetime capital gains exemption of $100,000, except for farms and small business corporations where the $500,000 limit continues to apply. (It had already eliminated real estate gains from the capital gains exemption in February, 1992.)

Even without the lifetime exemption, capital gains are still effectively taxed at a lower rate than interest income because only 75 per cent of the gain is taxable. For example, if you have $50,000 realized capital gains, only $37,500 or 75 per cent would be taxable. This $37,000 would be taxable at your marginal rate.

Make your investments tax-effective

It is important to note that inside RRSPs — the largest if not the only major savings program for many people — investment income compounds untaxed. However, when money is withdrawn from an RRSP either directly or in payments from an annuity or registered retirement income fund, the money is fully taxable whether it reflects interest income, dividends or capital gains.

Consequently, you should structure your total savings and investment package to reflect this tax treatment of investment income. In fact, many people don't do this and end up paying more tax than they should. Many people hold interest-paying investments such as CSBs and guaranteed investment certificates outside their RRSPs and growth mutual funds inside their plans. They pay tax on the interest earned outside their RRSPs. The capital gains inside their RRSPs grow untaxed but they will eventually be fully taxed when withdrawn from the RRSP.

If these people restructured their holdings so that their growth assets were outside their RRSPs and their interest-paying assets were inside their RRSPs they would reduce their taxes. They would still own the same assets, but the interest would compound untaxed inside their RRSPs while any capital gains earned would be eligible for the lifetime capital gains exemption.

If you currently hold interest-paying assets outside your RRSP and growth assets inside your RRSP you can switch them around dollar-for-dollar using a self-directed RRSP available through virtually all investment dealers and most trust companies.

CHAPTER 8

How to Meet Your Objectives

ONCE YOU HAVE STRUCTURED your savings and investments, the next step is to list your specific investment objectives. They could include saving for the down payment on a house, saving for retirement, saving for your children's education, investing for current income or simply investing for long-term growth.

Investment objectives can generally be categorized as short-term, medium-term or long-term. For our purposes, short-term means up to a couple of years, medium-term means three to 10 years, and long-term is anything longer than that.

Generally, short-term savings objectives are best met with money market funds simply because they are virtually risk-free. If you know that you will need the money fairly soon for a specific purpose, then a money market fund is for you.

If you won't need the money for three years or more, you have far more leeway. You can use fixed-income funds without too much worry. Even in years with sharp increases in interest rates, most fixed-income funds show positive returns. Over a three-year period, virtually all fixed-income funds show positive returns.

Whether you use equity funds really depends on how much risk you are willing to take. There is nothing wrong with using equity funds for medium-term investment objectives, provided you can accept the risk. It depends largely on whether you might find yourself forced to sell your holdings in a period when prices are down.

For long-term objectives, consider equity funds, which have traditionally outperformed fixed-income and money market funds over most periods of a decade or more.

Your investment objectives should be considered as flexible guidelines. There will be times when even long-term investors may want a heavy portion of assets invested in income and money market funds because of nervousness about the stock market. There will be other times when stocks seem very inexpensive and conservative investors who would normally invest for income may move into growth funds. Saving for the down payment on a home is usually considered a short-term objective; your strategy for saving for children's education will depend on the children's ages. If you start the program when your child is born it's a long-term program. If you wait until the child is in his or her teens, it's a short- to medium-term program. Similarly, a 20-year-old's RRSP is a long-term savings program while a 63-year-old's RRSP is a short-term program.

The rule of thumb is that the shorter the term of the savings program, the more conservative you should be and the less risk you should take.

Meeting short-term objectives

If you're going to need your money soon, perhaps within a year or so, it is probably best to play it safe and invest in a money market fund. You'll earn, at least in most periods, a relatively low return and pay tax on the interest earned but you'll know that you are not taking any risk and you'll get all your money back, plus interest.

Alternatively, you may want to look closely at preferred dividend funds. Many have had relatively stable returns. Depending on your income and tax bracket, the difference in rate of return between a money market fund and dividend fund can be significant. But remember: dividend funds, while relatively stable, are still more volatile than money market funds. Indeed, all dividend funds had negative rates of return in the six months ended June 30, 1994, an exceptional period for interest rates.

Generally, equity funds, and to a lesser extent bond funds, are too volatile to meet short-term savings objectives, particularly if a decline in capital will affect your lifestyle. If you're saving for the down payment on a home, don't invest in equity funds if a decline in the value of your investment will keep you out of that home. If you do invest in equity funds, particularly a specialty fund, in the hope of significant short-term performance, realize that you are a speculator — possibly even a gambler — betting that the market will perform as you expect.

Meeting medium-term objectives

If you are a conservative investor your best bet is probably a fixed-income fund, either a bond or mortgage fund for an RRSP, or a preferred dividend fund if you are trying to maximize your after-tax return.

You can, of course, go into asset allocation or growth funds, too. It all depends on where the market is. A lot can happen in relatively short periods of time. During the first three months of 1987 the Toronto Stock Exchange 300 total return index gained 22.8 per cent. But the stock market doesn't always move up, as many investors learned when the index plunged 31 per cent between its August peak and October trough. Unless you've got a crystal ball, or more than enough financial assets to meet your medium-term objectives, you should look at fixed-income funds rather than equities.

Meeting long-term objectives

If you won't need the money for more than a decade, go for growth using equity-based funds. Even if you measure performance using a market bottom as an ending date, such as the summer of 1982, almost all equity funds show positive returns over a 10-year period.

Of course, it makes little sense to jump into equity funds at a market top. So if you are a bit nervous about the near-term direction of the market, act conservatively and put only part of your money into equity funds and place the rest in money market funds.

Alternatively, look for funds that have heavy cash components, indicating that the manager has the same concerns as you. You should also consider balanced, or asset-allocation, funds because managers of these funds change asset mixes to reflect market conditions, increasing or decreasing equities according to market outlook. And remember, there are always exceptions to the rules. Many investors have had better returns from bond funds than from equity funds over the past decade. This reflects the downward trend in interest rates.

Meeting personal objectives

The following pages outline six common savings and investment objectives and how mutual funds can be used to meet them.

1. Saving for the down payment on a home

If you're saving for a home, you are probably hoping to buy within a couple of years. This makes your savings program relatively short term and you can't risk having to redeem your holdings when the market is down. Consequently, your investments should be confined to low-risk funds — funds in which the investment policies virtually guarantee your principal and interest.

Money market funds are the only funds that meet these requirements. They should be used exclusively if you expect to need your money within a year or so.

If you don't intend to buy a house for several years, you can accept more risk in the expectation of earning a higher rate of return. Look at dividend income funds or bond funds. While more volatile than money market funds, both are substantially less volatile than equity funds. Over most one-year periods, bond funds have done better than money market funds. In periods of sharply rising interest rates, a bond fund could do worse than a money market fund, as most did during the first half of 1994, even declining in value. Nevertheless, over a three-year period or longer you will almost certainly do better in dividend income or bond funds than in money market funds, if history holds true for the future.

Again, there are always exceptions and three-year returns from bond or dividend income funds for the three years ended June 30, 1990, were below rates from money market funds. Still, an investor who had started a medium-term program in the summer of 1987 using fixed-income funds might have switched into a money market fund partway during the three years locking in high rates of return.

You may be tempted to use equity funds to save for the down payment on a home. Indeed, long-term returns and some recent gains may make this a tempting option. Just remember that equity funds are volatile and that there will be some periods when prices will drop dramatically. If you can't afford to see the value of your savings drop, then don't go near equity funds.

2. Paying down your mortgage

Banks and trust companies may allow you to prepay the principal outstanding on your mortgage. The limit is generally 10 per cent of the principal annually on the anniversary of the mortgage, although some institutions allow 15 per cent. As well, you can pay off any or all of your mortgage at the renewal date.

Paying off your mortgage should be a priority before starting any long-term savings program other than your RRSP. You pay interest on your mortgage using after-tax dollars. This means that you have to earn about $1.72 to pay off every $1 of interest, if your taxable income is between $29,591 and $59,180 in 1995, depending on your province of residence. If it's higher, you have to earn at least $1.96 to pay $1 of interest after tax.

Therefore, if your mortgage rate is 10 per cent, you would have to earn more than 19 per cent on your investments before tax to break even. And remember, paying down your mortgage is a risk-free investment.

You can, of course, have your cake and eat it too by paying down your mortgage, borrowing against the equity in your home, then investing the capital. That way your mortgage interest is deductible. This strategy will be covered in detail in the next chapter.

3. Saving for your children's education

Since for most families saving for children's education is a medium- to long-term objective, mutual funds fit the bill. What you must remember is that any interest or dividends earned on the money you invest for your children, even if it is invested in their names, is taxable in your hands. However, any capital gains earned are attributed to the child. And interest or dividends earned on interest or dividends on which you paid tax is deemed to be your child's.

You should also keep in mind that if you have invested child tax credit cheques directly in your children's names, any interest or dividends earned are taxable in their hands, not yours. Each child can earn several thousand dollars of interest and dividends tax-free, so it makes sense to use child tax benefits as the cornerstone of any education savings program if you qualify.

If you prefer to be on the conservative side when it comes to investing your children's money, use a bond or a mortgage fund. Alternatively, choose a balanced fund. If university or college is a decade or more away, consider growth funds to give you a higher expected rate of return.

Many families use a combination of income and growth funds. Child tax credit cheques, inheritances and gifts from other than immediate family are invested in bond and mortgage funds while other capital is invested for growth. Just remember, when the children are a few years away from university, educational savings become a short-term objective. You may want to lock in your profits from growth funds and move into income or money market funds.

You can also consider a mutual fund registered education savings plan, a RESP. The capital contributed to a RESP (limited to $2,000 a year for each child to a maximum of $42,000) is not deductible for tax purposes. However, any income earned within the RESP grows untaxed. The income is taxable in the child's hands when withdrawn to finance post-secondary education but the capital you invested originally is withdrawn tax-free. However, the child's total income will probably be low and many of the expenses of education can be deducted by the student, so little or no tax will likely be paid. There is one potential problem; the money must be used to finance post-secondary education. However, if the child who is named as beneficiary does not continue his or her education, you can name another beneficiary.

A number of mutual fund companies, including Mackenzie Financial Corp., offer RESPs through mutual fund dealers and brokers.

4. Saving for retirement through RRSPs

By far, the largest single use of mutual funds is in RRSPs. Some estimates indicate that up to half of the $180 billion that Canadians have invested in mutual funds is in RRSPs. Because of the federal government's requirement that limits the foreign component of RRSP assets, RRSPs are concentrated in Canadian equity and balanced funds, bond funds and mortgage funds.

However, as noted previously, investors are allowed 20 per cent foreign content in their RRSPs. To maximize foreign content, many people have mutual funds in their RRSPs that invest outside Canada. This can be done by holding your mutual funds in a self-directed RRSP. These are available from virtually every organization involved in marketing mutual funds.

An RRSP is an extremely tax-efficient way of saving for retirement. Your contribution is deductible from income for tax purposes and you are saving untaxed dollars. Also, income within an RRSP grows untaxed. It is not until you withdraw money from an RRSP, either by cashing in your plan or by using one of the retirement options, such as a registered retirement income fund (RRIF) or annuity, that the proceeds are taxed.

Your contribution limit is 18 per cent of the previous year's earned income up to a maximum contribution of $13,500. From this contribution limit you must subtract any contributions made to a pension plan by you or by your employer on your behalf.

Contributions must be made in the taxation year or within 60 days of year-end to get a deduction for the tax year. It is possible to build a hefty cache of savings in your RRSP. When investing these savings in mutual funds, there are two important questions you should ask yourself: How does your RRSP fit in with your other savings? How much risk are you willing to take?

Remember, when you withdraw money from an RRSP, it will be fully taxable whether your gains are interest, dividends or capital gains. If you are saving both inside and outside an RRSP and you have both growth and interest-paying investments, you should structure your holdings so that as much of the interest-paying portion as possible is inside your RRSP. Keeping the growth portion outside your RRSP allows you to benefit from the lower tax rate applied to capital gains.

Many people, however, use asset allocation funds in their RRSPs as well as for other savings. They should continue with this approach and ignore the tax consequences. While this route might have some impact on after-tax returns, they are likely to be minor compared with the benefits of asset allocation.

As far as risk is concerned, you have two basic strategies from which to choose, one that is active and one that is passive. The active strategy is to constantly change the mix of mutual funds within your RRSP, moving into growth funds when they offer the best values and into income funds and money market funds when the outlook for equities is cloudy. This strategy, if successful, will give you the best returns from growth and income while preserving capital.

The passive strategy reflects the view that your age dictates the type of mutual funds you hold — the younger you are the more risk you can afford to take, the closer you are to retirement the more conservative you should be. The following are some guidelines based on age for structuring your retirement savings between interest-paying and growth investments. They apply to your total retirement savings, including those outside your RRSP.

If you are in your 20s, you have at least three decades before retirement. You can accept volatility in your RRSP and should invest the bulk of your RRSP for growth. Over the years you'll experience some ups and downs. But over the long haul you will probably come out significantly ahead of what you would have by playing it safe.

If you're in your 30s, you still have many years to go before retirement, so you can still put the bulk of your assets into equity funds, as much as 80 per cent, and invest the remaining 20 per cent for income.

If you're in your 40s, you should become a bit more conservative and move to around 60 per cent in growth funds and 40 per cent in bond funds, mortgage funds or both.

Once you're in your 50s, retirement is in sight. Consider moving to 40 per cent growth and 60 per cent income.

When you're within a decade of retirement, your main objective should be preservation of capital rather than growth. Move to 80 per cent income and 20 per cent growth funds as a longer-term hedge against inflation.

But remember, these are only guidelines. People who are approaching retirement with substantial investment assets — more than enough to comfortably finance their retirements — may decide to keep most of their assets invested for growth. Indeed, someone who started investing in his or her 20s might well decide to remain in equities because of the wealth he or she would likely accumulate. Similarly, if you have an adequate pension plan you might opt to keep the bulk of your RRSP invested for growth.

You also have to consider market conditions. It doesn't make much sense to plunge into equity funds if it looks like the markets are due for a sharp correction, even if you won't be retiring for 30 years or more. Similarly, people approaching retirement may want to put more of their money in growth funds if the market has been declining and prices seem relatively cheap.

You should also consider the portfolio components of the funds you hold. For example, balanced funds hold a blend of growth and income investments. You may want to consider this in structuring your RRSP. A 50-year-old man or woman might hold 50 per cent to 60 per cent of his or her RRSP in a balanced fund and the remainder in bond funds, rather than 40 per cent in growth funds.

Just remember that the objective of retirement savings is to finance retirement. Therefore, it should be the most conservative portion of your portfolio.

5. Registered retirement income funds

You can't have an RRSP beyond Dec. 31 of the year in which you turn 69. You have to roll your RRSP into an annuity or registered retirement income fund (RRIF) or cash it in and pay tax on the proceeds.

The RRIF option meets the needs of most investors. With a RRIF you can hold the same investments as in an RRSP. Moving from an RRSP to a RRIF is a simple matter which involves filling out a form provided by your fund broker or the mutual fund company with which you have your RRSP.

You can withdraw as much from your RRIF each year as you want. The minimum amount you are allowed to withdraw is determined by your age. However, the rules changed at the beginning of 1993 and again in 1996.

Under the rules for 1992, which continue to apply to RRIFs set up prior to 1993, minimum RRIF withdrawals were based on the amount of money in a plan at the end of the previous year, divided by the difference between 90 and the RRIF owner's age, or spouse's age if it is lower. For example, someone who was 71 years old at the end of 1991 and has a RRIF which had $100,000 in it at the end of 1991 would be required to withdraw a minimum of 1/19 or $5,263 in 1992, 1/18 in 1993, 1/17 in 1994, and 1/16 in 1995.

Under new rules effective in plans commenced after 1992, a RRIF can be structured to provide a lifetime income. The new rules require moderately higher minimum withdrawals than under the old rules for people 71 to 77, and lower minimum withdrawals for people 79 to 89. For people younger than 71, the old fractions based on age or spouse's age from age 90 will continue to apply.

The March, 1996, budget cut maximum retirement age for RRIF purposes to 69 from 71 with transition rules for those individuals 69 and 70. The age-to-90 ratio must be applied until age 71 when the government tables begin to apply.

You can convert your RRSP to a RRIF at any age. But because you have to withdraw some capital from a RRIF each year, you should postpone rolling your RRSP into a RRIF until you retire and need income from your plan. The first payment may be received in the year in which you open your plan, but you have the option of starting payments in the following year. In fact, you can postpone receiving your first payment, if you want annual payments, to Dec. 31 of the year you turn 70.

Your RRIF should be invested conservatively with the objective of providing income rather than growth. Consequently, it should be invested primarily in bond and mortgage funds. A portion, however, can be invested in equity or balanced funds to give you a longer-term hedge against inflation.

Overall preservation of capital is of the utmost importance because you will be withdrawing money from your plan each year. If you had a significant portion invested in growth funds and the market turned down, you could find yourself redeeming fund units after prices have fallen. You could seriously erode your financial security.

Again, this is a general guideline. If you retire with substantial assets you may decide you can afford to accept the volatility associated with growth funds and keep a major portion of your assets in growth funds.

6. Financing retirement outside a RRIF

Circumstances sometimes offer the option of a unique solution. Someone with limited assets and income would generally opt for a safe solution such as investing in bond mutual funds. However, sometimes the safe solution isn't always the best. Take, for instance, a widow with $50,000 in capital and no income other than government benefits. If she invested for interest income she would get her basic government benefit. But if she invested for growth and cashed in a portion of her units each month her income would largely be a return of her own capital and she might qualify for the guaranteed income supplement because her "income" doesn't fit the government definition. Such strategies aren't for everyone and they should be examined against an individual's circumstances.

CHAPTER 9

Strategies and Gimmicks

MAKING $1 MILLION THROUGH mutual funds isn't difficult. All it takes is the ability to set aside money each year and a long time to do it. If you can set aside $4,000 a year and earn an average annual return of 12 per cent you'll have $1 million in less than 30 years. If you could earn an average of 16 per cent, you would have $1 million in less than 25 years.

Saving can be difficult because of the temptations to spend. So virtually every mutual fund company has a program to make saving less painful. Depending on the fund company or the salesperson, such plans are called dollar-cost-averaging plans, automatic-purchase plans or preauthorized-purchase plans. You decide how much you want to invest each month or every three months and in which funds, fill out a bank authorization form and supply a sample cheque marked "void." The fund company will do the rest. Each month on the same date, the amount you chose will come out of your bank or trust company account and be invested in the fund or funds you pick. The plans are available for RRSPs and non-sheltered savings.

A key advantage of such plans is that if the market declines, your purchases will buy more mutual fund units, lowering your average cost. Conversely, you'll raise your average cost in rising markets. But with these programs you're in funds for the long term and in the end you'll do well.

You can establish a savings plan with as little as $50 a month. Chart IV shows how your investment would have grown if you had contributed $100 a month to a typical equity fund invested in the Canadian market during the 10 years ended June 30, 1995. It assumes you purchased the fund either on a no-load basis or with a declining deferred redemption fee so that all your money is invested. The chart is based on monthly returns of a Canadian equity

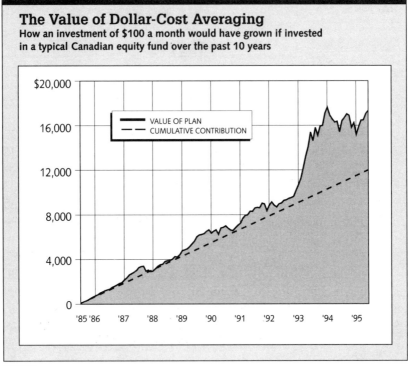

The Value of Dollar-Cost Averaging
How an investment of $100 a month would have grown if invested
in a typical Canadian equity fund over the past 10 years

VALUE OF PLAN
CUMULATIVE CONTRIBUTION

'85 '86 '87 '88 '89 '90 '91 '92 '93 '94 '95

CHART IV

fund and assumes contributions are made at the end of the month.
Different funds use different dates for investing contributions.

Withdrawal plans

A second type of plan offered by mutual fund companies is the
withdrawal plan. These plans allow you to invest a lump sum and
withdraw a constant amount each month. For example, you might
invest $100,000 in a typical equity fund with monthly withdrawals
of $833. Only a small portion of the $833 is regarded as realized
capital gain by the federal government in the early years of the plan
— most is seen as a return of capital.

The table in appendix one simulates the results over ten years of
a $833 monthly withdrawal plan from a Canadian equity fund
started with $100,000 on June 30, 1986. Acquisition and
redemption fees are ignored because many funds now allow such a
plan to be set up with no acquisition fees and ignore or reduce
substantially any redemption fees which might be applicable.

The fund in question had a 10 year return of just over 9 per cent. Consequently a withdrawal plan based on a higher amount would have resulted in a substantial decline of capital over the years. This isn't necessarily a bad thing, provided you don't outlive your capital. Many people, however, would likely prefer to withdraw less in the early years of such a plan to build a cushion in case of lower returns in subsequent years.

It is important to realize that different 10-year periods would provide different results. Stock markets were rising during much of the mid-1980s and 12 per cent withdrawal plans where relatively common. Given the volatilty of the stock and bond markets in recent years, withdrawal plans should be reviewed periodically and withdrawal amounts adjusted to reflect performance, that value of the plan, and short- and long-term cash needs.

It's important not to forget that a portion of your withdrawals could be taxable capital gain or dividend. This portion will vary from year to year depending on fund distributions as well as capital gains realized from selling units. In years of little or negative growth, much, if not all, of your withdrawals would simply be a return of your own capital and would not be taxable.

Leverage programs

Be very cautious about borrowing money to buy mutual funds. The use of borrowed money to invest, called leveraging, is a marginally profitable exercise in some cases and unprofitable in others. It can, however, be very profitable if used wisely. The key is to examine any proposal thoroughly and work out your projections on an after-tax basis. You must compare how you would fare with leverage and without.

Investing in growth funds with borrowed money is big business. In fact, it has been estimated in the industry that as much as a third of all mutual fund purchases made prior to the 1987 crash were made with borrowed money.

Of course, the reason for using borrowed money to invest is to make more money more quickly. If you can put $100,000 of the bank's money to work along with your own $100,000, you'll double your profit before interest expense and tax. Your interest is deductible. If the bank charges you 10 per cent and your marginal tax rate is 41 per cent, your after-tax cost of borrowing is 5.9 per cent or $5,900. (In fact, loan rates vary widely at different points in the economic cycle and were running at about 16 per cent during the first half of 1990 and about 5.75 per cent in mid-1996.) If you have $5,900 a year available for investment, instead of investing the money you could use it to finance a loan of $100,000.

Leverage has been extremely popular in the fund industry as a means of building business. Several major fund groups have arrangements with banks to finance leverage programs. Many individual salespeople make their own arrangements to bring clients to banks. Several years ago, one trust company, First City Trust, even produced a video on leverage designed to encourage investors to use borrowed money to buy mutual funds.

Leverage can be profitable in some situations but in many it is unlikely you will be compensated for the risk involved. If you are approached to buy funds using borrowed money, make some projections. In these projections, use several rates of return and various different interest rates for your cost of borrowing. By doing this you will have a range of possible results and can understand your potential risks and rewards. You should also determine the cushion you must have to protect yourself against a rise in interest rates or a fall in the market. Before implementing your leverage program, ask yourself whether you could afford to continue with a leverage program if interest rates rose sharply. Similarly, determine the magnitude of a market correction your bank will tolerate before asking you to put up additional security. In fact, you might want to have a generous credit line available to provide additional security.

The two examples in Table VI look at the results of leverage under certain circumstances and specific assumptions. In each case, we've allocated interest rates of 5.75 per cent which is a recent level and among the lowest prime rates of the past two decades and 13.75 per cent, the prevailing prime rate of only a few years ago. For rates of return we are using 10 per cent, 15 per cent, 30 per cent and -20 per cent. We've assumed that the investor's marginal tax rate is 50 per cent.

The cost and rates of return are realistic for one-year holding periods and reflect the experience of the past two decades. Just remember that only a handful of funds have managed to produce long-term rates of return in excess of 15 per cent and these are virtually all high risk funds.

If you wish to make your own projections using longer holding periods you should consider any taxes that might be payable on capital gains and dividend distributions. These could have a significant impact on your ability to continue your leverage program if you have limited cash flow and must take some profits to meet your tax bill.

We have made one important assumption that you shouldn't overlook. We have assumed that the investor who does not choose a leverage program will invest the cash flow which would otherwise be available for payment of interest. The interest on $100,000 using 5.75 per cent rate is of course $5,750 and has an after-tax cost of the $2,875, the amount the investor who does not use leverage has available for investment. Using the higher rate of 13.75 per cent or $13.750, the after-tax cost is $6,875.

If our investors borrow at 5.75 per cent, Table VI shows in the first set of examples a gain of 10 per cent on the capital invested over the year. The leveraged investor gets double the gain — $20,000 — and pays twice as much tax but earns double the after-tax profit of $12,500 (excluding interest costs). The investor who doesn't use leverage has an after-tax profit of $6,250 and in addition has the after-tax value of that interest to invest about $2,875. Consequently, his or her net worth grows by $9,125 over the year compared with $12,500 for the investor who borrows funds.

The next columns of the 5.75 per cent example show that the benefit of leverage increases with rates of return. In fact, with these three examples, the rates of return earned exceeds the cost of funds, a condition which is not guaranteed. The -20 per cent rate of return shows what can happen in a poor market — a significant loss, in this case 40 per cent of the investor's capital. The loss will be mitigated somewhat if our investor has taxable capital gains against which to apply a capital loss.

The second set of examples in Table VI uses a 13.75 per cent tax rate. It is apparent that the higher the interest rate the smaller the benefit from leverage. Over the past 10 years, the prime lending rate was in excess of 11 per cent about half the time as viewed monthly.

Before you go into any leverage program, determine what kind of cushion your bank requires in the event of a substantial decline in the value of your holdings or a major jump in the cost of money.

You should also ask any financial adviser recommending a leverage program to show you how someone would have fared on a month-by-month basis over the past 10 years using the specific fund or funds recommended and actual interest rates in place.

Borrowing to Invest — Two Examples

BORROWING TO INVEST AT 5.75% INTEREST

Return on your investment	10%		15%		30%		-20%	
	without leverage	with leverage	without leverage	with leverage	without leverage	with leverage	without leverage	with leverage
Equity	$100,000	$100,000	$100,000	$100,000	$100,000	$100,000	$100,000	$100,000
Loan	$0	$100,000	$0	$100,000	$0	$100,000	$0	$100,000
Total investment	$100,000	$200,000	$100,000	$200,000	$100,000	$200,000	$100,000	$200,000
Capital gain (loss)	$10,000	$20,000	$15,000	$30,000	$30,000	$60,000	($20,000)	($40,000)
Taxable gain (loss)	$7,500	$15,000	$11,250	$22,500	$22,500	$45,000	($15,000)	($30,000)
Tax	$3,750	$7,500	$5,625	$11,250	$11,250	$22,500	($7,500)	($15,000)
After-tax gain (loss)	$6,250	$12,500	$9,375	$18,750	$18,750	$37,500	($12,500)	($25,000)
Cash flow available for investment	$2,875	$0	$2,875	$0	$2,875	$0	$2,875	$0
Increase in equity	$9,125	$12,500	$12,250	$18,750	$21,625	$37,500	($9,625)	($25,000)

BORROWING TO INVEST AT 13.75% INTEREST

Return on your investment	10%		15%		30%		-20%	
	without leverage	with leverage	without leverage	with leverage	without leverage	with leverage	without leverage	with leverage
Equity	$100,000	$100,000	$100,000	$100,000	$100,000	$100,000	$100,000	$100,000
Loan	$0	$100,000	$0	$100,000	$0	$100,000	$0	$100,000
Total investment	$100,000	$200,000	$100,000	$200,000	$100,000	$200,000	$100,000	$200,000
Capital gain (loss)	$10,000	$20,000	$15,000	$30,000	$30,000	$60,000	($20,000)	($40,000)
Taxable gain (loss)	$7,500	$15,000	$11,250	$22,500	$22,500	$45,000	($15,000)	($30,000)
Tax	$3,750	$7,500	$5,625	$11,250	$11,250	$22,500	($7,500)	($15,000)
After-tax gain (loss)	$6,250	$12,500	$9,375	$18,750	$18,750	$37,500	($12,500)	($25,000)
Cash flow available for investment	$6,875	$0	$6,875	$0	$6,875	$0	$6,875	$0
Increase in equity	$13,125	$12,500	$16,250	$18,750	$25,625	$37,500	($5,625)	($25,000)

TABLE VI

You should also consider avoiding any leverage program that is based on the premise that you can cash in units to pay interest on the loan and that your returns will always exceed your cost of funds. A bear market and withdrawals could quickly erode your capital to the point that you would suffer permanent capital loss.

Borrowing against your home

Many Canadians are house-rich but cash-poor. They have a substantial net worth, but it's tied up in a single asset. Some mutual fund salespeople see this as an opportunity, both for the homeowner and for themselves. They might recommend that a homeowner borrow thousands of dollars using the home as collateral to invest in funds. A withdrawal plan would be used to finance the interest costs.

This type of program can be profitable, but what happens if interest rates skyrocket and the stock market plunges? This happened in 1981 when the prime lending rate reached a record 22.75 per cent and the stock market fell by 43 per cent over about 18 months. The hapless homeowner would find his equity dissipating if he has to sell his mutual fund investment after the market has dropped in order to pay the higher interest charges.

Unless you can handle the interest payments out of your personal income, not the cash flow from the mutual fund, you shouldn't be in a leverage program that uses your home as security. The risks are simply too great.

Leverage is sometimes used even by very conservative investors. For example, an individual with a locked-in investment, such as a GIC, might decide to borrow against it to buy equity funds with the intention of paying off the loan when the GIC matures.

Many people started leverage programs while the lifetime capital gains exemption was in place, often tying their leverage program to interest-generating investments. This allowed them to reduce their cumulative net investment loss to take full advantage of their lifetime exemption. With the end of the lifetime exemption such programs should be re-examined.

No "tax-free" withdrawals

A gimmick promoted by some fund salespeople — and one you should avoid — is the so-called "tax-free" withdrawal from RRSPs. It is a misnomer. Any money withdrawn from an RRSP is taxable.

What these salespeople really propose is a loan to purchase mutual funds. This loan is often secured by a mortgage although demand loans are also common with the interest payments financed by withdrawals from the client's RRSP. Because interest for investment purposes is deductible, the interest deduction offsets the increase in taxable income that stems from pulling money out of the RRSP. In the end, the client's tax bill remains the same — but the RRSP withdrawal is definitely taxable.

The idea behind the "tax-free" withdrawal, other than boosting sales commissions, is to convert a portfolio that will be fully taxed on withdrawal to one that will be taxed at capital gains rates.

This strategy is far too risky for most people, especially those approaching retirement and whose major investment assets are their RRSPs. It converts a conservative investment program which is designed to finance retirement to one that leaves the investor exposed to unpredictable results if interest rates move higher.

When to use leverage
Leverage can be used successfully in some circumstances to meet specific objectives. For example, you might decide that you want to use part of your investment assets for speculation, perhaps 10 per cent of the total. You could earmark these for specialty funds, such as gold funds, which you expect to do much better than broad-based funds in the short term. Alternatively, you might decide to borrow an amount equal to 10 per cent of your investment assets and use the loan to buy a specialty fund in the hope of making a substantial gain of 50 per cent or more within a year.

Just remember that the funds that are top performers in one period may turn out to be among the worst performers in a later period. As a result, be prepared to be nimble. And don't invest with borrowed funds for speculation unless you can afford to take a loss.

Also, don't second-guess your fund manager. It makes little sense to borrow money to buy a fund that is heavily invested in cash because its manager believes the market is vulnerable. The time to use leverage is when your fund manager is bullish.

Trading mutual funds
You can make a lot of money by simply buying funds and holding them for a long time. A single investment of $10,000 earning 12 per cent a year and held for 30 years would be worth almost $300,000.

Investing $2,000 a year for 30 years at an average return of 12 per cent would build to $540,000. In fact, most fund management companies recommend a buy-and-hold strategy.

Their argument is that the fund manager makes the decisions necessary to maximize gains and preserve capital, moving into those industry groups that offer the most potential at any given time and building cash when the market looks like it is going to move lower.

Some investors take a different tack. Rather than buying and holding, they trade funds. They try to buy in at the beginning of a trend and to sell at the top to lock in profits. People who invest this way are called market-timers. They may trade their whole fund portfolio. Or they may trade only the specialty funds such as gold funds, energy funds or Japanese funds — groups that tend to have wide swings in rates of return over relatively short periods. The success of market-timers depends on their own skills or those of their advisers. If you are going to trade funds, however, investigate trading costs before you start your program.

As a general rule, there is no charge to switch within a no-load group of funds. Among the groups selling load funds, the commission varies from group to group. Some do not charge for switching. Several have a maximum charge of 2 per cent. Some other fund management companies state that the maximum commission applies when switching. However, most commissions are negotiable and most switching within groups can be done for commissions of 2 per cent or less. Switching costs also vary among fund families with declining redemption fees. In some cases, there is a service charge for switching. In others, exchanges are not looked at as redemptions. It is all a matter of understanding the rules before you commit your funds.

If your fund portfolio includes funds of a number of management groups, your trading costs could be higher. Even so, you are unlikely to pay full commissions. Again, commissions are negotiable and you should be able to establish a rate with your dealer that reflects the volume of turnover in your portfolio. Some salespeople offer funds at zero commission but charge a transaction fee.

A bit of advice: If you are going to trade funds, become familiar with the portfolios of the funds you plan to trade. You wouldn't want to cash in a specific fund because of worries about market direction, only to find out later that the manager had similar concerns and had moved to a heavy cash position to preserve capital. In the same vein, you wouldn't want to sell 20 per cent of a Canadian equity fund to buy a gold fund, only to find out later that your manager had taken a 20 per cent position in gold stocks. You can get the portfolio information from the latest fund quarterlies or your fund sales representative.

Diversification

Diversification is a very important investment concept. By diversifying your investments, you spread your risk. If one investment goes sour, it is more than offset by the other investments you hold. Mutual funds are diversified portfolios — a mutual fund that invests in stocks would generally have a minimum of 20 different stocks.

Even so, you may want to diversify your fund holdings because you're concerned about tying your fortunes to a single manager, one market or one class of assets.

You can diversify a portfolio of mutual funds in two ways. The first is by asset mix, using different types of funds such as Canadian equity, American equity, fixed-income and global investments. The second is by using two or more funds of the same type but different investment strategies — if one manager does poorly the others will carry the day.

Diversification by asset mix is fairly common and makes sense. Many people will hold a Canadian equity fund and a fixed-income fund in their RRSP and hold a global fund and an American fund outside their RRSP. The actual mix depends largely on their age, the capital available and how much exposure they want in a given class of assets or a specific market.

Diversification within a specific type of fund also makes sense. However, many investors who diversify within a specific type of fund fail to meet their objective. They or their advisers neglect to look at the portfolios or the managers of the funds they buy. Consequently, they end up with two or more funds with similar portfolios and management styles. An extreme irony would be purchasing two Canadian equity funds offered by competing fund organizations but which, in fact, have the same fund manager.

CHAPTER 10

Fees, Loads and Commissions

IT'S IMPORTANT TO DEVELOP an understanding of all the fees and costs connected with mutual fund investment. First, they vary widely. Second, they can have a significant impact on the rate of return earned.

Fees and charges can be broken down into two broad categories: sales commissions and administrative and management fees. In some cases, they overlap so that part of the administrative fee is, in reality, ongoing compensation to a salesperson for either selling you a fund or for giving you continuing service. Until recently, many major fund groups withheld a portion of the commission paid when you purchased a fund with an acquisition fee. This was used to finance incentive programs and advertising. But whether costs are included as sales commissions or administrative fees, they affect your net returns from holding mutual funds.

Sales fees have become more complex in recent years. In addition to the traditional no-load funds, which don't charge any commission, and the front-end load funds, which can be bought only on payment of an acquisition fee, there are funds that have flat redemption fees, funds that have declining sales charges and funds that have ongoing sales charges. Some funds even combine two types of sales fees so you'll pay a fee when you buy and when you redeem. A number of groups give you the option of buying either with an acquisition fee or a declining deferred redemption fee. Others have cloned their front-end load funds and offer a group with declining sales charges but with higher management fees. A few funds have registration fees or administration fees.

Rates of return published in mutual fund performance tables do not take sales fees into consideration but do account for all administrative and management fees charged to the fund. If the published rate of return for a fund is 15 per cent and its management-expense ratio is 2 per cent, the fund actually returned 17 per cent. The return that investors realize is 15 per cent.

Management fees range from about 0.75 per cent to more than 3 per cent. They include the fees paid to the portfolio manager and they may also include the expenses of operating the fund. In some cases they reflect compensation paid to the salesperson. Funds must disclose all compensation and incentive arrangements in their prospectuses, a requirement introduced by the Ontario Securities Commission in 1987. Over the past decade, many mutual fund companies have offered various types of incentives to boost sales, a practice that is common in many industries. These incentives have ranged from giving salespeople small appliances for opening new accounts to providing fur coats or educational conferences on luxury ocean liners or in exotic foreign resorts. These incentives have disappeared. Instead, fund companies now tend to compete on commissions and on the provision of what is generally called marketing support.

No-load funds

Some funds do not carry any up-front sales fee or back-end redemption fee. Funds offered or sponsored by banks and trust companies generally, but not always, fall into this category. A few fund management companies offer these no-load funds through investment dealers as well as directly to investors. The fund companies compensate the dealer by paying them part of the management fee for as long as the client holds the fund. This payment, which ranges from 0.25 per cent to 1 per cent of the value of the client's holding, is called a "trailer." Most load funds also pay trailers.

Rear-end load funds

During late 1989 and early 1990, many fund companies modified their commission schedules and dealer compensation programs. Competition from banks and trust companies which do not charge acquisition fees on their own funds forced many fund companies to introduce declining deferred redemption fees as an option for purchasers. With these, you don't pay a commission when you buy into a mutual fund; all your money is invested for you. But, even though you don't pay an acquisition fee, the fund company pays your broker a commission of about 4 to 5 per cent. You will have to pay a redemption charge only if you redeem within a specific period. The fee is highest in the first year and tapers down to zero, usually after seven years. The fee differs between fund groups but usually ranges from about 5 per cent if you redeem within one year of purchase down to 1 per cent if you redeem in the seventh year. If you redeem after the seventh year, you won't have to pay any redemption fee. These fees vary widely and are not negotiable. The redemption fee on Maritime Life Growth Fund, for instance, is 10 per cent on first-year redemptions and declines by 1 per cent a year until it reaches zero after the 10th year.

Typical Back-End Charges	
Year of redemption	Charge
During first year	4.5%
During second year	4.0%
During third year	3.5%
During fourth year	3.0%
During fifth year	2.5%
During sixth year	2.0%
During seventh year	1.0%
After that	nil

TABLE VII

Some brokers and dealers were initially reluctant to introduce their clients to funds with deferred declining sales charges because they were used to charging up to 9 per cent. This reluctance has disappeared for the most part because of competitive pressures from banks and trust companies and their no-load funds. In fact, most funds sold in the past few years have been rear-end load.

Different fund groups have different bells and whistles. For instance, in some cases the redemption fee applies to the value of units at the time the investment was made, rather than the market value at the time of the redemption. Dividends reinvested may be exempt from the redemption fee and shares purchased with reinvested dividends are considered the first shares redeemed. You may also get exchange privileges within a fund group without triggering redemption fees. Also you may get the privilege of redeeming up to, say, 10 per cent of your holdings a year without triggering a redemption fee. This is an important privilege for someone who has an automatic withdrawal plan or who holds fund units inside a registered retirement income fund.

Load funds

No-load funds are a minority in Canada, but their numbers are growing as more banks and trust companies jump into the fund business. As well, declining deferred redemption fee sales have become increasingly important to funds which are sold by brokers and dealers. Still, a substantial portion of fund business written each year is in load funds — funds that pay a commission to the dealer or broker who places the order.

The most common form of load fund is the front-end load fund, which requires payment of a commission of up to a maximum 9 per cent. It is, however, rare for anyone to pay that per cent. Some firms routinely charge 2.5 per cent even on rela-

Typical Equity Fund Commission Schedule	
Amount paid	Maximum sales charge
Up to $14,999	9%
$15,000 to $24,999	8%
$25,000 to $49,999	7%
$50,000 to $99,999	5%
$100,000 to $249,999	4%
$250,000 to $499,999	3%
$500,000 to $999,999	2%
$1 million and over	1%

TABLE VIII

tively small amounts. Virtually all front-end load funds have tapered commission schedules, with the commission charged declining according to the size of the purchase.

There is no standard commission schedule and each mutual fund company can taper its commission rates in a different way. There can even be differences between the funds managed by one company. Typically, a fund would charge a maximum commission of 9 per cent on purchases of up to $24,999 and 7 per cent on purchases of $25,000 to $50,000; 5 per cent on purchases from $50,000 to $100,000; 3 per cent on $100,000 to $250,000; 2 per cent on $250,000 to $500,000; and 1 per cent on anything greater. Several preferred dividend funds have maximum commission rates of 5 per cent. Some dealers will add up the purchases made within a year for commission-calculating purposes to give clients the commission rate that would be paid if all the purchases had been made at once. Mutual Investco Inc. calculates sales charges on lifetime purchases of all funds in the Mutual group of funds.

Negotiating commissions

Commissions charged on front-end load funds are generally negotiable. The phrase in the prospectus is "maximum sales charge" or "not to exceed." This phraseology allows a salesperson to discount commission to reflect a client's purchase of several funds so that the commission charged would be the same as if the client put all of his or her money in one fund. As well, it creates a competitive environment in which some brokers and salespeople are more willing to cut commissions than others. They might, for instance, accept a 3 per cent commission on a $5,000 order rather than the maximum 9 per cent. Of course, a broker who accepts 3 per cent on a small order is unlikely to provide any service other than filling the forms and accepting your cheque.

Most people choose a deferred declining redemption fee fund. However, some people will choose front-end load funds for one of a variety of reasons. They might be active traders and a reduced front-end load is cheaper than redeeming a deferred-load fund after several months. Or, they might just want the flexibility of being able to move without concern about hefty penalties.

Discount stockbrokers will generally place an order for half or less of the maximum commission noted in a fund prospectus. But most dealers will cut commissions drastically if they aren't expected to provide any advice or service. As a group, stockbrokers are more likely to cut commissions than independent salespeople. But there are no hard rules. Many salespeople won't cut commissions other than to reflect the dollar value of a client's purchases. These salespeople usually provide detailed financial planning and feel they are compensated for their efforts only if they charge full commissions. Some financial planners do not charge any commission, receiving their compensation on a fee-for-service basis by the client and a trailer from the fund company.

The sale of load funds without the load is becoming very popular among sophisticated investors. These investors are well aware that they can buy no-load funds from banks and some fund companies and they believe that the size of their accounts justifies a substantial discount. Some dealers have been advertising the sale of load funds without a commission. In some cases they'll charge a one-time registration fee, perhaps $45, and provide little if any advice. Their compensation comes from the fund company through the payment of a trailer. The latest twist involves level-load funds for which the client pays a small acquisition fee, perhaps 1 per cent, when they buy and a small redemption fee if they sell within a year. In this case, the broker would receive an extra 1 per cent trailer each year.

Redemption fees

A handful of funds charge a flat fee when you redeem units. Most funds can charge a redemption fee of up to 2 per cent if an investor who paid less than 2 per cent commission then redeems within a short time, usually within one year of purchase. In some cases, management has the option of waiving this fee. This is often done as a good-will measure and depends on the circumstances.

Paying at both ends

A few fund groups charge a commission both when you buy and when you sell. Many fund groups apply a charge if you want to transfer your money to another fund within the group. Others allow transfers free of charge. While the fee can be as much as full commission rates, many groups charge a 2 per cent fee for a transfer.

Management expense ratio

All fees, other than direct and some indirect sales fees and specific fees such as RRSP trustee fees, are almost always reflected in the management expense ratio. This ratio, expressed as a percentage of total assets, includes the management fee and the expenses paid by the fund. Some funds pay all expenses out of the management fee. Others charge the expenses directly to the fund. However, the management expense ratio is all-inclusive and allows comparisons among funds.

There is one company that charges some fees, such as management fees, directly to the client rather than to the fund. (This is an exception to the rule.) However, its published rates of return are net of fees. Consequently, investors can make valid comparisons. Management expense ratios vary widely. For some equity funds they are as low as 0.75 per cent; others exceed 3 per cent. Most range from 1.5 per cent to 2.75 per cent. Indeed, management expense ratios have been rising in recent years. Management expense ratios for income funds are marginally lower. Many fund groups have raised their management fees in recent years to reflect rising costs, including sales costs such as trailer fees (see next section). Consequently, management expense ratios have been rising for some but not all funds. While management expense ratios are reflected in fund rates of return, it is important for investors to make any necessary adjustments to historical rates of return to keep them in perspective.

Funds disclose their latest five years' management expense ratios in their annual reports.

The management expense ratio is important because it is often the only part of a performance number that is predictable. For instance, few investors are going to worry about whether a management expense ratio is 1.5 per cent or 2.5 per cent if a fund's long-term rate of return is 15 or 16 per cent. But, in years when the markets are lacklustre or show negative returns, a one percentage point difference in management expense ratio becomes significant.

Trailer fees

Another shift in the mutual fund industry is toward trailer fees. Trailer fees are paid by management on an ongoing basis to the selling broker to encourage the broker to continue to service the client and to discourage switching. They are deferred sales commissions. Trailer fees are usually one-quarter of the management fee but can be as much as one-half.

If you've purchased your mutual fund units from one dealer and later switch your account to another firm, your trailer will move to the new firm provided your account shows you are dealing with the second firm. Therefore, a fund salesperson may insist you have all your dealings under one roof.

If you've purchased funds and aren't happy with the advice you're getting, find a salesperson with whom you feel comfortable. Even if you don't purchase additional funds, the salesperson may be happy to give you advice, provided the funds in question pay a trailer and he or she becomes involved with your account.

Trailers are a point of contention in the industry. Some want them banned entirely as a hidden charge, while others argue they are a payment made by the fund company, not the client, to encourage ongoing service. Provincial securities commissions are likely to require the fund industry to provide more detailed disclosure about trailers and the investors' rights, if any, to direct them.

Distribution fees

The move to funds sold with deferred declining redemption fees, or rear-end loads, has caused a profit squeeze on fund companies that sell through intermediaries. To cover the cost of paying sales commissions, some fund groups have raised management fees. Others have launched funds sold only with redemption fees and charge a heftier management fee than their comparable funds sold with acquisition fees. A few are trying a different approach. They continue to offer funds with either an acquisition fee or redemption fee; however, clients who choose to buy on the redemption fee basis are charged a distribution fee of about 0.5 per cent. This fee is taken from their accounts when the fund makes a dividend distribution. If the dividend is not high enough to cover the fee, units are redeemed from the client's account.

Additional fees

Depending on the funds you hold, you may face additional charges. A few funds have nominal charges for preauthorized purchases or cheques issued on redemption. Trustee fees for RRSPs are an additional charge for virtually all funds and are charged against your account or billed separately. The point is, fees vary widely, so you should know what they are before you commit to buy.

All fees are fully disclosed in a fund's prospectus and should be considered by an investor. If you examine a fund with a distribution fee, remember that it is not reflected in rates of return published in the business press. When comparing two funds sold with redemption fees – where one charges a distribution fee and the other does not – the rate of return for the fund with a distribution fee should be reduced by 0.5 per cent in order for the comparison to be valid.

Load versus no-load

Every fee you pay will affect your final return. Table XIII compares the growth of an investment of $10,000 over 30 years in three funds which have different types of sales charges. Each fund earns the same rate of return of 14 per cent before sales charges and management fees. The figures show what investors would receive if they redeemed at the beginning of any year.

The first fund is a front-end load fund with a management expense ratio of 2.3 per cent, so its compound rate of return is 11.7 per cent. The management expense ratio is the average for Canadian equity funds sold with front-end loads. We will assume the investor paid a 5 per cent front-end load.

The second fund has a deferred declining sales charge of 4.5 per cent in the first year decreasing by 0.5 per cent each year to zero in the ninth year. This fund has a management expense ratio of 2.6 per

Comparing Load and No-Load Funds

Year	Front-end load	Back-end load	No load	Year	Front-end load	Back-end load	No load
1	$ 9,500	$ 9,550	$10,000	16	$ 49,948	$ 50,498	$ 58,518
2	10,612	10,694	11,250	17	55,792	56,255	65,833
3	11,853	11,976	12,656	18	62,320	62,668	74,062
4	13,240	13,410	14,238	19	69,611	69,812	83,319
5	14,789	15,016	16,018	20	77,756	77,771	93,734
6	16,519	16,813	18,020	21	86,853	86,637	105,451
7	18,452	18,826	20,273	22	97,015	96,513	118,632
8	20,611	21,078	22,807	23	108,366	107,516	133,461
9	23,022	23,600	25,658	24	121,045	119,773	150,144
10	25,716	26,422	28,865	25	135,207	133,427	168,912
11	28,725	29,434	32,473	26	151,026	148,638	190,026
12	32,085	32,790	36,532	27	168,697	165,582	213,779
13	35,839	36,528	41,099	28	188,434	184,459	240,502
14	40,033	40,692	46,236	29	210,481	205,487	270,564
15	44,717	45,331	52,016	30	235,107	228,912	304,385

TABLE IX

cent (an actual average), so its compound rate of return to the investor is 11.4 per cent.

The third fund is a no-load fund with a management expense ratio of 1.5 per cent, so its compound rate of return is 12.5 per cent.

The table suggests that, all other things being equal, investors who expect to hold a fund for a long time and are choosing between a front-end load fund and a deferred declining-sales-charge fund with a higher management fee are better off paying the front-end load. Of course, if the fund company gives you a choice of front-end or rear-end load on the same fund, which is the trend, and you are a long-term investor, you are better off with the declining-sales-charge option, unless you can negotiate a zero front-end commission.

If the choice is between a front-end load fund and a no-load fund, the decision depends on the difference in management fees. A no-load fund has the advantage for at least 25 years, even if its management expense ratio is one-quarter point higher.

Your best buy is a no-load fund with a low management fee, ignoring the value of service and advice you receive when buying a load fund. Very few funds meet this description.

Don't shop on the basis of price alone. The decision to purchase a fund should be based on the securities in which the fund invests and the expertise of the manager. Arguments can be made for allowing costs to determine the choice of fund, but many people who haven't the time to continuously follow their investments are probably better off getting professional advice – and paying for it.

CHAPTER 11

Picking
Your Funds

ONCE YOU'VE SET YOUR OB-
jectives and developed an understanding of all the costs involved,
you will have to choose funds which meet your needs. Alternatively, you may want to choose an adviser who will do all the work
and tailor a portfolio of funds suitable to your requirements.

In this chapter I will recommend some funds to meet specific
needs and market scenarios. You (or your adviser) can and should
perform similar analyses using the most recent data at the time you
wish to invest or review your holdings. My recommendations are
primarily among funds invested in the Canadian market. While I
will comment on some funds which invest outside Canada,
particularly U.S. funds, readers should be aware that it is a lot
easier to obtain and interpret data on Canadian and U.S. holdings
than on foreign securities, especially in emerging markets.

I avoided the temptation to create "funds of the year" and
"managers of the year," and even "fund management companies of
the year." While such labels sell tons of books to the concerns noted
and are a great excuse for a party, they are of little use to the reader
in determining next year's winners. I prefer to provide some short
lists of funds which have decent performance but, more
importantly, are structured to perform well over the next year or so
under certain circumstances. The decision to invest in any
particular fund or funds, however, is yours alone and should be
based on your unique circumstances.

You may not find mention of some funds you own which you
consider excellent performers. That can happen if a fund company
declines to supply the portfolio data that Portfolio Analytics
Limited requires for the analyses I've requested. Getting access to
data has not been a problem, with the exception of a few fund
groups.

Also, the tables don't include any relatively new funds simply because their track records are relatively short. That in itself is not a reason to avoid a fund. If a fund company launches a new fund in an area in which it demonstrates expertise, by all means consider it. But if new product is simply there because competing families have one, be leery.

You should realize there is no way anyone can know for certain whether any one fund will outperform another over the short term or the long term. The best you can do is choose funds whose policies are compatible with your own and which have performed well over time, particularly in the same type of market conditions you currently face (or choose funds whose current managers have demonstrated acceptable performance under similar conditions).

Your views count

You can and should go one step further: Your choice of funds should reflect your views on where the markets are going. If you are unwilling to predict market movements you should pick funds that are broad-based or build a balanced portfolio. Your results may not be at the top of the pack. But they won't be at the bottom either.

My choices are based primarily on several criteria: How well a fund has performed in recent years; whether its performance is primarily a reflection of market movements or its manager's skills; the securities it held as of June 30 (or later if available); and anticipated market movements. Each of these criteria in turn has many components.

Far from perfect

Picking funds isn't rocket science. It is a lot more difficult to predict the future movement of a fund than the trajectory of a rocket. Picking funds involves a lot of guessing, assessing, judging and estimating, especially when all the information you want isn't available.

The weightings I've applied to each component or criteria will vary with type of fund and objective. For example, the only factors I care about in looking at money market funds are performance and costs. All money market funds invest in high-quality, short-term securities and treasury bills with average maturities of less than 90 days. As a result, returns before expenses shouldn't vary significantly among funds. Perhaps this is why only the rare individual outside a fund management company could name the manager of a money market fund.

While a manager's skills are of secondary importance in a money market fund, they are key in most equity funds, bond funds and asset-allocation funds. Consequently, I use what is called risk-adjusted past performance as a screen or filter in my choice of these types of funds.

If your manager leaves

The question this creates is how valid are these measurements if a fund manager leaves? The answer is probably less valid than they were. How much less valid is a matter of conjecture. Most fund management companies use a team approach to some extent, the team consisting of analysts and portfolio managers sharing views. Even the one-person shop gets some of his or her research from outside the organization and doesn't operate in a vacuum. In either case, a very key individual decides if and when to buy or sell a specific security; the team doesn't take a vote. Committees may work well for organizing mutual fund company staff parties. They don't work well when it comes to buying and selling stocks and bonds.

When a star goes to a new fund there are no guarantees he or she will maintain star status. If you follow one, be prepared to be nimble. And don't buy on a declining deferred redemption fee basis. The penalties for early redemption are too high. Instead, pay a low- or zero-acquisition fee, also known as a low-load or zero-load, in the case of funds which are sold through intermediaries (the dealer earns a hefty trailer fee).

If you stay with a fund whose star has shifted positions, watch performance closely. You might want to look at the star's new portfolio: Does it parrot the one he or she left behind? Likewise, has the new manager of the fund you hold made wholesale changes to the portfolio? In any event, the tables in Appendix 4 indicate the current manager's tenure.

Does the manager invest in the fund?

A fair question to ask your adviser or a fund company directly is whether the portfolio manager of the fund you are considering invests more than a token amount of his or her own money in the fund. This will be the case for more and more fund companies given the negative publicity some companies received last year about their managers' trading in new issues of junior securities. Whether or not you should invest with a fund group whose managers trade for their own account is up to you. The reality is that managers who trade for their own accounts are not going to jeopardize their careers by putting themselves in conflict with their clients. There will be exceptions just as there are exceptions in any profession or occupation.

The rules covering purchases of shares by fund managers are loose. But this is changing and by the time you read this paragraph, the Investment Funds Institute of Canada will likely have a policy for member companies. The vast majority of investment professionals in Canada are members of the Association for Investment Management and Research. These people have agreed to comply with AIMR's Code of Ethics and Standards of Professional Conduct. Managers, of course, should not put their interests in conflict with their clients so it is understood that a manager will not buy shares for his or her account in anticipation of the fund buying the same shares. The term given to these prohibited purchases is "front-running." Nor should a manager holding the same securities as a fund sell his or her shares in anticipation of the fund selling.

A manager cannot buy shares for his or her own account once the fund becomes a shareholder. However, there is no prohibition if the manager buys shares at an early stage in a company's development when it is too junior for a fund to consider.

Risk-adjusted performance

The risk-adjusted performance rankings I use were calculated by Portfolio Analytics Limited. These consider a fund's overall performance as well as the risk or volatility associated with that performance. For our purposes, risk is a measure of the magnitude of the variation in a fund's monthly rate of return, a fancy way of measuring the degree of uncertainty that next month's rate of return will be similar to this month's. This differs from the risk you assume if you put all your money in a penny gold stock with an exploration property in a politically unstable Third World country. Here you face the risk of losing all your money. It is unlikely you will experience permanent capital loss holding any mutual fund. Only one out of 196 mutual funds with 15-year track records had a negative rate of return; only one of 287 funds with 10-year track records lost money over that period.

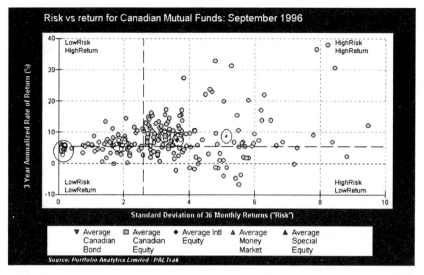

Risk vs return for Canadian Mutual Funds: September 1996

CHART V

The variation in a money market fund's return from month to month is generally quite moderate. Consequently, money market funds are low volatility or low risk as a group. At the other end of the spectrum we would find specialty mutual funds whose rates of return tend to vary widely on a month-to-month basis.

Another way of looking at risk is in terms of predictability of return. You can say with some certainty that a money market fund's performance in any one month will be very similar to its performance in the previous month. Performance of an equity fund on a month-to-month basis is a lot less predictable and the riskier the fund, the less certain the performance prediction.

Volatility is never used alone as the basis for choosing a fund. A fund that loses a small amount of money every month would show as a fund with low volatility. Volatility must be viewed against rates or return. The calculation should also consider whether a fund's performance and volatility are primarily the result of the types of holdings in the fund or the product of the fund manager's skills.

Volatility is often misused by investors and their advisers. It is quite common for advisers to recommend funds which have low volatility and high three-year returns as long-term investments, often using what are called scatter diagrams, such as Chart V to show the superiority of their choice on the basis of high three-year performance and low volatility.

But an examination of long-term performance of funds shows that most of the top performers over a 10-year period are funds which have above-average volatility. For the 10 years ended Sept. 30, 1996, only 73 out of 287 funds had 10-year compound rates of return of 10 per cent or better. Of these, 30 or 41 per cent were high-risk funds. Another 15 were medium-high risk. Fifteen were medium risk (of which several were fixed-income funds). Eleven of the 12 medium-low-risk funds were fixed-income funds — Cundill Value Fund was the exception. Only one fund, Dynamic Income Fund, was low risk.

The five top-performing funds were Marathon Equity Fund, Bullock American Fund, Multiple Opportunities Fund, AIC Advantage and Trimark Fund with rates ranging from 18 per cent to 15 per cent. Trimark's volatility has been declining.

Looking over the three years ended Sept. 30, 1996, 15 of the top 16 performing funds with returns ranging from 39.1 per cent to 18.7 per cent were high volatility (the 16th was medium-high).

It is a fact of investment life that the best performing funds within any classification during any period are unlikely to be the best performers in subsequent periods. There are exceptions. Some fund managers, either because of astute trading or astute analysis and buying, have provided performance far above their peers for several years so that even if their performance suffers in subsequent periods their clients will still have superior long-term rates of return. Of course, anyone buying on the basis of a track record is counting on that record continuing.

Past performance is important because it reflects how a specific manager fared under the market conditions of the period measured. However, performance figures can be misleading so it is important that investors understand how to interpret them. Moreover, there are many other factors that should be considered in determining which fund or funds meet each person's specific needs.

First to performance. Securities regulations require that any sales material or sales communication that uses rates of return include, as a minimum, one-year, three-year, five-year and 10-year annual compound rates of return. These provide a snapshot view of how a fund performed over specific periods. Investors should look closely at the underlying data to see the variation in performance.

For instance, one popular Canadian equity fund, Dynamic Canadian Growth Fund, had one-, three-, five- and 10-year returns

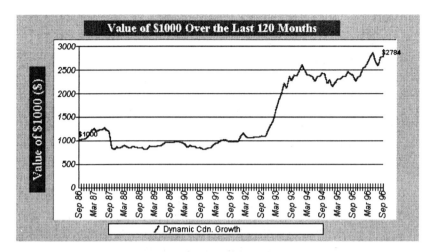

CHART VI

of 16.4 per cent, 7 per cent, 23.5 per cent and 10.8 per cent for periods ended Sept. 30, 1996. With the exception of its three-year compound rate where it fell in the third quartile or bottom 50 per cent (but above the bottom 25 per cent) of funds in terms of performance of other Canadian equity funds, the fund was first or second quartile in the other periods.

But as Charts VI and VII show, annual performance varied widely from year to year. The five- and 10-year rates are largely a reflection of a 107.6 per cent return in a single 12-month period. Moreover, the 10-year rate is most likely meaningless in that the fund was minuscule 10 years ago and did not yet have the management responsible for the superlative performance some years later.

Different ending eates bring different results

Returns and risk measures are snapshots in time. They reflect how specific managers have performed in their markets over certain periods. Different ending dates will almost always give different results. A decade earlier, the top-performing funds had 10-year rates in excess of 20 per cent and most of these were high risk.

The latest 10-year rates are taken from the relatively high base prior to the October, 1987, market decline. Ten-year rates for periods ended Oct. 31, 1997, will likely be higher than rates ended Sept. 30, 1996, reflecting the lower net-asset values from which returns will be measured.

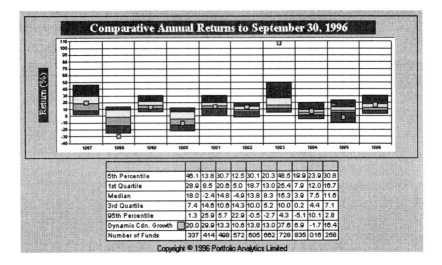

5th Percentile	46.1	13.8	30.7	12.5	30.1	20.3	48.5	19.9	23.9	30.8
1st Quartile	28.9	8.5	20.6	5.0	18.7	13.0	25.4	7.9	12.0	16.7
Median	18.0	-2.4	14.8	-4.9	13.8	8.3	15.3	3.9	7.5	11.6
3rd Quartile	7.4	14.6	10.6	14.3	10.0	5.2	10.0	0.2	4.4	7.1
95th Percentile	1.3	25.9	5.7	22.9	-0.5	-2.7	4.3	-5.1	10.1	2.8
Dynamic Cdn. Growth	20.0	29.9	13.3	10.6	13.8	13.0	37.6	6.9	-1.7	16.4
Number of Funds	337	414	498	572	605	662	728	835	916	268

Copyright © 1996 Portfolio Analytics Limited

CHART VII

Examine trailing rates of return

One way to avoid the problems of this so-called "end-date bias" is to examine the performance of mutual funds on what is called a trailing period basis. For example, if an investor wishes to examine what the five-year annualized rate of return has been for the latest period, she need only examine any of the monthly performance tables in The Globe and Mail or elsewhere. Since this figure can (and usually does) change each month, it is useful to examine the five-year rate of return over a wide range of ending dates. This would allow her to determine what the highest, lowest and average rate of return has been achieved for, in this case, a five-year holding period for the history of the fund. Using PAL*Trak* for Windows, Chart VIII illustrates the five-year trailing period returns for Trimark Canadian Fund, one of the most popular Canadian funds.

Note that this fund's worst five year average return over the past 10 years was 5.1 per cent and its best was 29.5 per cent. The average rate of return for a five-year holding period over the past 10 years was 13.5 per cent (annualized). These statistics emphasize that the figures reported each month are a single point in time and fail to present the range of rates that a longer term investor can expect. Summary tables covering trailing returns for most equity and bond funds are included in Appendix 3.

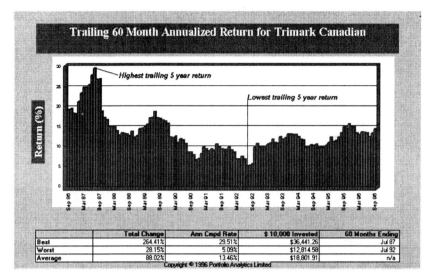

	Total Change	Ann Cmpd Rate	$ 10,000 Invested	60 Months Ending
Best	264.41%	29.51%	$36,441.26	Jul 87
Worst	28.15%	5.09%	$12,814.58	Jul 92
Average	88.02%	13.46%	$18,801.91	n/a

Copyright © 1996 Portfolio Analytics Limited

CHART VIII

It pays to take risk

What is apparent in examining performance over the past two decades is that specialty equity funds or funds concentrated in specific areas of the market tend to provide the highest returns and that the majority of these are high risk. The top long-term performers a decade ago were funds invested in the Japanese market. More recently, resource and small-cap funds have been the best performers. There are important exceptions. Very high returns can be earned in bond funds and by investing in equity funds holding interest-sensitive issues during periods of falling interest rates.

Keep in mind then that risk is just another tool an investor can use to meet his or her objectives. It can also be managed by combining several funds in a portfolio. A portfolio of several high-risk funds whose monthly rates of returns are not highly correlated will often have a volatility rating below the average of the individual funds. Often sophisticated investors will choose several managers whose methods of choosing stocks differ but whose expected long-term performance is high. The results are likely to be lower volatility, more diversification and superior long-term performance.

Only the starting point

Picking funds using a mathematical screen or filter is far from a perfect science. Using different ending dates will give somewhat different results. So it is imperative that an investor understand that using a risk-adjusted performance measure is only the starting point and other factors must be considered.

Such measures look only at the past. And as every mutual fund brochure, flyer and newsletter points out, "Past performance may not be indicative of future performance."

You should also look at how a fund manager has structured a portfolio at the time you are considering a purchase and on an ongoing basis. The key is to match your objectives with funds which have similar objectives and match your views about the markets with managers who share your views and have demonstrated superior performance in the past.

Future performance of any mutual fund reflects a number of factors. It reflects the skills of its manager. It reflects the behaviour of the overall markets in which a fund invests. It reflects the level of expenses charged the fund and any fees or commissions charged individual investors which other funds might charge the fund directly.

Take, for example, money market funds. As noted previously, few investors really care who manages a money market fund because all funds invest in the same pool of high-quality, short-term securities or treasury bills. As a result, gross returns will vary only slightly despite the skills of the manager. Management fees and sales commissions have a much greater bearing on the rate of return to client.

The direction of the markets also has a major bearing on performance. For instance, it is very difficult for a bond fund manager to outperform a money market fund during periods of rising interest rates. Conversely, it is very difficult for a money market fund to beat even an unmanaged bond fund when rates are falling.

CHAPTER 12

Fixed-Income Funds

FOR THE MOST PART, THE safety of the individual holdings in fixed-income mutual funds has not been an issue in Canada. Diversification and a bias toward quality minimizes capital risk. A few bond funds have held issues that have defaulted, but the impact on returns has been negligible.

One concern, however, is whether Quebec remains part of Canada. Parti Québécois economic policies pertaining to currency union are unrealistic. A worst-case scenario: An independent Quebec government facing a run on its securities requires financial institutions under its jurisdiction to sell federal securities in their control to provide the cash to support Quebec issues.

At this point in time I recommend a better-safe-than-sorry posture and the avoidance of fixed-income funds offered by Quebec institutions, especially for RRSPs (I do not consider Bank of Montreal, Royal Bank and other institutions which have their origins in Quebec but their major operations outside Quebec as Quebec institutions; similarly I am not concerned about Quebec-based counselling firms whose custodians are outside the province).

How to choose money market funds

If you are looking to buy money market funds, you are either investing for a relatively short term and want no risk to your accumulated capital or you are seeking a haven for your cash until you move it into a less predictable sector of the market. Consequently, you want to earn the most interest possible (while avoiding any risk to capital) and your choice of money market funds should be based on cost and return.

That's fairly easy. Don't buy any money market fund which requires you to pay a commission on purchase or a redemption fee on redemption. Buy no-load or zero per cent commission. Choose

Recommended Money Market Funds
Annualized Performance to Sept. 30, 1996

Fund	Assets ($mil)	MER	6M	1 Yr	2 Yr	3 Yr	5 Yr	10Yr
BPI T-Bill	138.6	0.65	2.29	5.37	5.81	5.25	5.52	7.83
Beutel Goodman M Mkt	87.6	0.59	2.32	5.31	5.89	5.48	6.11	
CIBC Premium Cdn T-Bill	1,510.9	0.58	2.17	4.88	5.61	5.15	5.37	
CT Everest M Mkt	1,043.8	1.07	1.88	4.38	5.01	4.62	4.95	
Cornerstone Govt Money	57.6	1.03	1.81	4.43	5.23	4.85	5.13	
Green Line Cdn T-Bill	661.6	0.82	2.18	4.94	5.49	5.03		
Green Line Cdn M Mkt	3,814.7	0.82	2.23	5.00	5.57	5.16		
Hongkong Bank M Mkt	394.4	0.90	2.16	4.88	5.47	4.87	5.04	
ICM Short-Term Inv	136.8	1.00	2.65	6.03	6.63	6.15		
InvesNat Corp Cash Mgmt	351.0	0.56	2.34	5.26				
InvesNat T-Bill Plus	312.3	0.81	2.20	5.00	5.58	5.08	5.41	
MD Money	301.6	0.53	2.30	5.27	5.86	5.40	5.60	7.49
Maxxum M Mkt	67.6	0.66	2.28	5.27	5.77	5.37	5.78	
Mutual MMkt	308.4	1.04	1.96	4.53	5.30	4.90	5.17	7.19
PH & N Cdn M Mkt	543.4	0.51	2.12	4.89	5.72	5.29	5.69	7.90
Royfund Cdn T-Bill	3,143.0	0.91	1.98	4.59	5.26	4.83	5.26	
Scotia Ex M Mkt	356.9	1.00	1.99	4.58	5.28	4.84	5.07	
Scotia Ex Premium T-Bill	1,218.8	0.52	2.21	4.99	5.71	5.24		
Scotia Ex T-Bill	487.1	1.00	1.97	4.50	5.29	4.88		
Templeton T-Bill	134.9	0.75	2.00	4.60	5.28	4.86	5.23	

SOURCE: PALTRAK FOR WINDOWS

TABLE X

funds which have low management expense ratios and an asset base of $50 million or more indicating some substance. In Table X, there are 20 funds that meet these criteria.

How to choose bond funds
Your choice of bond funds should reflect your views about the direction of interest rates at the time you make the purchase. For example, if you believe that Canadian interest rates are set to tumble and want to invest in bond funds for potential capital gains, then you would look for Canadian dollar bond funds which currently stress bonds with longer-term maturities. Should rates fall, as you expect, then these funds will show greater appreciation than funds which emphasize shorter maturities.

As at Sept. 30, 1996, the range of maturities among 124 Canadian bond funds was 0.3 years to 23.7 years with the average at 8 years. Only nine (actually five if you note that four funds are actually

Recommended Canadian Bond Funds with an Average Maturity Greater than 15 Years

Percentage Composition by Short-, Medium- and Long-Term Bonds, Cash, Canadian Bonds and Foreign Bonds at Sept. 30, 1996

Fund	Avg Matur	Shrt	Med	Long	Cash	Cdn	Fgn
Green Line Real Return Bond	23.7	3.1	0.0	96.9	1.8	96.9	0.0
Hyperion Fixed Income	17.8	0.0	44.5	55.5	1.8	98.4	0.0
Manulife VistaFund 1 Bond	19.9	14.8	13.6	71.6	5.5	72.7	15.9
Manulife VistaFund 2 Bond	19.9	14.8	13.6	71.6	5.5	72.7	15.9
Spectrum Govt. Bond A	20.1	0.0	0.0	100.0	8.7	91.5	0.0
Spectrum Govt. Bond B	20.1	0.0	0.0	100.0	8.7	91.5	0.0
Spectrum Govt. Bond C	20.1	0.0	0.0	100.0	8.7	91.3	0.0
Spectrum Govt. Bond D	20.1	0.0	0.0	100.0	8.7	91.4	0.0
United Canadian Bond	20.1	0.0	11.2	88.8	4.4	93.2	0.0

SOURCE: PALTRAK FOR WINDOWS

TABLE XI

identical funds, marketed under different names and commission structures) funds had average maturities beyond 15 years as noted in Table XI while 17 funds have average maturities between 10 and 15 years as shown in Table XII.

Cash in a portfolio can reflect recent purchases of units by investors, a cushion to fund redemptions or a decision of the fund manager to hold cash in anticipation of some movement in the market. In Tables XI, XII, XIII and XIV the impact of this cash component is reflected in the Average Maturity figure of the portfolio (cash is assumed to have a maturity of between 0 and 90 days and includes short-term notes and liquid bonds that mature within a year).

A hefty cash position can shorten the average maturity of a portfolio substantially. For instance, the bond component of Altamira Bond Fund's portfolio was 84.6 per cent invested in long-term bonds. However, 28.3 per cent of fund assets were in cash and cash equivalents so the average maturity of the total fund was "mid-term" at 11.8 years. In the previous quarter, Altamira's Canadian bond component was fully invested in so-called "long-term" bonds, but the hefty exposure to cash, which exceeded 25 per cent, kept it in the "mid-term" category.

Recommended Canadian Bond Funds with an Average Maturity Between 10 and 15 Years

Percentage Composition by Bond Type at Sept. 30, 1996

Fund	Avg Matur	Shrt	Med	Long	Cash	Cdn	Fgn
AGF Canadian Bond	11.1	22.5	50.0	27.5	1.4	97.2	0.0
AGF Canadian Bond B	11.1	22.5	50.0	27.5	1.4	97.2	0.0
AGF Canadian Bond C	11.1	22.5	50.0	27.5	1.4	97.2	0.0
Altamira Bond	11.8	15.4	0.0	84.6	28.3	70.5	0.0
Altamira Income	13.1	10.2	24.2	65.6	4.7	75.1	18.9
Batirente Sec Obligations	10.9	13.3	41.0	45.7	0.6	97.7	0.0
Elliott & Page Bond	10.1	52.8	12.6	34.5	12.8	86.1	0.0
HRL Bond	11.2	26.8	45.8	27.5	1.9	93.5	0.0
Industrial Bond	12.0	0.0	0.0	100.0	12.7	85.9	0.0
Leith Wheeler Fixed Income	10.5	47.6	16.3	36.1	1.7	96.1	0.0
Lotus Group Bond	10.6	32.6	39.7	27.7	4.3	88.2	0.0
McLean Budden Pooled Fxd Inc	10.1	27.7	36.5	35.7	7.5	92.1	0.0
McLean Budden Fixed Income	10.1	28.0	40.6	31.4	10.4	89.6	0.0
Optima Strat Cdn Fixed Income	13.9	20.2	28.7	51.1	3.2	96.8	0.0
Optimum Obligations	10.2	10.7	48.6	40.7	6.2	92.1	0.0
Sceptre Bond	10.4	31.3	41.0	27.7	4.2	95.8	0.0
Standard Life Bond	11.5	6.9	48.4	44.7	5.8	94.9	0.0

SOURCE: PAL*TRAK* FOR WINDOWS

TABLE XII

But what if your view is that interest rates will rise moderately over the next several months then decline. You might want to consider a fund that has an average maturity, of say, five to 10 years but has about half of its assets in shorter maturities and the remainder in long maturities. As rates rise, that manager might reinvest cash from bonds which mature and income in long-term bonds to raise the average coupon of the fund. As of Sept. 30, 1996, the funds in Table XIII met this criterion.

If you are concerned that interest rates may soon move higher but wish to remain in fixed income with as little capital risk as possible, search out funds with most of their assets in relatively near term maturities, say, under five years. Table XIV includes funds with impressive risk-adjusted performance histories to consider.

Without analyzing every transaction of a bond fund it is difficult to measure how often the fund manager adjusts the fund's term to maturity or actively manages the fund. Moreover, picking a single point in time to examine a portfolio may give a misleading result.

Recommended Canadian Bond Funds with Holdings Split Between Short and Long Bonds
Percentage Composition by Bond Type at Sept. 30, 1996

Fund	Avg Matur	Shrt	Med	Long	Cash	Cdn	Fgn
Colonia Life Bond	5.9	62.5	0.0	37.5	31.9	68.1	0.0
Templeton Canadian Bond	5.0	68.7	8.6	22.7	5.5	61.2	17.7
University Avenue Bond	6.3	61.8	3.8	34.5	15.7	105.5	0.0

SOURCE: PALTRAK FOR WINDOWS

TABLE XIII

Some managers are rate anticipators who will adjust their portfolios in advance of a move, sacrificing near-term performance in favour of higher medium-term and long-term performance. Others will make the adjustments after the market has moved. Which is the better method is a matter of preference.

It is important that you as an investor or an adviser to investors determine the fund's specific strategy at the time a purchase is considered. Needless to say, you or your adviser should monitor the fund continuously to determine if the fund manager's views continue to parallel your own.

Recommended Canadian Bond Funds with an Average Maturity Less Than or Equal to Five Years
Percentage Composition by Bond Type at Sept. 30, 1996

Fund	Avg Matur	Shrt	Med	Long	Cash	Cdn	Fgn
CIBC Cdn Short-Term Bond	3.7	97.9	2.1	0.0	1.2	95.9	0.0
CT Everest Bond	5.0	47.4	50.0	2.6	6.6	103.8	0.0
Dynamic Income	3.4	28.8	50.8	20.4	37.9	38.6	21.7
Fonds Professionals Bond	2.4	7.3	81.2	11.5	51.3	38.5	7.9
Industrial-Alliance Bonds	4.3	57.0	30.7	12.3	13.7	85.3	0.0
Industrial-Alliance Ecoflex Bond	4.3	57.0	30.7	12.3	13.7	85.3	0.0
Laurentian Government Bond	1.7	72.0	28.0	0.0	28.0	49.6	0.0
Mutual Life 2	4.4	44.8	52.4	2.7	5.2	60.9	0.0
Royal Trust Bond	4.7	63.9	22.6	13.5	16.7	82.1	0.0
Scotia Excelsior Defensive Income	1.8	100.0	0.0	0.0	28.3	62.5	8.1
Scotia Excelsior Income	3.8	37.2	56.5	6.3	26.2	69.3	3.9

SOURCE: PALTRAK FOR WINDOWS

TABLE XIV

Recommended Canadian Bond Funds with Good Long-, Medium- and Short-Term Performance

Annualized Performance to Sept. 30, 1996

Fund	1 Yr	3 Yr	5 Yr	10 Yr	Volatilty	MER
	Annualized compound returns					
AGF Canadian Bond	11.4	7.1	10.4	9.6	Med	1.40
Atlas Canadian Bond	10.5	6.8	9.2	8.8	Med-	1.98
Bissett Bond	12.7	8.8	9.9	9.9	Med-	0.75
Empire Group Bond	12.2	9.4	11.3	10.9	Med-	1.28
Industrial-Alliance Bonds	10.5	7.0	8.8	9.5	Med-	1.61
Investors Government Bond	10.8	7.6	9.2	9.4	Med-	1.91
PH & N Bond	12.2	8.9	10.9	11.1	Med-	0.60
Sceptre Bond	10.6	7.5	9.4	9.8	Med-	1.25
Talvest Bond	10.4	7.3	9.3	9.7	Med-	1.99
Average Cdn bond fund	10.2	7.1	9.2	9.6		1.59

SOURCE: PALTRAK FOR WINDOWS

TABLE XV

Of course many investors prefer to be passive. Table XV lists bond funds that have tended to provide good long-, medium- and short-term performance relative to bond funds in general and which would meet the needs of such investors.

Some investors want bond funds with large portions of assets invested in corporate bonds because they expect these to perform better than government issues in periods of economic growth when confidence in corporate profits is high. Table XVI lists several funds with high per centages of assets in corporate issues.

Recommended Canadian Bond Funds That Invest in Corporate Bonds

Percentage Composition by Cash, Canadian Bonds, Corporate Bonds, Federal Government Bonds and Other Government Bonds

Fund	Report date	Cash	Cdn	Canadian bond analysis		
				Corp	Fed	Other
Atlas Cdn. High Yield Bond	Sep-96	9.6	81.5	100.0	0.0	0.0
Green Line Canadian Bond	Sep-96	0.9	95.4	75.6	6.5	17.9
Guardian Canadian Income	Sep-96	44.3	41.5	100.0	0.0	0.0
Mawer Cdn High Yield Bond	Aug-96	4.9	89.3	97.0	3.0	0.0
Navigator Canadian Income	Aug-96	5.8	91.8	95.7	4.3	0.0
O'Donnell High Income	Sep-96	13.7	82.9	100.0	0.0	0.0

SOURCE: PALTRAK FOR WINDOWS

TABLE XVI

Recommended Canadian Bond Funds That Invest in Derivatives
Holdings at Aug. 31, 1996

Fund	Type	Primary use of derivatives	1 Yr	2 Yr	3 Yr
C.I. Global Bd RSP	Int'l	Access to foreign countries/ currencies & some currency hedging	10.8	10.9	6.1
Global Strategy Bd	Cdn	Domestic interest rate hedging	9.1	8.5	
Global Strat Div Fgn	Int'l	Access to foreign countries/currencies	9.2		
Guardian Fgn Inc A	Int'l	Access to foreign countries/currencies	9.5	9.1	
Royal Trust Int'l Bd	Int'l	Foreign currency hedge	7.6	8.6	5.3
Average Cdn bond			9.8	10.3	6.0
Average int'l bond			8.0	8.0	4.8

SOURCE: PAL*TRAK* FOR WINDOWS

TABLE XVII

Foreign currency bond funds

Investors who want a portion of their bond fund invested in currencies other than the Canadian dollar have a wide selection among RRSP and non-registered funds as can be seen in Appendix 3. Risk-adjusted performance of these tends to reflect whether or not the managers use what are called derivatives to moderate the impact of currency swings. Table XVII lists some of the better performing bond funds which had derivatives in their portfolios as at Aug. 31, 1996.

If you want to invest in bond funds but would rather not form an opinion on the direction of interest rates, consider a portfolio of several funds. Table XVIII and Chart IX show returns of three funds with very different management styles plus the returns of a portfolio made up of equal positions in the three funds. The combined fund portfolio has very stable returns: only Dynamic Income fund has a lower standard deviation, while the portfolio has outperformed Dynamic overall. This is an example of how diversifying even within a fund category can sometimes lead to overall lower volatility levels, while optimizing performance.

As noted, each of the three funds has a different management style. On a short-term basis this means their returns are unlikely to be highly correlated. Historically, however, their longer-term returns have tended to be similar. By holding equal positions of the three in a portfolio you are likely to get a more stable monthly

A Diversified Portfolio of Canadian Bond Funds
Performance to Sept. 30, 1996

Fund	1 Yr	2 Yr	3 Yr	5 Yr	MER	5 Yr Std Deviation
Altamira Bond	11.1	16.2	8.0	11.6	1.31	2.6
Dynamic Income	8.1	10.4	8.4	10.0	1.68	1.2
PH & N Bond	12.2	13.2	8.9	10.9	0.60	1.9
Portfolio of above 3 bond funds	10.5	13.3	8.4	10.8		1.7

SOURCE: PAL*TRAK* FOR WINDOWS

TABLE XVIII

return, an advantage in a withdrawal plan, without any sacrifice of longer term returns.

Chart IX compares the cumulative performance of the three funds plus a portfolio combining the three over a 60-month period. Chart X plots bond fund rates of return against risk with the three funds and the combined portfolio highlighted.

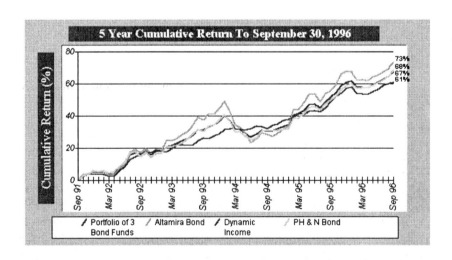

CHART IX

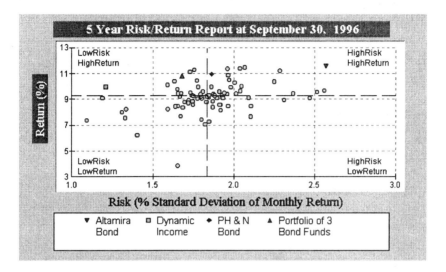

CHART X

Emerging-market bond funds

You should consider funds which invest in bonds issued by emerging-market countries speculative and buy them only if you are willing to hold what might prove to be very volatile funds. While they will potentially provide high returns, they will almost certainly prove to be high risk. Just remember that these countries have to earn foreign exchange to make their payments and that many do not have diversified economic bases leaving them vulnerable to, say, higher energy or food prices. It wasn't too many years ago that many Latin American and Eastern European countries could pay the interest on their bonds only because consortiums of banks were willing to lend them the money they needed to pay the interest. The banks did this so they wouldn't have to show the loans in default.

Some of the emerging-market countries have U.S. dollar denominated bonds outstanding. A number of these issues have their principal amounts (but not their interest) secured by U.S. Treasury zero coupon bonds. These are called Brady bonds after the former U.S. treasury secretary Nicholas Brady who developed a debt-restructuring plan for countries whose debt load required restructuring. These bonds tend to trade like strip bonds which are single amounts payable at some future specified date. Strips are extremely volatile with small moves in interest rates resulting in

Canadian Mortgage Funds with the Best Volatility-Adjusted Returns
Annualized Performance to Sept. 30, 1996

Fund	Assets ($mil)	Volatility	6 M	1 Yr	2 Yr	3 Yr	5 Yr	10 Yr
CIBC Mortgage	1,392	Low	5.2	9.9	9.6	7.6	8.9	9.6
CT Everest Mortgage	668	Low	3.7	7.4	8.2	7.1	8.1	9.1
First Cdn Mortgage	2,031	Low	4.5	9.7	9.8	7.6	8.9	9.9
GWL Mortgage (G) A	639	Low	5.5	9.1	9.6	6.2	8.1	8.7
Green Line Mortgage	912	Low	4.0	7.9	8.5	6.6	8.2	9.5
Investors Mortgage	2,969	Low	4.4	8.3	8.9	6.2	7.2	8.5
Royal Trust Mortgage	877	Low	3.8	8.0	8.3	5.9	7.0	8.6
Royfund Mortgage	1,023	Low	4.6	9.1	8.8	7.4		
Scotia Ex Mortgage	525	Med-	4.9	9.6	10.0	7.9		

SOURCE: PAL*TRAK* FOR WINDOWS

TABLE XIX

huge gains or declines in their prices. An emerging-market bond fund with a substantial holding of Brady bonds is more likely to move in sympathy with U.S. interest rates than with the fortunes of the emerging-market countries which issued the bonds.

Consequently, make sure you understand what is in the portfolios of an emerging-market bond fund before buying. Does it have bonds whose principal amounts are guaranteed by the U.S. government? If so, get your adviser to determine what each 1 per cent rise or decline in U.S. interest rates will mean to the value of the fund units. If you expect U.S. interest rates to rise, you may not wish to be in such a fund.

You should also be aware that some of the emerging-market countries lack Canada's traditions of fairness and freedom. A case in point is Nigeria whose bonds are held in at least one emerging-market bond fund. A country whose leaders are willing to execute their political opponents are unlikely to care much about your property rights. I have no recommendations in this area.

Mortgage funds

Mortgage interest rates are almost always higher than interest rates on bonds with similar terms. Consequently, they are suitable for individuals who require interest income for current needs and for people seeking a conservative investment for retirement savings.

Recommended Dividend Funds with a Focus on Preferred Shares

Percentage Composition by Cash, Common and Preferred Shares.
Annualized Performance to September 30, 1996

Fund	Cash	Com	Pref	6 M	1 Yr	2 Yr	3 Yr	5 Yr	10 Yr
Ind Alliance Int'l	2.9	0.0	97.1	6.7					
InvesNat Dividend	17.5	21.1	55.9	5.9	12.5	11.1	8.2		
Dynamic Dividend	0.0	29.0	46.6	7.4	14.1	12.4	8.7	10.0	8.7
MD Dividend	8.6	31.6	42.6	7.0	13.4	11.5	9.2		
Scotia Ex Dividend	21.1	46.3	39.3	10.4	18.4	13.6	9.7	9.3	
Guardian Mthly Div	11.0	23.4	39.0	6.2					
Maritime Life Div	13.3	42.2	33.1	7.9	12.8				
Altamira Dividend	17.5	43.4	26.3	9.1	16.0	14.5			
Spectrum Dividend	3.3	37.0	25.4	8.6	13.6				

SOURCE: PAL*TRAK* FOR WINDOWS

TABLE XX

Most mortgage funds offered by lending institutions invest in insured residential mortgages. Others hold mortgage-backed securities. A few funds hold commercial mortgages. My preferences are larger funds with broad geographical portfolio bases which have demonstrated an ability to earn high returns with low volatility. Table XIX includes some funds which fit this description.

I would specifically avoid funds whose portfolios are primarily in Quebec because of the uncertainties associated with future property values and currency should Quebec separate.

Dividend funds

Most investors who invest in dividend funds use them to earn higher after-tax returns than available from bond and mortgage funds. Given this objective, I have based my choices on returns, volatility and yield.

Investors who wish maximum dividend income or return should invest in funds with major portions of the assets invested in preferred shares. Those who want a rising income stream over time should consider funds which have large portions of their holdings in dividend-paying common shares and the expectation of rising dividends. Current income will be less than with a fund holding primarily preferreds. Total returns from the second group should be at least comparable and possibly higher. Table XX lists dividend

Recommended Dividend Funds with a Focus on Common Shares

Percentage Composition by Cash, Common and Preferred Shares.
Annualized Performance to Sept. 30, 1996

Fund	Cash	Com	Pref	6 M	1 Yr	2 Yr	3 Yr	5 Yr	10 Yr
Stan Life Cdn Div	4.5	95.7	0.0	15.1	24.0				
20/20 Dividend	7.1	91.1	0.0	8.5	17.0	15.2	13.1	12.2	9.90
First Cdn Div Income	6.8	86.7	1.9	12.7	21.3				
Green Line Dividend	5.1	82.0	10.9	11.7	17.9	8.2	7.4	9.5	
Concorde Dividendes	0.0	81.1	0.0	14.9	25.7				
Royfund Dividend	1.0	79.1	7.1	12.4	19.8	15.0	11.7		
Royal Trust Gth & Inc	1.6	78.0	6.8	13.5	22.7	14.1	10.5	9.1	6.8
Hongkong Bank Div	14.9	77.4	2.4	13.0	21.9				
Maxxum Dividend	11.0	76.0	3.8	9.8	20.3	15.4	13.6	17.2	
PH & N Div Income	14.7	72.7	6.1	13.3	21.1	15.4	13.1	12.8	10.5
Industrial Dividend	10.4	71.6	0.3	9.6	17.1	10.7	11.6	14.5	8.1

SOURCE: PAL*TRAK* FOR WINDOWS

TABLE XXI

funds which have the majority of their assets in preferred shares (or at least a tendency toward them); Table XXI lists funds which have the majority of their assets in dividend-paying common shares or convertible preferreds.

CHAPTER 13

Equity Funds

CANADIANS WHO WISH TO IN-
vest for growth can choose from among 660 mutual funds. The largest group, 303, invest primarily in the Canadian market (more later
on the definition of "primarily"). About 113 invest primarily in the
United States while over 50 invest in the Pacific Rim, including Japan, and about 30 invest in Europe. In addition, some three dozen
funds put their assets in the so-called emerging-market countries or
regions. There are a number of specialty funds which invest in narrow segments of the market such as gold or several segments such
as resources. Investors also have a choice of a number of global/in-
ternational funds which are free to invest in any or all markets.

Canadian equity funds

As an investor in the Canadian market you can take a passive
stance, buying and holding one or more funds based on a long-term
time horizon. Alternatively, you can take an active interest seeking
out those funds which you expect to perform well over the short or
medium term because of their portfolio holdings which mesh well
with your views about the market outlook, then switching when circumstances change. About half the Canadian funds available hold
some foreign content within the 20 per cent foreign property limit
allowed by Ottawa for RRSP-eligible funds. Many vary their cash
holdings according to how they view the outlook for the market.

If you want to take a passive stance, the funds listed in Table
XXII are likely to provide you with acceptable long-term returns
over time. You probably will not be among the market leaders. But
at the same time you are unlikely to be in the bottom quartile.

These funds tend to move in concert with the Toronto Stock
Exchange 300 index because they generally hold many of the same
stocks as the index. In fact, several of the funds noted as index

Recommended Canadian Equity Funds That Track the TSE 300

Annualized Performance to Sept. 30, 1996

Fund	1 Yr	2 Yr	3 Yr	5 Yr	R-Square	Beta
AMI Private Cap Equity	22.2	13.2	11.6	10.6	0.85	0.93
C.I. Canadian Growth	11.0	7.4	9.6		0.93	0.92
CIBC Canadian Equity	12.3	6.9	4.9	6.3	0.89	0.91
First Canadian Eq Index	17.5	11.0	10.4	10.2	0.98	1.00
GWL Eqty Index (G) A	16.1	9.7	9.5	9.6	1.00	1.00
Green Line Cdn Index	17.8	11.5	11.1	10.9	1.00	1.00
Investors Retirement	17.7	10.1	10.5	9.9	0.83	0.92
Laurentian Cdn Equity	13.0	7.3	7.0	8.4	0.85	0.93
PH & N Cdn Equity	22.0	14.1	14.3	12.4	0.91	0.92
Scotia Ex Cdn Blue Chip	16.7	8.2	6.4	8.5	0.87	0.92
TSE 300	19.4	12.8	12.4	12.2	1.00	1.00

SOURCE: PALTRAK FOR WINDOWS

TABLE XXII

funds have the identical holdings as the index. Their differences in returns from the index stem from their management expense ratios.

The table includes two measures, R square and beta. R square measures how closely correlated a fund's portfolio is with the index portfolio. Beta measures portfolio volatility relative to the TSE index volatility. Index funds have identical beta to the index. The variance in the others can largely be explained by the cash portion of the portfolios.

Not all equity funds tend to move together. Rather performance of funds with similar management philosophies tend to be correlated with each other. To moderate risk you may want to hold several funds with different management philosophies.

If you have specific views about the markets, then buy funds whose holdings reflect your views. For instance, many investors believe that the Canadian equity market will be among the world leaders over the next several years. This view (which I share) reflects the expanding world economy and in particular the expansion that is taking place in Asia and to a lesser extent in Latin America, Eastern Europe and the countries of the former Soviet Union. As these economies grow, their demand for energy, metals, forest products and resources in general will grow at a much faster

Recommended Canadian Equity Funds with Substantial Holdings in Resource Shares
Annualized Perfomance to Sept. 30, 1996

Resource Funds	1 Yr	2 Yr	3 Yr	5 Yr	10 Yr	15 Yr	MER	Std Dev*
AGF Cdn Resources A	41.4	17.0	9.5	22.7	13.2	7.3	2.56	5.6
BPI Cdn Resource Inc	39.6	13.1	6.6	22.2	12.4	10.6	2.72	6.1
Cambridge Resource	91.1	32.9	16.5	30.9	12.3	12.9	3.00	7.6
Universal Cdn Resource	39.1	9.3	8.2	26.4	12.4	9.2	2.40	5.8

						%	%	%
Equity Funds	1 Yr	2 Yr	3 Yr	5 Yr	10 Yr	Cash	Cdn	Resource
AGF Cdn Equity A	20.0	11.4	9.2	10.4	5.4	8.9	87.9	56.3
Altafund Investment	34.9	15.5	13.1	20.7		13.9	73.9	68.8
Altamira Capital Gth	3.5	3.5	8.2	12.6	9.4	5.4	77.8	69.4
Altamira Equity	14.1	9.6	9.8	22.5		11.7	75.8	66.8
C.I. Cdn Growth	11.0	7.4	9.6			22.1	74.0	57.5
CDA Common Stock	6.3	4.5	6.3	9.2	8.5	3.8	77.2	71.6
Colonia Life	64.1	34.4	24.2			13.7	83.8	55.4
Dynamic Cdn Gth	16.4	7.0	7.0	23.5	10.8	3.8	78.3	64.8
Fidelity Capital Builder	16.0	9.9	7.8	10.0		1.7	83.9	61.4
Industrial Growth	9.7	4.2	7.0	9.7	7.8	1.0	79.6	62.6
Industrial Horizon	10.0	5.3	9.2	9.8		8.4	82.9	67.8
Manulife VistaFd1Cap Gns	9.2	6.0	5.9	11.5	9.0	6.1	92.7	63.8
Manulife VistaFd1 Eqty	7.9	6.1	7.3	9.0	7.6	0.9	80.4	63.5
Multiple Opportunities	49.5	48.8	34.3	38.4	16.7	63.6	36.4	67.7
University Ave Cdn	17.4	8.9	6.4	18.1		33.8	46.7	58.7

* Monthly Standard Deviation for 120 months ending Sept. 30, 1996

SOURCE: PAL*TRAK* FOR WINDOWS

TABLE XXIII

pace than supply. This essentially dictates higher prices for resources and higher profits and share prices for Canadian producers. This in turn will be reflected in high returns for Canadian mutual funds with significant resource exposures.

Table XXIII includes Canadian equity funds with high risk-adjusted performance and substantial portions of their holdings in resource shares relative to the general Canadian market. If you wish to fine-tune your choices, use the tables in Appendix 3 or examine the individual portfolio holdings.

Gold is a special case. It is a resource product. It is used primarily in manufacturing jewelry. Demand for high karat gold jewelry has been growing in emerging-market countries where

Recommended Canadian Precious Metals Funds

Percentage Compositon by Cash, Canadian Equities and Canadian Precious Metals Stocks. Annualized Performance to Sept. 30, 1996

Fund	1 Yr	2 Yr	3 Yr	5 Yr	10 Yr	Cash	Cdn	Precious
Royal Prec Metals	71.9	50.7	39.1	30.6		2.4	68.3	72.6
Maxxum Prec Metals	80.9	37.3	33.2	32.1		17.6	60.0	64.9
Global Strat Gold Plus	71.9	35.4	33.1			6.5	74.2	71.3
Dynamic Prec Metals	36.6	11.5	17.4	24.6	12.2	8.0	48.1	66.2
Scotia Ex Prec Metals	49.6	18.4				19.0	69.5	78.5

SOURCE: PALTRAK FOR WINDOWS

TABLE XXIV

people have little trust in government securities and the banking system and use gold as a form of savings. At the same time demand has been rising, supply from mining has been falling.

Recommended Canadian Equity Funds That Invest in the Financial Services Industry

Percentage Contribution by Cash, Canadian Equities and Financial Services Stocks. Annualized Performance to Sept. 30, 1996

Fund	1 Yr	2 Yr	3 Yr	5 Yr	10 Yr	Cash	Cdn	Fin
AIC Advantage	59.6	37.7	26.3	27.9	15.5	2.8	81.3	71.3
AMI Private Cap Eqty	22.2	13.2	11.6	10.6		3.5	78.6	26.0
Atlas Cdn L-Cap Gth	21.1	14.9	12.0	8.5	6.6	7.0	74.9	21.5
Canadian Investment	20.2	13.6	10.9	8.6	6.2	11.1	76.1	29.2
CIBC Dividend	15.0	10.0	6.9	8.3		34.5	61.0	39.5
Confed Life	22.3	13.2	13.2	12.9	9.3	2.8	82.7	25.4
Ethical Growth	17.4	15.0	11.7	10.4	10.0	13.4	87.6	21.5
Global Strat Can Gth	18.2	12.1	7.6			8.1	75.1	23.9
Green Line Value	34.0	19.9				14.0	68.1	21.5
Industrial Pension	15.2	10.1	12.5	13.3	6.9	10.0	60.9	25.1
Ivy Canadian	17.1	14.8	12.5			32.9	52.7	37.5
Leith Wheeler Cdn Eqty	16.4	8.3				5.4	94.1	25.7
McLean Bud Eqty Gth	29.3	17.3	11.4	12.6		7.3	91.8	25.8
McLean Bud Pld Cdn Eq	32.5	19.8	13.3	15.0	11.2	3.8	97.1	26.0
MD Equity	13.1	5.7	8.0	11.4	9.3	18.9	56.7	21.4
Optima Strat Cdn Eqty	18.2	16.7	13.7			9.3	71.7	30.5
PH & N Cdn Eqty	22.0	14.1	14.3	12.4	9.8	3.6	95.4	22.5
PH & N Pld Pen Tr	23.6	15.2	14.3	12.8	10.0	2.5	81.7	22.5
Trans-Canada Value	19.1	7.3	3.6	8.4	7.1	15.6	61.4	62.1
Trimark Select Cdn Gth	11.9	8.6	11.4			22.3	60.5	26/5

SOURCE: PALTRAK FOR WINDOWS

TABLE XXV

Recommended Canadian Equity Small-Cap Funds

Percentage Composition by Cash, Canadian Equities and Average
Capitalization in Millions. Annualized Performance to Sept. 30, 1996

Fund	1 Yr	2 Yr	3 Yr	5 Yr	10 Yr	Cash	Cdn	Av Cap
Bissett Small Capital	34.9	20.7	15.9			0.4	94.9	180
BPI Cdn Small Co	49.7	32.9	21.2	23.9		12.1	55.7	100
Cambridge Growth	19.9	4.9	1.2	10.6	10.4	2.5	92.8	60
Cambridge Resource	91.1	32.9	16.5	30.9	12.3	7.4	83.2	60
Ethical Special Equity	13.1					6.2	82.4	80
Global Strat Cdn Small	22.7					10.0	90.0	160
Multiple Opportunities	49.5	48.8	34.3	38.4	16.7	63.6	36.4	60
Resolute Growth	40.4	20.0				11.2	88.5	160
Royal Cdn Small Cap	15.3	9.5	6.3			8.2	76.6	120
Royal Life Cdn Gth	17.8					28.7	69.4	160
Saxon Small Cap	13.3	9.8	7.2	13.7	6.6	11.1	89.1	70

SOURCE: PALTRAK FOR WINDOWS

TABLE XXVI

Bullion prices have been depressed by central bank selling. While this continues to be a threat, many analysts believe it is only a matter of time before gold prices move substantially higher.

You have two ways of holding gold in your portfolio. You can choose a fund which already has a hefty gold position. Or you can hold precious metals funds as part of your portfolio position. Appendix 3 notes the percentage of assets which Canadian funds have invested in gold. Table XXIV includes gold funds and resource funds which have substantial portions of their assets in gold and which have tended to provide better performance within the group.

Is a gold fund which provides a return of 100 per cent over one year any better than a fund that provides a return of 60 per cent? Only if you bought one at the beginning of the year with the intention of redeeming one year later. Major differences in performance can reflect the movements of one or two holdings over a short period of time.

You should examine the different philosophies of gold fund managers before buying a fund. Look at how they choose their holdings. Do they send analysts around the world to look at properties? Or do they use brokerage house reports as their source? Do they limit their holdings in exploration companies to any specific level? Do they maintain major positions in senior

Recommended Canadian Growth Funds

Percentage Composition by Canadian Equities with Average Capitalization in Billions, Average Dividend Yield, Average Price/Book Ratio and Average P/E Ratio. Annualized Performance to Sept. 30, 1996

Fund	1 Yr	2 Yr	3 Yr	5 Yr	10 Yr	Cdn	Cap	Div	PB	PE
20/20 Cdn Gth	7.8	7.6	8.6	8.3		81.0	5.6	1.1	2.2	21.3
AGF Gth Eqty	24.1	13.2	9.0	19.6	9.9	90.1	1.6	0.6	2.5	24.6
Altamira Cap Gth	3.5	3.5	8.2	12.6	9.4	77.8	4.3	1.0	2.1	23.6
Altamira Spec Gth	27.2	13.6	4.9	18.2	11.6	82.9	0.3	0.3	2.3	21.9
Apex Eqty Gth	19.1	12.6				91.6	3.4	0.8	2.3	21.7
Bullock Gth	20.1	14.5	9.7	15.2	8.7	68.9	0.3	0.2	2.0	21.7
C.I. Cdn Gth	11.0	7.4	9.6			74.0	5.0	0.7	2.2	27.6
Desjardins Gth	13.9	10.3				80.1	1.0	0.5	2.5	29.2
GBC Cdn Gth	30.1	19.8	12.6	19.3		78.9	0.7	0.4	3.2	28.5
Manu Cab Cdn Gth	37.9	17.7				81.4	0.3	0.3	2.2	20.4
Manu Cab Emer Gth	33.5	16.5				67.5	0.3	0.3	2.2	20.4
Maxx Cdn Eqty Gth	20.1	19.0	11.8	17.8	10.6	85.3	3.63	1.1	2.0	20.7
Metlife Mvp Gth	24.0	16.5	12.3			78.0	0.4	0.7	2.8	22.1
Mutual Premier Gth	20.3	18.3	14.3			83.6	0.4	0.7	2.1	26.2
Scotia Ex Cdn Gth	25.6	20.0	16.3	14.4	10.4	92.7	3.82	1.1	2.1	20.7
United Cdn Gth	24.3	21.9	17.7	21.6	11.3	67.7	0.7	0.2	2.2	22.2
TSE 300	19.4	12.8	12.4	12.2	9.2	100	6.3	1.8	1.9	20.1
TSE Paper & Forest	-9.1	-3.2	4.0	7.4	5.0	100	1.4	1.7	1.2	8.4
TSE Fin Services	37.6	26.8	19.5	15.5	12.3	100	8.3	2.8	1.7	11.0
TSE Utilities	28.0	13.5	13.3	12.0	10.7	100	10.9	4.3	1.8	19.9
TSE Merchandise	4.9	11.0	2.9	2.6	4.7	100	1.6	1.4	1.9	90.1
TSE Metals & Min	4.3	11.8	22.9	14.2	12.1	100	5.5	1.2	1.9	18.4
TSE Industrial	25.4	14.3	16.1	15.2	8.8	100	6.1	1.0	2.8	20.6
TSE Gold & Silver	5.2	1.2	10.0	20.3	9.3	100	5.5	0.6	3.2	57.6

SOURCE: PAL*TRAK* FOR WINDOWS

TABLE XXVII

producers? All these have a bearing on performance and risk. In addition, look carefully at the geographical diversification of the exploration and mining efforts of the companies in the portfolio. There are political risks in investments in emerging markets. Consequently, you want to see geographical diversification.

Alternatively you may believe that the largest gains will be made by financial services stocks and consequently desire funds that have hefty investments in this segment of the market. See Table XXV for funds to consider.

Recommended Canadian Value Funds and Their Value-Growth Orientation
Annualized Performance to Sept. 30, 1996

Fund	1 Yr	3 Yr	5 Yr	10 Yr	VGO* Min	Avg	Max	# of Periods
Associate Investors	19.9	9.8	9.4	7.7	0.67	0.78	0.89	19
Atlas Cdn L-Cap Value	7.0				0.78	0.91	0.98	15
Canadian Investment	20.2	10.9	8.6	6.2	0.66	0.84	1.00	43
CIBC Dividend	15.0	6.9	8.3		0.66	0.76	0.88	33
Global Strat Can Gth	18.20	7.6			0.64	0.78	0.93	23
Ind Alliance Ecoflex A	13.2	11.8			0.70	0.82	0.93	26
Ind Alliance Stocks	13.8	12.2	13.3	9.7	0.75	0.84	0.93	18
Investors Ret Gth Port	16.7	10.0	10.3		0.97	0.99	1.00	6
Ivy Canadian	17.1	12.5			0.58	0.79	0.92	31
Leith Wheeler								
Cdn Eqty	16.4				0.60	0.78	0.84	22
Mawer New Canada	37.2	15.4	21.3		0.88	0.94	0.99	12
Talvest Growth	8.0	8.3	7.9	8.3	0.67	0.89	0.98	35
Transamerica Growsafe								
Eqty	15.5				0.77	0.83	0.93	11
Westbury Cdn Life A	18.9	12.9	12.9	9.6	0.70	0.87	0.97	32

* Value-Growth Orientation is a numerical assessment of the relative Price/Earnings, Price/Book and Dividend Yield as measured against the TSE 300 index. In this context, a value of 1 would indicate that the stocks on balance had the same style fundamentals as did the TSE 300. A value greater than 1 would indicate a tendency to more growth oriented stocks, while, as in this case, a value of less than 1 indicates that stocks with traditionally value oriented characteristics prevail.

SOURCE: PAL*TRAK* FOR WINDOWS

TABLE XXVIII

Size of the companies within a portfolio may have a major bearing on performance. If you expect that the best performance in the Canadian market will develop from companies with market capitalizations of less than $200 million, Table XXVI includes some funds to consider.

Some managers pick stocks on the basis of above-average growth. These funds tend to have stocks with low dividend yields and relatively high price-earnings ratios. Table XXVII lists funds which fall into this category.

Alternatively, you may wish funds whose managers take what is called a value approach and find stocks which appear relatively undervalued. Generally such funds have holdings with relatively low price-earnings ratios, price to book ratios and relatively high

Recommended Blue Chip Equity Funds

Percentage Composition by Cash, Canadian Equities and Foreign Equities with Average Capital Size and Average Dividend Yield. Annualized Performance to Sept. 30, 1996

Fund	1Yr	2Yr	3Yr	5Yr	10Yr	Cash	Cdn	Fgn	($bil) Cap	Div
BNP (Canada) Eqty	17.4	11.8	10.3	9.7		2.6	84.7	12.8	6.4	1.8
Canadian Invest	20.2	13.6	10.9	8.6	6.2	11.1	76.1	1.3	7.6	3.2
CIBC Dividend	15.0	10.0	6.9	8.3		34.5	61.0	0.0	7.7	3.6
Empire Elite Eqty	17.4	12.3	9.3	11.3	7.0	3.7	77.2	18.6	7.5	1.9
Empire Group Eqty	20.2	13.5	11.0	12.7	9.5	3.1	76.9	19.4	7.5	1.9
Empire Life 3	19.6	13.8	11.3	12.8	9.6	0.8	79.7	19.0	7.7	1.9
Empire Premier Eqty	18.6	12.8	10.8	12.1	9.5	1.3	78.8	19.4	7.4	1.9
Green Line Cdn Idx	17.8	11.5	11.1	10.9	7.8	0.1	99.9	0.0.	6.4	1.8
Hongkong Bnk Eqty	22.2	8.7	8.1	13.2		5.1	80.4	14.5	6.5	1.2
Ivy Cdn	17.1	14.8	12.5			32.9	52.7	14.3	7.8	2.2
McLean Bud Eqty	29.3	17.3	11.4	12.6		7.3	91.8	0.9	6.3	1.3
Nat'l Tr Cdn Eqty	13.5	8.7	6.4	8.6	7.4	3.4	96.9	0.0	7.3	2.0
NN Cdn 35 Index	17.4	10.7	12.3	8.7		3.5	96.5	0.0	9.0	2.3
NN Cdn Gth	15.8	8.8	8.3	7.7	4.4	5.0	80.7	14.3	6.5	1.7
Scotia Ex Cdn B Chip	16.7	8.2	6.4	8.5		7.5	82.3	9.0	6.4	1.8
Spectrum Cdn Eqty	14.5	9.8	9.2	8.2		8.6	82.3	9.0	6.4	1.8
Top 50 Eqty	16.2	8.1	6.9	6.7		2.7	97.3	0.0	6.4	2.0
Westbury Cdn Life A	18.9	13.2	12.9	12.9	9.6	0.7	99.3	0.0	6.9	2.3
Westbury Cdn Life Eq	16.0	8.8	8.8	8.5		4.5	95.5	0.0	6.3	2.1

SOURCE: PAL*TRAK* FOR WINDOWS

TABLE XXIX

dividend yields as noted in the following table. Table XXVIII lists these funds.

It is of course possible for a fund to invest in growth companies which are undervalued yet have above-average revenue and earnings growth.

Some people prefer to invest in so-called blue chip stocks, or in mutual funds that invest in blue chip stocks. Blue chip stocks refer to those companies that are generally characterized as being well established, large (in terms of market capitalization), and generally provide a better than average dividend yield. Generally speaking, one does not expect rapid capital growth from a blue chip stock, but rather a steady income and conservative capital growth. In Table XXIX, Portfolio Analytics Limited has assembled some of the better

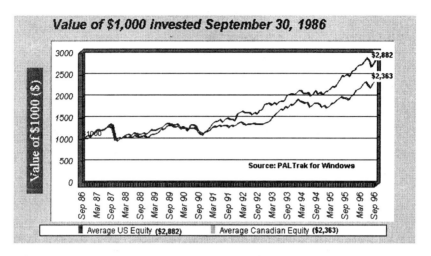

Value of $1,000 invested September 30, 1986

Source: PALTrak for Windows

■ Average US Equity ($2,882)   ▧ Average Canadian Equity ($2,363)

CHART XI

known mutual funds that have a tendency towards these types of stocks. Notice the Average Capital Size and Average Dividend Yield refer to the average capitalization and the average dividend yield of the underlying securities. Mutual funds allow investors to access Canadian blue chip stocks in a diversified portfolio as in Table XXIX.

Recommended U.S. Small-Cap Funds
Annualized Performance to Aug. 30, 1996

Fund	1 Yr	2 Yr	3 Yr	5 Yr	10 Yr	Vol	MER	($mil) Assets
20/20 Aggressive Gth	6.3	16.9	12.9			High	2.54	268.9
AGF Int'l Grp Spec A	-1.1	8.9	8.4	10.8	9.6	High	2.38	110.9
Altamira Select Amer	12.4	13.1	14.8	21.3		High	2.32	258.4
Atlas Amer Emerg Value	0.5						2.69	1.0
BPI Amer Small Co	11.6	16.8	17.5	22.5		High	2.97	81.5
Bullock American D	17.3	18.2	10.4	13.8	15.2	High	2.26	284.3
Cambridge Amer Gth	-11.2	-1.5	-7.3			High	3.00	0.7
Fidelity Small Cap Amer	2.1	14.5					2.59	56.6
GT Global America Gth	1.7						2.95	16.6
United American Gth	26.9	25.9	19.2	20.0	12.0	High	2.30	68.4
Universal US Emerg Gth	20.8	29.6	22.1			High	2.40	310.3
Zweig Strategic Growth	11.7	13.1	10.4			Med-	2.62	156.7

SOURCE: PAL*TRAK* FOR WINDOWS

TABLE XXX

Recommended U.S. Large-Cap Funds
Annualized Performance to Aug. 30, 1996

Fund	1 Yr	2 Yr	3 Yr	5 Yr	10 Yr	Vol	MER	($Mil) Assets
AGF Int'l Grp Amer Gth A	13.0	16.2	13.8	14.4	9.4	Med+	2.37	117.1
AGF Int'l Grp Amer Gth B	12.7						2.85	457.9
Altamira US Larger Co	9.2	16.9	15.3			High	2.36	92.0
Atlas Amer L Cap Gth	20.2	16.7	12.6	11.7	7.6	Med	2.70	7.8
Atlas Amer L Cap Value	22.0						2.69	2.1
Bissett American Eqty	12.0	13.4	12.0	12.6	8.5	Med	1.50	7.2
BPI Amer Eqty Value	14.4	12.5	2.1	12.5		Med+	2.64	55.4
Bullock Optimax USA A	13.2	12.2					2.33	6.3
Century DJ	6.2	4.7	3.8	4.2	3.4	Low	1.80	0.3
Cornerstone US	15.6	13.4	11.9	12.0	6.4	Med	2.59	23.4
CT Everest Amerigrowth	15.9	18.6	13.6			Med	1.41	234.6
Green Line US Index	17.4	18.6	13.7	12.0		Med	0.77	63.0
Industrial American	9.1	7.4	9.1	11.7	8.9	Med+	2.38	249.0
Mclean Budden Amer Gth	13.4	14.7	13.1	11.6		Med+	1.75	12.4

SOURCE: PAL*TRAK* FOR WINDOWS

TABLE XXXI

Recommended U.S. Index and Index-like Funds
Annualized Performance to Sept. 30, 1996

Fund	1 Yr	2 Yr	3 Yr	5 Yr	10Yr	R-Square	Beta
AGF Intl Grp-Amer Gth	20.0	24.3	16.1	17.4	11.3	0.82	1.03
Atlas Amer L Cap Gth	19.5	22.1	14.7	13.2	8.7	0.87	0.94
Bissett Amer Equity	13.3	18.8	13.7	14.1	9.7	0.91	1.01
CIBC US Equity	20.9	17.0	12.3	13.6		0.77	0.92
Cornerstone US	18.1	18.7	13.8	14.0	7.8	0.92	0.88
Green Line US Index	19.1	23.4	16.1	13.6		0.81	0.88
Investors US Growth	16.1	18.2	13.3	16.8	13.0	0.77	0.66
Laurentian American Eqty	13.2	14.1	11.9	13.7	9.2	0.82	0.94
McLean Bud Amer Gth	16.8	21.5	15.6	13.7		0.91	1.14
McLean Bud Pld Am Eqty	18.8	23.6	18.1	16.1	13.6	0.91	1.14
PH & N US Equity	25.5	20.6	15.4	17.7	13.9	0.81	0.95
PH & N US Pld Pens	27.2	22.0	16.8	18.8	15.0	0.81	0.94
Royal Trust Amer Stock	11.6	17.4	12.8	14.5	11.8	0.82	0.86
Talvest US Growth	18.7	19.1	13.6	14.3	12.0	0.81	0.98
S & P 500	22.0	25.9	18.2	19.5	14.8	1.00	1.00

SOURCE: PAL*TRAK* FOR WINDOWS

TABLE XXXII

Three US Equity Fund Portfolios
Percentage Composition by Cash and US Equities with Five-Year Standard Deviation and Similarity. Annualized Performance to Sept. 30, 1996

Fund	1 Yr	2 Yr	3 Yr	5 Yr	Cash	US	Std Dev	Sim*
Beutel Goodman Amer Eq	11.7	10.8	11.0	14.3	9.8	90.2	3.0	62.8
Green Line US Index	17.4	18.6	13.7	12.0	0.0	98.3	2.7	100.0
Investors US Gth	18.3	13.9	12.6	16.3	8.5	87.0	2.6	47.5
US Eqty Portfolio, Mar. 1991	15.7	14.2	12.4	14.2	6.3	91.5	2.4	

* Similarity measures how closely one fund performed relative to others. Similarity=100 means they are identical. In the above example, Green Line U.S. Index was used as the first pick, while the others were picked using their relative dissimilarity while providing above average returns.

Fund	1 Yr	2 Yr	3 Yr	5 Yr	Cash	US	Std Dev	Sim*
Altamira Select American	12.4	13.1	14.8	21.3	6.4	88.3	4.5	100.0
Atlas Am Large Cap Gth	20.2	16.7	12.6	11.7	5.2	88.6	3.1	33.6
Investors US Growth	18.3	13.9	12.6	16.3	8.5	87.0	2.6	26.1
US Equity Portfolio, July 1991	16.3	14.3	16.8	6.8	88.0	3.1		

* Similarity measures how closely one fund performed relative to others. Similarity=100 means they are identical. In the above example, Altamira Select American was used as the first pick, while the others were picked using their relative dissimilarity while providing above average returns.

Fund	1 Yr	2 Yr	3 Yr	5 Yr	Cash	US	Std Dev	Sim*
AGF Intl Grp-Special A	-1.1	8.9	8.4	10.8	9.1	90.3	4.7	70.2
AIC Value	30.7	23.9	15.1	19.2	5.6	65.8	4.2	76.7
Altamira Select Amer	12.4	13.1	14.8	21.3	6.4	88.3	4.5	72.5
BPI Amer Small Co	11.6	16.8	17.5	22.5	4.2	94.0	4.1	76.3
Bullock American D	17.3	18.2	10.4	13.8	11.7	81.8	4.9	69.2
Cambridge Americas	44.0	17.8	9.3	13.2	10.9	89.1	5.9	59.4
Dynamic Americas	28.7	16.5	10.6	12.5	0.0	71.8	3.5	60.5
General Trust US Equity	8.4	8.1	4.8	12.3	12.6	85.9	4.6	68.2
Guardian Amer Eqty A	6.6	12.9	11.7	15.2	9.5	83.8	3.9	81.6
Hyperion Value Line Eqty	13.0	20.9	13.6	17.7	5.9	91.4	4.2	77.6
Mclean Bud Amer Gth	13.4	14.7	13.1	11.6	1.2	98.8	3.6	89.3
United Amer Gth	26.9	25.9	19.2	20.0	15.8	79.5	3.7	71.2
Average Values	17.7	16.5	12.4	15.8			4.3	
US Eqty Portfolio, July 1991	16.6	16.5	12.6	16.1	7.8	84.9	3.7	84.9
Average US Equity	12.6	14.0	10.9	13.1	14.4	80.0	3.5	86.9
S&P 500	21.0	20.0	16.3	17.7	0.0	100.0	0.0	100.0

* Similarity measures how closely one fund performed relative to other funds or indexes. Similarity=100 means they are identical. In the above example, The Standard and Poor's 500 Index was used as the benchmark. The above shows a portfolio of 12 funds, generally more than anyone needs, but is used to illustrate a point. Unlike previous portfolios, the member funds were chosen by 5-year volatility (higher values), in an effort to illustrate that multiple funds with relatively high volatility levels, when combined together, can actually produce lower over-all volatility (see the Std Dev column). The average 5 year standard deviation for the member funds was about 4.3, while the portfolio achieved better than average returns with a standard deviation of 3.7.
Note: This portfolio, as in the previous two, were constructed by assuming a $1,000 investment in each fund on the date of portfolio inception (in this case, July 31, 1991).

SOURCE: PAL*TRAK* FOR WINDOWS

TABLE XXXIII

Picking U.S. funds

It's no wonder many Canadians choose to invest a portion of their holdings in mutual funds which invest in the U.S. market: They have a broader variety of funds from which to choose, especially in areas such as technology and health. The U.S. economy is much larger than Canada's. The tax system is less oppressive. The political system seems more pro-business. Moreover, U.S. funds on average have performed better than Canadian funds, as Chart XI shows. While there are no guarantees that this will continue, U.S. funds are an important investment alternative.

Table XXX includes funds which invest primarily in small capitalization companies. Table XXXI includes funds which invest primarily in larger companies. Table XXXII includes U.S. index funds and funds which have tended to provide returns similar to the general market. Table XXXIII includes three fund portfolios consisting of funds whose month to month performance figures are not highly correlated.

International funds

Almost 300 equity funds invest outside Canada and the U.S. Some restrict their investing to specific countries such as Japan, Germany or India. Others are regional investing in the Pacific Rim, Latin America, or Southeast Asia. Still others are global in nature. A growing number invest in emerging-economy countries. More than 20 are 100 per cent RRSP-eligible. These funds hold the bulk of their assets, say, 85 per cent or more, in treasury bills and the remainder in futures and options.

As noted earlier, your returns from such funds reflect currency movements against the Canadian dollar as well as the performance of the underlying securities and the markets in which they operate.

Many fund managers subcontract the management of their foreign funds to foreign fund managers to save money and because they lack managers who have hands-on expertise with the various markets. Others take a more hands-on approach and manage from home. Both methods seem to work.

Being in the right international markets at the right time can be very rewarding. Japanese funds outperformed almost every other fund for more than a decade ending in the mid-1980s, providing average annual returns in excess of 20 per cent. Many investors

Recommended International Funds

Percentage Composition by Canada, the United States, Japan, Pacific Rim, Europe and Latin America. Annualized Performance to Sept. 30, 1996

Fund	1Yr	2Yr	3Yr	5Yr	Can	US	Jpn	Pac	Euro	LA
20/20 Int'l Value	11.9	10.5	10.3	13.3	3.6	26.8	7.3	3.2	50.6	7.5
BPI Glbl Eqty	12.4	9.1	10.9	12.3	7.3	36.5	14.8	3.6	34.8	3.0
BPI Glbl Small Co	8.6	4.4	12.8		8.8	29.5	4.5	9.8	45.7	1.6
Beutel Good Int'l	11.6	3.8	8.1		12.3	2.0	22.0	21.3	37.2	5.3
Can Life US & Int'l	15.6	15.0	13.7	16.4	12.0	43.0	14.0	4.2	23.9	1.6
Capstone Int'l Inv	21.2	10.6	10.9	13.7	13.6	77.3	0.0	0.0	2.5	6.6
Cornerstone Global	14.6	12.5	11.7	13.7	0.9	46.6	16.6	3.8	28.9	3.3
Fidelity Int'l Port	12.7	11.9	10.2	14.4	12.9	38.5	22.6	7.5	18.5	0.0
Fonds Prof Int'l Eq	14.6	11.5	9.1		18.8	26.4	5.5	1.2	48.1	0.0
Guardian Glbl Eq A	13.5	10.1	11.4	10.3	4.5	22.7	23.4	11.5	31.6	4.3
Investors Global	12.2	11.5	10.5	11.7	8.9	27.2	19.2	12.6	31.5	0.0
Investors Gth Port	14.1	12.6	10.8	13.6	30.8	65.9	0.0	2.1	0.7	0.2
MD Gth Invest	13.8	11.7	12.8	16.6	9.7	29.2	2.2	11.2	41.4	5.1
Mawer Wrld Invest	13.0	6.5	10.4	12.5	2.0	5.8	11.7	15.2	51.2	10.2
Mutual Prem Int'l	11.4	8.2	9.4		7.6	2.4	22.7	12.5	54.8	0.0
Royal Int'l Eqty	10.4	8.1	9.2		15.3	2.4	6.3	24.8	49.4	1.7
Sceptre Int'l	11.8	5.3	10.7	18.1	1.6	23.8	15.0	28.2	24.9	3.6
Templeton Glbl Sm	9.4	13.0	12.0	16.0	30.1	19.9	0.6	11.1	33.0	4.1
Templeton Gth	9.3	10.6	11.9	17.0	18.3	31.1	1.9	8.6	33.2	6.1
Templeton Int'l Sto	14.1	10.8	13.7	19.1	12.9	1.8	3.2	14.9	62.5	4.2
Trimark Select Gth	8.8	12.9	14.2	19.2	12.0	65.8	6.9	1.9	13.3	0.1

Remaining investments are in regions such as Asia, Africa and the Middle East. Regional asset allocation does not account for regional exposure due to derivative products. It includes all assets including cash, which may be classified as a Canadian asset.

SOURCE: PALTRAK FOR WINDOWS

TABLE XXXIV

search the international economies seeking to duplicate that performance.

If you are interested in funds that are free to move into any or all international markets, consider the ones listed in Table XXXIV. They have tended to provide superior returns in the past.

If you believe that Japanese funds are poised for renewed strength you have a choice of about 15 funds with half or more of their assets in Japanese securities. As a group their returns have been dismal for much of the past decade. Performance has improved lately with the decline of the yen and a roaring market.

How a fund handles currency risk has a major bearing on performance. The best performing fund over the 12 months ended

Recommended European Equity Funds

Percentage Composition of European Equities. Annualized Performance to Sept. 30, 1996

Fund	1 Yr	2 Yr	3 Yr	5 Yr	Euro	MER	($mil) Assets
Altamira European Equity	14.2	13.6	12.6		93.8	2.41	140.6
Dynamic Europe	15.6	14.7	13.3	11.0	83.6	2.70	59.8
Hyperion European	12.0	12.1	10.1	12.1	93.6	3.03	26.4
InvesNat European Eqty	13.4	12.1	11.9		95.6	2.25	13.5
Investors European Gth	14.2	13.9	11.8	11.7	93.6	2.46	874.8
National Global Equities	14.2	9.1	9.1	13.6	99.1	2.40	33.9
Vision Europe	15.9	16.1	12.8		98.6	3.24	24.5

SOURCE: PALTRAK FOR WINDOWS

TABLE XXXV

June 30, 1996, was Regent Nippon with a return exceeding 40 per cent. Altamira Japanese Opportunity Fund was up almost 24 per cent. Both had the same portfolio manager over the period, Peter Everington (he is no longer involved with Regent Nippon). The funds, however, had different policies toward currency hedging which were reflected in the returns. Regent Nippon was fully hedged against a declining yen while the Altamira fund was not. Hedging can be quite expensive and often the cost is prohibitive.

Table XXXIV lists some of the better performing funds that hedge currency movements and some that do not. It also lists funds which hold treasury bills primarily and use derivatives to participate in the markets.

Europe has attracted much investor attention in recent years as it moved toward a single market economy and about three dozen funds are available. Table XXXV includes my choices; these represent some of the better risk-adjusted returns for this category. You may want to fine-tune your own selection based on holdings by country which you can obtain from the funds themselves.

Emerging markets

Over the past few years, fund companies have introduced several dozen funds which invest in the so-called emerging market countries or regions. The expectations are that such economies and investments in them will grow at a much faster pace than the North American or European economies and markets. Many of the emerg-

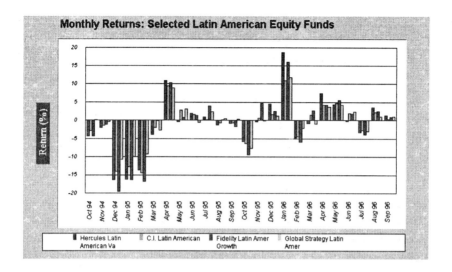

Monthly Returns: Selected Latin American Equity Funds

CHART XII

ing-market funds build similar portfolios seeking out construction, telecommunications, transportation and other companies involved in building a country's infrastructure.

There are, however, some differences among markets which must be considered. Some are quite embryonic. For instance, if money pours into the Canadian stock market, pushing up prices, many listed companies will tap this source of capital by issuing shares while some private companies may go public with initial public offerings. These issues tend to sop up some of the investment capital. The emerging markets are not yet as efficient. Consequently, prices can rise to significant premiums as cash moves in or tumble as cash moves out. Latin American funds, for example have been fairly volatile as Chart XII shows.

Currency movements have been a major factor in both positive and negative performance of emerging-market funds as a group.

To quote from Fidelity International Funds prospectus, one of the easier to understand:

"The ability . . . . to assess foreign markets may be adversely affected because issuers in such markets may not be subject to uniform and extensive accounting, auditing and financial reporting standards and practices, and other disclosure requirements such as are found in Canada and the United States. There may be difficulty in enforcing legal rights. In addition, foreign markets may be less liquid or more volatile than Canadian markets and may offer less protection to investors in such funds.

"Settlement of transactions in some markets may be delayed or may be less frequent than in Canada and the U.S., which will affect the liquidity of the fund's portfolio. A fund's investments in debt securities may include corporate debt securities and debt instruments issued by governments or government agencies. Lower-quality foreign government securities are often considered to be speculative and involve greater risk of default or price changes, or they may already be in default. These risks are in addition to the general risks associated with foreign securities.

"Security prices in emerging markets may be significantly more volatile than in the more developed nations of the world, reflecting the greater uncertainties of investing in less established markets and economies. In particular, emerging-market countries may have relatively unstable governments, present the risk of nationalization of businesses, restrict foreign ownership, or prohibit the repatriation of assets, and they may have less protection of property rights than more developed countries. The economies of emerging-market countries may be predominantly based on only a few industries, may be highly vulnerable to changes in local or global trade conditions, and may suffer from extreme and volatile debt burdens or inflation rates. Local securities markets may trade a small number of securities and may be unable to respond effectively to increases in trading volume, potentially making prompt liquidation of substantial holdings difficult or impossible at times. Securities of emerging-market issuers may have limited marketability and may be subject to more abrupt or erratic price movements.

"In recent years, there have been significant improvements in some emerging-market economies. However, others continue to experience problems, including high inflation rates and high interest rates. The emergence of emerging market economies and securities markets will require economic and fiscal discipline, as well as stable political and social conditions. Development may also be influenced by international economic conditions, particularly those in the United States, by the world prices for oil and other commodities, and by international trade agreements. There can be no assurance of continued favourable developments in emerging markets.

RRSP Eligible International Equity Funds That Invest in Derivatives

Annualized Performance to Sept. 30, 1996

Fund	RRSP	6 M	1 Yr	2 Yr	3 Yr
20/20 RSP Int'l Equity Alloc	Yes	2.8	14.5	10.5	
CT Everest Amerigrowth	Yes	5.9	17.5	23.2	15.9
CT Everest Asiagrowth	Yes	-2.3	9.3	1.8	
CT Everest Euro Growth	Yes	7.2	17.5	12.5	
First American	Yes	-4.7	-0.3	2.8	-0.1
Global Strategy Diversified Asia	Yes	-3.0	5.5	-3.2	
Global Strategy Diversified Europe	Yes	7.3	14.9	12.4	8.0
Global Strategy Diversified Japan	Yes	-6.3	-1.6	-6.0	
Global Strategy Diversifed Latin Amer	Yes	13.3	16.3	-9.5	
NN Can-American	Yes	5.3	16.0	22.0	14.8
NN Can-Asian	Yes	3.0	19.6	7.6	8.1
O.I.Q. Ferique Int'l	Yes	2.6	11.2	5.5	
Scotia Canam Growth	Yes	6.0	17.4	23.1	
Talvest Global RRSP	Yes	3.4	12.2	4.5	5.6
Universal World Growth RRSP	Yes	5.5	15.0	10.1	

SOURECE: PAL*TRAK* FOR WINDOWS

TABLE XXXVI

"Security prices in Latin American markets may be significantly more volatile than in the more developed nations of the world, reflecting the greater uncertainties of investing in less established markets and economies. In particular, Latin American countries may have relatively unstable governments, may present the risk of nationalization of businesses, restrictions on foreign ownership, or prohibitions on the repatriation of assets, and may have less protection of property rights than more developed countries. The economics of Latin American countries may be predominantly based on only a few industries, may be highly vulnerable to changes in local or global trade conditions, and may suffer from extreme and volatile debt burdens or inflation rates. Local securities markets may trade a small number of securities and may be unable to respond effectively to increases in trading volume, potentially making prompt liquidation of substantial holdings difficult or impossible at times. Securities of Latin American issuers may have limited marketability and may be subject to more abrupt or erratic price movements.

"In recent years, there have been significant improvements in some Latin American economies. However, others continue to experience problems, including high inflation rates and high interest rates. The emergence of Latin American economies and securities markets will require economic and fiscal discipline, as well as stable political and social conditions. Development may also be influenced by international economic conditions, particularly those in the United States, by the world prices for oil and other commodities, and by international trade agreements.

International funds that hold derivatives

A number of funds invest abroad by using derivatives. Typically, a fund will hold 90 per cent or more of its assets in Canadian T-Bills, and the remainder in derivatives tied to a foreign stock exchange index. Such funds are 100 per cent RRSP eligible, and tend to reduce if not eliminate currency risk. Table XXXVI lists some of these funds. Given the youthfulness of many of the funds, I'll hold my recommendations for another year or so.

CHAPTER 14

Asset Allocation and Balanced Funds

THE VAST MAJORITY OF IN-vestors should consider a portfolio of funds that includes fixed income, Canadian equity and international exposure and possibly some specialty funds. The actual mix will vary over time to reflect the outlook of the various markets and your specific needs. This diversification reduces portfolio risk. You can construct this mix yourself, use one of the asset allocation services available or pick off-the-shelf asset allocation or balanced funds.

Many investors are unaware that there is strong theoretical and empirical evidence that effective asset allocation, in the long term, is by far the most important aspect to the overall performance of a portfolio. Pension fund managers have known this for decades and in many cases apply the lion's share of their strategy to fine-tuning the so-called "asset mix."

What is asset allocation?

Asset allocation is the process in which different classes of assets such as stocks, bonds and cash, and different management styles are combined with a view to maximizing portfolio return while reducing overall portfolio risk (usually measured by the volatility of monthly returns). The concept can be used to build a wide variety of portfolios, including a purely domestic portfolio (one that only invests in Canadian assets) or an international portfolio. In addition, depending on the investment objectives of an individual, various asset allocation strategies can be devised to best suit individual needs.

Why is asset allocation so important?

Studies have shown, and practitioners can attest, that up to 90 per cent of a portfolio's return can be attributed to the asset allocation decisions — the percentages of various classes of assets in the portfolio as distinct from the fund manager's stock-picking ability. In the last year, it would have been unusual, even improbable, for a small-cap equity fund manager to generate returns of less than 10 per cent. This is because small-cap stocks outperformed as a group larger-capitalization stocks. Any asset allocation strategy that included small-cap stocks would have benefited from this. That is not to say that stock-picking doesn't matter — it does — but in the long run there is evidence that the decision to hold small-cap stocks was more important than which small-cap companies were selected for a fund portfolio. By combining different asset classes and investment styles, the overall volatility of the fund can be reduced. The reason, simplified to a single sentence (there are books on asset allocation) is that to a certain extent, when the return from one class of assets declines, returns from another class of asset to some degree or another, increases, reducing the magnitude of large swings in monthly returns.

There are two basic approaches to asset allocation: *strategic asset allocation* and *tactical asset allocation*.

Strategic asset allocation

Strategic asset allocation is based on the theory that given a certain tolerance for risk, a portfolio can be optimized by carefully constructing an asset mix that performs within the risk-tolerance level. Practitioners assume that it is impossible to time moves in and out of markets successfully over the long term to catch swings in prices. In other words, an asset mix is constructed to meet with the performance/volatility (risk/reward) expectations of the investor and is not adjusted in anticipation of short-term market changes. If the bond market is expected to rise dramatically in the next six months, the strategic asset allocator will pay little heed since he or she cannot be sure that that in fact will happen and doubts that jumping in and out of bonds will provide superior long-term returns. Many "balanced" funds use a strategic asset allocation policy of maintaining a reasonably stable asset mix. This is distinct from the so-called "asset allocation" funds which typically take a more tactical asset allocation approach. In many balanced fund prospectuses, the manager is restricted to working within a tight range of investment levels for each basic asset class (stocks, bonds, cash).

Of the strategic balanced funds available in Canada, Table XXXVII lists my picks — along with their current asset mix.

Recommended Strategic Balanced Funds

Percentage Composition by Cash, Canadian Equities, Foreign Equities, Canadian Bonds, Foreign Bonds, Preferred Equities and Mortgage-Backed Securities. Annualized Performance to Sept. 30, 1996

Fund	1 Yr	2 Yr	3 Yr	5 Yr	10 Yr	Cash	Cdn Eqty	Fgn Eqty	Cdn Bnd	Fgn Bnd	Pref Eqty	MBS
Bissett Retirement	18.7	16.7	11.8	13.0		5.3	36.3	22.4	33.1	0.0	0.0	2.3
Guardian Canadian Balanced A	10.8	9.4	7.9	9.6	9.9	31.6	31.0	6.4	18.7	8.4	0.2	2.1
Hongkong Bank Balanced	17.2	11.5	8.8	12.2		10.0	35.5	13.9	38.6	0.0	0.0	0.0
PH & N Balanced	16.2	13.2	11.0	11.7		5.6	34.0	14.2	42.0	0.0	0.2	0.0
Saxon Balanced	17.8	16.6	11.9	15.7	6.7	15.8	59.1	2.0	21.4	0.0	0.0	0.0
Sceptre Balanced Growth	25.4	17.6	13.8	13.1	10.8	5.2	37.7	11.4	34.2	2.1	1.9	0.0
Trimark Select Balanced	12.1	11.0	10.3	12.3		11.8	39.4	20.4	27.3	0.0	0.0	1.2
United Canadian Portfolio	15.6	13.7	10.0	12.4		14.4	31.5	18.1	33.0	0.0	0.1	0.9

SOURCE: PALTRAK FOR WINDOWS

TABLE XXXVII

Becoming more popular now is the asset allocation service, of which there are many, with the number growing each day it seems. These services typically use combinations of mutual funds to construct an asset mix rather than a single fund that combines, within its portfolio, stocks, bonds and T-bills. Perhaps the most prominent asset allocation service that is unambiguously strategic in nature is Mackenzie's STAR program, which is managed by asset allocation expert Gordon Garmaise of Garmaise Investment Technologies. This program has managed to attract a very large group of investors. Mr. Garmaise, using technology and sophisticated analytics, has constructed various portfolios of mutual funds that are aimed at various types of investors (as to their tolerance for risk and performance expectations). Since market timing is not involved, there is no need to constantly change the asset mix on an ongoing basis.

There is, however, from time to time, a need to "rebalance" the portfolio to ensure that the original asset mix and objectives are maintained. For example, Canadian stocks may become overweighted in one of the portfolios as a result of better performance in that sector. The strategic asset allocator will ensure that the portfolio is rebalanced to reflect the original intended asset mix. Mr. Garmaise also notes that other situations can give rise to a rebalancing exercise, including changes in the long-term investment strategy of one of the component funds or fundamental changes in the risk/return profile of a particular market.

Recommended Tactical Asset Allocation Funds

Percentage Composition by Cash, Canadian Equities, Foreign Equities, Canadian Bonds, Foreign Bonds, Preferred Equities and Mortgage-Backed Securities. Annualized Performance to Sept. 30, 1996

Fund	1 Yr	2 Yr	3 Yr	5 Yr	Cash	Cdn Eqty	Fgn Fgn	Cdn Bnd	Fgn Bnd	Pref Eqty	MBS
20/2 Cdn Tactical Asset Alloc	11.7	9.1	7.9	8.7	0.3	60.0	18.7	19.7	0.0	0.1	0.0
ADMAX Asset Allocation	10.9	7.1	6.7		18.0	44.2	0.0	36.5	0.0	0.3	0.0
Bullock Asset Strategy D	12.0	9.6	7.1		24.5	32.6	16.2	20.7	1.9	0.0	2.8
Dynamic Partners	9.8	8.4	8.4	14.8	15.5	37.4	12.3	20.0	14.0	0.0	0.0
First Canadian Asset Alloc	13.3	11.6	7.2	8.2	3.3	45.7	9.6	41.2	0.0	0.0	0.0
Scotia Ex Total Return	11.0	10.6	9.4	12.0	14.0	49.5	19.0	17.9	0.0	0.5	0.0

SOURCE: PAL*TRAK* FOR WINDOWS

TABLE XXXVIII

Tactical asset allocation

Tactical asset allocation is an allocation process that is based on the belief that the markets can be "timed" and that investors can exploit anticipated increases and declines in a market. For instance, if he or she believes the Canadian stock will outperform the bond market in the coming months, the tactical asset allocation manager will over-weight his or her portfolio in Canadian stocks in order to capitalize on the expected growth. Of course, if the anticipated growth does not materialize, the asset mix may not be optimal in the short term.

This is the basic strategy behind the so-called "asset allocation funds." These fund managers are given much more latitude in the size of the portion of the portfolio that can be devoted to each asset class than in the typical balanced fund. For example, if a manager of a tactical asset allocation fund is extremely bearish on the equity markets, he or she is usually able to rid the portfolio entirely of stocks and place the assets in, say, cash instruments.

Of the tactical asset allocation funds available in Canada, Table XXXVIII lists my picks — along with their current asset mix.

As mentioned above, asset allocation services that essentially are "funds of funds" are becoming a popular means by which to take advantage of an asset allocation program. Of the tactical asset allocation services available, perhaps the most prominent is the service offered by AGF. AGF utilizes a proprietary computer model that constantly evaluates expected rates of returns on cash, stocks and bonds relative to more than 20 years of historical data. Each week, the computer will recommend adjustments in the current asset mix in order to accommodate these expected rate changes. If the recommended adjustments exceed a 10 per cent threshold from its current position, then the portfolio is adjusted to reflect the suggested weighting.

Computer models, portfolio theory, technical analysis, and risk tolerance assessment are just some of the tools used in the asset allocation process. Sometimes, especially when using mutual funds as the main vehicle in which to achieve an asset mix, the results differ from the intended mix. That's because mutual funds are generally a combination of at least two asset classes — one usually being cash. In an asset allocation fund or balanced fund, the manager is working with the actual securities and has a tighter control on the overall mix of the portfolio.

Asset allocation using mutual funds

Asset allocation can be a very tricky exercise. While there are several tools available to professional planners and services available to the general public, one of the ongoing problems is matching your asset allocation requirements with appropriate mutual funds. As noted earlier, effective asset allocation can account for up to 90 per cent of portfolio return so it is important to choose appropriate funds according to the asset allocation required.

One problem involves the makeup of Canadian equity funds, a component in the asset allocation of most Canadians. The difficulty is that all Canadian equity funds have cash balances, many have significant foreign equity holdings, and some even hold fixed-income instruments. Professional money managers can "optimize" this problem through sophisticated software and the ability to trade at the security level. For the typical mutual fund investor, this can be a daunting task.

To help reduce this predicament, the focus of the tables at the back of this book is on portfolio content as much as it is on historical returns. If you deal with a financial adviser who talks about asset allocation using mutual funds, make sure that he or she has access to up-to-date portfolio information from the fund managers. Without this information your adviser cannot determine whether the funds selected, in fact, are appropriate for your specific asset allocation needs.

An example

To examine the dynamics of this problem, let's take an example of an individual about to embark on an investment strategy using mutual funds as the primary vehicle. A hypothetical investor we'll call Mr. Smith has recently come into an inheritance of $100,000 and has decided it is time that he start investing for his retirement. Let's assume for the moment that he is actively employed, in his early 30s and has no immediate need for these new-found funds. He has consulted with his trusted and professionally accredited financial adviser, who, upon assessing Mr. Smith's tolerance for risk, objectives and current needs, has suggested a specific asset mix. Consideration was given to Mr. Smith's generally bullish outlook on equities (for the long term) and therefore this asset class would be emphasized in his portfolio. Diversification and safety also figure prominently so fixed-income products such as solid bond and money market (cash) funds are deemed essential. Mr. Smith will place the money in an RRSP account, but insists on maximizing his exposure to international markets. Currently, RRSPs can hold up to 20 per cent of book value as foreign property. Higher levels can be effectively achieved by investing 20 per cent in foreign funds and some portion of the remaining 80 per cent in domestic funds that also invest in foreign assets typically up to a maximum of 20 per cent. For RRSP-related tax purposes these funds are treated as 100 per cent Canadian assets. Mr. Smith and his adviser agree that the suggested mix should be:

Canadian stocks	45%
Canadian bonds	20%
Foreign stocks	20%
Cash	15%

In many respects, the hard work is done. Which mutual funds are chosen to accommodate this or any other asset mix will be, ironically, of less importance to the long-term performance of his portfolio. This is true more or less to the extent that the funds chosen actually approximate the above mix. This is an important point: Don't be concerned if current asset mix is a little high in cash or shy in equities a bit. Mutual funds are constantly changing their holdings. The key to successful asset allocation is to select funds that have demonstrated a long-term commitment to a particular investment style or objective (some funds allow their managers generous latitudes in investment styles). Make sure that the fund not only states clearly the investment objective of the fund, but that that statement is supported by current and historical holdings and unit-holder reports.

To continue with our hypothetical case, Mr. Colin Smith is keen to select proven funds with solid management, which meet with some of the finer points of his and his financial adviser's recommendations.

The tables in the appendixes of this book provide much of the information an investor can use to decide which funds to choose. Mr. Smith used as a measure of the various funds the risk-adjusted performance of these funds, insisted that they have a history of at least three years and preferably five, and wanted diversification within each asset class in order to lower his overall risk.

Let's examine Mr. Smith's selections, one asset class at a time.

Canadian stocks (45 per cent)

Mr. Smith wanted to select funds that had a broad-based selection of stocks in them as well as some funds that invest in specific sectors that might enhance his overall returns. Mr. Smith is bullish on the resource sector, but is advised not to place the entire 45 per cent of his Canadian equity investment in resource-only funds. He decides that 10 per cent will be placed in resource and precious metals funds, 10 per cent in a fund that is overweight in the financial services sector another sector for which he is bullish) and the remainder in broad-based funds. Using the data available to him he came up with the following selections, based on past risk-adjusted performance, availability, RRSP eligibility, and portfolio content:

Resource and precious metals:

Maxxum Natural Resources	5.0%	$ 5,000
Global Strategy Gold Plus	5.0%	$ 5,000

Financial services:

AIC Advantage	10.0%	$10,000

Broad-based:

Bissett Canadian Equity	12.5%	$12,500
Trimark Canadian	12.5%	$12,500

Let's examine the individual funds as to current portfolio content. Note that in the following pie charts only the Canadian equity (stock) portion is broken down into the various industry sectors. The possible sectors are: Metals and minerals; Gold and silver; Oil and gas; Paper and forest products; Consumer products;

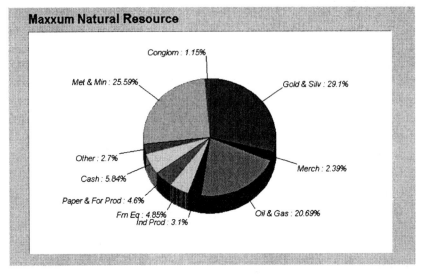

CHART XIII

Industrial products; Real estate and construction; Transportation and environmental services; Pipelines; Utilities; Communications and media; Merchandising; Financial servicesl and Conglomerates

As you can see in the Chart XIII, the Maxxum Natural Resource fund is clearly overweighted in gold and silver companies as well as the related mines and minerals sector. Oil and gas, yet another

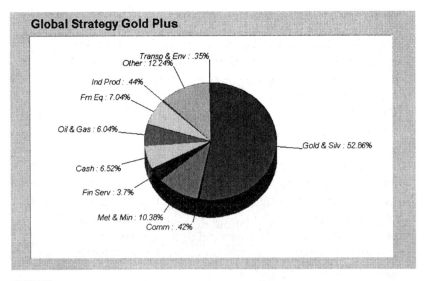

CHART XIV

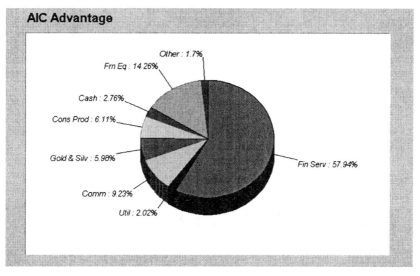

AIC Advantage

Other : 1.7%
Frn Eq : 14.26%
Cash : 2.76%
Cons Prod : 6.11%
Gold & Silv : 5.98%
Comm : 9.23%
Util : 2.02%
Fin Serv : 57.94%

CHART XV

resource sector also figures prominently. Paper and forest products round out the resource-based stocks. Note that the investment in this fund is neither a pure equity investment nor a pure resource equity investment. As with all mutual funds, there is a cash component. This particular fund also has a modest exposure to foreign assets (4.9 per cent) as well as some minor investment in merchandising (2.5 per cent) and industrial products stocks. Although this fund definitely suits Mr. Smith's more tactical requirements, the overall mix will be affected.

Now let's look at the Global Strategy Gold Plus fund in Chart XIV. Again it is clear that other sectors are represented — indeed other asset classes such as foreign equity and cash — but the emphasis is clearly gold and silver companies.

The other choice for a sector-specific fund is AIC Advantage, Chart XV. Although not mandated to invest in the financial services sector, it is clearly overweighted in these types of companies and has been for some time. This is a useful example of how all equity funds may not be as they appear; this fund will be much more sensitive to the financial services sector than a typical diversified equity fund. This is good, if as in Mr. Smith's case, that is a desirable outcome; it is less desirable if an investor is unwilling to emphasize a particular sector because of the potential risks that might lie ahead for a particular sector.

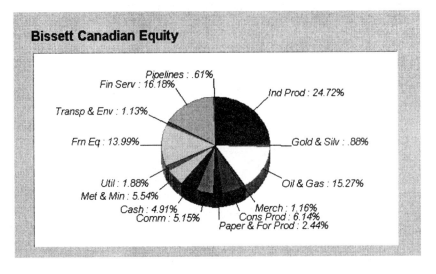

CHART XVI

Note also that foreign equity plays a part in AIC — a characteristic Mr. Smith desires — even though this fund, as with the other Canadian equity funds, is treated as pure Canadian assets for RRSP purposes.

As to the two broad-based Canadian equity funds, Bissett Canadian Equity and Trimark Canadian, these funds avoid emphasizing specific sectors and try to have significant

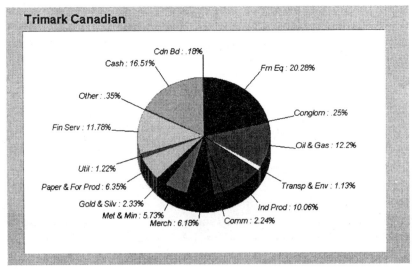

CHART XVII

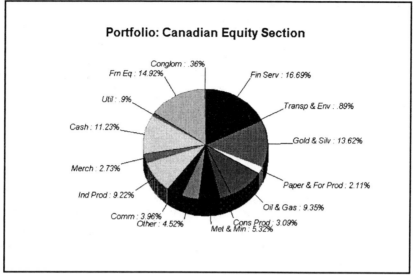

Portfolio: Canadian Equity Section

Conglom : .36%
Frn Eq : 14.92%
Fin Serv : 16.69%
Util : .9%
Transp & Env : .89%
Cash : 11.23%
Gold & Silv : 13.62%
Merch : 2.73%
Ind Prod : 9.22%
Paper & For Prod : 2.11%
Comm : 3.96%
Other : 4.52%
Oil & Gas : 9.35%
Cons Prod : 3.09%
Met & Min : 5.32%

CHART XVIII

representation in most of the TSE's 14 industry groups. These two were picked not only because of diversification and superior risk-adjusted performance, but because Mr. Smith wanted the foreign equity portion of his portfolio emphasized.

Trimark sponsors a fund that routinely maximizes its foreign content, has provided superior returns and provides a well diversified Canadian equity component. Its portfolio can be seen in Chart XVII.

Using the PAL*Trak* software, we combine the above funds in the amounts specified. Mr. Smith's Canadian equity portion of his portfolio is revealed in Chart XVIII.

Not surprisingly, Mr. Smith's Canadian equity section is well diversified with some emphasis on resources and financial services. Also note that on an overall basis, this particular combination of funds produced a 14 per cent exposure to foreign stocks. This exposure is in addition to the 20 per cent foreign content allowed in RRSPs.

Canadian bonds (20 per cent)
Mr. Smith chose three Canadian bond funds, based on risk-adjusted performance as well as variety in investment style. Altamira Income fund has been a fairly aggressive interest rate anticipator. In con-

Canadian Bonds Analysis
Percentage Composition by Cash, Canadian Bonds, Foreign Bonds,
Canadian Federal Bonds, Other Canadian Government Bonds, Corporate
Bonds and Short, Medium and Long Bonds

| | | | | | Canadian bond analysis | | | | |
| | | | | | Issuer Type | | Maturity Analysis | | |
Fund	Cash	Cdn Bnd	Fgn Bnd	Fed Bnd	Oth Gov't	Corp	Sht	Med	Long
Altamira Income	4.7	75.1	18.9	68.0	32.0	0.0	10.2	24.2	65.6
Dynamic Income	37.9	38.6	21.7	50.9	20.3	28.8	28.8	50.8	20.4
Green Line Cdn Bond	0.9	95.4	1.0	6.5	17.9	75.6	43.4	35.2	21.4
Colin's Bond Portion	15.0	69.4	13.6	35.1	23.0	42.0	29.8	34.7	25.5

SOURCE: PAL*TRAK* FOR WINDOWS

TABLE XXXIX

trast, the Green Line Canadian Bond fund has tended to concentrate on the so-called "spreads" in interest rates between corporate and government issuers. Corporate bonds can often provide better income yields because they are less secure than their government cousins. The additional "risk" is rewarded to the bond investor in the form of higher effective interest rates. This fund, as compared to the Altamira Income, more closely tracks the general bond market (as defined by the ScotiaMcLeod Bond Universe Index). The third fund, Dynamic Income, has provided the lowest volatility of any bond fund. Let's examine Mr. Smith's choices:

Dynamic Income	7%	$3,500
Green Line Canadian Bond	7%	$3,500
Altamira Income	6%	$3,000

As you can see in Table XXXIX, exposure to international markets is evident. The weighted bond portfolio has a balance of federal and other government issues and corporate bonds as well as a range of terms to maturity.

Foreign stocks (20 per cent)
As indicated earlier, Mr. Smith has decided to maximize his allowable exposure to non-Canadian markets. In addition to the international exposure he has achieved through the Canadian equity portion of his portfolio, he now decides to choose three well-

Foreign Stocks Analysis

Percentage Composition by Cash, Foreign Equities, Canada, the United States, Japan, Pacific Rim, Europe, Mexico, South and Central America and Africa

Fund	Cash	Fgn Eqty	Can	US	Geographic Allocation Jpn	Pac	Euro	Mex	S Am	Afr
Cundill Value	25.1	57.0	38.7	10.8	11.2	4.2	34.5	0.0	0.3	0.0
Trimark Fund	10.5	85.6	12.9	66.5	7.1	1.6	11.9	0.0	0.0	0.0
Templeton Growth	17.6	72.0	18.3	31.1	1.9	8.6	33.2	2.1	4.0	0.5
Colin's Foreign Equity Portion	17.7	71.5	23.6	36.4	7.0	4.6	26.2	0.6	1.3	0.1

* Geographic allocation includes Canadian cash

SOURCE: PALTRAK FOR WINDOWS

TABLE XL

known, high risk-adjusted performance leaders for his portfolio. They are:

Cundill Value	7%	$3,500
Trimark Fund	7%	$3,500
Templeton Growth	6%	$3,000

Examining the individual funds and the weighted combination of those funds, Table XL illustrates the geographic exposure..

Note that the cash levels for these funds are, at this point in time, quite high. This will, of course, affect the overall cash component of the portfolio. More importantly, if this was the only source of foreign stocks (remember we want about 20 per cent), Mr. Smith's portfolio at this point in time would only provide 71.5 per cent of the 20 per cent foreign content or about 14.3 per cent.

Cash (15 per cent)

Now, to round out his portfolio, Mr. Smith has decided on choosing a couple of money market funds that have strong, risk-adjusted money market performance, and relatively low expense ratios. Also, in that interest rates in the U.S. were becoming more and more attractive relative to the Canadian market, Mr. Smith wishes to select at least one manager that is taking advantage of the 20 per cent foreign asset limit without introducing any meaningful additional risk. The following are Mr. Smith's picks:

Capstone Cash Management	7.5%	$7,500
Beutel Goodman Money Mkt	7.5%	$7,500

Cash Portfolio Analysis
Percentage Composition by Security Type

Fund	General	Cdn T-Bills	US T-Bills	Provincial	Corporate
Capstone Cash Management	0.5	82.0	7.3	0.0	0.0
Beutel Goodman Money Mkt	0.9	62.1	0.0	1.5	35.5
Colin's Cash Portfolio	0.7	72.1	8.7	0.8	17.8

SOURCE: PAL*TRAK* FOR WINDOWS

TABLE XLI

Table XLI provides an analysis of the cash component of Mr. Smith's portfolio.

Mr. Smith's hypothetical portfolio

Now comes the telling moment. I asked Portfolio Analytics to combine all of these funds in the prescribed amounts to come up with Mr. Smith's hypothetical portfolio. Note that diversification among fund managers, asset class and geographic allocation are important characteristics of this portfolio.

First, let's take a look at the basic asset allocation of Mr. Smith's portfolio, Chart XIX. Note that the cash level is actually *much higher* than the prescribed allocation. This is because cash is held in all mutual funds for a variety of reasons. The above asset allocation analysis was performed using the PAL*Trak* for Windows software, which, among other things, allows investment professionals and investors alike to examine the current status of a mutual fund portfolio's asset allocation. Note also that the foreign equity (20.6 per cent) plus the foreign bond (3 per cent) provides a current (non-U.S. cash) foreign exposure of almost 24 per cent — higher than the 20 per cent ceiling for a specific fund but perfectly allowable in this scenario since some of the 100 per cent RRSP-eligible funds have foreign components. Certainly it is higher than would have been provided by investment in the foreign equity funds alone.

Here's the problem: Remember how important the asset allocation was to the exercise of optimizing performance? Mr. Smith chose equity funds in the prescribed amount (45 per cent) as well as the other classes. But his actual asset allocation differs: Canadian stocks are underweighted at 35 per cent against the desired 45 per

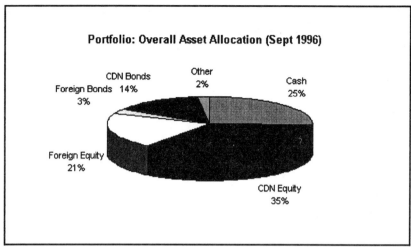

CHART XIX

cent while bonds are 14 per cent of the portfolio rather than 20 per cent. The cash component, unquestionably the hardest to control, is 25 per cent rather than 15 per cent.

These variations are significant, but within tolerance. The lesson to be learned here is that when embarking on an asset allocation process, ensure that you are up to date and fully informed not only about the current content of the funds you wish to use but the *intended* content of these funds. In other words, will the fund

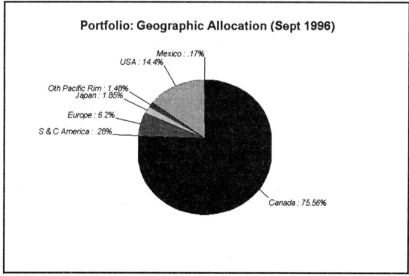

CHART XX

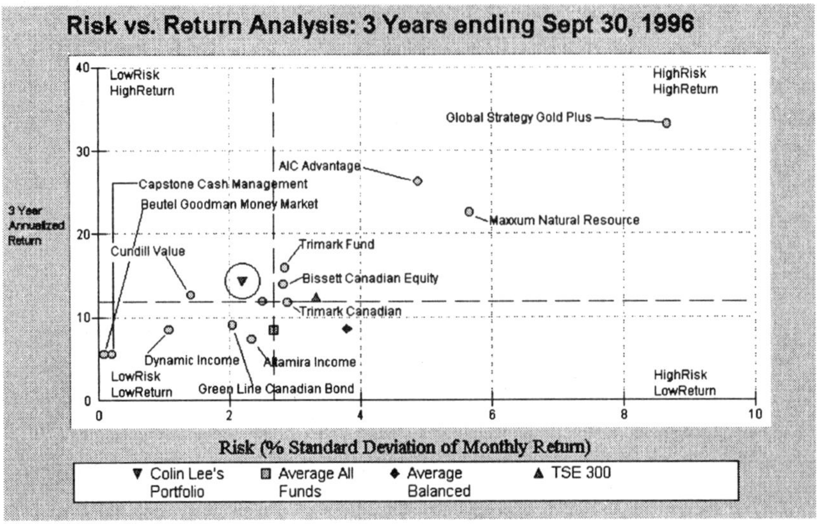

Risk vs. Return Analysis: 3 Years ending Sept 30, 1996

Risk (% Standard Deviation of Monthly Return)

▼ Colin Lee's Portfolio   ▣ Average All Funds   ◆ Average Balanced   ▲ TSE 300

CHART XXI

manager or managers be increasing or decreasing the portions invested in the various asset classes? Insist that your investment advisor or financial planner has access to this information.

Let's now take a look at the overall geographic allocation of Mr. Smith's portfolio, Chart XX. Remember, that Canadian cash and U.S. cash are considered Canadian and U.S. assets, respectively. Note that the above portfolio, though 100 per cent RRSP-eligible, has in fact only 75.6 per cent Canadian assets instead of the 80 per cent minimum required if using more primary investments.

Past performance (and volatility) is not necessarily indicative of future performance (or volatility). It does, however, provide useful insights into the benefit of investing in a diverse collection of mutual funds. Let's take Mr. Smith's portfolio, in the prescribed amounts, and assume we invested them exactly three years ago from Sept. 30, 1996.

What can we learn? Well, the single most important lesson is something professional money managers have known for years: Diversification often provides better performance with more stability or lower volatility. Chart XXI displays the component funds of Mr. Smith's portfolio as well as the portfolio itself. Note that the portfolio *outperformed* nine of the component 13 funds (69 per cent) while remaining *less volatile* than eight of the 13 funds (62 per cent), in some cases, *much less volatile*. If the past serves as a proxy for the future, then Mr. Smith will reap the benefits of diversification.

In addition to reducing the overall risk inherent in the funds selected individually, this particular fund combination outperformed the average balanced fund as well as the TSE 300 composite index — with a substantially reduced volatility level! You can expect to achieve these types of results whenever you combine a diverse group of risk-adjusted high performers that concentrate on diverse asset classes and geographic locations. Remember that diversification should be sought on various levels, including: Manager and management style; asset class (cash, stocks, bonds, etc.) and geographic (domestic and international).

Table XLII lists new funds that started up in the summer of 1996.

Mutual Funds That Started Up in the Summer of 1996
Percentage Return as of Sept. 30, 1996

Fund	Type	RRSP	Return	MER	($mil) Assets
Altamira Global Small Co	Int'l Eqty	N	1.2	2.5	6.2
C.I. Glo Financial Ser Sec	Int'l Eqty	N	12.3		11.3
C.I. Glo Health Sci Sector	Int'l Eqty	N	3.0		9.7
C.I. Glo Technology Sector	Int'l Eqty	N	14.		6.3
C.I. Glo Telecom Sector	Int'l Eqty	N	3.2		3.5
C.I. Global Resource Sect	Spec Eqty	N	2.9		4.9
CIBC Canadian Index Fund	Cdn Eqty	Y	7.6	1.0	49.2
CIBC Energy	Spec Eqty	Y	9.9	2.0	9.4
CIBC Precious Metal	Spec Eqty	Y	(0.1)	2.0	11.2
CIBC U.S. Index RRSP	US Eqty	Y	6..5	1.0	11. 0
Friedberg Diversified	Spec Eqty	N	0.3	3.9	1.6
Friedberg Foreign Bond	Int'l Bnd	N	(1.5)	0.9	5. 0
Hansberger Dev Markets Sec	Int'l Eqty	N	3.5		1.6
Hansberger Glo Small Cap S	Int'l Eqty	N	0.5		1.6
Hansberger Intl Sector	Int'l Eqty	N	-(0.6)	2.6	4.8
Hansberger Value Sector	Int'l Eqty	N	0.5	2.6	14.2
IG BG Canadian Small Cap	Cdn Eqty	Y	8.3	2.7	12.7
IG Beutel Goodman Cdn Bal	Bal	Y	2.6	2.7	7.4
IG Beutel Goodman Cdn Eq	Cdn Eqty	Y	2.9	2.7	3.4
IG Sceptre Canadian Bond	Cnd Bnd	Y	2.0	2.0	1.0
IG Sceptre Canadian Equity	Cdn Eqty	Y	6.1	2.7	22.6
IG Sceptre Cdn Balanced	Bal	Y	3.1	2.7	9.8
Investors Cdn Natural Res	Spec Eqty	Y	3.5	2 .7	21.0
Investors Cdn Small Cap	Cdn Eqty	Y	10.0	2.7	32.3
Investors Latin Amer Grth	Int'l Eqty	N	4.2	2.8	10.2
Investors N.A. High Yield	Int'l Bnd	N	(0.1)	2.2	4.4
Investors US Opportunities	US Eqty	N	4.8	2.7	23.4
Pursuit Growth	Int'l Eqty	N	5.4	1.8	0.2
Scudder US Growth & Income	US Eqty	N	5.7	1.3	1.0

SOURCE: PAL*TRAK* FOR WINDOWS

TABLE XLII

CHAPTER 15

How to Pick an Adviser

THE MAJORITY OF FUND owners in Canada buy funds through an intermediary. It can be an investment dealer or stockbroker, a mutual fund specialist, a trust company employee, or an insurance agent selling insurance company segregated funds or mutual funds.

Some intermediaries will sell funds offered by several fund management companies; others will sell only a single group of funds. Firms that advertise themselves as independent dealers, such as Regal Capital Planners Ltd., offer funds from many of the major fund management companies. In contrast, sales representatives employed by Investors Group, or its subsidiary Investors Syndicate Ltd., will offer only the Investors funds, although this may be changing. Similarly, many insurance agents will sell only the specific family of funds that is affiliated with their insurance company. Stockbrokers will generally offer funds from the major fund management companies. In addition, some will offer funds affiliated with their firms. It's expected that brokerage houses owned by banks may soon be distributing bank-managed mutual funds along with other funds.

Should you use an adviser who offers a single family of funds or someone who offers many? All advisers will, or should, offer you the best they have. The question is whether a sales representative handling a single family of funds has the best. Similarly, many independents handle only a few fund groups which may or may not be the best for you. While many fund companies have top performers, none has a monopoly on top performance in all types of funds — RRSP equity, RRSP bond, foreign equity, specialty funds and so on. An independent salesperson who handles many funds has access to a wider range than a captive representative who has only a single family to offer. Further, many of the top-performing funds are available only through independent salespeople. But as the ranking table indicates, some of the funds sold only through captive sales forces have done quite well, as have some of the no-load funds.

Of course, there is nothing stopping you from dealing with more than one sales organization and indeed many people do have several dealers.

Much depends on the individual sales representative and whether he or she can tailor a fund portfolio to suit your needs. The key point is that if you are going to need advice and guidance, the salesperson you choose must be an expert. A mutual fund specialist, whether employed by an investment dealer, independent fund sales organization, insurance agency or part of a captive sales force should have a detailed understanding of how to use funds to meet clients' objectives. He or she should monitor fund performance closely and be in touch with fund management companies to be aware of any changes in strategy or investment personnel that may have an impact on client returns.

While there is a tendency among many fund salespeople not to second-guess portfolio managers, some salespeople demand detailed explanations of current investment policy. This helps them determine whether specific funds continue to meet the criteria on which they base their recommendations. Take the time to choose your fund adviser carefully and with thought. Making the wrong choice can be financially and emotionally expensive.

Licencing requirements

Sales of mutual funds are regulated by provincial securities commissions. Firms selling mutual funds must meet certain capital requirements and their officers and managers must demonstrate specific levels of expertise. Individuals selling mutual funds must also meet certain standards.

To receive registration to sell mutual funds, individuals must complete an investment course. Salespeople who are employed by investment dealers must have completed the Canadian Securities Course. This course covers the investment spectrum but includes a section on mutual funds. It also meets the requirement for licencing of people employed by mutual fund dealers. The Canadian Investment Funds Course is designed specifically for people seeking registration to sell mutual funds and as additional education for people who are registered to sell securities. The banking and trust companies associations have their own educational programs which meet licencing requirements for their employees.

The Canadian Investment Funds Course is sponsored by the education division of the Investment Funds Institute of Canada. IFIC is the umbrella organization of the fund industry and is recognized as such by provincial securities commissions. The educational standards of the industry are constantly being upgraded. However, the quality of people giving advice on mutual funds varies widely, just as in any other profession. It's up to you to determine whether a specific fund salesperson meets your needs.

If you do most of your own work and know specifically which funds you want, almost any dealer can handle your order at a discounted commission. If you only want your purchase order executed and nothing else, expect to pay between one-third and one-half of the maximum commission in the fund prospectus for the amount of money you're investing, although some firms will execute the order at zero commission plus a handling fee of $25. If you buy funds with a declining deferred redemption fee you will not get a break on the redemption fee whether you buy from a full service or discount broker.

If you want full service, including detailed advice and monitoring of your holdings, and you are buying funds sold only with an acquisition fee, expect to pay higher commissions — up to, but not necessarily, the full rates. Full service should include an analysis of your investment objectives and needs along with recommendations on the funds that meet your requirements. Many sales representatives will confine their analysis to your investment needs; others will extend their analysis to every aspect of your finances including your life insurance needs, tax returns, pension plans and personal balance sheet.

You should determine in advance what type of ongoing service you can expect from a fund salesperson. Is his or her analysis of funds limited to reviewing rates of return? Or does the analysis include reviews of portfolio managers' investment strategies and comparisons with other funds? Many fund salespeople do this on their own, while others depend on specialists within their firms to do this work. It is essential that your adviser have access to this type of information on a continuous basis in order to advise you when conditions have changed. Your adviser should be able to give you detailed explanations behind all purchase recommendations, especially those that involve switching funds. He or she should also provide you with periodic statements of your holdings and their performance, generally monthly or quarterly, depending on how active you are in the market.

The use of personal computers has allowed many fund salespeople to develop their own report packages. These often include monthly statements showing how your funds have performed. Other reports include such items as projected returns using recent performance figures along with account histories and performance summaries of each fund held plus a detailed portfolio summary and performance comparison of clients' holdings.

Not every investor wants detailed reports. What it really comes down to is making sure that you are comfortable with the salesperson you choose. Do his or her recommendations fit your investment objectives? Do they take into consideration your other investment holdings? Have the risks been explained in detail? Will your situation be monitored constantly and, if so, how? Will you get service even if you don't make any subsequent purchases? Does your adviser have substantial investment or business experience? Unfortunately, many fund salespeople may not fully appreciate the risks involved in the strategies they recommend.

Financial planning

Many people selling funds call themselves financial planners. However, financial planning is unregulated except in Quebec. Anyone can call himself or herself a financial planner, whether or not he or she has any financial expertise. This will likely change. As noted in the introduction, eight associations whose members deal with the personal finances of individuals — the Canadian Association of Financial Planners, the Canadian Institute of Chartered Accountants, the Canadian Institute of Financial Planners, the Canadian Securities Institute, the Certified General Accountants Association of Canada, the Credit Union Institute of Canada, the Life Underwriters Association of Canada and the Society of Management Accountants of Canada have formed the Financial Planners Standards Council of Canada.

Don't be shy about asking financial planners about their credentials. Are they Certified Financial Planners or taking courses leading to that designation? Do they have any other professional designations which indicate expertise in financial planning?

Avoiding commissions

Should you buy a no-load fund and avoid commissions? The answer depends on your own personal situation. In some cases the answer is "absolutely." In other cases it's a definite "no." In many cases it's a "maybe." It all depends on your objectives, how much work you do on your own and whether you need professional advice. Moreover, with the choice of funds available with deferred declining sales charges, redemption fees, or zero loads, the question is becoming academic in many cases, especially when management fees are comparable.

Some no-load fund groups have employees who can provide advice. But the majority of fund specialists sell load funds or funds with redemption fees and are paid commissions. If you decide to use a broker or fund specialist, make sure the person you pick has the expertise and can provide a level of service that justifies the commission you pay.

As far as performance is concerned, no-loads, as a group, are just as good as load funds. Both groups include funds that are excellent performers as well as funds that are poor performers. In fact, some investment managers manage both types of funds, but the funds are marketed through different distribution companies.

If you are a sophisticated, experienced investor who knows what you want, then by all means buy no-load funds and save yourself the commission (or negotiate the commission on a load fund down to a handling fee). Even if you aren't an investment wizard but have a good idea which funds suit your objectives — perhaps you want a bond fund for your RRSP or a mortgage fund for income — then check out the no-loads offered by the banks and trust companies with which you deal. Just make sure the portfolios are compatible with your view on the direction of interest rates.

The vast majority of no-loads are offered by banks and trust companies. However, a handful of investment counsellors such as Sceptre Investment Counsel Ltd. offer no-loads directly to the public. As well, several organizations such as the Canadian Medical Association and Ontario Teachers' Group offer families of funds to their members.

If you buy a fund from a bank, trust company or credit union, the quality of advice you'll get, if any, depends on the expertise of the individual who comes to the counter. This can be a hit-or-miss situation, depending on the experience and education of the institution's employee. Recognizing the need for quality information, most financial institutions have made significant investments in training their employees.

Securities regulators have taken steps to improve the proficiency of bank and trust company funds salespeople. As well as the IFIC mutual fund course and the Canadian Securities Institute course, regulatory authorities accept for registration requirements courses offered by the Institute of Canadian Bankers and Trust Companies Institute.

The onus is on you to determine whether the person advising you has sufficient training and experience. It is generally a good idea to ask for the manager. And don't be too shy to ask what training he or she has. Just remember that if you use no-load funds you've assumed the responsibility of monitoring performance and making changes to your fund portfolio when necessary. You've also assumed the task of making sure the portfolio of funds you've chosen meets your needs and objectives.

CHAPTER 16

Inside the Prospectus

WHILE VIRTUALLY EVERY fund uses glossy sales material to promote itself, the offer to sell fund shares or units is made only through the fund's prospectus. This is a legal document that discloses all pertinent information about the fund.

When you first inquire about a fund you may be given the prospectus or, more likely, the condensed prospectus summary statement. No-load funds routinely send out prospectuses in response to requests for information. But many load funds do not because their salespeople prefer to stick with the more easily understood brochures.

When you actually get down to buying a fund, the seller is required by law to provide a prospectus, the latest annual financial statements and subsequent quarterly statements, if any. Generally, these will be mailed to you along with the slip confirming your purchase order.

Most people don't bother to read prospectuses and financial statements and, frankly, most people are not any worse off since they can get enough information from sales material or their salesperson. Nevertheless, you might take the time to at least skim through the prospectus.

Each fund actually files two prospectuses, the second being a shorter form or summary statement of the first. This summary prospectus includes the main points of the full prospectus in plain language.

The shorter version was introduced in response to requests from the fund industry in the belief that a condensed version would not only save the funds money on postal and printing costs but would also more likely be read by investors.

If you request a prospectus or agree to invest in a fund, you'll almost certainly receive the shorter version. Even if you don't want to read it thoroughly, leaf through the first couple of pages of the section that summarizes the document.

There are a number of areas you can look at quickly. Make sure the fund's investment policies and objectives are compatible with yours. It's also important that you understand the sales charges, if any, and whether they are negotiable. You should also be aware of ongoing management fees. Every fund has management fees that, with the rare exception, are charged to the fund and not to individual investors. Management fees cover the cost of portfolio management and certain other expenses of running a fund. Since they can vary widely and have a significant impact on the rate of return you receive, you should look at the explanation of how these fees are calculated and paid.

Some funds absorb all expenses, such as legal and audit fees, as part of their management fees. Others charge certain expenses directly to the fund. If you want to compare directly expenses of different funds, check the management expense ratio. This takes into account all fees charged to the fund, excluding brokerage commissions, and allows for direct comparisons among funds in most cases. A few funds charge some ongoing sales fees directly to their clients.

The summary prospectus begins by telling you that it is only an outline of the information you should have before making a decision to buy and that additional information is available in the prospectus or annual information form, which you can get by writing to the issuer.

The summary prospectus also explains your statutory rights. Generally speaking, you can back out of an agreement to buy mutual fund shares or units within two days after receipt of the simplified prospectus or within 48 hours of receiving the confirmation of the purchase of such securities. Very few people use this right of rescission. But if you read the prospectus and you find that the fund's investment objectives aren't compatible with yours or that the fund is undesirable for any other reason, you have the right to withdraw from your agreement to purchase.

You have other rights, too. Some provinces provide for cancelling the purchase and allow for damages if the prospectus includes misrepresentations. There are time limits, however, on exercising these rights.

The next item in a prospectus is the name and address of the fund and information on its incorporation. This is followed by a brief summary of the fund's investment policies.

The summary statement may include a section outlining risks. This isn't included in all short-form prospectuses. Rather, it is required only if a fund is speculative or has significant risk factors. The value of all funds, including money market funds on rare occasions, will fluctuate with changes in the value of their underlying securities. This is disclosed in all summary prospectuses. However, not every fund calls this a risk factor.

Following the summary statement is a description of the shares or units, which provides information on dividend rights, voting rights and the like.

Other important items include how the manager calculates the price at which sales are offered and redeemed, how the shares will be distributed, as well as information on minimum purchases and sales charges, management fees, dividend records, the tax consequences of sales, rules governing dividends and redemptions. Every prospectus will provide the name and address of the auditor.

Since the rules on exactly where all this information must appear aren't rigid, some of this information may be found in the annual report, rather than the summary statement.

CHAPTER 17

Directory of Fund Management Companies

ABC Funds
8 King Street East, Suite 500
Toronto, Ontario M5C 1B5
(416) 365-9696
Fax: (416) 365-9705
ABC American Value Fd
ABC Fully-Managed Fd
ABC Fundamental Value Fd

Acadia Investment Funds Inc.
295 St. Pierre Blvd. West
Box 5554
Caraquet, New Brunswick
E1W 1B7
(506) 727-1345 (800) 351-1345
Acadia Balanced Fd
Acadia Bond Fd
Acadia Money Market Fd
Acadia Mortgage Fd

ADMAX Regent International Management Ltd.
150 King Street West Suite 1802
Toronto, Ontario M5H 1J9
(416) 408 2222 (800) 667-2369
Fax: (416) 408-1228
ADMAX American Select Growth Fd
ADMAX Asset Allocation Fd
ADMAX Canadian Performance Fd
ADMAX Canadian Select Growth Fd
ADMAX Cash Performance Fd
ADMAX Global Health Sciences Fd
ADMAX Dragon 888 Fd
ADMAX Europa Performance Fd
ADMAX International Fd
ADMAX Korea Fd
ADMAX Nippon Fd
ADMAX Tiger Fd
ADMAX World Income Fd

AGF Management Limited
66 Wellington Street West
Toronto-Dominion Bank Tower
31st Floor, P.O. Box 50
Toronto-Dominion Centre
Toronto, Ontario M5K 1E9
(416) 367-1900 (800) 268-8583
Fax: (416) 865-4155
AGF American Growth Fd Ltd.A
AGF American Growth Fd Ltd. B
AGF American Growth Fd Ltd. C
AGF Asian Growth Fd Ltd. A
AGF Asian Growth Fd Ltd. B
AGF Asian Growth Fd Ltd. C
AGF Canadian Bond Fd A
AGF Canadian Bond Fd B
AGF Canadian Bond Fd C
AGF Canadian Equity Fd A
AGF Canadian Equity Fd B
AGF Canadian Equity Fd C

AGF Canadian Resources Fd A
AGF Canadian Resources Fd B
AGF Canadian Resources Fd C
AGF China Focus Fd Ltd. A
AGF China Focus Fd Ltd. B
AGF China Focus Fd Ltd. C
AGF European Growth Fd Ltd. A
AGF European Growth Fd Ltd. B
AGF European Growth Fd Ltd. C
AGF Germany Fd Class A
AGF Germany Fd Class B
AGF Germany Fd Class C
AGF Germany Fd Class D
AGF Global Government Bond Fd A
AGF Global Government Bond Fd B
AGF Global Government Bond Fd C
AGF Growth & Income Fd A
AGF Growth & Income Fd B
AGF Growth & Income Fd C
AGF Growth Equity Fd Ltd. A
AGF Growth Equity Fd Ltd. B
AGF Growth Equity Fd Ltd. C
AGF High Income Fd A
AGF High Income Fd B
AGF High Income Fd C
AGF International Short Term Fd A
AGF International Short Term Fd B
AGF International Short Term Fd C
AGF Japan Fd Ltd. A
AGF Japan Fd Ltd. B
AGF Japan Fd Ltd. C
AGF Money Market Account Fd A
AGF Money Market Account Fd B
AGF Money Market Account Fd C
AGF RSP Global Income Fd A
AGF RSP Global Income Fd B
AGF RSP Global Income Fd C
AGF Special Fd Ltd. A
AGF Special Fd Ltd. B
AGF Special Fd Ltd. C

AGF U.S. Dollar Money Market Fd
AGF U.S. Income Fd A
AGF U.S. Income Fd B
AGF U.S. Income Fd C
AGF World Equity Fd A
AGF World Equity Fd B
AGF World Equity Fd C

AIC Limited
1 Markland Street
Hamilton, Ontario L8P 2J5
(905) 529-5500
(800) 263-2144 (Ontario only)
Fax: (905) 529-6436
AIC Advantage Fd
AIC Diversified Canada Fd
AIC Emerging Markets Fd
AIC Money Market Fd
AIC Value Fd
AIC World Equity Fd

All-Canadian Management Inc.
P.O. Box 7320
Ancaster, Ontario L9G 3N6
(905) 648-2025
Fax: (905) 648-5422
All-Canadian CapitalFund
All-Canadian Compound
All-Canadian ConsumerFund
All-Canadian Resources Corporation

Altafund Investment Corp.
See Altamira Investment Services Inc.

Altamira Investment Services Inc.

250 Bloor Street East, Suite 200
Toronto, Ontario M4W 1E6
(416) 925-1623
(800) 263-2824 (Ontario only)
Fax: (416) 925-5352
Altafund Investment Corp.
Altamira Asia Pacific Fd
Altamira Balanced Fd
Altamira Bond Fd
Altamira Capital Growth Fd
Altamira Dividend Fd Inc.
Altamira Equity Fd
Altamira European Equity Fd
Altamira Global Bond Fd
Altamira Global Discovery Fd
Altamira Global Diversified Fd
Altamira Global Small Company Fd
Altamira Growth & Income Fd
Altamira Japanese Opportunity Fd
Altamira North American Recovery Fd
Altamira Precious & Strategic Metal Fd
Altamira Resource Fd
Altamira Science and Technology Fd
Altamira Select American Fd
Altamira Short-Term Global Income Fd
Altamira Short-Term Gov't Bond Fd
Altamira Special Growth Fd
Altamira U.S. Larger Company Fd

AMI Partners Inc.

26 Wellington Street East
Suite 900
Toronto, Ontario M5E 1S2
(416) 865-1985
Fax: (416) 865-9241
AMI Private Capital Equity Fd
AMI Private Capital Income Fd
AMI Private Capital Money Market Fd
AMI Private Capital Optimix Fd

APEX Funds

See Seaboard Life Insurance Company

Associate Investors Limited

8 King Street East, Suite 2001
Toronto, Ontario M5C 1B6
(416) 864-1120
Fax: (416) 864-1491
Associate Investors Ltd.

Atlas Capital Group

110 Yonge Street, Suite 500
Toronto, Ontario M5C 1T4
(416) 369 4525 (800) 463-2857
Fax: (416) 369-8176
Atlas American Advantage Fd
Atlas American Emerging Value Fd
Atlas American Money Market Fd
Atlas American Opportunity Fd
Atlas American Large Cap Value Fd
Atlas Canadian Balanced Fd
Atlas Canadian Bond Fd
Atlas Canadian Diversified Fd
Atlas Canadian Emerging Growth Fd
Atlas Canadian Emerging Value Fd
Atlas Canadian High Yield Bond Fd
Atlas Canadian Large Cap Growth Fd
Atlas Canadian Large Cap Value Fd
Atlas Canadian Money Market Fd
Atlas Canadian T-Bill Fd
Atlas Global Equity Fd
Atlas Managed Futures Fd
Atlas NAFTA Fd
Hercules Emerging Markets Debt Fd
Hercules European Value Fd
Hercules Global Short-Term Fd

Hercules Latin American Value Fd
Hercules Pacific Basin Value Fd
Hercules World Bond Fd

Azura Funds

See Societe Financiere Azura Inc.

Bank of Montreal Investment Management Limited

100 King Street West, P.O. Box 1
Toronto, Ontario M5X 1A1
(416) 927-6000
Fax: (416)867-7305
First Canadian Asset Allocation Fd
First Canadian Bond Fd
First Canadian Dividend Income Fd
First Canadian Emerging Markets Fd
First Canadian Equity Index Fd
First Canadian European Growth Fd
First Canadian Far East Growth Fd
First Canadian Growth Fd
First Canadian Int'l Growth Fd
First Canadian International Bond Fd
First Canadian Japanese Growth Fd
First Canadian Money Market Fd
First Canadian Mortgage Fd
First Canadian NAFTA Advantage Fd
First Canadian Resource Fd
First Canadian Special Growth Fd
First Canadian T-Bill Fd
First Canadian U.S. Growth Fd

Batirente Funds

See Corp. Financiers du St. Laurent

Beutel Goodman Managed Funds Inc.

20 Eglinton Avenue West
Suite 2000
Toronto, Ontario M4R 1K8
(416) 932-6400 (800) 461-4551
Fax: (416) 485-8194
Beutel Goodman American Equity Fd
Beutel Goodman Balanced Fd
Beutel Goodman Canadian Equity Fd
Beutel Goodman Income Fd
Beutel Goodman Int'l Equity Fd
Beutel Goodman Money Market Fd
Beutel Goodman Private Balanced Fd
Beutel Goodman Small Cap Fd

Bissett & Associates Investment Management Ltd.

500 4th Avenue S.W.
Suite 1120
Calgary, Alberta T2P 2V6
(403) 266-4664
Fax: (403) 237-2334
Bissett American Equity Fd
Bissett Bond Fd
Bissett Canadian Equity Fd
Bissett Dividend Income Fd
Bissett Money Market Fd
Bissett Multinational Growth Fd
Bissett Retirement Fd
Bissett Small Cap Fd

BNP (Canada) Valeurs Mobiliers Inc.
1981 McGill College Avenue
Suite 500
Montreal, Quebec H3A 2W8
(514) 285-2920
Fax: (514) 285-7598
BNP (Canada) Bond Fd
BNP (Canada) Cdn Money Market Fd
BNP (Canada) Equity Fd
Strategic Value Fd

BPI Capital Management Corporation
161 Bay Street, Suite 3900
Toronto, Ontario M5J 2S1
(416) 861-9811 (800) 263-2427
Fax: (416) 861-9415
BPI American Equity Value Fd
BPI American Small Companies Fd
BPI Canadian Balanced Fd
BPI Canadian Bond Fd
BPI Canadian Equity Value Fd
BPI Canadian Opportunities RSP Fd
BPI Canadian Resource Fd Inc.
BPI Canadian Small Companies Fd
BPI Emerging Markets Fd
BPI Global Balanced RSP Fd
BPI Global Equity Fd
BPI Global Opportunities Fd
BPI Global RSP Bond Fd
BPI Global Small Companies Fd
BPI Income Fd
BPI International Equity Fd
BPI North American Balanced RSP Fd
BPI T-Bill Fd
BPI U.S. Money Market ($US) Fd
Vengrowth Investment Fund Inc.

Bullock Funds
See Spectrum United Financial Services

Burgeonvest Investment Counsel
1 King St. W., Suite 1101
Hamilton, Ontario L8N 3P6
(905) 528-6505
Fax: (905) 528-3540
Burgeonvest T-Bill Fd
Dolphin Growth Fd
Dolphin Income Fd
Marlborough Canadian Balanced Fd
Marlborough Int'l Balanced Fd

Caldwell Securities Ltd.
150 King Street West, Suite 1710, P.O Box 47
Toronto, Ontario M5H 1J9
(416) 862-7755
Fax: (416) 862-2498
Caldwell Securities Associate Fd
Caldwell Securities International Fd

Cambridge Funds
See Sagit Investment Management Ltd.

Canada Life Investment Management Ltd.
330 University Avenue
Toronto, Ontario M5G 1R8
(416) 597-1456 (800) 387-4447
Fax: (416) 597-9674
Canada Life Asia Pacific Fd
Canada Life Canadian Equity S-9 Fd
Canada Life European Equity S-37 Fd
Canada Life Fixed Income S-19 Fd

Canada Life Int'l Bond S-36 Fd
Canada Life Managed Fd S-35 Fd
Canada Life Money Market S-29 Fd
Canada Life U.S. & Int'l Equity S-34 Fd

Canada Trust Funds
See CT Fund Services Inc.

Canadian Anaesthetists Mutual Accumulating Fund Ltd.
94 Cumberland Street, Suite 503
Toronto, Ontario M5R 1A3
(416) 925-7331 (800) 267-4713
Fax: (416) 920-7843
Canadian Anaesthetists Mutual
  Accumulating Fd

Canadian Dental Association
100 Consilium Place, Suite 710
Scarborough, Ontario M1H 3G8
(416) 296-9401 (800) 591-9401
Fax: (416) 296-8920
CDA Aggressive Equity Fd
CDA Balanced Fd
CDA Bond and Mortgage Fd
CDA Common Stock Fd
CDA Emerging Markets Fd
CDA European Fd
CDA International Equity Fd
CDA Money Market Fd
CDA Pacific Basin Fd

Canadian International Fund Management Inc.
151 Yonge Street, 8th Floor
Toronto, Ontario M5C 2Y1
(416) 364-1145 (800) 563-5181
Fax: (416) 364-6299
C.I. American Fd
C.I. American RSP Fd
C.I. Canadian Balanced Fd
C.I. Canadian Bond Fd
C.I. Canadian Growth Fd
C.I. Canadian Income Fd
C.I. Convington Labour Sponsored Fd
C.I. Emerging Markets Fd
C.I. Global Bond RSP Fd
C.I. Global Equity RSP Fd
C.I. Global Fd
C.I. International Balanced Fd
C.I. International Balanced RSP Fd
C.I. Latin American Fd
C.I. Money Market Fd
C.I. New World Inc.
C.I. Pacific Fd
C.I. Sector American Fd
C.I. Sector Canadian Fd
C.I. Sector Emerging Markets Fd
C.I. Sector Global Fd
C.I. Sector Global Financial Service Fd
C.I. Sector Global Health Sciences Fd
C.I. Sector Global Resource Shares Fd
C.I. Sector Global Tech. Shares Fd
C.I. Sector Global Telecom Shares Fd
C.I. Sector Latin American Fd
C.I. Sector Pacific Fd
C.I. Sector Short-Term Fd
C.I US Money Market Fd ($US)
C.I. World Bond Fd
Hansberger Asian Fd
Hansberger Asian Sector Shares
Hansberger Developing Markets Fd

Hansberger Developing Mrkt Sector
Hansberger European Fd
Hansberger European Sector Shares
Hansberger Global Small-Cap Fd
Hanberger Global Small-Cap Sector
Hansberger International Fd
Hansberger Int'l Sector Shares
Hansberger Value Fd
Hansberger Value Sector Shares

Canadian Investment Fund

See Spectrum United Financial Services

Canadian Medical Discoveries Fund

Talvest Fund Management Inc.

Canadian Protected Fund

See Guardian Timing Services Inc.

Capital Alliance Management Inc.

60 Queen Street, Suite 1202
Ottawa, Ontario K1P 5Y7
(613) 567-3225 (800) 304-2330
Capital Alliance Ventures Inc.

Capstone Consultants Limited

401 Bay Street, Suite 1102
P.O Box 25
Toronto, Ontario M5H 2Y4
(416) 863-0005
Fax: (416) 863-0841
Capstone Cash Management Fd
Capstone Int'l Investment Trust
Capstone Investment Trust

Cassels Blaikie & Co. Limited

1 Adelaide Street East, Suite 200
Toronto, Ontario M5C 2W8
(416) 941-7500
Fax: (416) 867-9821
Cassels Blaikie American Fd (US $)
Cassels Blaikie Canadian Fd

CCPE Funds

See Manulife Financial

CDA Funds

See Canadian Dental Association

Century DJ Fund

4 King Street West, Suite 301
Toronto, Ontario M5H 1B6
(416) 608-0727
Century DJ Fd

Chou Associates Management

70 Dragoon Crescent
Scarborough, Ontario M1V 1N4
(416) 299-6749
Fax: (416) 412-1898
Chou Associates Fd
Chou RRSP Fd

C.I. Funds

See Canadian International Mutual
Fund Management Inc.

CIBC Securities Inc.

Commerce Court Postal Station
P.O. Box 51
Toronto, Ontario M5L 1A2
(416) 980-3863 (800) 465-3863
Fax: (416) 351-4440
CIBC Balanced Income and Growth Fd
CIBC Canadian Bond Fd
CIBC Canadian Equity Fd
CIBC Canadian Index Fd
CIBC Canadian Income Fd
CIBC Canadian Resource Fd
CIBC Canadian T-Bill Fd
CIBC Capital Appreciation Fd
CIBC Emerging Economies Fd
CIBC Energy Fd
CIBC Equity Income Fd
CIBC European Equity Fd
CIBC Far East Prosperity Fd
CIBC Global Bond Fd
CIBC Global Equity Fd
CIBC Global Technology Fd
CIBC Japanese Equity Fd
CIBC Money Market Fd
CIBC Mortgage Investment Fd
CIBC Precious Metals Fd
CIBC Premium T-Bill Fd
CIBC U.S. Dollar Money Market Fd
CIBC U.S. Equity Fd
CIBC U.S Index RRSPFund
CIBC U.S Opportunities Fd

Clarington Capital Management Inc.

181 University Ave.
Suite 1010
Toronto, Ontario M5H 3M7
(416) 860-9880 (888) 860-9888
Clarington Canadian Balanced Fd
Clarington Canadian Equity Fd
Clarington Cdn Global Opp Fd
Clarington Money Market Fd
Clarington U.S. Equity Fd
Clarington U.S. Smaller Co. Gth Fd

Clean Environment Mutual Funds Inc.

65 Queen Street West
Suite 1800
Toronto, Ontario M5H 2M5
(416) 366-9933 (800) 461-4570
Fax: (416) 366-2568
Clean Environment Balanced Fd
Clean Environment Equity Fd
Clean Environment Income Fd
Clean Environment Int'l Equity Fd

Colonia Life Insurance Company

2 Street Clair Avenue East
Toronto, Ontario M4T 2V6
(416) 960-3601 (800) 463-9297
Fax: (416) 323-0934
Colonia Bond Fd
Colonia Equity Fd
Colonia Money Market Fd
Colonia Mortgage Fd
Colonia Special Growth Fd
Colonia Strategic Balanced Fd

Common Sense Funds
See Primerica Financial Services

Concorde Funds
See Groupe Financier Concorde

Confederation Life Insurance Company
1 Mount Pleasant Road
10th Floor
Toronto, Ontario M4Y 2Y5
(902) 453-4300
Fax: (416) 323-4191
Confed Equity Fd
Confed Fixed Income Fd
Confed Life B Fd
Confed Life C Fd

Co-operators Life Insurance Co.
1920 College Avenue
Regina, Saskatchewan S4P 1C4
(306) 347-6211 (800) 667-8164
Co-operators Balanced Fd
Co-operators Cdn Equity Fd
Co-operators Fixed Income Fd
Co-operators U.S. Equity Fd

Cornerstone Funds
See Laurentian Bank Investment
  Services Inc.

Corp. Financiers du St. Laurent
425 de Maisonneuve boul ouest
Suite 1740
Montreal, Quebec H3A 3G5
(514) 288-7545
Fax: (514) 288-4280
Batirente - Section Actions
Batirente - Section Diversifiee
Batirente - Section Marche Monetaire
Batirente - Section Obligations

Cote 100
561 Beaumont Street East
St. Bruno, Quebec J3V 2R2
(514) 461-2826
(800) 454-2683 (Quebec only)
Fax: (514) 461-2177
Cote 100 Amerique
Cote 100 Amerique REER
Cote 100 EXP
Cote 100 REA- Action

CSA Management Enterprises Ltd.
145 King Street West, Suite 2700
Toronto, Ontario M5H 1J8
(416) 865-0326 (800) 363-3463
Fax: (416) 865-9636
Goldfund Ltd.
Goldtrust

CT Fund Services Inc.
161 Bay Street, 3rd Floor
Toronto, Ontario M5J 2T2
(416) 361-3757 (800) 668-8888
Fax: (416) 361-5333
Canada Trust Everest Amerigrowth Fd
Canada Trust Everest Asiagrowth Fd
Canada Trust Everest Balanced Fd

Canada Trust Everest Bond Fd
Canada Trust Everest Dividend Inc Fd
Canada Trust Everest Emerg Mkts Fd
Canada Trust Everest EuroGrowth Fd
Canada Trust Everest International Fd
Canada Trust Everest Int'l Bond Fd
Canada Trust Everest Money Mkts Fd
Canada Trust Everest Mortgage Fd
Canada Trust Everest North Amer Fd
Canada Trust Everest Special Equity Fd
Canada Trust Everest Stock Fd
Canada Trust Everest U.S. Equity Fd

Peter Cundill & Associates Ltd.
1100 Melville Street
1200 Sun Life Plaza
Vancouver, BC V6E 4A6
(604) 685-4231 (800) 663-0156
Fax: (604) 689-9532
Cundill Security Fd
Cundill Value Fd

Deacon Capital Corporation
320 Bay Street
Toronto, Ontario M5H 4A6
(416) 350-3232 (800) 361-2680
Resolute Growth Fund

Desjardins Trust Inc.
1 Complexe Desjardins, C.P. 34
Montreal, Quebec H5B 1E4
(514) 286-3100
Fax: (514) 849-3328
Fonds Desjardins Actions
Fonds Desjardins Croissance
Fonds Desjardins Dividendes
Fonds Desjardins Divers. Audacieux
Fonds Desjardins Divers. Modere
Fonds Desjardins Divers. Secure

Fonds Desjardins Environnement
Fonds Desjardins Equilibre
Fonds Desjardins Hypotheques
Fonds Desjardins International
Fonds Desjardins Marche Americain
Fonds Desjardins Mondial Equilibre
Fonds Desjardins Monetaire
Fonds Desjardins Obligations

DGC Entertainment Ventures Corp.
387 Bloor Street East, Suite 401
Toronto, Ontario M4W 1H7
(416) 972-1158 (800) 382 1159
Fax: (416) 972-0820
DGC Entertainment Ventures Corp.

Dolphin Funds
See Burgeonvest Investment Counsel

Dominion Equity Resource Fund Inc.
205 - 5th Avenue S.W., Suite 1710
Bow Valley Square Two
Calgary, Alberta T2P 2V7
(403) 531-2657
Fax: (403) 264-5844
Dominion Equity Resource Fd Ltd.

Dynamic Mutual Funds
Scotia Plaza,
Suite 5500
40 King Street West
Toronto, Ontario M5H 4A9
(416) 363-5621 (800) 268-8186
Fax: (416) 365-2558
Dynamic Americas Fd
Dynamic Canadian Growth Fd

Dynamic Dividend Fd
Dynamic Dividend Growth Fd
Dynamic Europe Fd
Dynamic Far East Fd
Dynamic Fd of Canada
Dynamic Global Bond Fd
Dynamic Global Millennia Fd
Dynamic Global Partners Fd
Dynamic Global Precious Metals Fd
Dynamic Global Resources Fd
Dynamic Government Income Fd
Dynamic Income Fd
Dynamic International Fd
Dynamic Money Market Fd
Dynamic Partners Fd
Dynamic Global Precious Metals Fd
Dynamic Real Estate Equity Fd
Dynamic Team Fd

Elliott & Page Limited
120 Adelaide Street West
Suite 1120
Toronto, Ontario M5H 1V1
(416) 365-8300 (800) 363-6647
Fax: (416) 365-2143
Elliott & Page American Growth Fd
Elliott & Page Asia Growth Fd
Elliott & Page Balanced Fd
Elliott & Page Bond Fd
Elliott & Page Emerging Markets Fd
Elliott & Page Equity Fd
Elliott & Page Global Balanced Fd
Elliott & Page Global Bond Fd
Elliott & Page Global Equity Fd
Elliott & Page Money Fd
Elliott & Page T-Bill Fd

The Empire Financial Group
259 King Street East
Kingston, Ontario K7L 3A8
(613) 548-1881
Fax: (613) 548-4104
Empire Asset Allocation Fd
Empire Balanced Fd
Empire Bond Fd
Empire Elite Equity Fd 5
Empire Equity Growth Fd 3
Empire Foreign Currency Cdn Bond Fd
Empire International Fd
Empire Money Market Fd
Empire Premier Equity Fd 1

Enterprise Fund
See FESA Enterprise Venture Capital

Equitable Life of Canada
1 Westmount Road North, P.O
Box 1603
Waterloo, Ontario N2J 4C7
(519) 886-5110 (800) 387-0588
Fax: (519) 886-5314
Equitable Life Asset Allocation Fd
Equitable Life Canadian Bond Fd
Equitable Life Canadian Stock Fd
Equitable Life International Fd
Equitable Life Money Market Fd
Equitable Life Mortgage Fd
Equitable Life Seg Accum Income Fd
Equitable Life Seg Common Stock Fd

Ethical Funds Inc.
510-815 West Hastings Street
Vancouver, B.C., V6C 1B4
(604) 331-8350 (800) 267-5019
Fax: (604) 331-8399
Ethical Balanced Fd
Ethical Global Bond Fd
Ethical Growth Fd
Ethical Income Fd
Ethical Money Market Fd
Ethical North American Equity Fd
Ethical Pacific Rim Fd
Ethical Special Equity Fd

Ferique Funds
See Ordre des Ingenieurs du Quebec

FESA Enterprise Venture Capital
65 Queen Street West
Suite 1404
Toronto, Ontario M5H 2M5
(416) 362-9009 (800) 563-3857
Fax: (416) 360-8286
The Enterprise Fund

Fidelity Investments Canada Limited
Ernst & Young Tower
222 Bay Street, Suite 900
Toronto, Ontario M5K 1P1
(416) 307-5200 (800) 263-4077
Fax: (416) 307-5508
Fidelity Asset Manager Fd
Fidelity Canadian Asset Allocation Fd
Fidelity Canadian Bond Fd
Fidelity Canadian Growth Company
Fidelity Canadian Income Fd
Fidelity Canadian Short-Term Asset Fd

Fidelity Capital Builder Fd
Fidelity Emerging Markets Bond Fd
Fidelity Emerging Markets Portfolio Fd
Fidelity European Growth Fd
Fidelity Far East Fd
Fidelity Growth America Fd
Fidelity International Portfolio Fd
Fidelity Japanese Growth Fd
Fidelity Latin American Growth Fd
Fidelity North American Income Fd
Fidelity RSP Global Bond Fd
Fidelity Small Cap American Fd
Fidelity True North Fd
Fidelity U.S. Money Mkt Fd ($US)

First American Fund
See Guardian Timing Services Inc.

First Canadian Funds
See Bank of Montreal Investment
    Management Limited

First Heritage Fund
See Gordon Daly Grenadier Securities

First Marathon Securities Ltd.
P.O. Box 21, The Exchange
Tower
2 First Canadian Place
Suite 3200
Toronto, Ontario M5X 1J9
(416) 869-3707 (800) 661-3863
Fax: (416) 869-6405
Marathon Equity Fd

First Ontario LSIF Ltd.
234 Eglinton Ave E, Suite 310
Toronto, Ontario M4P 1K5
(416) 487-5444 (800) 777-7506
First Ontario LSIF Ltd.

Fonds D'Investissement REA
See Gentrust Investment Counsellors

Fonds Desjardins
See Desjardins Trust Inc.

Fonds des Professionnels du Quebec Inc.
2 Complexe Desjardins, P.O Box 216
Montreal, Quebec H5B 1G8
(514) 350-5055 (800) 363-6713
Fax: (514) 350-5051
Fonds des Prof Balanced Fd
Fonds des Prof Bond Fd
Fonds des Prof Canadian Equity Fd
Fonds des Prof Growth and Income Fd
Fonds des Prof Int'l Equity Fd
Fonds des Prof Short-Term Fd

Fonds Ficadre
See Sogefonds MFQ Inc.

Friedberg Commodity Management Inc.
181 Bay St, Ste 250, PO Box 866,
Toronto, Ontario M5J 2T3
(416) 364-1171 (800) 461-2700
Friedberg Currency Fd
Friedberg Double Gold Plus Fd

GBC Asset Management Inc.
55 University Avenue, Suite 616
Toronto, Ontario M5J 2H7
(800) 668-7383
Fax: (416) 366-6833
GBC Canadian Bond Fd
GBC Canadian Growth Fd
GBC International Growth Fd
GBC Money Market Fd
GBC North American Growth Fd Inc.

General Trust of Canada Funds
See National Bank Securities Inc.

Gentrust Investment Counsellors
1000 University, 11th Floor
Montreal, Quebec H3B 2G7
(514) 871-7162 (800) 341-1419
Fonds D'Investissement REA

Global Strategy Financial Inc.
33 Bloor Street East, Suite 1600
Toronto, Ontario M4W 3T8
(416) 966-8667 (800) 387-1229
Fax: (416) 927-9168
Global Strat Asia Fd
Global Strat Bond Fd
Global Strat Canada Growth Fd
Global Strat Cdn Small Cap Fd
Global Strat Diversified Asia Fd
Global Strat Diversified Bond Fd
Global Strat Diversified Europe Fd
Global Strat Diversified Foreign Bd Fd
Global Strat Diversified Japan Plus Fd
Global Strat Diversified Latin Fd
Global Strat Diversified World Eqty Fd
Global Strat Europe Plus Fd
Global Strat Foreign Bond Fd

Global Strat Gold Plus Fd
Global Strat Income Plus Fd
Global Strat Japan Fd
Global Strat Latin America Fd
Global Strat Money Market Fd
Global Strat U.S. Equity
Global Strat World Bond Fd
Global Strat World Emerging Cos Fd
Global Strat World Equity Fd

GlobeInvest Funds
   Management Inc.
20 Queen Str W, Suite 3206
Toronto, Ontario M5H 3R3
(416) 369-4592 (800) 387-0784
GFM Emerg Mkts Country Fd (SUS)
Globelnvest Emerg Mkts Country Fd

GFM Emerging Markets
   Country Fund
See Globelnvest Funds Management
   Inc.

Goldfund/Goldtrust
See CSA Management Enterprises Ltd.

Gordon Daly Grenadier
   Securities
224 Richmond Street West
Toronto, Ontario M5V 1V6
(416) 593-0144 (800) 268-9165
Fax: (416) 593-8753
First Heritage Fd

Great-West Life Assurance
   Company
60 Osborne Street North
P.O. Box 6000
Winnipeg, Manitoba R3C 3A5
(204) 946-1190 (800) 665-0049
Fax: (204) 946-8622
GWL Canadian Resource Fd (A)
GWL Balanced Fd (B)
GWL Balanced Fd (M)
GWL Balanced Fd (S)
GWL Bond Fd (B)
GWL Bond Fd (M)
GWL Bond Fd (S)
GWL Canadian Bond Fd
GWL Canadian Equity
GWL Diversified RS Fd
GWL Equity Fd (M)
GWL Equity Fd (S)
GWL Equity Index Fd
GWL Equity Bond Fd
GWL Government Bond
GWL Growth Equity Fd (A)
GWL Growth and Income Fd (M)
GWL Income Fd
GWL International Bond Fd
GWL International Equity Fd
GWL Larger Co. Fd (M)
GWL Money Market Fd
GWL Mortgage Fd
GWL Money Market Fd
GWL Mortgage Fd
GWL N.A Equity (B)
GWL Smaller Company (M)
GWL Strategic Inc. (A)
GWL U.S. Equity Fd

Green Line Funds
See Toronto-Dominion Securities Inc.

Greystone Funds

See Managed Investments Ltd.

Groupe Financier Concorde

850 Place d'Youville
Quebec, Quebec G1R 3P6
(418) 692-1221
Fax: (418) 692-1679
Concorde Croissance
Concorde Dividendes
Concorde Hypotheques
Concorde Marche Monetaire
Concorde Revenu

Growsafe Funds

See Transamerica Life Insurance Co.
of Canada

GS Funds

See Investors Group Inc.

G.T. Global Canada Inc.

77 King Street West, Suite 4001
Toronto, Ontario M5K 1K2
(416) 594-4300 (800) 588-5684
Fax: (416) 594-0656
G.T. Global America Growth Fd
G.T. Global Canada Growth Fd
G.T. Global Canada Income Fd
G.T. Global Growth and Income Fd
G.T. Global Health Care Fd
G.T. Global Infrastructure Fd
G.T. Global Latin America Fd
G.T. Global Natural Resources Fd
G.T. Global Pacific Growth Fd
G.T Global Short-Term Income Fd A
G.T Global Short-Term Income Fd B

G.T. Global Telecommunications Fd
G.T Global World Bond Fd

Guardian Group of Funds Limited

Commerce Court West
Suite 3100, P.O. Box 201
Toronto, Ontario M5L 1E8
(416) 364-8341 (800) 668-7327
Fax: (416) 947-0601
Guardian American Equity Fd A
Guardian American Equity Fd B
Guardian Asia Pacific Fd A
Guardian Asia Pacific Fd B
Guardian Canadian Balanced Fd A
Guardian Canadian Balanced Fd B
Guardian Canadian Income Fd A
Guardian Canadian Income Fd B
Guardian Cdn Money Market Fd A
Guardian Cdn Money Market Fd B
Guardian Cdn Emerging Markets Fd A
Guardian Cdn Emerging Markets Fd B
Guardian Enterprise Fd A
Guardian Enterprise Fd B
Guardian Foreign Income Fd A
Guardian Foreign Income Fd B
Guardian Global Equity Fd A
Guardian Global Equity Fd B
Guardian Growth Equity Fd A
Guardian Growth Equity Fd B
Guardian International Balanced Fd A
Guardian International Balanced Fd B
Guardian International Income Fd A
Guardian International Income Fd B
Guardian Monthly Dividend Fd A
Guardian Monthly Dividend Fd B
Guardian U.S. Money Mkt Fd ($US) A
Guardian U.S. Money Mkt Fd ($US) B

Guardian Timing Services Inc.
130 Adelaide Street West
Suite 3303
Toronto, Ontario M5H 3P5
(416) 960-4890
Fax: (416) 364-3752
Canadian Protected Fd
First American Fd
Protected American Fd

GWL Funds
See Great-West Life Assurance
    Company

Hercules Funds
See Atlas Capital Group

John D. Hillery Investment
    Counsel Inc.
2842 Bloor St West, Suite 203
Etobicoke, Ontario M8X 1B1
(416) 234-0846
Fax: (416) 234-0846
Margin of Safety Fd

Hodgson Roberton Laing
    Limited
One Queen Street East
Suite 2300
Toronto, Ontario M5C 2Y5
(416) 364-4444 (800) 268-9622
Fax: (416) 955-4878
HRL Balanced Fd
HRL Bond Fd
HRL Canadian Fd
HRL Instant $$ Fd
HRL Overseas Growth Fd

Hongkong Bank Securities Inc.
885 West Georgia Street
Suite 400
Vancouver, B.C. V6C 3E9
(604) 641-3088 (800) 830-8888
Fax: (604) 641-3096
Hongkong Bank Americas Fd
Hongkong Bank Asian Growth Fd
Hongkong Bank Balanced Fd
Hongkong Bank Canadian Bond Fd
Hongkong Bank Dividend Income Fd
Hongkong Bank Emerging Markets Fd
Hongkong Bank Equity Fd
Hongkong Bank European Growth Fd
Hongkong Bank Global Bond Fd
Hongkong Bank Money Market Fd
Hongkong Bank Mortgage Fd
Hongkong Bank Small Cap Growth Fd

Howson Tattersall Investment
    Counsel
20 Queen St. West, Suite 1904
P.O. Box 95
Toronto, Ontario M5H 3R3
(416) 979-1818 (888) 287-2966
Fax: (416) 979-7424
Saxon Balanced Fd
Saxon Small Cap Fd
Saxon Stock Fd
Saxon World Growth Fd

HRL Funds
See Hodgson Roberton Laing Limited

Hyperion Funds
See Talvest Fund Management Inc.

ICM Funds
See Integra Capital Management Corp.

Imperial Life Assurance Company of Canada
95 St. Clair Avenue West
Toronto, Ontario M4V 1N7
(416) 324-1617
Fax: (416) 324-1617
Imperial Growth Canadian Equity Fd
Imperial Growth Diversified Fd
Imperial Growth Money Market Fd
Imperial Growth North Amer Eqty Fd
Millennia III American Equity Fd 1
Millennia III American Equity Fd 2
Millennia III Cdn Balanced Fd 1
Millennia III Cdn Balanced Fd 2
Millennia III Cdn Equity Fd 1
Millennia III Cdn Equity Fd 2
Millennia III Income Fd 1
Millennia III Income Fd 2
Millennia III Int'l Equity Fd 1
Millennia III Int'l Equity Fd 2
Millennia III Money Mkt Fd 1
Millennia III Money Mkt Fd 2

Industrial Alliance Life Insurance Company
1080 Chemin St- Louis
C.P. 1901
Quebec, Quebec G1K 7M3
(418) 684-5000 (800) 268-8882
Fax: (418) 684-5161
Industrial Alliance Bond Fd
Industrial Alliance Diversified Fd
Industrial Alliance Ecoflex Fd A
Industrial Alliance Ecoflex Fd B
Industrial Alliance Ecoflex Fd D
Industrial Alliance Ecoflex Fd H
Industrial Alliance Ecoflex Fd I
Industrial Alliance Ecoflex Fd M
Industrial Alliance Int'l Fd
Industrial Alliance Money Market Fd
Industrial Alliance Mortgage Fd
Industrial Alliance Stocks Fd

Industrial Group of Funds
See Mackenzie Financial Corporation

Integra Capital Management Corporation
55 University Avenue
Suite 1100, P.O. Box 42
Toronto, Ontario M5J 2H7
(416) 367-0404
Fax: (416) 367-0351
ICM Balanced Fd
ICM Short Term Investment Fd

Integrated Growth Fund Inc.
135 Queens Plate Dr, Suite 540
Etobicoke, ON M9W 6V1
(416) 745-5355 (800) 420-5399
Integrated Growth Fund

InvesNat Funds
See National Bank Securities Inc.

Investors Group Inc.
One Canada Centre
447 Portage Avenue
Winnipeg, Manitoba R3C 3B6
(204) 943-0361 (888) 746-6344
Fax: (204) 949-1340
GS American Equity Fd
GS Canadian Balanced Fd

GS Canadian Equity Fd
GS International Bond Fd
GS International Equity Fd
Investors Asset Allocation Fd
Investors Canadian Equity Fd
Investors Corporate Bond Fd
Investors Dividend Fd
Investors European Growth Fd
Investors Global Bond Fd
Investors Global Fd
Investors Government Bond Fd
Investors Growth Plus Portfolio Fd
Investors Growth Portfolio Fd
Investors Income Plus Portfolio Fd
Investors Income Portfolio Fd
Investors Japanese Growth Fd
Investors Money Market Fd
Investors Mortgage Fd
Investors Mutual of Canada Fd
Investors North American Growth Fd
Investors Pacific Int'l Fd
Investors Real Property Fd
Investors Retirement Gth Portfolio
Investors Retirement Mutual Fd
Investors Retirement Plus Portfolio
Investors Special Fd
Investors Summa Fd
Investors U.S. Growth Fd
Investors World Growth Portfolio
Merrill Lynch Canadian Equity Fd
Merrill Lynch Capital Asset Fd
Merrill Lynch Emerging Markets Fd
Merrill Lynch World Allocation Fd
Merrill Lynch World Bond Fd

Ivy Funds
See Mackenzie Financial Corporation

Jones Heward Investment Management Inc.
Royal Trust Tower
77 King Street West, Suite 4200
Toronto, Ontario M5K 1J5
(416) 359-5000 (800) 361-1392
Fax: (416) 359-5040
Jones Heward American Fd
Jones Heward Bond Fd
Jones Heward Canadian Balanced Fd
Jones Heward Fd Ltd.
Jones Heward Money Market Fd

Laurentian Bank Investment Services Inc.
151 Yonge Street, 3rd Floor
Toronto, Ontario M5C 2W7
(416) 865-5832
Fax: (416) 947-5116
Cornerstone Balanced Fd
Cornerstone Bond Fd
Cornerstone Canadian Growth Fd
Cornerstone Global Fd
Cornerstone Government Money Fd
Cornerstone U.S. Fd

Laurentian Funds Management Inc.
95 St. Clair Avenue West
Toronto, Ontario M4V 1N7
(416) 324-1617
Fax: (416) 324-1670
Laurentian American Equity Fd Ltd.
Laurentian Asia Pacific Fd
Laurentian Canadian Balanced Fd
Laurentian Canadian Equity Fd Ltd.
Laurentian Commonwealth Fd Ltd.
Laurentian Dividend Fd Ltd.
Laurentian Emerging Markets Fd

Laurentian Europe Fd
Laurentian Global Balanced Fd
Laurentian Government Bond Fd
Laurentian Income Fd
Laurentian International Fd Ltd.
Laurentian Money Market Fd
Laurentian Special Equity Fd

Leith Wheeler Investment Counsel Ltd.

400 Burrard Street, Suite 1500
Vancouver, British Columbia
V6C 3A6
(604) 683-3391
Fax: (604) 683-0323
Leith Wheeler Balanced Fd
Leith Wheeler Canadian Equity Fd
Leith Wheeler Fixed Income Fd
Leith Wheeler Money Market Fd
Leith Wheeler U.S. Equity Fd

London Life Insurance Company

255 Dufferin Avenue
London, Ontario N6A 4K1
(519) 432-5281
Fax: (519) 432-2851
London Life Bond Fd
London Life Canadian Equity Fd
London Life Diversified Fd
London Life International Equity Fd
London Life Money Market Fd
London Life Mortgage Fd
London Life U.S. Equity Fd

Loring Ward Investment Counsel Ltd.

360 Main Street, Suite 1501
Winnipeg, Manitoba R3C 3Z3
(204) 957-1730 (800) 267-1730
Fax: (204) 947-2103
Optima Strategy Canadian Equity Fd
Optima Strategy Cdn Fixed Income Fd
Optima Strategy Global Fixed Inc Fd
Optima Strategy Int'l Equity Fd
Optima Strategy ST Income Fd
Optima Strategy U.S. Equity Fd

Lotus Funds

See M.K. Wong & Associates Ltd.

Mackenzie Financial Corporation

150 Bloor Street West
Suite M111
Toronto, Ontario M5S 3B5
(416) 922-5322 (800) 387-0615
Fax: (416) 922-0399
Industrial American Fd
Industrial Balanced Fd
Industrial Bond Fd
Industrial Cash Management Fd
Industrial Dividend Fd Ltd.
Industrial Equity Fd Ltd.
Industrial Future Fd
Industrial Growth Fd
Industrial Horizon Fd
Industrial Income Fd
Industrial Mortgage Securities Fd
Industrial Pension Fd
Industrial Short-Term Fd
Industrial Strategic Cap Protection Fd
Ivy Canadian Fd
Ivy Enterprise Fd

Ivy Foreign Equity Fd
Ivy Growth and Income Fd
Ivy Mortgage Fd
Mackenzie Sentinal Global Fd
Mackenzie Sentinel Canada Equity Fd
STAR Cdn Bal Gth & Income Fd
STAR Cdn Maximum Eqty Gth Fd
STAR Foreign Bal Gth & Income Fd
STAR Foreign Maximum Eqty Gth Fd
STAR Foreign Maximum LT Gwth Fd
STAR Inv Bal Gth & Income Fd
STAR Inv Conservative Inc & Gth Fd
STAR Inv Max Long-Term Growth Fd
STAR Inv. Long-Term Growth Fd
STAR Reg Bal Gth & Income Fd
STAR Reg Conservative Inc & Gth Fd
STAR Reg Long-Term Gth Fd
STAR Reg Maximum Eqty Gth
STAR Reg Max Long-Term Gth Fd
Universal Americas Fd
Universal Canadian Growth Fd Ltd.
Universal Canadian Resource Fd
Universal European Opportunities Fd
Universal Far East Fd
Universal Growth Fd
Universal Japan Fd
Universal U.S. Emerging Growth Fd
Universal U.S. Money Market Fd
Universal World Asset Allocation Fd
Universal World Balanced RRSP Fd
Universal World Emerging Growth Fd
Universal World Equity Fd
Universal World Growth RRSP Fd
Universal World Income RRSP Fd
Universal World Precious Metals Fd
Universal World Science & Tech Fd
Universal World Tactical Bond Fd

Majendie Securities Ltd.
200 Burrard Street, Suite 320
Vancouver, B.C. V6C 3L6
(604) 682-6446
Fax: (604) 662-8594
Top Fifty Equity Fd
Top Fifty T-Bill/Bond Fd
Top Fifty U.S. Equity Fd

Managed Investments Ltd.
10104 - 103 Avenue, Suite 555
Edmonton, Alberta T5J 0H8
(403) 423-3544 (800) 287-5211
Fax: (403) 426-0506
Greystone Managed Global Fd
Greystone Managed Wealth Fd

**Mandate Management
  Corporation**
1285 West Broadway, 8th Floor
Vancouver, BC V6H 3X8
(604) 731-2899
Mandate National Mortgage Corp.

Manulife Financial
5650 Yonge Street
North York, Ontario M2M 4G4
(416) 229-4515
Fax: (416) 229-6594
CCPE Diversified Growth Fd R
CCPE Fixed Income Fd
CCPE Global Equity Fd
CCPE Growth Fd R
CCPE Money Market Fd
CCPE U.S. Equity Fd

Manulife Financial
500 King Street North
Waterloo, Ontario N2J 4C6
(519) 747-7000
Fax: (519) 747-9835
Manulife Vistafund 1 Amer Stock Fd
Manulife Vistafund 1 Bond Fd
Manulife Vistafund 1 Cap Gain Gth Fd
Manulife Vistafund 1 Diversified Fd
Manulife Vistafund 1 Equity Fd
Manulife Vistafund 1 Global Bond Fd
Manulife Vistafund 1 Global Equity Fd
Manulife Vistafund 1 ST Sec Fd
Manulife Vistafund 2 Amer Stock Fd
Manulife Vistafund 2 Bond Fd
Manulife Vistafund 2 Cap Gain Gth Fd
Manulife Vistafund 2 Diversified Fd
Manulife Vistafund 2 Equity Fd
Manulife Vistafund 2 Global Bond Fd
Manulife Vistafund 2 Global Equity Fd
Manulife Vistafund 2 ST Sec Fd
NAL Balanced Growth Fd
NAL Canadian Bond Fd
NAL Canadian Diversified Fd
NAL Canadian Equity Fd
NAL Canadian Money Market Fd
NAL Equity Growth Fd
NAL Global Equity Fd
NAL U.S. Equity Fd

Manulife Securities International Ltd.
500 King Street North
Waterloo, Ontario N2J 4C6
(519) 747-7000 (800) 265-7401
Fax: (800) 265-5123
Manulife Cabot Blue Chip Fd
Manulife Cabot Canadian Equity Fd
Manulife Cabot Canadian Growth Fd
Manulife Cabot Diversified Bond Fd
Manulife Cabot Emerging Growth Fd
Manulife Cabot Global Equity Fd
Manulife Cabot Money Market Fd

Marathon Equity Fund
See First Marathon Securities Ltd.

Margin of Safety Fund
See John D. Hillery Investment
  Counsel Inc.

Maritime Life Assurance Company
2701 Dutch Village Road
P.O. Box 1030
Halifax, Nova Scotia B3J 2X5
(902) 453-4300
Fax: (902) 453-7041
Maritime Life Amer Gth & Income Fd
Maritime Life Balanced Fd
Maritime Life Canadian Equity Fd
Maritime Life Dividend Income Fd
Maritime Life Global Equities Fd
Maritime Life Bond Fd
Maritime Life Growth Fd
Maritime Life Money Market Fd
Maritime Life Pacific Basin Fd
Maritime Life S&P 500 Fd

Marlborough Funds
See Burgeonvest Investment Counsel

Mawer Investment Management
603 - 7th Avenue S.W.
Suite 600, Manulife House
Calgary, Alberta T2P 2T5
(403) 262-4673
Fax: (403) 262-4099
Mawer Cdn Bal Retirement Savings Fd
Mawer Canadian Bond Fd
Mawer Cdn Diversified Investment Fd
Mawer Canadian Equity Fd
Mawer Canadian Income Fd
Mawer Canadian Money Market Fd
Mawer High Yield Bond Fd
Mawer New Canada Fd
Mawer U.S. Equity Fd
Mawer World Investment Fd

Maxxum Group of Funds
33 Yonge Street, Suite 320
Toronto, Ontario M5E 1G4
(888) 4-MAXXUM
Fax: (888) MAXXUM-1
Maxxum American Equity Fd
Maxxum Canadian Balanced Fd
Maxxum Canadian Equity Growth Fd
Maxxum Dividend Fd
Maxxum Global Equity Fd
Maxxum Income Fd
Maxxum Money Market Fd
Maxxum Natural Resources Fd
Maxxum Precious Metals Fd

McDonald Financial
Corporation
40 King Street West
Toronto, ON M5H 3Y2
(416) 594-1979
McDonald Asia Plus Fd
McDonald Canada Plus Fd

McDonald Emerging Economies Fd
McDonald Enhanced Bd Fd
McDonald Euro Plus Fd
McDonald New America Fd
McDonald New Japan Fd

McLean Budden Ltd.
145 King Street West, Suite 2525
Toronto, Ontario M5H 1J8
(416) 862-9800
Fax: (416) 862-0167
McLean Budden American Growth Fd
McLean Budden Balanced Fd
McLean Budden Equity Growth Fd
McLean Budden Fixed Income Fd
McLean Budden Money Market Fd
McLean Budden Pooled Amer Eqty Fd
McLean Budden Pooled Balanced Fd
McLean Budden Pooled Cdn Eqty Fd
McLean Budden Pooled Fixed Inc Fd
McLean Budden Pooled Offshore Eqty

MD Management Limited
1867 Alta Vista Drive
Ottawa, Ontario K1G 3Y6
(613) 731-4552 (800) 267-4022
Fax: (613) 526-1352
MD Balanced Fd
MD Bond Fd
MD Bond and Mortgage Fd
MD Dividend Fd
MD Emerging Markets Fd
MD Equity Fd
MD Global Bond Fd
MD Growth Fd
MD Money Fd
MD Select Fd
MD U.S. Equity Fd

Merrill Lynch Funds
See Investors Group Inc.

Metropolitan Life Insurance Company of Canada
50 O'Connor, Suite 1226
Ottawa, Ontario K1P 6L2
(800) 267-9375
Fax: (613) 560-6926
Metlife MVP Balanced Fd
Metlife MVP Bond Fd
Metlife MVP Equity Fd
Metlife MVP Growth Fd
Metlife MVP Money Market Fd
Metlife MVP U.S. Equity Fd

Middlefield Resource Management Ltd.
One First Canadian Place
58th Floor, P.O. Box 192
Toronto, Ontario M5X 1A6
(416) 362-0714
Fax: (416) 362-7925
Middlefield Growth Fund

Millennia III Funds
See Imperial Life Assurance Company
of Canada

Millennium Funds
See Morrison Williams Investment
Management Ltd.

MOF Management Ltd.
609 Granville Street, 20th Floor
P.O. Box 10379
Vancouver, B.C. V7Y 1G8
(604) 643-7416 (800) 663-6370
Fax: (604) 687-6532
Multiple Opportunities Fd
Special Opportunities Fd Ltd.

Montreal Trust Co. of Canada
510 Burrard Street,
Vancouver, B.C. V6C 3B9
(604) 661-9535
Teachers'RSP - Equity Section

Montrusco Associates Inc.
1501 McGill College, Suite 2800
Montreal, Quebec H3A 3N3
(514) 842-6464
Quebec Growth Fund

Morrison Williams Investment Management Ltd.
1 Toronto Street, Suite 405
P.O. Box 21
Toronto, Ontario M5C 2V6
(416) 777-2922
Fax: (416) 777-0954
Millennium Diversified Fd
Millennium Next Generation Fd

Multiple Opportunties Fund
See MOF Management Ltd.

Mutual Investco Ltd.
227 King Street South
Waterloo, Ontario N2J 4C5
(519) 888-3863
Fax: (519) 888-3646
Mutual AmeriFund
Mutual Bond Fd
Mutual Diversifund 40
Mutual EquiFund
Mutual Money Market Fd
Mutual Premier American Fd
Mutual Premier Blue Chip Fd
Mutual Premier Bond Fd
Mutual Premier Emerging Markets Fd
Mutual Premier Diversifund Fd
Mutual Premier Growth Fd
Mutual Premier International Fd
Mutual Premier Mortgage Fd

NAL Funds
See Manulife Financial

National Bank Securities Inc.
1100 University Street, 4th Floor
Montreal, Quebec H3B 2G7
(514) 394-8642 (800) 363-3511
Fax: (514) 394-8804
Genl Trust of Canada Balanced Fd
Gen Trust of Canada Bond Fd
Gen Trust of Canada Cdn Equity Fd
Gen Trust of Canada Growth Fd
Gen Trust of Canada International Fd
Gen Trust of Canada Money Mrkt Fd
Gen Trust of Canada Mortgage Fd
Gen Trust of Canada U.S. Equity Fd
InvesNat Blue Chip American Eqty Fd
InvesNat Canadian Bond Fd
InvesNat Canadian Equity Fd
InvesNat Corp Cash Mgmt Fd

InvesNat Dividend Fd
InvesNat European Equity Fd
InvesNat Far East Equity Fd
InvesNat In't RSP Bond Fd
InvesNat Japanese Equity Fd
InvesNat Money Market Fd
InvesNat Mortgage Fd
InvesNat Retirement Balanced Fd
InvesNat Short-Term Gov't Bond Fd
InvesNat Treasury Bill Fd
InvesNat U.S. Money Mkt Fd ($US)
Vision Europe Fd

National Life of Canada
522 University Avenue
Toronto, Ontario M5G 1Y7
(416) 585-8094 (800) 242-9753
Fax: (416) 598-0728
National Life Balanced Fd
National Life Equities Fd
National Life Fixed Income Fd
National Life Global Equities Fd
National Life Money Market Fd

National Trust Funds
See Natrusco Investment Funds
Limited

Natrusco Investment Funds Limited
1 Financial Place
1 Adelaide Street East, 7th Floor
Toronto, Ontario M5C 2W8
(416) 361-3863 (800) 563-4683
Fax: (416) 361-5563
National Trust American Equity Fd
National Trust Balanced Fd
National Trust Canadian Bond Fd
National Trust Canadian Equity Fd

National Trust Dividend Fd
National Trust Emerging Markets Fd
National Trust International Equity Fd
National Trust Int'l RSP Bond Fd
National Trust Money Market Fd
National Trust Mortgage Fd
National Trust Special Equity Fd

Navigation Fund Company Ltd.

444 St. Mary Avenue
Suite 1500
Winnipeg, Manitoba R3C 3T1
(204) 942-7788 (800) 665-1667
Fax: (204) 942-5100
Navigator Amer Value Investments Fd
Navigator Asia Pacific Fd
Navigator Canadian Income Fd
Navigator Latin America Fd
Navigator Value Investment Retire Fd

NN Life Insurance Company of Canada

One Concorde Gate
Don Mills, Ontario M3C 3N6
(416) 391-2200
Fax: (416) 391-8415
NN Balanced Fd
NN Bond Fd
NN Can-Am Fd
NN Can-Asian Fd
NN Can-Emerge Fd
NN Canadian 35 Index Fd
NN Canadian Growth Fd
NN Can-Euro Fd
NN Can-Global Bond Fd
NN Dividend Fd
NN Elite Fd
NN Money Market Fd
NN T-Bill Fd

O'Donnell Investments Management Corp.

2 First Canadian Place,
Suite 1010, Box 447
Toronto, Ontario M5X 1E4
(416) 214-2214
O'Donnell American Sector Gth Fd
O'Donnell Cdn Emerging Gth Fd
O'Donnell Growth Fd
O'Donnell High Income Fd
O'Donnell Money Market Fd
O'Donnell Short Term Fd
O'Donnell U.S. Mid-Cap Fd

OHA Investment Management Ltd.

Suite 2501, 200 Front St. W.
Toronto, Ontario M5V 3L1
(416) 205-1455 (800) 268-9597
Fax: (416) 205-1440
OHA Balanced Fd
OHA Bond Fd
OHA Canadian Equity Fd
OHA Foreign Equity Fd
OHA Short Term Fd

Ontario Teachers Group

57 Mobile Drive
Toronto, Ontario M4A 1H5
(416) 752-9410 (800) 263-9541
Fax: (416) 752-6649
Ont Teachers Group Balanced Fd
Ont Teachers Group Diversified Fd
Ont Teachers Group Fixed Value Fd
Ont Teachers Group Global Fd
Ont Teachers Group Growth Fd
Ont Teachers Group Mortgage Inc

Optima Strategy Funds
See Loring Ward Investment Counsel
    Ltd.

Optimum Placements Inc.
425 boul. de Maisonneuve ouest
bureau 1120
Montreal, Quebec H3A 3G5
(514) 288-1600 (888) OPTIMUM
Fax: (514) 288-3317
Optimum Fonds Actions
Optimum Fonds Epargne
Optimum Fonds Obligations
Optimum Fonds Equilibre
Optimum Fonds Internationales

Orbit Mutual Fund
    Management Ltd
4141 Sherbrooke Street West
Suite 240
Montreal, Quebec H3Z 1B8
(514) 932-3000
Fax: (514) 989-2132
Orbit North American Equity Fd
Orbit World Fd

Ordre des Ingenieurs du Quebec
2020 University Street
18th Floor
Montreal, Quebec H3A 2A5
(514) 845-6141
Fax: (514) 845-1833
Ferique American Fd
Ferique Balanced Fd
Ferique Bond Fd
Ferique Equity Fd
Ferique Growth Fd
Ferique International Fd
Ferique Short Term Income Fd

Pacific Capital Management
    Inc.
2460 - 666 Burrard Street
Vancouver, BC V6C 2X8
(604) 682-5338 (800) 662-5338
Pacific Special Equity Fund

Phillips, Hager & North Ltd.
1055 West Hastings Street
Suite 1700
Vancouver, BC V6E 2H3
(604) 691-6781 (800) 661-6141
Fax: (604) 685-5712
PH & N Balanced Fd
PH & N Bal Pension Trust Fd
PH & N Bond Fd
PH & N Canadian Equity Fd
PH & N Canadian Money Market Fd
PH & N Dividend Income Fd
PH & N International Equity Fd
PH & N North American Equity Fd
PH & N RSP/RIF Equity Fd
PH & N Short Term Bd & Mortgage Fd
PH & N U.S. Equity Fd
PH & N $U.S. Money Market Fd
PH & N Vintage Fd

Primerica Financial Services
350 Burnhamthorpe Road
Suite 300
Mississauga, Ontario L5B 3J1
(905) 848-7731 (800) 387 7876
Fax: (905) 270-7096
Common Sense Asset Builder Fd 1
Common Sense Asset Builder Fd 2
Common Sense Asset Builder Fd 3
Common Sense Asset Builder Fd 4
Common Sense Asset Builder Fd 5

Prosperity Capital Corporation

3365 Cider Mill Place
Mississauga, Ontario L5L 3H6
(416) 867-3863
Fax: (905) 569-6693
Prosperity American Performance

Protected American Fund

See Guardian Timing Services Inc.

Pursuit Financial Management Corp.

1200 Sheppard Avenue East
Suite 402
Willowdale, Ontario M2K 2S5
(416) 502-9300 (800) 253-9619
Fax: (416) 502-9394
Pursuit Canada Bond Fd
Pursuit Canadian Equity Fd
Pursuit Global Bond Fd
Pursuit Global Equity Fd
Pursuit Growth Fd
Pursuit Income Fd
Pursuit Money Market Fd

Quebec Growth Fund

See Montrusco Associates Inc.

Resolute Growth Fund

See Deacon Capital Corporation

Retrocom Growth Fund Inc.

89 The Queensway, #226
Mississauga, Ontario L5B 2V2
(905) 848-2430 (888) 743-5627
Retrocom Growth Fd

Royal Bank Investment Management Inc.

Royal Trust Tower,
P.O Box 7500
77 King Street West, 5th Floor
Toronto, Ontario M5W 1P9
(416) 955-3612 (800) 463-3863
Fax: (416) 955-3630
Royal Asian Growth Fd
Royal Balanced Fd
Royal Canadian Growth Fd
Royal Canadian Small Cap Fd
Royal Energy Fd
Royal European Growth Fd
Royal Income Fd
Royal International Equity Fd
Royal Japanese Stock Fd
Royal Latin American Fd
Royal LePage Comm Real Estate Fd
Royal Life Science & Tech Fd
Royal Precious Metals Fd
Royal Trust Advantage Balanced Fd
Royal Trust Advantage Growth Fd
Royal Trust Advantage Income Fd
Royal Trust American Stock Fd
Royal Trust Bond Fd
Royal Trust Canadian Money Mkt Fd
Royal Trust Canadian Stock Fd
Royal Trust Canadian T-Bill Fd
Royal Trust Growth and Income Fd
Royal Trust International Bond Fd
Royal Trust Mortgage Fd
Royal Trust U.S. Money Mkt Fd ($US)
RoyFund Bond Fd
RoyFund Canadian Equity Fd
RoyFund Canadian Money Market Fd
RoyFund Canadian T-Bill Fd
RoyFund Dividend Fd
RoyFund International Income Fd
RoyFund Mortgage Fd

RoyFund U.S. Equity Fd
Roy Fd U.S. Dollar Money Market Fd
Zweig Global Managed Assets Fd
Zweig Strategic Growth Fd

Royal LePage Commercial Real Estate
See Royal Mutual Funds Inc.

Royal Life Insurance Company of Canada
277 Lakeshore Road East
Suite 300
Oakville, Ontario L6J 1H9
(905) 842-6200 (800) 263-1747
Fax: (905) 842-6294
Royal Life Balanced Fd
Royal Life Canadian Growth Fd
Royal Life Equity Fd
Royal Life Income Fd
Royal Life International Equity Fd
Royal Life Money Market Fd

RoyFund Funds
See Royal Mutual Funds Inc.

Sagit Investment Management Ltd.
789 West Pender Street
Suite 900
Vancouver, BC V6C 1H2
(604) 685-3193 (800) 663-1003
Fax: (604) 681-7536
Cambridge American Growth Fd
Cambridge Americas Fd
Cambridge Balanced Fd
Cambridge China Fd
Cambridge Global Fd
Cambridge Growth Fd
Cambridge Pacific Fd
Cambridge Precious Metals Fd
Cambridge Resource Fd
Cambridge Special Equity Fd
Trans-Canada Bond Fd
Trans-Canada Dividend Fd
Trans-Canada Money Market Fd
Trans-Canada Pension Fd
Trans-Canada Value Fd

Saxon Funds
See Howson Tattersall Investment Counsel

Sceptre Investment Counsel Limited
26 Wellington St. East
Suite 1200
Toronto, Ontario M5E 1W4
(416) 360-4826 (800) 265-1888
Fax: (416) 367-5938
Sceptre Asian Growth Fd
Sceptre Balanced Growth Fd
Sceptre Bond Fd
Sceptre Equity Growth Fd
Sceptre International Fd
Sceptre Money Market Fd

Scotia Securities Inc.
Scotia Plaza, 40 King St. West
5th Floor
Toronto, Ontario M5H 1W1
(416) 866-2018 (800) 268-9269
Fax: (416) 933-2735
Scotia CanAm Growth Fd
Scotia CanAm Income Fd
Scotia Excelsior American Growth Fd
Scotia Excelsior Balanced Fd
Scotia Excelsior Canadian Blue-Chip Fd

Scotia Excelsior Canadian Growth Fd
Scotia Excelsior Dividend Fd
Scotia Excelsior Global Bond Fd
Scotia Excelsior Income Fd
Scotia Excelsior International Fd
Scotia Excelsior Latin America Fd
Scotia Excelsior Money Market Fd
Scotia Excelsior Mortgage Fd
Scotia Excelsior Pacific Rim Fd
Scotia Excelsior Precious Metals Fd
Scotia Excelsior Premium T-Bill Fd
Scotia Excelsior T-Bill Fd
Scotia Excelsior Total Return Fd

Scudder Funds of Canada

161 Bay Street, Box 712
Toronto, Ontario M5J 2S1
(800) 850-3863
Fax: (416) 350-2018
Scudder Canadian Equity Fd
Scudder Canadian Short Term Bond Fd
Scudder Emerging Markets Fd
Scudder Global Fd
Scudder Greater Europe Fd
Scudder Pacific Fd

Seaboard Life Insurance Company

2165 West Broadway
P.O. Box 5900
Vancouver, B.C. V6B 5H6
(604) 737-9107 (800) 363-2166
Fax: (604) 734-7207
APEX Asian Pacific
APEX Balanced Allocation Fd
APEX Equity Growth Fd
APEX Fixed Income Fd
APEX Money Market Fd
APEX Mortgage Fd

Societe Financiere Azura Inc.

1260 boul Lebourgneuf, Ste 150
Quebec, Quebec G2K 2G2
(418) 624-3000 (800) 231-6539
Azura Balanced Pooled Fd
Azura Balanced RSP Pooled Fd
Azura Conservative Pooled Fd
Azura Growth Pooled Fd
Azura Growth RSP Pooled Fd

Sogefonds MFQ Inc.

625, rue Saint Amable
Quebec, Quebec G1R 2G5
(418) 692-1221 (800) 667-SOGE
Fonds Ficadre Actions
Fonds Ficadre Equilibree
Fonds Ficadre Hypotheques
Fonds Ficadre Marche Monetaire
Fonds Ficadre Obligations

Special Opportunites Fd

See MOF Management Ltd.

Spectrum United Financial Services

145 King Street West, Suite 300
Toronto, Ontario M5H 1J8
(416) 352-3050 (800) 263-1851
Fax: (416) 360-2203
Bullock American Fd A
Bullock American Fd B
Bullock American Fd C
Bullock American Fd D
Bullock Asian Dynasty Fd A
Bullock Asian Dynasty Fd B
Bullock Asian Dynasty Fd C
Bullock Asset Strategy Fd A
Bullock Asset Strategy Fd B
Bullock Asset Strategy Fd C

Bullock Asset Strategy Fd D
Bullock Emerging Markets Fd A
Bullock Emerging Markets Fd B
Bullock Emerging Markets Fd C
Bullock European Enterprises A
Bullock European Enterprises B
Bullock European Enterprises C
Bullock Global Bond Fd A
Bullock Global Bond Fd B
Bullock Global Bond Fd C
Bullock Growth Fd A
Bullock Growth Fd B
Bullock Growth Fd C
Bullock Growth Fd D
Bullock Optimax USA Fd A
Bullock Optimax USA Fd B
Bullock Optimax USA Fd C
Canadian Investment Fd
Spectrum Canadian Equity Fd A
Spectrum Canadian Equity Fd B
Spectrum Canadian Equity Fd C
Spectrum Canadian Equity Fd D
Spectrum Cash Reserve Fd A
Spectrum Cash Reserve Fd B
Spectrum Cash Reserve Fd C
Spectrum Cash Reserve Fd D
Spectrum Diversified Fd A
Spectrum Diversified Fd B
Spectrum Diversified Fd C
Spectrum Diversified Fd D
Spectrum Dividend Fd A
Spectrum Dividend Fd B
Spectrum Dividend Fd C
Spectrum Dividend Fd D
Spectrum Government Bond Fd A
Spectrum Government Bond Fd B
Spectrum Government Bond Fd C
Spectrum Government Bond Fd D
Spectrum Interest Fd A
Spectrum Interest Fd B

Spectrum Interest Fd C
Spectrum Interest Fd D
Spectrum International Bond Fd A
Spectrum International Bond Fd B
Spectrum International Bond Fd C
Spectrum International Bond Fd D
Spectrum International Equity Fd A
Spectrum International Equity Fd B
Spectrum International Equity Fd C
Spectrum International Equity Fd D
Spectrum Savings Fd
Trillium Growth Capital Fd
United American Equity Fd
United American Growth Fd Ltd.
United Canadian Bond Fd
United Canadian Equity Fd
United Canadian Growth Fd
United Canadian Interest Fd
United Canadian Mortgage Fd
United Canadian Portfolio of Funds
United Global Equity Fd
United Global Growth Fd
United Global Portfolio of Funds
United Global Telecommunications Fd
United U.S. Dollar Money Market Fd

Sportfund Inc.
2892 South Sheridan Way
Suite 301
Oakville, Ontario L6J 7G9
(905) 970-7767 (800) 970-SPORT
Sportfund Inc.

Standard Life Mutual Funds Ltd.

1245 Sherbrooke Street West
Montreal, Quebec H3G 1G3
(514) 499-4188 (800) 665-6237
Fax: (514) 499-4466
Standard Life Balanced Mutual Fd
Standard Life Bond Mutual Fd
Standard Life Canadian Dividend Fd
Standard Life Equity Mutual Fd
Standard Life Growth Equity Fd
Standard Life International Bond Fd
Standard Life International Equity Fd
Standard Life Money Market Fd
Standard Life Natural Resource Fd
Standard Life U.S. Equity Fd
Standard Life Ideal Balanced Fd
Standard Life Ideal Bond Fd
Standard Life Ideal Equity Fd
Standard Life Ideal Money Market Fd

STAR Funds

See Mackenzie Financial Corporation

Strategic Value Fund

See BNP (Canada) Valeurs Mobiliers
Inc.

Stone & Co. Limited

155 University Ave, Suite 710
Toronto, Ontario M5H 3B7
(800) 336-9528
Fax: (416) 350-2018
Stone & Co. Flagship Stock Fd

Talvest Fund Management Inc.

130 King Street West
Suite 2200
Toronto, Ontario M5X 1B1
(416) 364-5620 (800) 268-8258
Fax: (416) 368-4243
Canadian Medical Discoveries Fd
Hyperion Asian Fd
Hyperion Aurora Fd
Hyperion European Fd
Hyperion Fixed Income Fd
Hyperion Value Line Equity Fd
Talvest Bond Fd
Talvest Diversified Fd
Talvest Foreign Pay Canadian Bond
Talvest Global Diversified Fd
Talvest Global RRSP Fd Inc.
Talvest Growth Fd Inc.
Talvest Income Fd
Talvest Money Fd
Talvest New Economy
Talvest U.S. Diversified Fd
Talvest U.S. Growth Fd Ltd.

Teachers' RSP - Equity Section

See Montreal Trust Co. of Canada

Templeton Management Ltd,

4 King Street West
P.O. Box 4070, Station A
Toronto, Ontario M5W 1M3
(416) 364-4672 (800) 387-0830
Fax: (416) 364-1163
Templeton Balanced Fd
Templeton Cdn Asset Allocation Fd
Templeton Canadian Bond Fd
Templeton Canadian Stock Fd
Templeton Emerging Markets Fd
Templeton Global Balanced Fd

Templeton Global Bond Fd
Templeton Global Smaller Cos Fd
Templeton Growth Fd Ltd.
Templeton International Balanced Fd
Templeton International Stock Fd
Templeton Treasury Bill Fd

Toronto-Dominion Securities Inc.

Toronto-Dominion Centre
P.O. Box 100
Toronto-Dominion Bank Tower
26th Floor
Toronto, Ontario M5K 1G8
(416) 982-6432 (800) 268-8166
Fax: (416) 982-6625
Green Line Asian Growth Fd
Green Line Balanced Growth Fd
Green Line Balanced Income Fd
Green Line Blue Chip Equity Fd
Green Line Canadian Bond Fd
Green Line Canadian Equity Fd
Green Line Canadian Gov't Bond Fd
Green Line Canadian Index Fd
Green Line Cdn Money Market Fd
Green Line Canadian T-Bill Fd
Green Line Dividend Fd
Green Line Emerging Markets Fd
Green Line Energy Fd
Green Line European Growth Fd
Green Line Global Gov't Bond Fd
Green Line Global RSP Bond Fd
Green Line Global Select Fd
Green Line International Equity Fd
Green Line Japanese Growth Fd
Green Line Latin American Growth Fd
Green Line Mortgage-Backed Fd
Green Line Mortgage Fd
Green Line North Amer Growth Fd A
Green Line Precious Metals Fd

Green Line Real Return Bond Fd
Green Line Resource Fd
Green Line Science & Technology Fd
Green Line Short Term Income Fd
Green Line U.S. Index Fd ($US)
Green Line U.S. Money Mkt Fd (US$)
Green Line Value Fd

Top Fifty Funds

See Majendie Securities Ltd.

Tradex Management Inc.

45 O'Connor Street, Suite 1860
Ottawa, Ontario K1P 1A4
(613) 233-3394 (800) 567-FUND
Fax: (613) 233-8191
Tradex Bond Fd
Tradex Emerging Markets Country Fd
Tradex Equity Fd Limited

Trans-Canada Funds

See Sagit Investment Management
Ltd.

Transamerica Life Insurance Co. of Canada

300 Consilium Place
Scarborough, Ontario M1H 3G2
(416) 290-2818
Fax: (416) 290-2896
Growsafe Balanced Fd
Growsafe Canadian Bond Fd
Growsafe Canadian Equity Fd
Growsafe Canadian Money Market Fd
Growsafe International Balanced Fd
Growsafe U.S Equity Fd

Triax Growth Fund Inc.
1 University Ave, Suite 600
Toronto, Ontario M5J 2P1
(416) 362-2929 (800) 407-0287
Triax Growth Fd

Trillium Growth Capital Inc.
See Spectrum United Financial Services

Trimark Investment Management Inc.
One First Canadian Place
Suite 5600, P.O. Box 487
Toronto, Ontario M5X 1E5
(416) 362-7181 (800) 387-9845
Fax: (416) 368-6331
Trimark - The Americas Fd
Trimark Advantage Bond Fd
Trimark Canadian Bond Fd
Trimark Canadian Fd
Trimark Discovery Fd
Trimark Fd
Trimark Government Income Fd
Trimark Income Growth Fd
Trimark Indo-Pacific Fd
Trimark Interest Fd
Trimark RSP Equity Fd
Trimark Select Balanced Fd
Trimark Select Canadian Growth Fd
Trimark Select Growth Fd

Trust Pret et Revenu du Canada
850 Place d'Youville
Quebec, Quebec G1R 3P6
(418) 692-1221 (800) 667-7643
Fax: (418) 692-1679
Trust Pret & Revenu American Fd
Trust Pret & Revenu Bond Fd
Trust Pret & Revenu Canadian Fd

Trust Pret & Revenu Dividend Fd
Trust Pret & Revenu H Fd
Trust Pret & Revenu International Fd
Trust Pret & Revenu Money Mkt Fd
Trust Pret & Revenu Retirement Fd
Trust Pret & Revenu World Bond Fd

United Funds
See Spectrum United Financial Services

Universal Funds
See Mackenzie Financial Corporation

University Avenue Management Ltd.
40 University Ave.
Toronto, Ontario M5J 1T1
(416) 351-1617 (800) 465-1812
Fax: (416) 366-2700
University Avenue Bond Fd
University Avenue Canadian Fd
University Avenue Growth Fd

Vengrowth Investment Fd Inc.
See BPI Capital Management
  Corporation

Vision Europe Fund
See National Bank Securities Inc.

M. K. Wong & Associates Ltd.
33 Yonge Street, Suite 1050
Toronto, Ontario M5E 1S9
(416) 361-3370 (800) 665-9360
Fax: (416) 361-6345
Lotus Balanced Fd
Lotus Bond Fd
Lotus Canadian Equity Fd

Lotus Income Fd
Lotus International Bond Fd

Westbury Canadian Life Insurance Co.
21 King Street West
Suite 1100
Hamilton, Ontario L8N 3R5
(905) 528-6766 (800) 263-9241
Westbury Canadian Balanced Fd
Westbury Canadian Bond Fd
Westbury Canadian Equity Fd

Working Opportunity Fund
1055 West Georgia Street
Suite 2901
P.O. Box 11170, Royal Centre
Vancouver, BC V6E 3R5
(604) 688-9631
Fax: (604) 669-7605
Working Opportunity Fd

Working Ventures Investment Services Inc.
250 Bloor St. East, Suite 1600
Toronto, Ontario M4W 1E6
(416) 922-5479 (800) 268-8244
Fax: (416) 929-2752
Working Ventures Canadian Fund Inc.

20/20 Funds Inc.
690 Dorval Drive Suite 700
Oakville, Ontario L6K 3X9
(905) 339-2020 (800) 268-8690
Fax: (905) 339-3863
20/20 Aggressive Growth Fd
20/20 Amer Tactical Asset Alloc Fd
20/20 Asia Pacific Fd
20/20 Canadian Growth Fd

20/20 Cdn Tactical Asset Alloc Fd
20/20 Dividend Fd
20/20 European Asset Allocation Fd
20/20 Foreign RSP Bond Fd
20/20 Income Fd
20/20 India Fd
20/20 International Value Fd
20/20 Latin America Fd
20/20 Managed Futures Value Fd
20/20 Money Market Fd
20/20 Multimanager Emerg Mkts Fd
20/20 RSP Aggressive Equity Fd
20/20 RSP Int'l Equity Allocation Fd
20/20 US Short-term High Yield Fd
20/20 World Bond Fd
20/20 World Fd

Zweig Funds
See Royal Mutual Funds Inc.

The Growth of an Investment

This table shows:

1. How an investment of $100 a month (ignoring acquisition fees) would have grown if invested in a typical Canadian equity fund during the 10 years ended June 30, 1996, and,

2. A withdrawal plan in which $100,000 (ignoring any acquisition or redemption fees) was invested at June 30, 1986, and $833 a month was withdrawn for the subsequent 10 years.

Month	Return	Cumulative contribution	Value of plan	Cumulative withdrawal	Value of plan
Jul-86	-3.2%	$100	$97	$833	$95,980
Aug-86	4.5%	$200	$206	$1,667	$99,509
Sep-86	-0.2%	$300	$305	$2,500	$98,452
Oct-86	1.1%	$400	$409	$3,333	$98,655
Nov-86	1.5%	$500	$517	$4,167	$99,288
Dec-86	-1.2%	$600	$610	$5,000	$97,291
Jan-87	7.0%	$700	$759	$5,833	$103,276
Feb-87	3.4%	$800	$889	$6,667	$105,948
Mar-87	6.8%	$900	$1,056	$7,500	$112,301
Apr-87	0.6%	$1,000	$1,163	$8,333	$112,158
May-87	1.0%	$1,100	$1,275	$9,167	$112,391
Jun-87	2.0%	$1,200	$1,402	$10,000	$113,825
Jul-87	4.9%	$1,300	$1,577	$10,833	$118,619
Aug-87	-0.3%	$1,400	$1,673	$11,667	$117,488
Sep-87	-2.1%	$1,500	$1,736	$12,500	$114,213
Oct-87	-15.4%	$1,600	$1,554	$13,333	$95,825
Nov-87	-0.4%	$1,700	$1,647	$14,167	$94,628
Dec-87	-7.5%	$1,80C	$1,616	$15,000	$86,678
Jan-88	-1.3%	$1,900	$1,693	$15,833	$84,685
Feb-88	3.4%	$2,000	$1,854	$16,667	$86,722
Mar-88	3.6%	$2,100	$2,024	$17,500	$89,016
Apr-88	1.0%	$2,200	$2,146	$18,333	$89,099
May-88	-1.6%	$2,300	$2,211	$19,167	$86,870

Month	Return	Cumulative contribution	Value of plan	Cumulative withdrawal	Value of plan
Jun-88	4.1%	$2,400	$2,406	$20,000	$89,630
Jul-88	-1.1%	$2,500	$2,480	$20,833	$87,838
Aug-88	-1.7%	$2,600	$2,536	$21,667	$85,513
Sep-88	0.3%	$2,700	$2,644	$22,500	$84,948
Oct-88	3.1%	$2,800	$2,828	$23,333	$86,709
Nov-88	-3.0%	$2,900	$2,839	$24,167	$83,240
Dec-88	2.4%	$3,000	$3,008	$25,000	$84,364
Jan-89	5.7%	$3,100	$3,286	$25,833	$88,359
Feb-89	-0.5%	$3,200	$3,368	$26,667	$87,061
Mar-89	-0.2%	$3,300	$3,463	$27,500	$86,096
Apr-89	1.7%	$3,400	$3,625	$28,333	$86,761
May-89	3.1%	$3,500	$3,838	$29,167	$88,575
Jun-89	2.5%	$3,600	$4,035	$30,000	$89,916
Jul-89	5.1%	$3,700	$4,348	$30,833	$93,708
Aug-89	0.9%	$3,800	$4,490	$31,667	$93,754
Sep-89	-0.9%	$3,900	$4,550	$32,500	$92,112
Oct-89	-0.4%	$4,000	$4,631	$33,333	$90,908
Nov-89	1.6%	$4,100	$4,808	$34,167	$91,542
Dec-89	0.5%	$4,200	$4,933	$35,000	$91,181
Jan-90	-5.7%	$4,300	$4,745	$35,833	$85,125
Feb-90	1.0%	$4,400	$4,893	$36,667	$85,144
Mar-90	0.4%	$4,500	$5,011	$37,500	$84,612
Apr-90	-7.3%	$4,600	$4,736	$38,333	$77,573
May-90	7.4%	$4,700	$5,193	$39,167	$82,466
Jun-90	-0.6%	$4,800	$5,263	$40,000	$81,165
Jul-90	0.5%	$4,900	$5,390	$40,833	$80,737
Aug-90	-4.5%	$5,000	$5,244	$41,667	$76,296
Sep-90	-4.0%	$5,100	$5,130	$42,500	$72,404
Oct-90	-2.2%	$5,200	$5,117	$43,333	$70,003
Nov-90	2.5%	$5,300	$5,349	$44,167	$70,940
Dec-90	1.8%	$5,400	$5,549	$45,000	$71,414
Jan-91	0.8%	$5,500	$5,693	$45,833	$71,137
Feb-91	4.9%	$5,600	$6,075	$46,667	$73,764
Mar-91	2.1%	$5,700	$6,302	$47,500	$74,451
Apr-91	-0.6%	$5,800	$6,366	$48,333	$73,188
May-91	2.7%	$5,900	$6,639	$49,167	$74,320
Jun-91	-1.3%	$6,000	$6,653	$50,000	$72,542
Jul-91	2.4%	$6,100	$6,913	$50,833	$73,422
Aug-91	-0.6%	$6,200	$6,974	$51,667	$72,178
Sep-91	-1.5%	$6,300	$6,969	$52,500	$70,278
Oct-91	3.5%	$6,400	$7,316	$53,333	$71,903
Nov-91	-1.7%	$6,500	$7,289	$54,167	$69,830

Month	Return	Cumulative contribution	Value of plan	Cumulative withdrawal	Value of plan
Dec-91	-7.8%	$6,600	$6,812	$55,000	$63,548
Jan-92	4.6%	$6,700	$7,232	$55,833	$65,652
Feb-92	2.1%	$6,800	$7,483	$56,667	$66,172
Mar-92	-4.1%	$6,900	$7,271	$57,500	$62,617
Apr-92	-3.0%	$7,000	$7,149	$58,333	$59,899
May-92	2.0%	$7,100	$7,395	$59,167	$60,274
Jun-92	-0.2%	$7,200	$7,478	$60,000	$59,303
Jul-92	1.4%	$7,300	$7,688	$60,833	$59,329
Aug-92	-0.5%	$7,400	$7,747	$61,667	$58,183
Sep-92	0.3%	$7,500	$7,871	$62,500	$57,526
Oct-92	-0.3%	$7,600	$7,947	$63,333	$56,519
Nov-92	0.1%	$7,700	$8,053	$64,167	$55,729
Dec-92	4.7%	$7,800	$8,532	$65,000	$57,490
Jan-93	3.9%	$7,900	$8,969	$65,833	$58,898
Feb-93	4.5%	$8,000	$9,479	$66,667	$60,732
Mar-93	7.5%	$8,100	$10,299	$67,500	$64,463
Apr-93	7.6%	$8,200	$11,185	$68,333	$68,501
May-93	5.4%	$8,300	$11,893	$69,167	$71,357
Jun-93	8.5%	$8,400	$13,013	$70,000	$76,589
Jul-93	-5.6%	$8,500	$12,374	$70,833	$71,442
Aug-93	7.4%	$8,600	$13,395	$71,667	$75,881
Sep-93	-5.0%	$8,700	$12,819	$72,500	$71,251
Oct-93	4.7%	$8,800	$13,532	$73,333	$73,795
Nov-93	-0.3%	$8,900	$13,594	$74,167	$72,758
Dec-93	6.1%	$9,000	$14,535	$75,000	$76,394
Jan-94	2.5%	$9,100	$15,001	$75,833	$77,471
Feb-94	-4.5%	$9,200	$14,421	$76,667	$73,146
Mar-94	-2.6%	$9,300	$14,142	$77,500	$70,404
Apr-94	-2.3%	$9,400	$13,917	$78,333	$67,965
May-94	-0.2%	$9,500	$13,992	$79,167	$67,013
Jun-94	-6.3%	$9,600	$13,211	$80,000	$61,988
Jul-94	5.7%	$9,700	$14,075	$80,833	$64,711
Aug-94	1.0%	$9,800	$14,317	$81,667	$64,526
Sep-94	1.4%	$9,900	$14,619	$82,500	$64,597
Oct-94	-1.3%	$10,000	$14,524	$83,333	$62,908
Nov-94	-6.9%	$10,100	$13,617	$84,167	$57,744
Dec-94	1.9%	$10,200	$13,979	$85,000	$58,014
Jan-95	-6.9%	$10,300	$13,104	$85,833	$53,163
Feb-95	3.8%	$10,400	$13,700	$86,666	$54,326
Mar-95	3.0%	$10,500	$14,216	$87,500	$55,131
Apr-95	-0.4%	$10,600	$14,260	$88,333	$54,082

Month	Return	Cumulative contribution	Value of plan	Cumulative withdrawal	Value of plan
May-95	2.7%	$10,700	$14,754	$89,166	$54,733
Jun-95	1.0%	$10,800	$14,996	$90,000	$54,421
Jul-95	2.4%	$10,900	$15,457	$90,833	$54,890
Aug-95	-1.6%	$11,000	$15,308	$91,666	$53,179
Sep-95	0.5%	$11,100	$15,485	$92,500	$52,612
Oct-95	-3.5%	$11,200	$15,043	$93,333	$49,946
Nov-95	2.8%	$11,300	$15,572	$94,166	$50,529
Dec-95	1.7%	$11,400	$15,942	$95,000	$50,566
Jan-96	2.9%	$11,500	$16,502	$95,833	$51,184
Feb-96	-1.2%	$11,600	$16,411	$96,666	$49,761
Mar-96	1.5%	$11,700	$16,764	$97,500	$49,691
Apr-96	4.3%	$11,800	$17,588	$98,333	$50,989
May-96	1.3%	$11,900	$17,923	$99,166	$50,835
Jun-96	-4.1%	$12,000	$17,281	$100,000	$47,909

APPENDIX 2

Survey of Annual Fund Performance

THIS SURVEY SIMPLY SHOWS the year-over-year annual returns for the funds for the past 20 years. Its purpose is to show the historical range of annual returns. Compounded returns as shown in Appendix 4 (which are the most commonly published rates of return and are often used for advertising purposes) can often hide year-over-year volatility. Tables © Portfolio Analytics Limited, 1996.

Fund	1996	1995	1994	1993	1992	1991	1990	1989	1988	1987	1986	1985	1984	1983	1982	1981	1980	1979	1978	1977
20/20 Aggressive Growth	14.5	32.0	1.4																	
20/20 Amer Tac Asset Alloc	9.7	21.8	-5.1	22.3	21.1	14.0	0.1													
20/20 Asia Pacific	5.6	-12.7	19.6																	
20/20 Canadian Growth	7.8	7.4	10.6	17.5	-0.8	13.8	-9.0													
20/20 Cdn Tac Asset Alloc	11.7	6.6	5.4	14.8	5.6	15.8	-1.3													
20/20 Dividend	17.0	13.4	9.0	17.5	4.7	14.8	-7.2	17.1	0.5	15.2										
20/20 Emerg Mkts Value	-2.0	-23.7																		
20/20 European Asset Alloc	9.7	7.5	1.8																	
20/20 Foreign RSP Bond	5.4	11.5	-7.1																	
20/20 Income	8.3	11.2	-2.5	12.7	11.9	17.0	-1.0	12.9	0.5	10.2										
20/20 India	-33.8																			
20/20 Int'l Value	11.9	9.2	10.0	23.2	12.5	15.6	1.7													
20/20 Latin America	8.2	-21.9																		
20/20 Managed Futures Val	13.5																			
20/20 Money Market	5.3	5.9	4.3	5.5	7.2	10.4														
20/20 RSP Aggressive Equity	60.4	24.1																		
20/20 RSP Int'l Equity Alloc	14.5	6.6																		
20/20 US S-T High Yield	8.4	5.9																		
20/20 World	6.6	-5.5	12.1	37.3	4.3	19.2	-19.6	19.0	-2.4											
20/20 World Bond	6.4	13.5	-9.7																	
ABC Fully-Managed	20.4	6.8	16.5	47.9	3.7	17.2	1.4	23.8												
ABC Fundamental Value	18.9	2.4	25.7	91.5	7.3	25.8	-2.2													
Acadia Balanced	6.4																			
Acadia Bond	6.8																			
Acadia Money Market	4.5																			
Acadia Mortgage	3.7																			
ADMAX Amer Select Growth	2.3	16.4	-0.1	9.7																
ADMAX Asset Allocation	10.9	3.3	6.1	15.8																
ADMAX Cdn Performance	17.2	6.4	3.0	20.7	2.7	3.7														
ADMAX Cash Performance	4.3	5.4	3.5																	
ADMAX Cdn Select Growth	4.3	9.1	-1.5	9.7	-3.7															
ADMAX Dragon 888	-4.9	-11.6																		

Fund	1996	1995	1994	1993	1992	1991	1990	1989	1988	1987	1986	1985	1984	1983	1982	1981	1980	1979	1978	1977
ADMAX Europa Perform	9.3	6.4	3.4	-2.5																
ADMAX Global Health & Sci	31.7	58.8	4.9																	
ADMAX International	-5.2	3.8	20.0	35.6	9.6	8.4	-18.7	19.0												
ADMAX Korea	-29.2	-0.2	33.4	22.4	-12.3															
ADMAX Nippon	12.8	-4.0	-3.2	17.2																
ADMAX Tiger	-16.4	-12.7	27.7	37.6	12.3	15.9														
ADMAX World Income	11.9	6.4	1.9	19.9																
AGF Cdn Bond A	11.4	14.4	-3.5	14.4	16.4	20.4	1.1	11.3	17.4	-4.2	21.7	21.4	11.6	20.6	33.6	-4.5	-0.4	3.4	7.7	14.0
AGF Cdn Bond B	10.8																			
AGF Cdn Bond C	10.8																			
AGF Cdn Equity A	20.0	3.4	5.0	21.1	4.1	5.6	-21.4	18.5	-12.2	19.3	24.1	20.9	8.0	59.1	-2.0	-3.4	33.3	30.2	40.8	11.0
AGF Cdn Equity B	19.4																			
AGF Cdn Equity C	19.1																			
AGF Cdn Resources A	41.4	-3.2	-4.2	83.2	15.6	-15.4	6.3	14.8	-29.6	70.7	-9.3	-6.1	-10.6	40.8	-22.1	-23.8	53.8	60.2	37.0	30.9
AGF Cdn Resources B	40.9																			
AGF Cdn Resources C	40.5																			
AGF Cdn Asset Alloc Serv A	12.2	8.5	3.0	18.6	11.0	13.6														
AGF Cdn Asset Alloc Serv B	10.4																			
AGF Cdn Asset Alloc Serv C	10.4																			
AGF Global Gov't Bond A	9.2	10.3	-3.0	7.2	25.5	9.2	14.3	3.9	7.9											
AGF Global Gov't Bond B	8.6																			
AGF Global Gov't Bond C	8.4																			
AGF Growth & Income A	30.8	6.1	8.9	18.3	7.3	15.8	-13.2	14.7	-2.5	18.2	7.1	17.8	5.0	46.0	4.4	-2.1	16.0	17.7	22.4	10.0
AGF Growth & Income B	30.8																			
AGF Growth & Income C	31.0																			
AGF Growth Equity A	24.1	3.3	1.1	63.2	15.8	10.9	-16.2	16.6	-24.6	28.4	27.2	18.0	-3.3	59.3	-19.8	-17.3	56.3	56.0	54.8	24.7
AGF Growth Equity B	23.6																			
AGF Growth Equity C	23.2																			
AGF High Income A	11.9	9.0	3.8	7.6	13.4	10.4	6.6													
AGF High Income B	11.2																			
AGF High Income C	11.3																			
AGF Int'l Grp Germany A	18.1																			

Fund	1996	1995	1994	1993	1992	1991	1990	1989	1988	1987	1986	1985	1984	1983	1982	1981	1980	1979	1978	1977
AGF Int'l Grp Germany B	17.2																			
AGF Int'l Grp Germany C	17.2																			
AGF Int'l Grp Germany M	18.9																			
AGF Int'l Grp Amer Gth A	20.0	28.7	1.3	26.5	12.8	20.4	-15.7	25.7	-15.9	22.1	24.3	13.8	7.0	47.7	13.7	3.8	39.5	12.4	30.2	1.0
AGF Int'l Grp Amer Gth B	19.6																			
AGF Int'l Grp Amer Gth C	19.1																			
AGF Int'l Grp Asia Growth A	4.5	-0.3	37.4	36.1																
AGF Int'l Grp Asia Growth B	4.0																			
AGF Int'l Grp Asia Growth C	4.0																			
AGF Int'l Grp China Focus A	-1.1	-9.1																		
AGF Int'l Grp China Focus B	-1.6	-9.6																		
AGF Int'l Grp China Focus C	-1.5	-9.8																		
AGF Int'l Grp Euro Growth A	16.7	8.4																		
AGF Int'l Grp Euro Growth B	16.5	7.7																		
AGF Int'l Grp Euro Growth C	16.4	8.1																		
AGF Int'l Grp Japan A	4.0	-13.7	0.7	41.7	-12.3	10.3	-26.4	17.0	-9.1	34.6	76.0	35.3	11.4	68.7	-20.6	20.4	28.7	-12.6	55.1	20.5
AGF Int'l Grp Japan B	3.7																			
AGF Int'l Grp Japan C	3.4																			
AGF Int'l Grp S-T Income A	3.4																			
AGF Int'l Grp S-T Income B	2.8																			
AGF Int'l Grp S-T Income C	2.9																			
AGF Int'l Grp Special A	3.8	27.0	-0.6	23.2	13.4	37.4	-17.3	24.0	-12.5	24.3	24.6	16.8	-4.3	77.2	14.8	-9.8	53.0	22.5	59.9	23.5
AGF Int'l Grp Special B	3.1																			
AGF Int'l Grp Special C	3.3																			
AGF Int'l Grp World Eq A	7.8																			
AGF Int'l Grp World Eq B	7.2																			
AGF Int'l Grp World Eq C	7.2																			
AGF Money Market Acct A	4.5	5.9	4.0	4.9	6.4	10.2	12.3	11.3	8.6	7.9	8.9	10.4	9.9	10.2	16.9	17.3	13.7	10.5	7.2	6.6
AGF Money Market Acct B	3.9																			
AGF Money Market Acct C	4.5																			
AGF RSP Global Income A	5.9	8.4	-0.3																	
AGF RSP Global Income B	5.1																			

Fund	1996	1995	1994	1993	1992	1991	1990	1989	1988	1987	1986	1985	1984	1983	1982	1981	1980	1979	1978	1977
AGF RSP Global Income C	5.4																			
AGF US Asset Alloc Serv A	7.7	11.9	-3.7																	
AGF US Asset Alloc Serv B	7.2																			
AGF US Asset Alloc Serv C	7.1																			
AGF US Income A	3.8	8.4	-8.4																	
AGF US Income B	3.3																			
AGF US Income C	3.3																			
AGF US$ Money Mkt Acct	4.6	4.8	3.0	2.7	3.9															
AIC Advantage	59.6	18.7	6.2	43.6	18.5	31.7	-26.1	22.4	-18.0	24.9										
AIC Diversified Canada	50.6																			
AIC Emerging Markets	8.8	-20.4																		
AIC Money Markets	4.3	5.8																		
AIC Value	33.8	27.6	1.7	33.7	15.4	40.1														
AIC World Equity	7.7	2.7																		
All-Canadian Capital	5.1	7.9	20.9	15.8	5.2	-0.4	0.7	9.9	-10.7	23.8	15.2	10.3	5.0	29.3	12.1	15.6	18.4	10.7	29.2	13.5
All-Canadian Compound	4.5	7.6	20.7	15.8	5.1	-0.3	0.7	9.9	-10.6	23.6	15.3	10.4	4.9	29.1	12.1	15.5	18.4	10.5	29.3	13.5
All-Canadian Consumer	2.8	2.3	12.4																	
All-Canadian Res Corp	-2.1	3.6	34.4	35.4	4.5	-14.4	-19.7	2.8	-18.3	45.4	1.0	-1.1	-9.8	24.8	4.8	1.8	28.2	15.2	27.9	14.3
Altafund Invest Corp	34.9	-1.1	8.6	46.4	20.6															
Altamira Asia Pacific	-16.8	-14.5	26.6	33.2																
Altamira Balanced	7.2	5.6	0.7	29.4	10.8	1.8	-9.3	15.3	-16.9	18.3	20.2									
Altamira Bond	11.1	21.6	-6.7	17.4	17.0	19.6	4.6	9.6												
Altamira Capital Growth	3.5	3.6	18.1	19.5	19.8	7.7	-6.3	26.2	-8.4	16.3	8.0	9.8	-3.2	39.6	15.5	-4.6	21.7	27.9	34.9	10.4
Altamira Dividend	16.0	13.5																		
Altamira Equity	14.1	5.2	10.1	44.5	44.3	14.0	9.0	48.7												
Altamira European Equity	14.2	13.0	10.5																	
Altamira Global Bond	7.5	12.9	-5.6																	
Altamira Global Discovery	6.0	-16.6																		
Altamira Global Diversified	17.0	3.7	7.8	16.0	8.4	2.7	-19.4	14.4	-25.3	15.0	29.2									
Altamira Growth & Income	9.5	-6.1	19.3	16.4	13.9	14.8	1.0	16.8	8.8	11.5										
Altamira Income	8.0	17.3	-2.5	16.4	18.3	22.4	7.3	11.1	14.9	4.5	11.3	16.0	7.8	19.0	24.7	6.6	7.7	7.6	7.4	11.4
Altamira Japanese Opp	7.1	-15.0																		

Fund	1996	1995	1994	1993	1992	1991	1990	1989	1988	1987	1986	1985	1984	1983	1982	1981	1980	1979	1978	1977
Altamira NA Recovery	14.5	-4.4	16.6	...	...	...	...	...	...	...	...	...	...	...	...	...	...	...	...	...
Altamira P&S Metals	39.8	21.0	...	...	...	...	...	...	...	...	...	...	...	...	...	...	...	...	...	...
Altamira Resource	25.5	-10.0	-0.2	75.6	60.7	7.9	...	...	...	...	...	...	...	...	...	...	...	...	...	...
Altamira S-T Global Income	4.7	0.3	5.5	6.9	21.7	...	...	...	...	...	...	...	...	...	...	...	...	...	...	...
Altamira S-T Govt Bond	8.1	14.0	...	...	...	...	...	...	...	...	...	...	...	...	...	...	...	...	...	...
Altamira Science & Tech	26.7	...	...	...	...	...	...	...	...	...	...	...	...	...	...	...	...	...	...	...
Altamira Select American	14.7	18.1	11.8	47.4	21.1	...	...	...	...	...	...	...	...	...	...	...	...	...	...	...
Altamira Spec High Yield B	14.8	...	...	...	...	...	...	...	...	...	...	...	...	...	...	...	...	...	...	...
Altamira Special Growth	27.2	1.5	-10.7	46.1	37.3	17.9	-5.2	27.1	-21.5	16.5	...	...	...	...	...	...	...	...	...	...
Altamira US Larger Co	10.9	33.5	6.4	...	...	...	...	...	...	...	...	...	...	...	...	...	...	...	...	...
AMI Private Cap Equity	22.2	4.8	8.5	19.5	-0.4	6.0	-17.9	22.9	...	...	...	...	...	...	...	...	...	...	...	...
AMI Private Cap Money Mkt	5.3	6.3	4.4	5.6	7.0	10.7	11.6	10.3	...	...	...	...	...	...	...	...	...	...	...	...
AMI Private Cap Optimix	16.8	8.6	3.6	15.1	7.0	13.3	-5.9	15.2	...	...	...	...	...	...	...	...	...	...	...	...
AMI Private Capital Income	10.9	12.0	-0.9	12.4	14.2	19.6	2.7	9.8	...	...	...	...	...	...	...	...	...	...	...	...
Apex Asian Pacific	5.1	-0.2	...	...	...	...	...	...	...	...	...	...	...	...	...	...	...	...	...	...
Apex Balanced Allocation	10.3	8.4	...	...	...	...	...	...	...	...	...	...	...	...	...	...	...	...	...	...
Apex Equity Growth	19.1	6.6	...	...	...	...	...	...	...	...	...	...	...	...	...	...	...	...	...	...
Apex Fixed Income	9.8	11.3	...	...	...	...	...	...	...	...	...	...	...	...	...	...	...	...	...	...
Apex Money Market	4.5	6.1	...	...	...	...	...	...	...	...	...	...	...	...	...	...	...	...	...	...
Apex Mortgage	7.4	...	...	...	...	...	...	...	...	...	...	...	...	...	...	...	...	...	...	...
Asset Builder I	11.9	12.1	...	...	...	...	...	...	...	...	...	...	...	...	...	...	...	...	...	...
Asset Builder II	12.2	11.7	...	...	...	...	...	...	...	...	...	...	...	...	...	...	...	...	...	...
Asset Builder III	13.1	10.4	...	...	...	...	...	...	...	...	...	...	...	...	...	...	...	...	...	...
Asset Builder IV	12.7	9.7	...	...	...	...	...	...	...	...	...	...	...	...	...	...	...	...	...	...
Asset Builder V	12.9	10.0	...	...	...	...	...	...	...	...	...	...	...	...	...	...	...	...	...	...
Associate Investors	19.9	7.7	2.5	17.2	1.3	12.0	-11.5	17.1	-1.2	16.9	12.2	20.5	4.1	49.1	-7.3	-8.8	22.9	32.8	25.0	14.5
Atlas Amer Large Cap Gth	19.5	24.7	1.2	4.1	18.6	28.7	-10.3	11.3	-17.7	16.7	...	...	...	...	...	...	...	...	...	...
Atlas Amer Money Market	4.5	4.7	2.7	2.1	3.3	5.9	7.6	7.8	6.3	...	...	...	...	...	...	...	...	...	...	...
Atlas Amer Advan Value	17.6	...	...	...	...	...	...	...	...	...	...	...	...	...	...	...	...	...	...	...
Atlas Canadian Balanced	14.2	13.1	2.2	10.7	7.0	15.3	-5.9	...	...	...	...	...	...	...	...	...	...	...	...	...
Atlas Canadian Bond	10.5	12.4	-1.8	11.8	13.9	16.9	3.6	8.5	13.1	0.7	13.8	...	...	...	...	...	...	...	...	...
Atlas Canadian Money Mkt	4.6	5.9	4.1	4.8	6.4	10.0	12.6	10.6	8.5	7.8	9.3	...	...	...	...	...	...	...	...	...

Fund	1996	1995	1994	1993	1992	1991	1990	1989	1988	1987	1986	1985	1984	1983	1982	1981	1980	1979	1978	1977
Atlas Canadian T-Bill	4.4	5.7	3.8	4.6	6.1	9.7	12.2	10.6	9.4											
Atlas Cdn Large Cap Growth	21.1	9.0	6.5	9.8	-2.4	14.8	-14.2	19.1	-11.4	20.4										
Atlas Cdn Large Cap Value	7.0																			
Atlas Cdn Emerg Growth	43.0																			
Atlas Cdn Emerg Value	26.7																			
Atlas Cdn High Yield Bond	12.4																			
Atlas European Value	16.6	12.5																		
Atlas Global Value	9.5	4.1	13.6	25.1	11.8	10.2														
Atlas Latin Amer Value	24.7	-39.6																		
Atlas Managed Futures	-3.3																			
Atlas Pacific Basin Value	-3.4	-10.0																		
Atlas World Bond	11.3	12.5																		
Azura Balanced Pooled	9.5																			
Azura Conservative Pooled	8.2																			
Azura Growth Pooled	12.2																			
Batirente Sec Diversifee	13.2	13.4	0.2	14.4	9.9	17.4	-3.3	13.4												
Batirente Sec Marche Monet	4.3	5.9	4.2	5.5	7.0	11.5	11.7	9.9												
Batirente Sec Obligations	12.8	15.9	-0.5	15.0	15.0	22.8	0.4	12.2												
Batirente Section Actions	16.6	6.2																		
Beutel Goodman Amer Eqty	12.8	15.3	6.2	27.7	17.3															
Beutel Goodman Balanced	12.0	6.8	9.8	14.1	6.8															
Beutel Goodman Cdn Equity	13.5	1.4	20.4	12.7	-4.4															
Beutel Goodman Income	11.4	14.7	-2.7	12.2	15.4															
Beutel Goodman Int'l Equity	11.6	-3.5	17.3	47.2																
Beutel Goodman Money Mkt	5.3	6.5	4.7	5.6	8.5															
Beutel Goodman Private Bal	14.1	11.9	5.8	16.8	14.8	19.4														
Beutel Goodman Small Cap	40.4																			
Bissett American Equity	13.3	24.6	4.2	10.3	19.1	22.8	-12.6	22.1	-17.8	20.9	8.3									
Bissett Bond	12.7	14.1	0.3	12.2	11.0	20.4	3.9	10.5	13.6	1.7										
Bissett Canadian Equity	26.5	12.7	3.7	31.0	7.9	14.9	-12.3	22.7	-9.8	22.2	18.4	15.6	2.2							
Bissett Dividend Income	22.0	16.3	4.4	15.3	5.5	15.0	-12.2	14.0												

Fund	1996	1995	1994	1993	1992	1991	1990	1989	1988	1987	1986	1985	1984	1983	1982	1981	1980	1979	1978	1977
Bissett Money Market	5.8	6.7	4.7	5.6	6.8															
Bissett Multinational Growth	23.8	18.7																		
Bissett Retirement	18.7	14.6	2.6	20.6	9.5															
Bissett Small Capital	34.9	8.1	6.9	102.4																
BNP Canada Bond	10.8	12.9	-1.3	12.4	15.6															
BNP Canada Money Market	4.7	5.7	3.9	4.5	7.3															
BNP Canada Equity	17.4	6.5	7.4	14.0	3.2															
BPI Amer Equity Value	13.2	21.1	5.3	15.5	13.1	22.6	-4.3													
BPI America Small Co	15.6	27.3	7.3	63.0	11.0	30.1	-12.0	2.0												
BPI Cdn Balanced	11.2	5.2	0.1	21.0	10.2	14.4	-6.6	16.2												
BPI Cdn Bond	4.4	7.5	-1.7	11.6	11.9	18.1	4.7													
BPI Canadian Equity Value	21.9	6.6	-1.8	28.5	6.7	13.2	-7.6													
BPI Canadian Small Co	49.7	18.0	0.8	47.3	11.5	18.0	-19.6	14.0												
BPI Canadian Opp RSP	87.9																			
BPI Cdn Resource Fund Inc	39.6	-8.3	-5.4	78.0	26.3	-0.2	-3.7	22.9	-29.7	42.9	0.5	-4.6	6.1	45.3	-5.5	-10.1	41.5	58.6	36.8	13.4
BPI Global Balanced RSP	5.4	4.1	10.2	31.1	8.5	6.8	-0.8	-0.3												
BPI Global Equity	12.4	5.9	14.6	21.5	7.7	9.2	-0.5	21.1												
BPI Global Opportunities	13.5																			
BPI Global RSP Bond	11.0																			
BPI Global Small Cos	8.6	0.3	31.6																	
BPI Income	17.6	14.7	5.3	4.8	3.9	16.2	-2.9	8.2	7.1	4.0	7.8	10.7	6.6	22.1	28.3	-0.9	7.7	3.7	2.5	17.4
BPI Income	17.6	14.7	5.3	4.8	3.9	16.2	-2.9	8.2	7.1	4.0	7.8	10.7	6.6	22.1	28.3	-0.9	7.7	3.7	2.5	17.4
BPI Int'l Equity	10.7	-2.1	12.2	20.3	10.8	20.1	-4.1													
BPI North Amer Bal RSP	6.1	11.1	3.5																	
BPI T-Bill	5.4	6.3	4.1	5.1	6.7	10.2	12.5	11.4	8.8	8.0	9.2	10.3	9.9	9.8						
C.I. American	18.0	21.3	8.1	54.2																
C.I. American Sector	17.5	20.7	8.5																	
C.I. Canadian Balanced	10.0	7.5	12.2																	
C.I. Canadian Bond	13.7	13.4	-1.5																	
C.I. Canadian Growth	11.0	3.8	14.1																	
C.I. Canadian Income	13.8																			
C.I. Canadian Sector	10.7	3.5	14.3	35.9	-3.1	-2.9	-19.5	16.0												

Fund	1996	1995	1994	1993	1992	1991	1990	1989	1988	1987	1986	1985	1984	1983	1982	1981	1980	1979	1978	1977
C.I. Covington	8.4																			
C.I. Emerging Markets	3.2	-26.5	35.7	30.6	15.7															
C.I. Emerg Markets Sector	2.8	-26.6	35.5																	
C.I. Global	11.4	-0.9	10.5	29.9	15.2	24.2	-12.8	16.5	-18.1	25.4										
C.I. Global Bond RSP	10.4	13.9	-3.6																	
C.I. Global Equity RSP	10.4	1.0	4.1																	
C.I. Global Sector	10.9	-1.3	10.6	29.7	14.7	23.4	-12.6	15.3												
C.I. Int'l Balanced	10.6																			
C.I. Int'l Balanced RSP	9.4																			
C.I. Latin America	14.5	-32.1	32.9																	
C.I. Latin America Sector	14.3	-31.7																		
C.I. Money Market	5.0	6.5	4.4	5.0	7.3															
C.I. New World Income	23.7	1.3																		
C.I. Pacific	8.3	-11.6	25.8	46.9	12.4	10.1	-11.3	24.4	-16.8	32.5	110.6	7.4	15.3	45.8						
C.I. Pacific Sector	7.9	-11.9	25.6	46.0	12.1	9.7	-11.6	23.9												
C.I. Short-term Sector	2.6	3.4	2.6	3.4	3.4	6.5	6.8	5.8												
C.I. US Money Market	4.9																			
C.I. World Bond	10.0	11.5	-2.1	15.0																
Caldwell Securities Assoc	15.9	7.4	26.6	14.9	-5.0															
Caldwell Securities Int'l	11.8	5.1	19.7	13.7																
Cambridge Amer Growth	-4.6	-0.2	-19.1	25.4																
Cambridge Americas	45.3	-0.4	-5.1	27.0	12.4	19.7	-14.6	20.1	-17.8											
Cambridge Balanced	15.6	-5.6	-3.1	39.0	10.2	12.9	2.2	10.1	7.1	8.4	31.9	19.6	4.2	19.6	21.7	4.8	5.5	9.2	16.8	14.9
Cambridge China	-3.5	2.4																		
Cambridge Global	37.7	-11.0	1.2	30.8	10.7	12.4	-22.1	12.5	6.9	19.7	33.6	20.6	1.5	27.2	11.6	-1.9	11.3	17.3	14.2	3.7
Cambridge Growth	19.9	-8.3	-5.6	46.6	9.0	6.0	2.2	16.5	-0.9	29.1	35.6	21.7	5.5	40.3	3.8	2.3	9.9	11.1	28.7	6.3
Cambridge Pacific	10.7	-17.6	9.6	27.4	10.8	-2.2	4.7	-45.4	-24.4	17.9	15.8	1.6	13.5							
Cambridge Resource	91.1	-7.6	-10.5	159.1	-6.2	-10.8	-22.8	5.5	-14.0	33.3	20.3	2.3	-0.8	38.1	14.5	-14.9	10.1	18.3	15.8	16.8
Cambridge Special Equity	42.5	1.3	-12.5	110.5	-21.6	-8.7	-24.7	25.6	-6.8											
Canada Life Cdn Equity	16.1	9.5	3.8	22.3	3.3	13.4	-19.7	25.0	-6.1	25.8	19.4	15.8	6.8	44.6	3.1	-9.0	25.9	33.9	25.4	2.2
Canada Life E-2	17.3	9.8	4.5	24.4	4.6	14.7	-18.4	23.8	-8.6	28.9	23.1	17.1	7.1	46.4	4.5	-8.3	25.7	34.6	26.5	3.5
Canada Life Fixed Income	9.9	12.3	-2.1	11.9	12.9	18.5	4.1	8.9	10.9	1.3	15.2	17.6	7.9	23.1	34.3	-3.4	-1.6	2.6	6.9	14.2

Fund	1996	1995	1994	1993	1992	1991	1990	1989	1988	1987	1986	1985	1984	1983	1982	1981	1980	1979	1978	1977
Canada Life Int'l Bond	6.4	13.5																		
Canada Life Managed	13.6	11.1	2.0	17.4	8.9	15.7	-8.8	17.1	0.8	15.8	18.4	16.5								
Canada Life Money Market	4.6	5.5	3.8	5.2	5.9	10.6	11.6	10.6	7.5	6.1	7.5	9.0	9.7	10.4	16.2	17.2	12.5	10.0	6.7	7.4
Canada Life US & Int'l	15.6	14.4	11.1	26.7	15.0	26.0	-13.0	31.3	-9.8	25.4	24.7	13.6								
Cdn Medical Discovery	6.8																			
Canadian Protected	4.4	5.9	-2.1	22.2	5.7	7.3	7.0	5.5	5.3	15.7	14.1									
Capital Alliance Ventures	8.8																			
Capstone Cash Management	5.0	6.9	4.7	6.0	7.1	10.8	12.8	11.0												
Capstone Int'l Invest Trust	21.2	0.9	11.6	21.7	14.5	28.4	-10.3	16.0	-4.6											
Capstone Invest Trust	18.8	5.8	3.9	16.4	4.5	15.5	-3.2	15.8	-14.5	18.1	22.0	16.9	1.6	24.5	13.4	7.5				
Cassels Blaikie American	19.0	30.5	-2.8	7.6	3.2	37.4	-11.9	45.7	-19.5	36.0	39.9	18.5	-14.4	60.5						
Cassels Blaikie Canadian	14.3	11.3	4.6	11.5	10.4	16.8	-1.8	15.4	2.6	9.3	15.7	18.6								
CCPE Diversified	15.5	9.2	4.1	12.4	7.3	16.7	-4.4	15.9	2.0	10.3										
CCPE Fixed Income	11.0	13.0	-0.8	12.8	15.3	18.8	5.5	9.7	8.6	-1.2										
CCPE Global Equity	6.2																			
CCPE Growth R	15.2	7.1	12.0	11.6	-2.7	12.6	-12.7	21.7	-5.0	21.5										
CCPE Money Market	5.3																			
CCPE US Equity	12.4	18.3																		
CDA Aggressive Equity	23.0	0.7																		
CDA Balanced	14.8	10.0	4.1	11.6	10.3	15.6	-3.6	17.5	0.2	13.8	17.5	18.1	4.6	36.8	-0.2	-7.6	0.5	11.6		
CDA Common Stock	6.3	2.8	9.8	22.9	5.2	13.1	-13.0	25.8	-9.9	30.8	23.3	19.7	4.9	45.7	4.9	-6.7	16.6	28.4	26.7	-2.6
CDA Emerging Markets	2.5																			
CDA European	14.2																			
CDA Int'l Equity	10.6																			
CDA Money Market	5.4	6.6	4.7	5.6	7.1	10.4	12.7	11.2	8.7	7.3	9.4	10.3	10.2	9.9	15.6	15.0	12.7	8.4	7.6	7.9
CDA Pacific Basin	10.0																			
Cdn Anaes Mutual Accum	20.6	7.1	6.4	12.8	1.1	3.7	-11.9	19.8	-8.4	29.4	16.9	17.5	5.3	45.3	-2.6	-2.1	36.4	47.9	33.9	7.5
Century DJ	6.3	2.8	2.4	7.9	3.9	42.5	-23.5	16.5	-23.6	22.3										
Champion Growth	14.6	9.6																		
Chou Associates	19.2	25.7	-6.1	22.5	19.3	23.3	-15.7	18.4	-4.8											
Chou RRSP	10.9	10.0	-0.4	12.4	5.8	9.3	-15.0	16.4	3.9											
CIBC Balanced	11.5	8.2	0.2	15.1	3.9	14.9	-2.3	15.6												

Fund	1996	1995	1994	1993	1992	1991	1990	1989	1988	1987	1986	1985	1984	1983	1982	1981	1980	1979	1978	1977
CIBC Canadian Bond	10.8	13.6	-4.9	12.1	14.2	21.8	3.3	11.0	...	...	...	...	...	...	...	...	...	...	...	...
CIBC Canadian Equity	12.3	1.7	0.9	21.5	-2.9	2.1	-7.6	...	...	...	...	...	...	...	...	...	...	...	...	...
CIBC Canadian Res	8.9	...	...	...	...	...	...	...	...	...	...	...	...	...	...	...	...	...	...	...
CIBC Canadian S-Term Bond	9.8	11.5	0.2	...	...	...	...	...	...	...	...	...	...	...	...	...	...	...	...	...
CIBC Canadian T-Bill	4.4	5.7	3.6	4.3	5.8	...	...	...	...	...	...	...	...	...	...	...	...	...	...	...
CIBC Capital Appreciation	9.6	3.8	-3.8	40.1	24.1	...	...	...	...	...	...	...	...	...	...	...	...	...	...	...
CIBC Dividend	15.0	5.1	1.1	20.4	1.1	...	...	...	...	...	...	...	...	...	...	...	...	...	...	...
CIBC Far East Prosperity	11.0	-11.9	22.3	...	...	...	...	...	...	...	...	...	...	...	...	...	...	...	...	...
CIBC Global Bond	6.7	...	...	...	...	...	...	...	...	...	...	...	...	...	...	...	...	...	...	...
CIBC Global Equity	10.2	2.6	5.0	17.3	18.3	12.9	-11.2	18.0	...	...	...	...	...	...	...	...	...	...	...	...
CIBC Japanese Equity	3.0	...	...	...	...	...	...	...	...	...	...	...	...	...	...	...	...	...	...	...
CIBC Money Market	4.4	5.8	3.6	3.9	6.5	10.1	12.6	...	...	...	...	...	...	...	...	...	...	...	...	...
CIBC Mortgage	9.9	9.3	3.6	4.7	17.5	15.5	8.9	12.1	7.1	7.8	10.2	14.0	9.5	16.7	22.7	4.1	7.2	7.1	8.0	11.8
CIBC Premium Cdn T-Bill	4.9	6.4	4.2	4.9	6.5	...	...	...	...	...	...	...	...	...	...	...	...	...	...	...
CIBC US Equity	20.9	13.2	3.6	10.6	20.6	...	...	...	...	...	...	...	...	...	...	...	...	...	...	...
CIBC US$ Money Market	4.3	4.7	2.7	2.2	3.4	...	...	...	...	...	...	...	...	...	...	...	...	...	...	...
Clean Environment Bal	14.1	9.6	-1.0	43.1	...	...	...	...	...	...	...	...	...	...	...	...	...	...	...	...
Clean Environment Equity	19.5	15.1	-2.9	47.0	...	...	...	...	...	...	...	...	...	...	...	...	...	...	...	...
Clean Environment Income	6.8	3.7	...	...	...	...	...	...	...	...	...	...	...	...	...	...	...	...	...	...
Clean Environment Int'l Eq	13.6	3.7	...	...	...	...	...	...	...	...	...	...	...	...	...	...	...	...	...	...
Co-operators Bal	13.3	14.2	4.5	18.1	...	...	...	...	...	...	...	...	...	...	...	...	...	...	...	...
Co-operators Canadian Eq	12.0	4.4	10.1	23.5	...	...	...	...	...	...	...	...	...	...	...	...	...	...	...	...
Co-operators Fixed Income	11.2	15.1	-1.9	13.2	...	...	...	...	...	...	...	...	...	...	...	...	...	...	...	...
Co-operators US Equity	20.7	57.6	...	...	...	...	...	...	...	...	...	...	...	...	...	...	...	...	...	...
Colonia Life Bond	8.5	11.9	0.8	8.8	...	...	...	...	...	...	...	...	...	...	...	...	...	...	...	...
Colonia Life Equity	16.5	2.8	-1.4	13.3	...	...	...	...	...	...	...	...	...	...	...	...	...	...	...	...
Colonia Life Money Mkt	4.7	6.5	3.5	6.1	...	...	...	...	...	...	...	...	...	...	...	...	...	...	...	...
Colnia Life Mortgage	8.3	9.7	2.6	7.0	...	...	...	...	...	...	...	...	...	...	...	...	...	...	...	...
Colonia Life Special Growth	64.1	10.1	6.2	...	...	...	...	...	...	...	...	...	...	...	...	...	...	...	...	...
Concorde Croissance	19.7	10.7	6.0	17.6	...	...	...	...	...	...	...	...	...	...	...	...	...	...	...	...
Concorde Dividendes	25.7	...	...	...	...	...	...	...	...	...	...	...	...	...	...	...	...	...	...	...
Concorde Equilibre	14.9	...	...	...	...	...	...	...	...	...	...	...	...	...	...	...	...	...	...	...

Fund	1996	1995	1994	1993	1992	1991	1990	1989	1988	1987	1986	1985	1984	1983	1982	1981	1980	1979	1978	1977
Concorde Hypotheques	7.0	7.9	3.0	8.7	12.0	...	...	...	...	...	...	...	...	...	...	...	...	...	...	...
Concorde Int'l	9.6	...	...	...	...	...	...	...	...	...	...	...	...	...	...	...	...	...	...	...
Concorde Monetaire	4.6	6.0	4.3	5.0	...	...	...	...	...	...	...	...	...	...	...	...	...	...	...	...
Concorde Revenu	9.0	11.8	-0.9	10.5	...	...	...	...	...	...	...	...	...	...	...	...	...	...	...	...
Confed Equity	21.9	3.5	10.0	17.5	5.6	9.3	-18.1	20.1	-3.8	21.7	13.8	21.0	1.9	56.1	-3.7	-13.1	...	...	...	...
Confed Fixed Income	9.5	12.6	-1.3	10.6	13.3	18.4	2.7	10.0	17.2	3.2	14.0	29.1	20.3	19.3	35.7	-5.0	...	...	...	...
Confed Life A	22.3	4.8	13.1	18.2	7.1	12.2	-17.2	22.6	-3.2	20.4	16.0	23.1	4.7	56.7	-1.0	-10.4	22.3	37.4	28.4	6.0
Confed Life B	22.6	4.5	10.7	18.6	6.8	10.8	-17.3	21.4	-2.8	22.9	15.0	22.3	2.9	57.7	-2.6	-12.2	22.4	40.9	27.0	3.4
Confed Life C	9.8	13.2	-1.0	11.2	13.9	19.1	3.3	10.6	17.9	3.7	14.7	29.9	21.0	19.7	36.9	-4.7	1.0	3.7	9.4	16.6
Contrarian Strategy FUT LP	-11.8	9.0	26.5	43.0	-2.6	...	...	...	...	...	...	...	...	...	...	...	...	...	...	...
Cornerstone Balanced	17.2	6.7	3.8	13.9	5.5	13.1	-5.1	14.9	-19.5	18.8	17.8	9.8	1.5	31.5	-5.8	-6.4	15.8	28.1	37.0	12.4
Cornerstone Bond	9.8	13.1	-0.4	11.8	11.5	17.5	9.8	10.4	17.1	...	...	...	...	...	...	...	...	...	...	...
Cornerstone Cdn Growth	20.7	6.5	9.4	19.1	8.2	19.1	-20.5	19.1	-18.0	...	...	...	...	...	...	...	...	...	...	...
Cornerstone Global	14.6	10.4	10.2	18.1	15.5	17.9	-2.1	17.9	-24.5	49.2	...	...	...	...	...	...	...	...	...	...
Cornerstone Gov't Money	4.4	6.0	4.1	4.6	6.5	10.3	...	...	...	...	...	...	...	...	...	...	...	...	...	...
Cornerstone US	18.1	19.4	4.4	12.6	16.4	16.1	-4.8	18.2	-27.2	15.7	24.7	4.9	4.1	48.8	19.6	-5.7	29.5	10.1	55.4	4.5
Cote 100 Amerique	31.6	14.2	-4.7	...	...	...	...	...	...	...	...	...	...	...	...	...	...	...	...	...
Cote 100 Amerique REER	27.3	12.3	-4.7	...	...	...	...	...	...	...	...	...	...	...	...	...	...	...	...	...
Cote 100 EXP	29.6	17.4	...	...	...	...	...	...	...	...	...	...	...	...	...	...	...	...	...	...
CT Everest Amerigrowth	17.5	29.3	2.5	...	...	...	...	...	...	...	...	...	...	...	...	...	...	...	...	...
CT Everest Asiagrowth	9.3	-5.1	...	...	...	...	...	...	...	...	...	...	...	...	...	...	...	...	...	...
CT Everest Balanced	11.9	9.2	0.2	20.1	9.7	12.4	-1.3	16.9	...	...	...	...	...	...	...	...	...	...	...	...
CT Everest Bond	9.6	13.5	-2.1	11.0	14.2	18.0	7.1	11.3	13.8	...	...	...	...	...	...	...	...	...	...	...
CT Everest Dividend Income	19.6	...	...	...	...	...	...	...	...	...	...	...	...	...	...	...	...	...	...	...
CT Everest Emerging Market	6.4	...	...	...	...	...	...	...	...	...	...	...	...	...	...	...	...	...	...	...
CT Everest Eurogrowth	17.5	7.8	...	...	...	...	...	...	...	...	...	...	...	...	...	...	...	...	...	...
CT Everest Int'l	12.6	-5.2	8.8	28.2	-1.5	1.4	6.7	30.6	...	...	...	...	...	...	...	...	...	...	...	...
CT Everest Int'l Bond	6.0	...	...	...	...	...	...	...	...	...	...	...	...	...	...	...	...	...	...	...
CT Everest Money Market	4.4	5.6	3.9	4.1	6.8	10.8	12.9	12.0	8.7	...	...	...	...	...	...	...	...	...	...	...
CT Everest Mortgage	7.4	9.0	5.0	6.0	13.4	13.1	9.9	12.3	8.3	7.3	10.7	14.7	9.9	15.8	23.3	5.6	9.7	5.6	7.5	13.9
CT Everest North American	11.7	1.0	1.2	29.9	8.4	11.7	-13.5	20.4	-17.9	27.4	21.2	14.3	1.7	59.6	-6.3	-14.1	29.3	40.4	24.3	-2.9
CT Everest Special Equity	14.7	-0.3	-5.6	41.1	16.4	8.7	-7.7	15.1	-21.6	...	...	...	...	...	...	...	...	...	...	...

Fund	1996	1995	1994	1993	1992	1991	1990	1989	1988	1987	1986	1985	1984	1983	1982	1981	1980	1979	1978	1977
CT Everest Stock	11.8	4.5	2.6	32.3	8.3	8.1	-10.2	14.3	...	...	...	...	...	...	...	...	...	...	...	...
CT Everest US Equity	10.3	18.5	-4.7	20.3	11.5	...	...	...	...	...	...	...	...	...	...	...	...	...	...	...
Cundill Security	12.4	15.2	18.0	31.8	-12.1	-2.4	-10.6	13.2	-2.8	27.3	9.8	24.9	0.8	49.8	-5.0	13.1	9.3	22.5	65.0	22.0
Cundill Value	11.9	11.5	14.6	35.4	8.1	1.7	-6.8	11.9	4.2	31.5	14.7	12.3	6.9	59.7	20.7	-6.0	24.7	33.2	29.6	4.2
Desjardins Actions	14.9	4.9	8.7	15.5	4.2	6.8	-15.9	23.6	-13.2	18.0	8.5	14.3	-3.3	50.8	-2.1	-9.3	-3.5	4.5	9.2	13.9
Desjardins Bond	12.6	14.2	-0.8	14.1	14.9	22.6	4.8	13.7	15.5	1.6	16.5	22.5	10.8	23.2	41.7	...	...	...	...	...
Desjardins Divers Audaciou	11.8	...	...	...	...	...	...	...	...	...	...	...	...	...	...	...	...	...	...	...
Desjardins Divers Moderate	10.7	...	...	...	...	...	...	...	...	...	...	...	...	...	...	...	...	...	...	...
Desjardins Divers Secure	7.6	...	...	...	...	...	...	...	...	...	...	...	...	...	...	...	...	...	...	...
Desjardins Diversified	13.8	9.9	4.6	18.0	9.9	17.2	...	...	...	...	...	...	...	...	...	...	...	...	...	...
Desjardins Dividend	15.1	10.9	...	...	...	...	...	...	...	...	...	...	...	...	...	...	...	...	...	...
Desjardins Environnement	12.1	6.6	10.8	9.7	3.3	...	...	...	...	...	...	...	...	...	...	...	...	...	...	...
Desjardins Equilibre	12.0	8.5	4.4	16.4	10.3	12.9	-4.3	14.7	0.2	6.2	...	...	...	...	...	...	...	...	...	...
Desjardins Growth	13.9	6.8	...	...	...	...	...	...	...	...	...	...	...	...	...	...	...	...	...	...
Desjardins Hypotheque	7.9	9.3	3.5	6.2	12.0	13.3	10.0	10.6	9.3	8.0	11.0	15.5	8.4	18.8	24.7	5.0	8.4	5.5	7.0	13.1
Desjardins Int'l	10.8	6.5	10.2	25.6	16.1	16.5	-4.5	17.9	-20.0	36.9	29.2	6.2	7.0	25.6	10.3	0.0	6.6	8.1	34.4	14.5
Desjardins Marche Monetair	4.3	5.6	3.9	5.0	6.4	9.8	11.9	...	...	...	...	...	...	...	...	...	...	...	...	...
Desjardins Mortgage	9.4	10.1	3.3	8.1	10.3	14.3	10.1	14.0	11.0	6.7	13.6	16.4	11.0	17.3	23.6	0.8	9.7	6.4	9.4	14.7
Desjardins Obligations	10.5	13.0	-1.3	11.3	13.3	18.7	2.3	10.0	14.3	-1.8	15.7	19.2	4.8	20.5	43.9	-14.3	-3.9	0.8	4.4	14.7
Desjardins Stock	16.8	7.0	9.0	23.1	4.2	16.1	-17.3	21.1	-14.1	29.0	30.6	16.8	1.0	48.3	-1.8	-4.2	31.7	35.9	32.6	2.9
DGC Entertainment Ventures	9.8	0.8	...	...	...	...	...	...	...	...	...	...	...	...	...	...	...	...	...	...
Dolphin Growth	2.8	3.7	11.2	18.4	5.4	8.5	-17.4	18.5	-5.8	22.2	23.0	20.8	2.3	54.1	-3.2	-12.1	21.5	48.4	35.3	4.2
Dolphin Income	17.3	7.6	3.6	6.0	18.8	13.4	10.0	10.3	9.3	8.4	11.0	13.7	12.2	18.8	23.6	5.8	10.0	6.3	5.5	16.1
Dominion Equity Resource	33.3	-20.0	-13.2	119.1	18.9	-19.7	4.8	5.6	-55.2	39.3	-20.2	-2.1	-13.1	33.1	-27.0	-25.4	32.7	44.1	27.2	2.1
Dynamic Americas	32.0	9.9	-2.7	24.2	7.2	17.0	-11.5	20.6	-11.0	26.8	30.7	17.1	10.4	50.0	7.4	8.5	...	...	...	...
Dynamic Canadian Growth	16.4	-1.7	6.9	107.6	13.0	13.8	-10.6	13.3	-29.9	20.0	...	...	...	...	...	...	...	...	...	...
Dynamic Dividend	14.1	10.7	1.8	14.9	8.8	15.5	-2.6	9.9	8.9	6.8	12.1	...	...	...	...	...	...	...	...	...
Dynamic Dividend Growth	19.9	10.2	5.7	16.9	8.8	6.0	-6.4	8.2	7.8	-0.1	...	...	...	...	...	...	...	...	...	...
Dynamic Europe	15.6	13.9	10.6	9.0	6.3	0.2	...	...	...	...	...	...	...	...	...	...	...	...	...	...
Dynamic Far East	10.5	3.4	...	...	...	...	...	...	...	...	...	...	...	...	...	...	...	...	...	...
Dynamic Fund of Canada	9.8	-2.5	4.8	44.4	6.9	11.4	-11.4	21.4	-6.6	27.3	18.7	14.7	-4.9	48.0	-7.1	-5.6	30.1	34.0	53.3	16.3
Dynamic Global Bond	7.1	19.5	-1.7	12.9	24.2	4.4	7.4	3.0	...	...	...	...	...	...	...	...	...	...	...	...

Fund	1996	1995	1994	1993	1992	1991	1990	1989	1988	1987	1986	1985	1984	1983	1982	1981	1980	1979	1978	1977
Dynamic Global Millennia	37.4	-1.7	-9.5	36.4	-4.7	0.7	-10.9	17.6	-17.7											
Dynamic Global Partners	12.3	8.1																		
Dynamic Global Resource	66.4																			
Dynamic Government Inc	11.1	10.1																		
Dynamic Income	8.1	12.8	4.6	8.8	16.0	19.4	4.5	13.6	8.6	6.1	13.5	19.9	10.7	18.7	35.4	-7.3	19.7			
Dynamic International	18.3	3.5	8.5	32.3	6.4	13.0	-12.5	8.1	-38.4	46.1										
Dynamic Money Market	4.5	6.4	4.1	4.5	7.0	10.5	12.4	9.4	8.4	7.5	8.6	9.6								
Dynamic Partners	9.7	7.0	8.5	37.3	14.1	14.8	-2.7													
Dynamic Precious Metals	36.6	-9.0	30.0	57.9	17.5	-13.4	0.2	4.9	-26.9	58.6										
Dynamic Real Estate Equity	43.4																			
Dynamic Team	16.1	4.9	4.7	34.7	9.6	10.3	-7.1	15.6	-6.2	20.4										
Elliott & Page Amer Growth	12.8	17.0	8.7	10.5	15.6	12.2	-4.9	18.2	-26.6	36.1	23.7	7.9	-7.4	38.5	23.7	-9.1	23.8	11.0	41.5	33.9
Elliott & Page Asian Growth	4.6	2.7																		
Elliott & Page Balanced	15.3	7.5	6.5	30.2	9.5	13.8	-6.4	17.7												
Elliott & Page Bond	8.5	9.4	-3.9	10.3	11.8	17.1	6.3	11.6												
Elliott & Page Emerg Market	-1.0	-16.5																		
Elliott & Page Equity	21.2	7.6	9.7	28.4	15.7	13.7	-16.2	32.6												
Elliott & Page Global Bal	7.6	9.8																		
Elliott & Page Global Bond	5.5	13.8																		
Elliott & Page Global Equity	12.1	8.0																		
Elliott & Page Money	4.9	6.3	4.7	5.8	6.7	11.4	13.0	11.5	9.1	8.5	9.9	10.4								
Elliott & Page T-Bill	3.6	4.4																		
Empire Asset Allococation	12.4	6.7																		
Empire Balanced	12.9	9.9	2.2	16.8	5.8	16.3	-3.2													
Empire Bond	9.3	11.8	-1.1	10.4	11.8	21.4	4.1	9.6	10.4											
Empire Elite Equity	17.4	7.4	3.5	19.5	9.7	11.6	-17.3	18.9	-16.6	25.3	23.4	23.9	12.5	56.7	-17.6	28.8	33.4	31.4	47.3	14.0
Empire Fgn Curr Cdn Bond	2.4	1.6																		
Empire Group Bond	12.2	14.1	2.2	14.5	13.8	23.3	4.2	11.4	8.5	6.3	14.9	16.4	10.5	19.6	32.4	-0.9	6.3	3.4	8.1	13.0
Empire Group Equity	20.2	7.2	6.2	26.3	5.1	12.8	-12.9	20.7	-6.8	23.5	34.5	13.3	-5.3	60.4	4.4	-7.2	33.3	44.3	31.9	3.9
Empire Int'l Growth	11.8	6.7	10.3	25.6	9.2	20.1	-2.3													
Empire Life 3	19.6	8.2	6.6	27.2	4.0	15.8	-18.2	25.6	-0.4	16.1	34.8	18.1	-5.5	63.8	8.4	-7.1	36.5	56.9	28.0	4.1
Empire Money Market	4.0	5.4	3.6	4.8	5.8	10.4	11.0													

Fund	1996	1995	1994	1993	1992	1991	1990	1989	1988	1987	1986	1985	1984	1983	1982	1981	1980	1979	1978	1977
Empire Premier Equity	18.6	7.2	6.9	19.6	9.0	8.7	-14.0	22.0	-2.7	26.1	22.5	17.6	1.2	60.3	-2.4	1.3	32.5	28.0	42.1	10.4
Equit Life Can Asset All	12.2																			
Equit Life Can Cdn Bond	10.6	10.8	-1.1	10.2																
Equit Life Can Cdn Stock	20.8	4.3	11.5	14.2																
Equit Life Can Com Stock	24.3	9.2	13.1	17.3	3.5	7.8	-16.4	19.3	-20.2	37.2	19.6	14.3	-3.0	61.0	-6.2	-19.3	29.9	43.0	37.9	1.2
Equit Life Can Int'l	14.8																			
Equit Life Can Money Mkt	4.0																			
Equit Life Can Mortgage	7.3																			
Equit Life Can Accum	12.3	13.3	-0.5	11.7	16.1	21.5	6.0	10.5	12.3	3.6	15.9	20.1	9.3	20.9	30.2	-1.5	1.6	3.4	8.3	13.5
Ethical Balanced	10.2	14.2	1.2	13.6	5.0	9.9	10.3													
Ethical Global Bond	6.8																			
Ethical Growth	17.4	12.7	5.5	19.7	-2.0	10.4	-3.7	23.2	9.0	10.7										
Ethical Income	10.9	15.1	-2.5	12.8	7.6	11.5	11.4	8.4	8.3	3.5	13.6	17.8								
Ethical Money Market	4.6	5.7	3.7	5.1	6.3	10.1	13.0	11.3	8.7	7.8	9.1	10.0								
Ethical North Amer Equity	12.5	31.2	-2.9	21.8	8.1	12.8	-17.3	19.6	-16.2	25.0	19.8	14.4	-1.2	40.4	5.3	-8.2	12.2	26.0	27.9	7.8
Ethical Pacific Rim	10.6																			
Ethical Special Equity	13.1																			
Ficadre Actions	19.2	11.0	5.4	15.7	5.4	7.1	-27.1	12.4	-25.9											
Ficadre Equilibre	14.4	12.5	3.9	7.9	9.5	15.4	-7.6	14.8	-12.1	17.4	24.7	18.8	6.1	28.7	16.4	-2.9	14.2	5.9	13.2	1.5
Ficadre Hypotheques	6.7																			
Ficadre Monetaire	4.9	5.6	3.8	5.6	6.8	10.1														
Ficadre Obligations	9.8	12.9	-1.1	8.7	12.6	21.0	2.4	9.4												
Fidelity Asset Manager	12.7	4.4	2.1																	
Fidelity Canadian Bond	10.6	8.0	-1.9	17.0	10.0	12.8	2.4	11.0												
Fidelity Canadian Income	10.0																			
Fidelity Capital Builder	16.0	4.2	3.7	23.1	4.4	13.9	-5.1	18.1												
Fidelity Canadian Asset Alloc	18.5																			
Fidelity Cdn Growth Co	22.0	23.9																		
Fidelity Cdn S-Term Asset	4.2	5.7	3.6	4.0	6.6															
Fidelity Emerg Mkts Ptl	20.3																			
Fidelity Emerg Mkts Bnd	37.3	-5.3																		
Fidelity European Growth	14.7	17.3	12.3	20.5																

Fund	1996	1995	1994	1993	1992	1991	1990	1989	1988	1987	1986	1985	1984	1983	1982	1981	1980	1979	1978	1977
Fidelity Far East	18.8	2.1	22.8	45.5	33.9															
Fidelity Growth America	8.8	36.3	-1.2	34.4	26.3	34.7														
Fidelity Int'l Portfolio	12.7	11.2	6.9	37.1	6.9	17.4	-14.2	32.9												
Fidelity Japanese Growth	-1.7	-12.1	3.0																	
Fidelity Latin Amer Growth	21.2	-39.2																		
Fidelity North Amer Income	6.8	-6.9	2.6																	
Fidelity RSP Global Bond	3.5	10.4																		
Fidelity Small Cap America	4.3	34.6																		
Fidelity US Money Market	4.3																			
First American	-0.3	5.9	-5.6	24.0																
First Canadian Asset Alloc	13.3	9.9	-1.0	14.4	5.3	16.2	-6.9	11.7												
First Canadian Bond	11.1	13.7	-1.4	11.6	14.0	21.2	2.3	8.7												
First Canadian Div Income	21.5																			
First Canadian Emerg Mkt	1.6																			
First Cdn Equity Index	17.5	4.8	9.3	21.3	-0.5	9.2	-17.8	21.4												
First Cdn Europe Growth	12.6																			
First Cdn FarEast Growth	10.6																			
First Canadian Growth	19.8	7.8	-0.8																	
First Canadian Int'l Bond	6.8	16.3	0.0																	
First Cdn Int'l Growth	9.8	1.5	11.6	32.5																
First Cdn Japan Growth	-0.6																			
First Canadian Money Mkt	4.6	5.8	3.9	4.7	6.8	10.0	11.7	9.8												
First Canadian Mortgage	9.7	9.9	3.4	5.2	16.7	16.2	9.8	11.3	9.6	7.8	11.4	15.5	10.4	16.4	25.9	3.9	8.9	5.9	8.3	11.7
First Canadian NAFTA Adv	16.0																			
First Canadian Resource	23.5	0.1	-0.7																	
First Cdn Special Growth	27.8	8.2	-12.6																	
First Canadian T-Bill	4.6	5.8	3.9																	
First Canadian US Growth	-2.9	29.4	-1.7																	
First Heritage	12.8	-7.4	10.2	44.2	10.1	-19.0	-8.2	13.1	-23.4	29.4										
First Ontario	1.6																			
Fonds De Crois Select	20.5	19.4	4.0																	
Fonds D'Investissement REA	11.4	2.2	-4.9																	

Fund	1996	1995	1994	1993	1992	1991	1990	1989	1988	1987	1986	1985	1984	1983	1982	1981	1980	1979	1978	1977
Fonds Professional Gth Inc	9.7																			
Fonds Professional Int'l Eqty	14.6	8.4	4.4	27.6																
Fonds Professionals Bal	11.3	10.6	1.7	11.7	10.8	17.3	3.0	12.3	6.3	6.4	14.9	18.3	8.3	19.2	29.1	1.5	8.3	7.0		
Fonds Professionals Bond	10.0	12.2	-0.2	10.4	13.6	17.5	5.7	10.8	10.7	4.7	14.6	18.5	8.4	18.6	29.2	1.6	8.3	7.1		
Fonds Professionals Cdn Eqty	14.9	8.0	3.6	16.5	-1.0	13.8	-16.0	18.6												
Fonds Professionals S-Term	6.2	6.9	4.8	6.3	7.9	12.4	10.6	10.3												
Formula Growth	25.7	36.1	1.5	72.4	20.0	66.5	-40.7	28.6	-24.4	28.1	34.6	13.7	-14.2	79.5	18.7	2.5	55.4	15.0	79.0	21.2
Friedberg Currency	26.2																			
Friedberg Double Gold Plus	-0.7	-9.6	23.0	12.4	0.3	-24.2	-5.2	-1.2												
GBC Canadian Bond	11.7	13.8	-0.7	13.1	14.2	23.2	2.0	11.2	13.8	1.8	16.1									
GBC Canadian Growth	30.1	10.4	-0.6	42.9	18.3	28.2	-8.7													
GBC Int'l Growth	4.7	-7.6	2.2	30.0	-7.0	11.6														
GBC Money Market	4.6	6.1	4.4	5.3	6.7	10.5	12.6													
GBC North Amer Growth	10.6	26.5	-6.1	50.0	15.1	31.4	-25.5	32.1	-17.0	28.0	16.8	20.4	-9.0	67.5	0.5	-1.8	45.1	27.5	69.7	27.2
Generall Trust Mortgage	6.5	7.1	4.9	5.8	13.1	13.3	10.7	9.7	8.6	7.7	12.2	17.3	11.4	18.2	25.8	1.9	5.4	5.0	9.1	12.7
General Trust Balanced	12.9	9.4	2.0	12.1	9.0	19.7	-10.0	14.8	-1.7											
General Trust Cdn Equity	17.0	6.1	9.3	12.2	-0.9	14.4	-19.9	19.2	-15.0	26.1	15.6	20.9	-3.1	44.7	-11.0	-11.7	25.4	39.1	39.1	-1.0
General Trust Growth	20.0	-4.4	-1.0	43.9	20.3	15.6	-22.3	28.0												
General Trust Int'l	7.3	-0.4	9.2	24.3	8.7	13.9	-12.2	19.3												
General Trust Money Market	4.6	5.9	4.1	5.1	7.3	11.0	11.9	9.9	9.5											
General Trust of Cdn Bond	11.6	12.0	-3.2	11.6	16.2	21.0	0.4	10.9	13.1	-0.6	19.2	22.8	7.7	20.5	33.7	-3.8	0.7	3.1	9.1	13.2
General Trust US Equity	13.2	15.1	-7.3	38.5	17.1	42.8	-21.1	36.1	-26.8	36.4	32.1	16.0	-2.0							
GFM Emerg Mkts Country	2.3																			
Global Strategy Asia	9.6	-9.3	25.7																	
Global Strategy Bond	9.1	8.7																		
Global Strategy Canada Gth	18.2	6.3	-0.9	20.6																
Global Strategy Cdn Small	22.7																			
Global Strategy Diver Asia	5.5	-11.1																		
Global Strategy Diver Bond	9.7	10.0	-7.1	11.8	19.8															
Global Strategy Diver Euro	14.9	10.0	-0.2																	
Global Strategy Diver Jap	-1.6	-10.1																		
Global Strategy Diver Fgn Bd	9.1	6.5																		

Fund	1996	1995	1994	1993	1992	1991	1990	1989	1988	1987	1986	1985	1984	1983	1982	1981	1980	1979	1978	1977
Global Strategy Diver Latin	16.3	-29.5																		
Global Strategy Diver World	10.5																			
Global Strategy Euro Plus	16.7																			
Global Strategy Gold Plus	71.9	6.6	31.8																	
Global Strategy Income Plus	21.8	8.4	3.5	17.9																
Global Strategy Japan	-3.5																			
Global Strategy Latin Amer	10.6	-18.5																		
Global Strategy Money Mkt	4.4	6.0	4.3	5.4	6.6	8.7	11.6	10.6												
Global Strategy US Equity	15.7																			
Global Strategy World Bal	7.8																			
Global Strategy World Bond	9.5	9.8	-7.9	13.9	19.9	13.9	-0.2	7.2												
Global Strategy World Emer	24.3																			
Global Strategy World Eqty	12.2																			
Globeinvest Emerg Mkt Co	4.8																			
Goldfund Limited	10.3	-14.5	24.3	66.2	9.6	-17.6	8.6	-5.0	-40.3	49.1	32.3	0.6	-5.6	27.8	-4.9	-38.2	154.7	65.1	29.6	69.0
Goldtrust	17.6	-14.3	17.0	49.8	18.5	-18.7	9.3	-5.8	-36.0	38.6	29.8	10.5	-5.2	30.5	-7.2	-37.0	94.1	36.1	30.1	57.1
GWL Cdn Bond (G) A	9.5	11.2	-1.9	10.6	13.1	20.0	1.9	9.1	12.4	0.7	16.4	18.7	6.1	15.8	33.0	-3.1				
GWL Cdn Equity (G) A	16.3	1.8	3.0	31.7	7.5	10.0	-9.0	19.2	-15.9											
GWL Diversified (G) A	11.4	7.1	1.2	16.4	7.5	12.9	-3.5	13.8												
GWL Equity Index (G) A	16.1	3.7	9.1	21.8	-1.3	9.3	-18.1	21.9	-14.4	32.1	13.6	11.5	-2.4							
GWL Equity/Bond (G) A	13.6	5.9	1.4	20.7	9.5	14.2	-2.5	13.8												
GWL Gov't Bond (G) A	9.1																			
GWL Income (G) A	13.2																			
GWL Int'l Bond (P) A	6.9																			
GWL Int'l Eq (P) A	11.0																			
GWL Money Market (G) A	3.7	5.2	3.4	4.6	5.7	9.7	12.2	10.7	7.9	7.1	8.7	9.8	9.3	9.4	16.3					
GWL Mortgage (G) A	9.1	10.1	-0.2	10.7	11.1	18.1	3.9	10.9	10.1	3.8	12.5	14.2	10.6	17.2	23.4	-1.1	4.3			
GWL US Equity (G) A	11.6																			
Green Line Asian Growth	6.6	-5.2																		
Green Line Balanced Growth	19.7	10.9	-1.0	9.2	8.0	15.5	-7.9	15.6	6.8											
Green Line Bal Income	13.9	8.1	1.7	10.2	7.0	15.4	-9.9	18.7												
Green Line Blue Chip Equity	18.3	5.3	5.8	11.5	3.2	9.5	-12.6	24.5	3.9											

Fund	1996	1995	1994	1993	1992	1991	1990	1989	1988	1987	1986	1985	1984	1983	1982	1981	1980	1979	1978	1977
Green Line Canadian Bond	13.1	15.1	-0.4	12.3	13.2	20.8	0.4	7.1												
Green Line Canadian Equity	16.4	5.5	4.8	29.7	-1.2	10.9	-19.2	27.7												
Green Line Canadian Index	17.8	5.5	10.4	23.0	-0.8	10.0	-17.9	22.7	-14.2											
Green Line Canadian T-Bill	4.9	6.1	4.1	4.5																
Green Line Cdn Gov't Bond	11.2	13.6	-0.2	10.1	11.4	20.9	-2.3	11.2	9.0											
Green Line Cdn Money Mkt	5.0	6.1	4.4	5.1	7.3	10.6	13.0	11.3												
Green Line Dividend	17.9	-0.7	5.8	15.2	10.3	23.5	-8.5	17.4	5.1											
Green Line Emerging Mkts	4.0	-20.5																		
Green Line Energy	34.7		37.9																	
Green Line European Growth	22.4																			
Green Line Global Govt Bnd	5.3	12.3	-1.0																	
Green Line Global RSP Bond	7.9	13.2																		
Green Line Global Select	15.9	6.5																		
Green Line Int'l Equity	11.1	-1.7	12.0																	
Green Line Japanese Growth	2.9																			
Green Line Latin Amer Gth	12.0																			
Green Line Mortgage	7.9	9.2	2.8	6.6	15.0	14.1	10.8	11.7	9.8	7.8	7.6	12.4	9.9	16.3	24.6	6.7	9.3	6.2	7.7	13.1
Green Line Mortgage Backed	8.2	8.7	2.4	5.9	12.5	13.0	13.0													
Green Line North Am Gth A	23.0	28.8																		
Green Line Precious Metals	82.8																			
Green Line Real Return Bnd	8.0																			
Green Line Resource	38.4	-3.4																		
Green Line Science & Tech	16.9	69.8																		
Green Line S-Term Income	8.8	8.4	2.3	5.7	7.8	10.2	12.5													
Green Line US Index	19.1	27.8	2.9	10.5	9.3	28.2	-9.8	28.8	-14.3											
Green Line US Money Mkt	4.4	4.7	2.6	2.2	3.5	6.1	7.6	8.4												
Green Line Value	34.0	7.3																		
Greystone Managed Global	15.8	10.8																		
Greystone Managed Wealth	7.1	7.1																		
GT Global - Can Gth Cl	47.7																			
GT Global America Growth	7.9																			
GT Global Gbl Infrastructure	20.4																			

Fund	1996	1995	1994	1993	1992	1991	1990	1989	1988	1987	1986	1985	1984	1983	1982	1981	1980	1979	1978	1977
GT Global Gbl Nat Resources	45.0																			
GT Global Gbl Telecomm	9.3																			
GT Global Growth & Income	11.5																			
GT Global Latin Amer Gth	26.2																			
GT Global Pacific Growth	18.7																			
GT World Bond	16.3																			
Guardian America Equity A	8.4	29.1	2.6	31.6	15.9	35.3	-17.1	20.9	-17.1	27.6	17.9	2.1	-4.1	32.6	2.3	-0.5	46.8	14.0	46.0	18.5
Guardian Asia Pacific A	3.9	3.4																		
Guardian Canadian Bal A	10.8	8.0	4.9	14.2	10.2	16.8	1.8	12.8	4.3	16.2	12.3	14.0	7.7	28.0	22.4	-8.0	8.5	14.4	19.3	11.5
Guardian Cdn Income A	8.0	9.1																		
Guardian Cdn Money Mkt A	4.5	6.0	4.2	5.2	6.4	10.4	13.2	11.7	8.9	7.6	9.1	10.0	10.0	9.7	17.1	16.4	11.5	7.2	7.7	10.1
Guardian Emerging Mkt A	11.9	2.2																		
Guardian Enterprise A	50.7	11.3	-0.5	26.3	2.5	6.5	-9.0	17.3	-13.0	26.8	14.2	14.3	6.7	64.6	2.4	-7.2	41.6	31.8	29.2	5.5
Guardian Foreign Income A	10.4	11.1																		
Guardian Global Equity A	13.5	6.9	14.0	21.8	-2.9	14.8	-27.2	30.5	-20.5	19.3	54.1	14.7	2.3	32.8	-4.2	3.5	45.3	3.7	53.1	13.0
Guardian Growth Equity A	26.0	0.4	2.9	38.9	10.3	7.4	-2.9													
Guardian Int'l Bal A	13.1	4.3	-2.4																	
Guardian Int'l Income A	10.3	12.8	-6.0	15.0	23.1	5.4	6.3	1.4	1.8											
Guardian Monthly Div A	11.5	9.6	-0.5	11.8	10.8	9.3	-0.4	8.3	6.7	5.2										
Guardian US Money Mkt A	4.5	4.9	3.0	2.5	3.6	6.1	8.2	13.5	6.3	5.9										
Hansberger Asian	2.9	-13.7	11.5																	
Hansberger Asian Sector	2.4	-13.8																		
Hansberger European	11.4	3.8	1.6	10.0	3.2															
Hansberger European Sector	10.9	3.5	1.9																	
Hemisphere Value	10.6																			
Hongkong Bank Americas	18.4																			
Hongkong Bank Asian Gth	7.8	-1.0																		
Hongkong Bank Balanced	17.2	6.1	3.7	20.5	14.6	8.7	-3.6													
Hongkong Bank Cdn Bnd	11.0																			
Hongkong Bank Dividend Inc	21.9																			
Hongkong Bank Emerg Mkt	1.9																			
Hongkong Bank Equity	22.2	-3.4	7.0	50.4	-2.1	8.5	-14.7													

Fund	1996	1995	1994	1993	1992	1991	1990	1989	1988	1987	1986	1985	1984	1983	1982	1981	1980	1979	1978	1977
Hongkong Bank Euro Gth	15.7																			
Hongkong Bank Global Bond	5.4																			
Hongkong Bank Money Mkt	4.9	6.1	3.7																	
Hongkong Bank Mortgage	10.4	10.1	8.2																	
Hongkong Bank S-Cap Gth	38.8																			
Horizons I Multi-Asset Fd	6.7	4.4																		
HRL Balanced	11.9	5.0	3.5	11.7	1.3	15.6	-4.1	13.9	3.3	14.9	14.8	10.6	7.5	25.1	18.9	0.6	19.3	23.9	20.5	3.9
HRL Bond	11.1	12.0	-1.5	10.9	12.6	17.8	0.0	10.6	7.6											
HRL Canadian	15.3	0.0	-2.8	22.9	-5.4	7.7	-6.9	14.6	0.2											
HRL Instant $$	5.3	6.4	4.4	5.1	6.7	10.5	12.3	11.2	8.3											
HRL Overseas Growth	11.0	-1.0	10.7																	
Hyperion Asian	13.6	-13.9	28.8	51.7	25.8	7.4														
Hyperion European	12.0	12.3	6.1	14.6	15.7	9.4														
Hyperion Global Sci & Tech	18.7	19.5	3.4	12.8	17.9	42.1	-15.9	37.5	-19.4	20.1	22.5	10.7	3.4	33.9	14.6	0.2	24.0	9.4	46.7	10.5
Hyperion High Yield Bond	10.9	15.3	-5.4	12.1	14.0	22.3														
Hyperion S-Cap Cdn Eqty	23.2	12.9																		
Hyperion Value Line US Eqty	14.8	37.6	-6.8	32.7	20.8															
ICM Balanced	13.4	9.4	3.8	18.3	11.8	17.9	-8.9	11.7												
ICM Short Term Investment	6.0	7.2	5.2	6.6																
Ideal Balanced	12.4	12.6	3.9	12.2	10.9	18.9	-3.5	12.6	-1.5											
Ideal Bond	9.8	13.0	-1.4	11.8	14.6	21.5	1.5	9.4	14.4											
Ideal Equity	24.8	9.0	10.1	15.9	3.4	12.4	-10.2	17.6	-16.7											
Ideal Money Market	5.6	7.1																		
Imperial Growth Cdn Equity	13.9	3.5	8.7	16.7	7.4	10.9	-10.9	24.7	1.1	63.3	18.4	17.5	-0.1	47.5	5.3	-11.2	25.4	42.6	23.7	2.3
Imperial Growth Diversified	12.2	8.4	4.2	10.5	10.5	12.8	-1.0													
Imperial Growth Money Mkt	3.8	5.4	3.4	4.5	5.7	9.5	10.7													
Imperial Gth N Amer Equity	14.2	15.0	10.5	20.5	14.2	5.7	-19.9	15.1	-17.0	45.7	18.4	16.3	-4.7	51.3	3.5	-11.3	25.5	41.0	23.2	2.0
Ind Alliance Bonds	10.5	12.6	-1.5	11.4	11.6	22.0	4.9	11.8	12.0	1.6	19.1	17.9	7.1	22.4	48.3	-11.3				
Ind Alliance Diversified	11.7	10.5	6.9	18.8	6.3	16.7	0.2	15.5	1.5											
Ind Alliance Ecoflex A	13.2	8.5	13.6																	
Ind Alliance Ecoflex B	9.9	12.0	-2.1																	
Ind Alliance Ecoflex D	11.1	9.9	6.3																	

Fund	1996	1995	1994	1993	1992	1991	1990	1989	1988	1987	1986	1985	1984	1983	1982	1981	1980	1979	1978	1977
Ind Alliance Ecoflex H	7.3	7.6	2.9																	
Ind Alliance Ecoflex M	4.2	5.2																		
Ind Alliance Money Market	4.2	5.2	3.1	5.2	5.5															
Ind Alliance Mortgages	7.9	8.2	3.5	6.3	12.0	14.2	9.9	10.6	9.8	9.2	12.5	15.5	11.6	17.4	25.1	4.5	5.0			
Ind Alliance Stocks	13.8	9.1	13.8	26.9	4.0	15.6	-11.5	23.9	-11.8	21.0	16.4	14.1	0.2	51.4	-0.6	-7.9	21.2	33.4	31.7	-1.6
Industrial American	11.4	10.9	9.1	21.1	13.0	18.0	-16.9	23.5	-14.6	30.8	24.0	18.4	6.7	41.9	17.6	5.8	20.5	15.2	46.6	16.5
Industrial Balanced	10.6	7.1	4.6	19.2	7.2															
Industrial Bond	11.6	14.3	-4.6	13.6	13.5	20.9	0.9													
Industrial Cash Management	4.9	6.4	4.5	5.4	6.7	10.3	12.9	11.4	8.4	7.6	9.2	10.2								
Industrial Dividend	17.1	4.6	13.4	43.2	-1.2	-6.7	-20.0	14.8	-6.3	38.1	15.6	25.8	6.8	60.8	2.0	-3.8	3.1	20.5	29.2	21.5
Industrial Equity	16.8	-10.7	4.6	80.8	9.7	-10.4	-22.0	5.9	-9.7	41.6	16.1	12.2	-1.9	67.6	5.1	-16.9	27.9	22.9	40.2	27.3
Industrial Future	7.7	16.6	13.6	39.7	-3.2	3.3	-15.4	19.6												
Industrial Growth	9.7	-1.0	12.8	34.4	-3.8	1.6	-14.8	18.0	-4.3	36.2	14.5	20.8	4.9	54.1	11.0	-13.5	32.0	24.4	24.3	36.9
Industrial Horizon	10.0	0.8	17.5	25.2	-2.0	5.3	-13.7	18.7	8.9											
Industrial Income	11.1	12.4	-1.0	15.0	11.6	19.0	-6.5	13.8	9.9	14.4	19.2	27.2	5.9	25.0	38.2	-14.4	-6.3	2.6	8.2	18.5
Industrial Mortgage Secur	11.6	7.3	0.5	16.5	10.7	20.3	-5.7	14.5	10.0	14.5	18.3	22.0	10.1	16.3						
Industrial Pension	15.2	5.3	17.4	30.2	0.7	-7.9	-21.4	15.3	-7.5	34.7	20.7	22.5	1.4	61.5	7.9	-7.4	0.1	18.1	34.0	29.0
Industrial Short-Term	4.2	5.5	3.5	4.2	5.4															
Integrated Growth	-16.5	-19.4																		
InvesNat Blue Chip Amer Eq	15.0	7.0	-4.8	5.2																
InvesNat Cdn Bond	10.9	10.5	-0.7	7.5																
InvesNat Cdn Equity	16.7	7.8	6.8	20.6	5.6	9.7	-9.8													
InvesNat Corp Cash Mgmt	5.3																			
InvesNat Dividend	12.5	9.6	2.7	9.3																
InvesNat European Equity	13.4	10.7	11.6	10.7																
InvesNat Far East Equity	16.8	2.0																		
InvesNat Int'l RSP Bond	6.3																			
InvesNat Japanese Equity	0.8	-10.5																		
InvesNat Money Mkt	4.7	5.9	4.0	5.0	6.6															
InvesNat Mortgage	8.8	9.1	4.8	6.6	14.3															
InvesNat Retirement Balance	12.4	10.1	1.8	12.1	10.3	15.1	-6.0													
InvesNat S-T Gov't Bond	10.3	9.2	0.8	8.2	12.2	19.0	3.8													

Fund	1996	1995	1994	1993	1992	1991	1990	1989	1988	1987	1986	1985	1984	1983	1982	1981	1980	1979	1978	1977
InvesNat T-Bill Plus	5.0	6.2	4.1	5.1	6.7															
InvesNat US Money Mkt	4.4	4.5	2.4	2.0	3.5															
Investors Asset Allocation	15.3	10.4																		
Investors Canadian Equity	18.6	2.3	9.7	30.1	5.0	15.7	-11.6	18.0	-11.1	17.6	24.7	12.5	-4.1							
Investors Corporate Bond	11.2	10.7																		
Investors Dividend	14.9	6.5	3.6	12.0	7.7	20.7	-3.0	12.7	7.5	5.5	11.9	17.3	4.1	39.4	15.2	-9.7	5.5	16.7	23.9	-3.3
Investors European Growth	14.2	13.7	7.8	11.7	11.1	2.3														
Investors Global	12.2	10.7	8.7	17.8	9.0	19.2	-7.5	14.5	-20.9											
Investors Global Bond	4.1	10.4	-2.9	13.4																
Investors Government Bond	10.8	13.6	-0.9	10.8	12.5	20.2	3.9	10.4	15.3	-0.8	15.8	20.7	6.5	18.0	30.2	-4.6	-5.6			
Investors Growth Plus Port	12.5	10.7	3.7	19.9	8.6	18.2	-8.4													
Investors Growth Portfolio	14.1	11.1	7.2	29.4	7.6	19.3	-15.8													
Investors Income Plus Port	11.1	8.9	1.3	8.7	9.1	17.2	1.9													
Investors Income Portfolio	9.9	11.6	-0.1	8.6	11.5	16.8	5.7													
Investors Japanese Growth	-1.4	-8.6	4.2	55.6	-7.6	19.1	-34.9	18.7	-3.3	23.0	96.6	8.1	13.8	58.3	-11.2	29.4	10.4	-20.8	64.7	30.3
Investors Money Market	4.5	6.1	4.1	4.8	6.1	10.0	12.2	10.9	8.5	7.3	8.8									
Investors Mortgage	8.3	9.5	0.9	6.8	10.8	13.8	8.8	10.9	9.4	6.6	10.9	15.4	10.3	17.4	25.4	3.6	8.3	5.1	8.6	13.8
Investors Mutual	14.2	4.3	8.5	22.0	6.2	17.3	-10.5	17.4	-4.9	23.5	11.9	9.3	0.8	49.5	7.0	-5.7	17.5	25.3	21.9	0.6
Investors North Amer Gth	12.3	12.2	6.7	26.7	8.6	33.6	-14.6	34.6	-15.2	31.9	20.2	14.7	1.2	46.0	2.9	-6.6	26.8	32.9	26.1	-6.1
Investors Pacific Int'l	5.0	-4.3	31.7	43.0	22.2	12.9														
Investors Real Property	4.3	4.6	0.2	-3.4	1.6	6.0	5.0	12.0	8.7	11.4	9.8	8.9								
Investors Retirement Gth	16.7	4.3	9.3	21.2	1.2	14.7	-12.7													
Investors Retirement Plus	12.2	6.5	5.5	15.8	5.4	15.6	-5.5													
Investors Retirement	17.7	3.0	11.3	21.5	-2.2	15.1	-16.9	18.7	-0.9	28.1	13.0	15.4	1.4	42.5	-2.6	-8.3	26.1	38.8	24.9	-3.3
Investors Special	11.3	10.5	0.2	37.2	6.4	41.1	-16.1	33.3	-16.5	31.7	15.0	9.1	-9.1	60.7	1.0	-8.6	34.6	31.2	26.7	-0.6
Investors Summa	19.6	10.0	2.3	18.3	3.6	25.2	-23.2	18.7	-3.3											
Investors US Growth	16.1	20.2	4.1	21.1	23.6	29.7	-11.4	24.3	-21.1	38.8	20.6	14.0	-2.8	53.3	4.9	-8.8	31.4	11.6	23.9	5.4
Investors World Growth Port	8.7	5.5	9.2																	
Ivy Canadian	17.1	12.6	8.1																	
Ivy Enterprise	20.5																			
Ivy Foreign Equity	10.0	18.0	6.8																	
Ivy Growth & Income	19.3	14.4	0.6																	

Fund	1996	1995	1994	1993	1992	1991	1990	1989	1988	1987	1986	1985	1984	1983	1982	1981	1980	1979	1978	1977
Ivy Mortgage	9.9	8.9																		
Jones Heward	15.2	5.6	-7.2	46.9	6.8	17.6	-21.2	19.3	-9.9	23.8	24.8	16.4	2.2	49.2	-5.5	-9.0	40.1	39.7	45.5	5.2
Jones Heward American	7.5	8.5	-7.1	27.0	14.6	28.3	-20.8	32.4	-19.1	33.8	25.3	14.3	8.5							
Jones Heward Bond	10.1	12.6	-2.9	11.2	12.0	16.6	5.0	10.0	6.8											
Jones Heward Canadian Bal	9.5	8.0	-1.5	23.9	10.9	13.1	-3.7	10.4	-3.8	13.1	18.9	11.0	10.2							
Jones Heward Money Mkt	4.9	6.2																		
Lasalle Balanced	9.4	10.2	1.2	18.3	6.9	12.4	-0.7	14.4												
Laurentian American Equity	13.2	15.0	7.7	18.2	14.7	11.4	-16.0	22.4	-11.3	25.0	38.7	16.8	1.3	43.7	0.4	3.4	18.3	15.8	31.0	21.3
Laurentian Asia Pacific	2.5																			
Laurentian Canadian Equity	13.0	1.9	6.4	18.8	2.9	6.1	-17.3	20.0	-7.7	20.9	16.3	14.7	3.6	47.6	2.8	-7.1	23.1	37.9	28.0	-2.9
Laurentian Cdn Balanced	11.2	7.2	2.9	11.4	6.4	12.3	-2.0													
Laurentian Commonwealth	6.9	4.2	7.7	20.6	12.5	13.1	-9.9	19.5	-5.6	25.1	32.3	15.3	4.3	48.5	6.0	13.7	10.2	7.3	21.7	16.3
Laurentian Dividend	13.2	7.2	3.6	11.5	5.8	16.5	-6.6	17.0	5.1	9.7	16.2	17.1	8.1	40.2	12.4	-7.5	8.8			
Laurentian Emerging Market	2.7																			
Laurentian Europe	12.1																			
Laurentian Global Balanced	7.8	8.3	0.2	21.5	8.3	9.4														
Laurentian Gov't Bond	8.4	8.6	1.6	8.1	10.3	15.3	6.6													
Laurentian Income	9.7	11.8	-0.9	11.2	10.9	18.8	4.3	8.6	14.3	0.7	17.1	21.8	8.0	20.7	37.1	-7.4	-6.9	0.6	5.9	12.6
Laurentian International	7.2	4.1	8.7	25.4	10.5	10.4	-10.7	17.1	-9.7	23.8	26.5	13.6	6.6	51.2	4.7	17.6	13.5	7.0	47.9	26.7
Laurentian Money Market	4.4	5.8	3.8	4.7	6.2	9.9	12.2	11.2	8.7	8.0	9.1									
Laurentian Special Equity	8.1	7.4	9.1	29.8	3.3	7.5														
Leith Wheeler Balanced	12.3	8.7	5.6	17.3	12.1	17.7	-6.3	9.8	13.3											
Leith Wheeler Cdn Equity	16.4	0.8																		
Leith Wheeler Fixed Income	10.8	12.6																		
Leith Wheeler Money Mkt	4.9	6.2																		
Leith Wheeler US Equity	12.7	21.7																		
London Life Bond	11.0	13.3	-2.3	10.7	13.6	17.3	0.4	11.4	12.3	-4.4	24.8	29.9	7.5	23.2	28.0	-0.6	1.9	3.3	7.1	13.4
London Life Canadian Equity	18.8	2.6	8.8	20.5	9.8	13.9	-23.1	23.8	-8.6	35.6	16.7	14.5	2.7	48.3	3.7	-6.8	26.6	38.1	29.1	-0.9
London Life Diversified	14.3	7.0	4.1	14.7	12.7	16.1	-8.9	17.8												
London Life Int'l Equity	7.9																			
London Life Money Market	5.1	6.1	4.1	4.7	9.3	10.5	12.4													
London Life Mortgage	8.3	9.3	2.9	7.3	15.6	13.5	6.5	12.9	9.2	7.8	13.9	18.3	11.2	29.3	30.9	-8.0	2.8	-1.8	7.5	17.5

Fund	1996	1995	1994	1993	1992	1991	1990	1989	1988	1987	1986	1985	1984	1983	1982	1981	1980	1979	1978	1977
London Life US Equity	16.8	10.5	2.3	14.2	16.4	24.2	-29.3	30.2												
Lotus Group Balanced	15.0	5.8	-1.1	26.7	7.4	15.2	-6.4	14.7	-9.8	15.8	17.6	15.8								
Lotus Group Bond	12.1	12.5																		
Lotus Group Canadian Equity	43.4	-6.6	7.7																	
Lotus Group Income	5.1	6.1	4.3	5.1	6.8	11.0	13.5	11.7												
Lotus Group Int'l Bond	-1.6	16.7																		
Lotus Int'l Equity	2.6																			
Mackenzie Sentinel Cdn Eqty	14.9	-6.6	30.8	39.2	-0.4	-7.2	-13.5	17.4	-15.5	40.6										
Mackenzie Sentinel Global	7.3	2.7	13.5	32.6	-2.5	2.2	-16.1													
Manulife Cabot Blue Chip	15.2	9.1																		
Manulife Cabot Cdn Equity	17.1	8.1																		
Manulife Cabot Cdn Growth	37.9	0.5																		
Manulife Cabot Divers Bond	7.5	9.8																		
Manulife Cabot Emerg Gth	33.5	1.8																		
Manulife Cabot Global Eqty	7.8	12.3																		
Manulife Cabot Money Mkt	4.1	6.0																		
Manulife VistaFd1 Cap Gns	9.2	2.9	5.6	28.9	12.7	13.1	-15.1	24.5	-15.9	36.6	12.0	17.4								
Manulife VistaFd1 Divers	8.3	8.2	3.2	15.5	8.5	14.3	-6.1	16.8	-3.8	20.3	12.7	13.7	2.6	29.6	20.6	-3.8				
Manulife VistaFd1 S-T Sec	5.2	6.3	4.1	5.6	5.5	10.4	12.3	11.0	8.5	7.4	8.5	10.0								
Manulife VistaFd2 Cap Gns	8.4	2.2	4.9	27.9	11.8	12.2	-15.8	23.6	-16.5	35.6	11.2	16.5								
Manulife VistaFd2 Divers	7.5	7.4	2.5	14.6	7.8	13.5	-6.8	15.9	-4.6	19.4	11.9	12.9	1.9	28.7	19.7	-4.5				
Manulife VistaFd2 S-T Sec	4.4	5.5	3.2	4.8	4.7	9.5	11.5	10.1	7.7	6.6	7.8	9.1								
Manulife VistaFd1 Am Stock	9.2																			
Manulife VistaFd1 Gbl Bond	5.5																			
Manulife VistaFd1 Gbl Eq	10.0																			
Manulife VistaFd2 Am Stock	8.4																			
Manulife VistaFd2 Gbl Bond	4.7																			
Manulife VistaFd2 Gbl Eq	9.2																			
Manulife VistaFd1 Equity	7.9	4.4	9.7	15.3	7.8	13.3	-14.9	22.8	-14.4	33.5	5.5	12.6	-2.1	43.1	5.7	-5.6	29.0	36.8	27.6	
Manulife VistaFd2 Equity	7.1	3.7	8.8	14.4	6.9	12.5	-15.6	21.9	-15.0	32.5	4.7	11.8	-2.8	42.1	4.9	-6.2				
Manulife VistaFd1 Bond	6.9	12.3	-5.2	12.9	16.8	19.6	4.1	10.7	14.2	1.6	14.9	17.2	6.5	21.5	34.8	3.0				-0.8
Manulife VistaFd2 Bond	6.1	11.5	-5.9	12.1	15.9	18.8	3.3	9.9	13.4	0.9	14.0	16.3	5.7	20.6	33.8	2.3				

Fund	1996	1995	1994	1993	1992	1991	1990	1989	1988	1987	1986	1985	1984	1983	1982	1981	1980	1979	1978	1977
Marathon Equity	52.1	44.4	7.6	91.0	33.7	-8.3	-5.3	37.4	-25.6	-1.9										
Margin of Safety	18.6	15.6	0.5	18.5	5.0	33.7	-13.5	27.4												
Maritime Life Amer Gth&Inc	19.3	17.7																		
Maritime Life Balanced	14.0	9.7	3.9	13.9	5.4	14.5	-4.4	14.4	0.6	13.0										
Maritime Life Bond	9.8	11.7	-1.3	11.2	13.1	19.5	3.0													
Maritime Life Cdn Equity	17.7																			
Maritime Life Dividend Inc	12.8																			
Maritime Life Global Equity	6.0																			
Maritime Life Growth	19.4	4.5	2.5	29.5	0.5	8.0	-18.7	22.2	-16.1	26.7	21.4	18.5	4.2	52.0	-2.9	-9.3	22.4	30.5	37.3	3.8
Maritime Life Money Mkt	3.9	4.5	2.8	4.8	7.1	9.5	11.4	10.0	7.8	6.8	8.4	9.7	9.3	9.5						
Maritime Life Pacific Basin	8.1	-9.7																		
Maritime Life S&P 500	17.1																			
Mawer Canadian Bond	11.8	13.1	-0.7	11.5																
Mawer Canadian Div Invest	12.7	10.7	2.3	14.8	8.4	17.1	-0.6													
Mawer Canadian Equity	8.5	6.2	5.3	21.0																
Mawer Canadian Income	13.7	10.8	0.7																	
Mawer Cdn Money Mkt	5.0	6.0	4.1	5.0	6.4	10.0	12.4													
Mawer Canadian Bal RSP	12.5	10.9	2.7	15.3	9.1	17.9	-0.7													
Mawer New Canada	37.2	0.1	11.8	57.1	8.8	8.4	6.8													
Mawer US Equity	21.1	21.6	1.2																	
Mawer World Investment	13.0	0.5	18.5	20.5	11.3	12.1	5.1													
Mawer American Equity	26.1																			
Maxxum Canadian Balanced	15.2	12.0	-1.5	23.4	13.1	16.3	-4.9	15.1												
Maxxum Cdn Equity Growth	20.1	17.8	-1.2	50.3	7.8	5.3	-12.6	22.0	-23.3	40.9	22.4	12.7	1.0	50.9	-5.4	-12.6	24.4	38.0	30.5	0.7
Maxxum Dividend	20.3	10.7	10.2	38.8	8.7	17.5	-17.6	1.4	11.2											
Maxxum Global Equity	7.1																			
Maxxum Income	9.5	15.8	-2.2	12.6	10.4	20.3	2.8	11.0	12.7	3.7	13.3	17.3	9.5	20.3	30.7	-2.5	1.9	2.5	6.6	12.8
Maxxum Money Market	5.3	6.3	4.6	5.4	7.3	10.8	12.6	10.7	9.0											
Maxxum Natural Resource	49.3	23.0	0.1	94.8	28.4	-10.3	2.4	44.1												
Maxxum Precious Metals	80.9	4.2	25.5	46.5	16.2	-12.4	-5.6	22.5												
McDonald Canada Plus	11.9	4.0																		
McLean Budden Amer Gth	16.8	26.4	4.5	6.0	16.3	31.3	-2.1	31.8												

Fund	1996	1995	1994	1993	1992	1991	1990	1989	1988	1987	1986	1985	1984	1983	1982	1981	1980	1979	1978	1977
McLean Budden Balanced	18.6	12.0	-0.4	18.5	8.4	18.2	-4.9	11.2	...	...	...	...	...	...	...	...	...	...	...	...
McLean Budden Equity Gth	29.3	6.5	0.5	26.0	3.6	14.7	-16.6	17.7	...	...	...	...	...	...	...	...	...	...	...	...
McLean Budden Fixed Inc	11.7	14.3	-1.7	13.9	12.4	20.6	6.1	9.0	...	...	...	...	...	...	...	...	...	...	...	...
McLean Budden Money Mkt	5.0	6.1	4.2	4.5	6.6	10.1	11.9	8.8	...	...	...	...	...	...	...	...	...	...	...	...
McLean Budden Pld Off Eq	12.1	-4.0	14.7	25.5	9.0	7.3	-16.5	21.7	...	...	...	...	...	...	...	...	...	...	...	...
McLean Budden Pld Cdn Eq	32.5	8.2	1.4	31.6	5.2	13.3	-15.1	24.5	-6.8	28.4	23.2	18.0	3.5	51.2						
McLean Budden Pld Am Eq	18.8	28.6	7.9	7.8	18.9	33.2	-8.3	31.4	-23.3	37.2	40.6	19.5	2.9							
McLean Budden Pld Bal	19.5	12.5	2.5	19.7	11.6	19.2	-3.7	16.9	-0.3	17.3	20.1	17.4	7.0							
McLean Budden Pld F-Inc	13.2	15.9	-0.5	14.4	14.7	21.4	5.1	11.5	13.4	3.4	16.2	19.0	10.1	19.7	35.8					
MD Balanced	13.5	11.0	6.0	14.2																
MD Bond	11.8	13.4	0.2	12.1	15.3	19.8	4.1	9.6												
MD Bond & Mortgage	8.5																			
MD Dividend	13.4	9.7	4.8	9.0																
MD Emerging Markets	6.0																			
MD Equity	13.1	-1.2	12.8	32.7	2.6	7.0	-12.1	19.8	-1.3	27.7	18.5	22.8	6.1	46.3	15.3	-8.0	21.0	22.9	25.6	-2.5
MD Global Bond	5.2																			
MD Growth Investments	13.8	9.5	15.3	34.4	11.6	15.4	-17.9	20.1	-13.2	41.4	37.2	21.8	5.1	60.3	14.5	-0.5	26.4	25.5	51.4	46.9
MD Money	5.3	6.5	4.5	5.1	6.7	10.5	11.7	9.9	7.9	7.2	8.6	9.9	9.9	9.9	16.3	15.7	13.1	10.9	7.9	8.4
MD Select	24.5	2.8																		
MD US Equity	15.4	31.9	-0.8	32.3																
Metlife Mvp Balanced	9.4	7.3	1.7	12.6	6.0	11.3	-4.3	13.5	-5.1											
Metlife Mvp Bond	6.3	12.4	-3.1	10.5	11.8	14.3	6.0	7.2	7.8											
Metlife Mvp Equity	12.1	1.8	6.7	16.3	-1.4	6.2	-14.3	22.1	-17.3											
Metlife Mvp Growth	24.0	9.4	4.4																	
Metlife Mvp Money Market	4.6	5.3	3.3	4.0	5.2															
Metlife Mvp US Equity	20.1	20.3	-3.8																	
Middlefield Growth	23.1	-5.8	-5.6	36.9	13.0															
Millennium Diversified	16.5	7.9																		
Millennium Next Generation	42.0	22.4																		
Multiple Opportunities	49.5	48.1	9.3	138.6	-11.9	-0.5	-13.6	13.2	-51.7	95.7	39.9									
Mutual Amerifund	14.6	18.2	-1.0	19.2	11.6	26.5	-24.0	20.2	-10.4	27.8										
Mutual Bond	9.2	11.5	-1.3	11.4	12.6															

Fund	1996	1995	1994	1993	1992	1991	1990	1989	1988	1987	1986	1985	1984	1983	1982	1981	1980	1979	1978	1977
Mutual Diversifund 40	14.5	10.4	3.0	13.9	5.8	17.4	-10.5	16.1	3.1	6.4	16.4									
Mutual Equifund	19.6	8.4	8.6	15.4	-1.7	13.4	-23.7	28.1	-11.6	19.8	17.9									
Mutual Life 2	12.4	12.1	2.2	13.2	9.3	20.5	5.5	10.6	13.1	3.1	17.7	21.9	8.8	20.3	32.1	0.1	3.6			
Mutual Life A	17.3	9.3	5.9	16.6	1.5	16.9	-23.8	24.6	-10.3	18.8	12.6	17.7	1.3	58.2	-2.6	-8.6	33.4	38.2	25.2	-0.1
Mutual Life B	17.5	9.6	4.5	17.3	0.0	16.3	-24.4	28.0	-7.2	17.7	18.6	18.6	2.7	60.2	-0.8	-4.6	33.6	41.4	25.5	-1.5
Mutual Money Market	4.5	6.1	4.1	4.9	6.2	9.5	11.5	10.5	7.8	6.8	7.9									
Mutual Premier America	13.8	17.7	-1.3																	
Mutual Premier Blue Chip	16.9	6.5	9.7																	
Mutual Premier Bond	9.6	12.0	-1.5																	
Mutual Premier Diversified	15.8	8.8																		
Mutual Premier Emerg Mkts	3.1																			
Mutual Premier Growth	20.3	16.4	6.6																	
Mutual Premier Int'l	11.4	5.0	11.9																	
Mutual Premier Mortgage	8.5	9.2	2.9																	
NAL-Balanced Growth	16.5																			
NAL-Canadian Bond	9.5	13.5	-0.2	11.2	12.5	19.8	1.6	9.9	14.0											
NAL-Canadian Diversified	17.6	9.5	4.4	18.0	5.0	12.9	-5.9	16.2	-0.2											
NAL-Canadian Equity	22.0	6.7	8.3	23.4	-0.9	7.7	-13.0	23.2	-13.0											
NAL-Canadian Money Mkt	4.6	5.5	3.3	4.8	6.7	9.9	12.7													
NAL-Equity Growth	23.3																			
NAL-Global Equity	5.6	4.9	14.5	32.5																
NAL-US Equity	11.8	17.8																		
National Life Balanced	14.8	9.8	3.2	15.0	1.8	12.4	-13.5	17.6	-12.0	32.5	14.4	14.5	2.1	43.2	-2.9	-10.5	25.6	32.2	27.3	-3.5
National Life Equities	18.3	9.7	8.8	23.4	13.2	19.3	4.3	9.7	11.9	1.5	14.8	17.7	10.2	19.8	36.5	-6.6	-0.3	0.9	5.6	11.4
National Life Fixed Income	10.5	12.6	-0.7	12.2	13.2	20.3	-5.7	19.2												
National LifeGlobal Equities	14.2	4.2	9.2	34.6	8.2															
National Life Money Market	3.9	5.5	3.3	4.2																
National Trust Special Equity	27.6	1.0	-5.6																	
National Trust Amer Equity	16.6	16.4	-3.5	16.1																
National Trust Balanced	13.8	10.2	1.6	15.9	9.2	19.2	0.8	10.0	10.8	3.5	16.9	18.8	6.1	23.7	38.9	-8.8	-4.5	5.3	7.4	12.6
National Trust Cdn Bond	11.2	14.3	-1.0	11.0	13.2	20.9														
National Trust Cdn Equity	13.5	4.1	1.9	23.0	2.0	16.9	-13.6	21.0	-19.2	36.9	18.3	14.2	0.2	39.3	2.7	-5.8	29.1	33.0	27.9	-3.7

Fund	1996	1995	1994	1993	1992	1991	1990	1989	1988	1987	1986	1985	1984	1983	1982	1981	1980	1979	1978	1977
National Trust Dividend	18.4	1.9	5.1																	
Nationall Trust Emerg Mkts	6.3	-29.0																		
National Trust Int'l Equity	10.7	2.1																		
National Trust Int'l RSP Bond	9.5	12.8																		
National Trust Money Mkt	4.7	5.6	3.7	5.0	6.2	9.7														
National Trust Mortgage	9.2	9.3	2.3																	
Navigator America Value	18.5																			
Navigator Asia Pacific	9.2																			
Navigator Canadian Income	12.6		11.1																	
Navigator Latin America	35.6																			
Navigator Value Invest Retire	47.1	18.1	16.8																	
NN Balanced	15.7	9.8	4.1	13.8	8.9	12.4	-6.8	11.3	-3.0											
NN Bond	11.8	13.8	-1.3	13.3	10.6	18.9	3.9	10.5	14.3											
NN Can-Am	16.0	28.3	1.5																	
NN Can-Asian	19.6	-3.1	9.0																	
NN Can-Euro	17.9																			
NN Canadian 35 Index	17.4	4.4	15.7	9.1	-1.8	8.6	-16.2													
NN Canadian Growth	15.8	2.2	7.2	14.6	-0.4	14.6	-15.8	15.5	-17.6	15.2	16.8	27.8	0.4	51.8	16.2	-3.8	22.1	28.3	26.5	3.3
NN Dividend	16.3	11.2																		
NN Money Market	5.1	6.4	4.4	5.2	7.0	10.5	10.4	9.3	7.0											
NN T-Bill	4.6	5.2	3.3	4.6	7.0	10.0	10.4	9.3	7.0											
O.I.Q. Ferique Actions	17.4	7.9	11.7	13.8	4.1	19.7	-16.8	24.1	-8.6	31.7	17.6	16.7	-3.3	60.1	-9.3	15.8				
O.I.Q. Ferique Equilibre	13.2	11.0	6.5	13.2	9.1	21.0	-3.3	14.3	3.4	15.9	16.1	18.3	2.5	36.9	3.7					
O.I.Q. Ferique Internation	11.2	0.2																		
O.I.Q. Ferique Obligations	11.5	13.3	0.1	11.8	16.0	18.0	5.2	10.4	12.4	2.4	14.8	18.5	8.6	23.4	46.7	-13.3				
O.I.Q. Ferique Revenu	5.6	6.9	5.0	5.8	7.5	11.4	12.0	10.6	8.4	7.9	9.1	10.8	10.2	12.1	17.7	14.7				
OHA Balanced	18.1	8.9	1.3	14.5																
OHA Bond	11.7	13.9	-2.1	11.4	15.7															
OHA Canadian Equity	22.9	2.4	-10.9	54.1	7.6															
OHA Foreign Equity	8.9	20.3	15.5	11.9																
OHA Short Term	4.9	6.1	4.2	6.0	6.6															
Optima Strat Cdn Equity	18.2	15.3	7.9																	

Fund	1996	1995	1994	1993	1992	1991	1990	1989	1988	1987	1986	1985	1984	1983	1982	1981	1980	1979	1978	1977
Optima Strat Cdn Fixed Inc	11.3	14.8	-1.4																	
Optima Strat Glo Fixed Inc	8.5	11.9																		
Optima Strat Int'l Equity	20.6	7.5																		
Optima Strat Short Term	8.4	7.8	2.8																	
Optima Strat US Equity	28.2	22.8																		
Optimum Actions	16.8	5.5																		
Optimum Epargne	4.3	6.3	4.3	5.8	7.4	10.7	12.2	9.7	8.9	8.1										
Optimum Equilibre	11.4	14.6	0.2	16.3	9.9	16.5	-3.9	12.3	9.4	2.8										
Optimum Int'l	6.2	17.2																		
Optimum Obligations	12.4	15.8	-1.3	15.2	15.9	19.9	1.3	11.5	13.0	1.8										
Orbit World	0.8	-9.5	16.5	16.7	6.7	5.5	-0.2													
OTGIF Balanced	14.4	8.8	4.2	15.3	9.8	13.1	-4.5	17.9	0.6	16.1										
OTGIF Diversified	17.9	5.0	8.4	15.1	1.7	7.5	-15.5	25.7	-10.9	29.6	16.8	19.4	3.6	46.3	0.2	-5.3	26.1	34.5	21.8	3.9
OTGIF Fixed Value	5.6	6.6	4.7	7.9	8.0	10.3	11.4	10.4	8.8	7.4	9.1	9.8	9.7	10.5	15.4	14.0				
OTGIF Global	12.1	9.6	6.9	16.3	9.9															
OTGIF Growth	14.0	5.8	4.6	15.9	0.5	7.8	-14.9	26.7	-11.1	30.5	20.2	22.7	3.8	50.0	-3.0	-1.9	25.9	36.1	22.3	0.4
OTGIF Mortgage Income	9.9	9.6	4.8	11.6	9.1	10.0	10.6	10.1	9.1	9.0	10.1	14.3	8.4	11.4	12.7	10.6				
Pacific Special Equity	27.9	39.4	-7.7																	
PH & N $US Money Mkt	5.1	5.4	3.2	2.7	4.1															
PH & N Bal Pension TR	17.5	10.8	6.3	16.0	10.7	19.8	-4.9	20.9												
PH & N Balanced	16.2	10.4	6.6	16.1	10.2															
PH & N Bond	12.2	14.2	0.7	13.8	14.4	22.1	5.0	12.0	14.1	4.1	20.0	23.1	5.2	24.1	42.8	-12.0	3.6	7.3	12.6	
PH & N Canadian Equity	22.0	6.8	14.7	18.0	1.7	9.5	-13.9	29.0	-9.0	28.5	23.1	18.0	0.2	67.4	-15.6	-3.6	33.4	28.5	42.6	9.0
PH & N Cdn Money Mkt	4.9	6.5	4.4	5.4	7.2	10.5	13.1	11.3	8.5	7.5										
PH & N Dividend Income	21.1	10.0	8.7	20.1	5.0	15.1	-10.1	21.4	0.7	17.7	13.4	11.9	2.3	44.4	16.7	-6.8	9.4	12.4	14.3	
PH & N Int'l Equity	11.2	5.1																		
PH & N North Amer Equity	31.9	-10.7	8.2	17.1	4.4	12.8	-14.8	26.7	-10.8	31.1	20.5	13.3	6.0	56.8	-5.8	-10.4	27.8	23.1	31.1	0.8
PH & N Pooled Pension Tr	23.6	7.4	12.6	17.1	4.4	12.8	-14.8	26.7	-10.8	31.1	20.5	13.3	6.0	58.0	12.2	11.8				
PH & N Pooled US Pension	27.2	17.1	7.1	27.7	16.4	40.1	-14.8	33.3	-17.2	30.0	22.1	16.2	2.2							
PH & N RSP/RIF Equity	20.4	8.6	12.1	20.2	3.3	11.6	-14.6	29.6	-12.3	28.8	24.3	16.4	-0.4	66.2	-13.2	-6.6	27.9	17.5	40.3	0.3
PH & N S-T Bond & Mtg	10.8	11.1																		
PH & N US Equity	25.5	15.9	5.7	26.4	16.1	38.7	-15.4	31.8	-18.6	29.1	22.4	14.6	-1.9	54.5	14.9	7.2	29.6	9.8	46.1	9.2

Fund	1996	1995	1994	1993	1992	1991	1990	1989	1988	1987	1986	1985	1984	1983	1982	1981	1980	1979	1978	1977
PH & N Vintage	33.2	12.9	9.3	24.8	11.2	20.4	-6.7	32.5	-15.0	35.9										
Pret et Revenu Americain	16.7	32.8	-2.0	8.5	23.5	24.7	-10.0	21.3	-25.1	37.2	24.2	10.0	6.2	27.7	6.4	-5.1	9.0	5.1	32.0	4.1
Pret et Revenu Canadien	18.0	12.1	4.3	26.1	6.2	13.7	-15.9	21.4	-20.8	32.6	7.7	2.3	-1.0	50.2	-6.0	-12.6	7.8	24.3	32.8	2.9
Pret et Revenu Dividendes	26.2																			
Pret et Revenu Hypotheque	8.0	8.3	2.3	8.6	11.8	13.8	9.4	10.6	9.7	6.2	11.4	14.6	10.8	14.1	22.5	6.5	8.7	6.0	8.5	12.8
Pret et Revenu Int'l	12.0																			
Pret et Revenu Mond Oblig	0.8																			
Pret et Revenu M Mkt	4.7	5.8	4.3	5.2	6.3	10.3	11.5													
Pret et Revenu Obligations	9.7	13.1	-0.2	11.6	13.8	19.6	2.9	9.1												
Prosperity American Perf	-9.5	17.7	0.9																	
Protected American	-0.3	4.3	-0.7	26.8	8.0	9.8	8.3													
Pursuit Canadian Bond	5.6	6.2	1.3	10.4	13.1	12.9	-1.7	2.0	8.9											
Pursuit Canadian Equity	22.0	10.2	-1.5	32.5	6.9	19.2	-17.4	6.6	-23.8	14.9	67.1	9.8	2.7							
Pursuit Global Bond	4.8																			
Pursuit Global Equity	14.2																			
Pursuit Money Market	5.5	6.3	4.8	6.0	7.2	11.0	12.1	10.5												
Quebec Growth Fund Inc	18.5	6.4	-7.4	41.2	43.3	48.3	-50.0	50.0	-44.8											
Resolute Growth	40.4	2.5																		
Retrocomm Growth	0.8	-7.5	20.2																	
Royal Asian Growth	10.4	7.7	4.7	18.7	12.9	11.6	-2.4	14.4												
Royal Balanced	12.2	4.5	0.3																	
Royal Canadian Growth	17.4	4.1	0.1																	
Royal Canadian Small Cap	15.3																			
Royal Energy	29.0	-13.3	-6.0	81.5	19.7	-18.7	16.2	23.6	-22.1	64.0	-21.3	-5.3	-5.5							
Royal European Growth	13.7	10.6	14.3	27.6	0.9	5.4	-17.3	15.2	-24.2											
Royal Int'l Equity	10.4	5.8	11.6																	
Royal Japanese Stock	-4.8	-14.7	6.3	48.5	-13.1	15.5	-34.2	9.0	-7.6	25.4	70.6			24.6	-14.2					
Royal Latin America	11.2																			
Royal Lepage Commercial	-0.9	2.6	5.9	-3.2	-2.5	4.9	9.8													
Royal Life Balanced	12.8	9.6	2.9	13.7	8.9	19.6														
Royal Life Canadian Growth	17.8																			
Royal Life Equity	16.4	6.4	11.0	15.4	4.1	21.7														

Fund	1996	1995	1994	1993	1992	1991	1990	1989	1988	1987	1986	1985	1984	1983	1982	1981	1980	1979	1978	1977
Royal Life Income	10.5	13.2	-2.9	10.7	12.8	14.3														
Royal Life Int'l Equity	10.8																			
Royal Life Money Market	5.9	6.4	4.7																	
Royal Life Science & Tech	17.2																			
Royal Precious Metals	71.9	32.1	18.4	23.4	14.5	-17.5	6.1													
Royal Trust $US Money Mkt	4.4	4.7	2.6	2.1	3.4	6.3														
Royal Trust Adv Balanced	11.5	8.7	2.9	15.4	9.4	13.9	-1.8	17.0	-2.3											
Royal Trust Adv Growth	12.8	7.4	3.4	17.7	7.5	12.4	-5.3	17.7	-8.3											
Royal Trust Adv Income	11.0	9.5	2.0	12.8	10.8	16.4	0.0	14.6	3.2											
Royal Trust American Stock	11.6	23.5	4.1	14.1	20.3	24.3	-9.6	30.7	-20.3	32.7	28.9	7.4	-3.3	36.4	11.6	-7.3	22.4	6.9	23.5	5.7
Royal Trust Bond	9.9	13.3	-1.5	12.3	13.5	20.9	3.1	9.9	14.3	-0.8	16.8	20.6	7.7	20.7	35.4	-3.8	-1.4	3.0	7.2	14.0
Royal Trust Cdn Money Mkt	4.3	5.6	3.7	4.4	6.6	10.3	11.8	10.3	8.2											
Royal Trust Canadian Stock	14.8	6.2	8.4	17.9	3.8	11.8	-16.7	23.5	-13.1	27.7	9.4	11.9	-1.8	53.0	-3.5	-13.2	28.5	38.8	27.0	-1.2
Royal Trust Canadian T-Bill	4.5	5.3	3.1	3.6																
Royal Trust Gth & Income	22.7	6.2	3.6	10.6	3.4	14.3	-7.2	9.7	6.7	0.4										
Royal Trust Int'l Bond	5.3	13.2	-4.1	17.5																
Royal Trust Mortgage	8.0	8.5	1.3	5.2	12.3	13.7	9.9	11.1	9.3	7.3	10.6	14.9	10.3	16.2	24.4	6.0	9.6	5.5	8.2	12.5
Royfund Bond	9.6	13.0	-0.8	10.3	14.9	21.0	3.5	8.3	10.8	3.7	16.6	17.8	5.1	16.0	20.6	2.1	7.9	5.7	6.9	13.1
Royfund Canadian Equity	15.0	6.2	9.9	29.0	1.7	-0.7	-13.8	20.8	-14.0	23.5	30.3	20.8	7.1	62.4	-16.0	-14.1	42.5	48.4	31.8	0.8
Royfund Cdn Money Mkt	4.3	5.7	3.6	4.5	7.2	10.1	12.7	10.8	8.0											
Royfund Canadian T-Bill	4.6	5.9	4.0	4.6	7.2															
Royfund Dividend	19.8	10.4	5.2																	
Royfund Int'l Income	5.2	12.5	-1.5																	
Royfund Mortgage	9.1	8.5	4.8	6.6																
Royfund US Equity	12.1	26.0	3.1	31.3																
Royfund US Money Market	4.4	4.6	2.6	2.0	3.4															
Saxon Balanced	17.8	15.4	3.2	36.6	8.0	11.0	-13.1	5.5	-14.8	6.7										
Saxon Small Cap	13.3	6.5	2.0	45.0	6.4	9.9	-25.0	15.6	-12.8	20.4										
Saxon Stock	22.3	15.4	3.4	48.9	6.6	8.1	-16.8	6.5	-16.7	10.8										
Saxon World Growth	9.5	24.3	13.4	51.7	2.7	30.8	-26.7	25.5	-18.0	41.2										
Sceptre Asian Growth	6.3	-11.7	37.7																	
Sceptre Balanced Growth	25.4	10.3	6.5	16.6	7.5	17.7	-6.3	14.8	1.6	17.0										

Fund	1996	1995	1994	1993	1992	1991	1990	1989	1988	1987	1986	1985	1984	1983	1982	1981	1980	1979	1978	1977
Sceptre Bond	10.6	12.6	-0.2	11.4	13.4	20.5	6.2	9.0	13.0	2.8										
Sceptre Equity Growth	38.5	23.4	25.6	24.7	-2.2	8.6	-12.5	23.5	-6.2											
Sceptre Int'l	11.8	-0.8	22.4	36.0	24.3	21.0	-11.0	27.3	-13.0											
Scotia Money Market	5.3	6.2	4.3	5.5	6.5	10.3	12.7	11.2												
Scotia Canam Growth	17.4	29.0																		
Scotia Canam Income	2.8	12.2	-4.4	7.5																
Scotia Ex Balanced	13.2	9.4	3.9	15.6	8.1	14.8	3.8													
Scotia Ex Canadian Growth	25.6	14.7	9.1	23.2	1.4	13.8	-15.3	20.2	-9.7	30.7	14.4	8.2	-1.9	45.7	0.6	-12.0	25.8	34.6	32.9	-2.2
Scotia Ex Canadian Blue Chip	16.7	0.4	2.8	19.7	4.2	17.3	-14.2	17.8	-15.8											
Scotia Ex Defensive Income	9.0	9.9	1.7	10.6	9.0	13.2	5.4	7.9	7.9											
Scotia Ex Dividend	18.4	9.0	2.3	10.6	6.7	20.5	-3.9	8.1	5.1											
Scotia Ex Global Bond	4.2																			
Scotia Ex Income	10.2	14.4	0.2	10.9	9.9	12.6	6.1	10.3	12.2											
Scotia Ex Int'l	7.8	5.7	8.0	25.6	13.7	18.9	-16.1	24.6	-21.3	28.0	37.6	23.6	0.9	36.6	11.9	4.1	21.2	6.8	38.7	7.8
Scotia Ex Latin America	32.2																			
Scotia Ex Money Market	4.6	6.0	4.0	4.3	6.5	10.0														
Scotia Ex Mortgage	9.6	10.3	3.8																	
Scotia Ex Pacific Rim	2.9																			
Scotia Ex Precious Metals	49.6	-6.2																		
Scotia Ex Premium T-Bill	5.0	6.4	4.3	5.8																
Scotia Ex T-Bill	4.5	6.1	4.1	4.4																
Scotia Ex Total Return	11.0	10.2	6.9	21.5	11.0	23.8	-2.4													
Scotia Ex American Growth	8.1	19.2	7.5	21.8	8.5	23.9	-8.1	7.9	-29.4											
Special Opportunities	15.4	5.9	2.8	27.0	3.1	0.9	-17.7	24.0												
Spectrum Utd Amer Eqty	25.1	27.7	-1.9	4.9	18.8	28.8	-17.6	29.3	-11.1	21.5	22.8	26.2	14.8	37.7	-2.9	1.6	32.9	44.1	22.4	-4.2
Spectrum Utd Amer Growth	30.2	34.8	1.6	29.1	18.6	36.3	-21.9	27.0	-15.5	18.2	17.3	24.3	11.2	44.6	8.4	2.0	10.9	15.1	25.5	15.0
Spectrum Utd Asian Dynasty	5.6	-6.2																		
Spectrum Utd Asset Alloc	12.0	7.2	2.3	15.6																
Spectrum Utd Canadian Eqty	18.6	3.6	11.0	32.8	8.6	18.4	-13.8	19.4	-1.2	9.2	17.0	31.1	5.2	48.1	-7.7	-2.9	33.8	44.7	42.3	-3.9
Spectrum Utd Cdn Growth	24.3	19.6	9.7	45.2	12.3	14.3	-22.9	16.2	-9.4	18.1	22.9	26.4	-3.0	60.1	-14.1	-14.6	53.6	53.6	43.8	-0.7
Spectrum Utd Canadian Inv	20.2	7.4	5.7	12.4	-1.5	8.1	-15.2	24.5	-14.5	24.4	11.9	13.9	1.1	46.5	4.6	-7.6	17.3	24.5	24.5	3.8
Spectrum Utd Cdn Portfolio	15.6	11.8	3.0	20.8	11.4	17.1	-5.3													

Fund	1996	1995	1994	1993	1992	1991	1990	1989	1988	1987	1986	1985	1984	1983	1982	1981	1980	1979	1978	1977
Spectrum Utd Cdn Stock	14.5	5.3	7.9	17.5	-2.8	12.8	-16.1	16.0	-7.0											
Spectrum Utd Cdn T-Bill	4.6	5.7	4.0	4.7	6.5	10.1	12.4	11.0	8.2											
Spectrum Utd Diversified	12.7	8.3	0.7	14.3	6.8	15.6	-5.6	12.4	2.4											
Spectrum Utd Dividend	13.9	8.1	3.0	13.8	3.3	16.3	-4.6	13.0	7.4											
Spectrum Utd Emerg Mkts	23.0	-14.8																		
Spectrum Utd European Gth	21.8																			
Spectrum Utd Gbl Telecomm	3.0	31.1																		
Spectrum Utd Global Bond	5.4	15.2																		
Spectrum Utd Global Diver	10.6	13.3	0.1	17.0	13.0	19.7	-8.6													
Spectrum Utd Global Equity	15.1	0.7	5.5	21.2	7.3															
Spectrum Utd Global Growth	-1.3	-4.0	5.1	40.2	14.4	18.6	-32.2	15.0	-14.0	8.7	18.9	25.5	-0.8	49.1	-7.8	-6.4	44.3	44.4	30.0	8.8
Spectrum Utd L-T Bond	10.0	14.8	-4.7	13.0	16.1	21.2	0.8													
Spectrum Utd M-T Bond	10.1	13.3	-3.0	11.8	14.3	16.6	5.9	8.4	11.7											
Spectrum Utd Optimax USA	13.7	18.2																		
Spectrum Utd RSP Int'l Bond	3.4	15.1	-3.1																	
Spectrum Utd Savings	4.6	6.0	4.1	4.5	6.7	10.2	12.6	11.3	8.5											
Spectrum Utd S-T Bond	8.8	9.8	0.5	6.1	10.3	12.5	8.5	7.7	6.8	7.8	8.6	13.1	10.2	13.7	18.9	9.8	10.1	7.2	8.8	14.2
Spectrum Utd US$ M Mkt	4.2	5.0	3.3	2.5	2.2	4.4	6.7	9.4												
Sportfund	17.6																			
SSQ - Actions Americaines	28.5	26.5	2.9	7.1	4.8	56.0	-11.1													
SSQ - Actions Canadiennes	18.7	10.1	0.8	16.2	6.7	20.0	-13.5	22.3	-17.0	28.7	11.7	6.3	-3.1	52.4	-10.9	7.8				
SSQ - Equilibre	15.9	11.9	1.9	13.3																
SSQ - Hypotheques	10.0	10.0	5.5	8.7	12.1	16.9	10.6													
SSQ - Marche Monetaire	6.1	7.0																		
SSQ - Obligations	13.3	13.9	1.5	12.3	15.1	23.7	6.1	12.6	14.2	2.8	17.3	21.3	11.7	23.9	38.2	-9.8				
Standard Life Balanced	14.9	11.6	1.6																	
Standard Life Bond	10.7	13.3	-0.9																	
Standard Life Cdn Dividend	24.0																			
Standard Life Equity	18.8	8.3	10.7																	
Standard Life Growth Equity	17.9																			
Standard Life Int'l Bond	2.1																			
Standard Life Int'l Equity	10.5																			

Fund	1996	1995	1994	1993	1992	1991	1990	1989	1988	1987	1986	1985	1984	1983	1982	1981	1980	1979	1978	1977
Standard Life Money Mkt	5.5	6.1	4.1	……	……	……	……	……	……	……	……	……	……	……	……	……	……	……	……	……
Standard Life Natural Res	28.6	……	……	……	……	……	……	……	……	……	……	……	……	……	……	……	……	……	……	……
Standard Life US Equity	15.0	……	……	……	……	……	……	……	……	……	……	……	……	……	……	……	……	……	……	……
STAR Fgn Bal Gth & Income	11.5	……	……	……	……	……	……	……	……	……	……	……	……	……	……	……	……	……	……	……
STAR Fgn Max Eqty Gth	11.7	……	……	……	……	……	……	……	……	……	……	……	……	……	……	……	……	……	……	……
STAR Fgn Maximum L-T Gth	13.4	……	……	……	……	……	……	……	……	……	……	……	……	……	……	……	……	……	……	……
STAR Inv Bal Growth & Inc	10.0	……	……	……	……	……	……	……	……	……	……	……	……	……	……	……	……	……	……	……
STAR Inv Conserv Inc & Gth	16.4	……	……	……	……	……	……	……	……	……	……	……	……	……	……	……	……	……	……	……
STAR Inv Long-Term Gth	11.1	……	……	……	……	……	……	……	……	……	……	……	……	……	……	……	……	……	……	……
STAR Inv Maximum L-T Gth	12.7	……	……	……	……	……	……	……	……	……	……	……	……	……	……	……	……	……	……	……
STAR Reg Bal Gth & Income	12.3	……	……	……	……	……	……	……	……	……	……	……	……	……	……	……	……	……	……	……
STAR Reg Conserv Inc & Gth	13.1	……	……	……	……	……	……	……	……	……	……	……	……	……	……	……	……	……	……	……
STAR Reg Long-Term Gth	12.7	……	……	……	……	……	……	……	……	……	……	……	……	……	……	……	……	……	……	……
STAR Reg Max Equity Gth	11.4	……	……	……	……	……	……	……	……	……	……	……	……	……	……	……	……	……	……	……
STAR Reg Max L-T Gth	13.1	……	……	……	……	……	……	……	……	……	……	……	……	……	……	……	……	……	……	……
Sunfund	17.8	6.1	9.1	18.5	-2.0	14.4	-15.2	19.0	-6.5	27.8	14.6	15.7	3.1	50.2	-2.6	-10.1	25.2	36.3	25.4	1.9
Talvest Bond	10.4	12.9	-0.8	12.2	12.3	18.6	4.2	10.3	15.0	3.1	15.8	20.6	9.5	24.0	37.4	-3.4	0.1	4.3	8.5	13.2
Talvest Canadian Asset Alloc	10.0	10.7	2.2	15.3	4.2	14.5	-2.6	15.9	4.6	14.1	……	……	……	……	……	……	……	……	……	……
Talvest Canadian Eqty Value	8.0	9.8	7.1	15.1	-0.2	21.8	-14.4	19.0	-5.7	30.4	16.3	16.7	2.4	38.3	-9.1	-3.1	22.7	29.5	30.4	-0.7
Talvest Dividend	14.4	……	……	……	……	……	……	……	……	……	……	……	……	……	……	……	……	……	……	……
Talvest Forgn Pay Cdn Bond	6.2	13.4	-4.7	……	……	……	……	……	……	……	……	……	……	……	……	……	……	……	……	……
Talvest Global Asset Alloc	6.5	1.8	7.2	26.3	10.7	4.3	-1.5	17.9	……	……	……	……	……	……	……	……	……	……	……	……
Talvest Global RRSP	12.2	-2.7	7.9	……	……	……	……	……	……	……	……	……	……	……	……	……	……	……	……	……
Talvest Income	10.5	9.4	2.0	10.3	10.3	16.1	6.6	9.7	9.6	6.3	10.6	15.6	8.4	17.0	24.1	4.2	7.9	5.5	8.1	12.8
Talvest Money	5.3	6.4	4.6	5.4	7.4	10.6	12.8	11.3	8.2	5.3	……	……	……	……	……	……	……	……	……	……
Talvest New Economy	16.7	13.9	……	……	……	……	……	……	……	……	……	……	……	……	……	……	……	……	……	……
Templeton Balanced	11.9	7.0	9.8	19.9	2.7	……	……	……	……	……	……	……	……	……	……	……	……	……	……	……
Templeton Canadian Bond	8.9	7.3	-0.9	9.3	13.6	13.8	……	……	……	……	……	……	……	……	……	……	……	……	……	……
Templeton Canadian Stock	15.8	3.3	13.7	21.5	-4.0	5.5	-16.4	……	……	……	……	……	……	……	……	……	……	……	……	……
Templeton Cdn Asset Alloc	12.6	……	……	……	……	……	……	……	……	……	……	……	……	……	……	……	……	……	……	……
Templeton Emerging Mkts	11.1	-10.4	21.9	46.3	4.1	……	……	……	……	……	……	……	……	……	……	……	……	……	……	……
Templeton Global Balanced	11.9	……	……	……	……	……	……	……	……	……	……	……	……	……	……	……	……	……	……	……

Fund	1996	1995	1994	1993	1992	1991	1990	1989	1988	1987	1986	1985	1984	1983	1982	1981	1980	1979	1978	1977
Templeton Global Bond	9.8	9.6	-2.4	11.3	18.7	8.4	12.9	7.3												
Templeton Global Small Co	9.4	16.7	10.0	37.5	8.6	26.4	-20.8													
Templeton Growth	9.3	11.8	14.5	29.3	20.9	24.8	-14.5	23.9	-13.7	29.4	27.5	20.8	10.7	54.7	2.3	-2.0	23.2	16.3	50.9	40.1
Templeton Int'l Stock	14.1	7.5	19.9	41.0	15.8	15.4	-13.7													
Templeton Int'l Balanced	12.1																			
Templeton T-Bill	4.6	6.0	4.0	5.0	6.6	10.3	12.5	11.0												
The Enterprise	0.0																			
Top 50 Equity	16.2	0.6	4.5	9.6	3.1	9.9	-16.5	19.4												
Top 50 T-Bill Bond	9.0	5.0	-9.3	6.0	9.7	17.5	10.7													
Top 50 US Equity	0.3	18.8	-7.7	30.9																
Tradex Bond	10.7	11.3	-4.1	9.7	11.6	13.4	11.1													
Tradex Emerg Mkts Country	4.9																			
Tradex Equity	31.6	9.6	10.8	19.3	1.5	7.6	-12.4	20.3	-8.0	28.1	15.9	17.1	5.7	48.0	-1.7	-3.6	31.6	46.7	37.7	18.5
Trans-Canada Bond	5.5	9.8	0.6	5.6	9.7	15.2	6.4	5.7	10.8											
Trans-Canada Dividend	14.5	7.7	13.5	3.9	-1.0	9.1	-12.1	15.3	2.7	18.1	30.3	20.6	2.4	23.3	5.2	7.3	10.6	9.7	15.4	3.1
Trans-Canada Money Mkt	5.3	6.2	4.9	4.8	6.9	10.0	11.2	5.9	2.9	6.4	8.6	10.1	9.5							
Trans-Canada Pension	19.2	-6.1	1.9	47.6	-10.1	9.2	-8.7	19.5	-12.1	24.5	21.6	14.9	13.4							
Trans-Canada Value	19.1	-3.3	-3.5	43.0	-6.1	5.3	-14.4	17.1	-1.4	27.6	43.2	21.8	6.2	42.2	2.5	-7.6	14.1	7.5	20.4	2.3
Transamerica B.I.G.	11.2	9.4	4.9	13.4	10.5	13.2	3.1	9.7	4.1	11.3	11.3	12.6	9.3	27.4	20.7	-3.1	2.7			
Transamerica Growsafe Bal	11.8	7.4																		
Transamerica Growsafe Bond	7.3	9.2																		
Transamerica Growsafe Eqty	15.5	6.8																		
Transamerica Growsafe Int'l	12.2	6.2																		
Transamerica Growsafe M	4.2	4.0																		
Trillium Gth Cap Income	0.2																			
Trimark Advantage Bond	13.7																			
Trimark Americas	16.4	-3.8	16.7																	
Trimark Canadian	14.7	3.8	17.2	25.2	12.0	16.9	-15.4	25.6	-5.7	33.0	13.2	22.1	4.8	70.3	-2.6					
Trimark Canadian Bond	12.4																			
Trimark Fund	9.5	19.5	18.9	31.8	27.3	31.9	-22.0	22.0	-6.7	32.5	28.7	14.9	4.5	68.6	15.4					
Trimark Government Income	9.2	10.0																		
Trimark Income Growth	11.7	12.0	8.0	25.4	9.5	20.8	-11.5	17.3	9.3											

Fund	1996	1995	1994	1993	1992	1991	1990	1989	1988	1987	1986	1985	1984	1983	1982	1981	1980	1979	1978	1977
Trimark Indo-Pacific	13.4																			
Trimark Interest	4.7	6.3	4.2	5.3	6.4	10.3	13.0	10.6	8.7											
Trimark RSP Equity	12.2	3.5	16.9	19.8	7.8	20.3	-15.2	17.0												
Trimark Select Balanced	12.1	9.9	9.1	21.3	9.7	20.8														
Trimark Select Cdn Growth	11.9	5.4	17.1																	
Trimark Select Growth	8.8	17.2	16.8	26.9	27.2	30.9	-17.9													
Trust Pret et Revenu retra	15.3	13.7	2.3	15.8	11.5	17.0	-2.5	12.8	-2.1	13.1	16.3	10.0	7.6	28.7	17.9	-10.3	5.1	18.1	21.0	4.8
Universal Americas	14.4	-9.6	18.7	26.2	12.6	16.1	-14.3	24.9	-13.4	30.0	22.4	18.6	10.1	36.6	25.9	12.7	4.9			
Universal Canadian Growth	13.2																			
Universal Canadian Resource	39.1	-14.1	6.2	135.4	8.2	-22.4	-7.4	9.7	-21.5	61.9	-11.2	1.2	-2.3	47.4	-10.6	-24.7	55.8	34.7		
Universal Euro Opportunity	29.9	25.4																		
Universal Far East	9.1	-10.4																		
Universal Growth	5.2																			
Universal Japan	-1.8	-8.9																		
Universal US Emerg Growth	24.1	44.4	4.0	50.0																
Universal US Money Market	3.8	4.0																		
Universal World Asst Alloc	2.4	4.2																		
Universal World Bal RRSP	14.1	6.9																		
Universal World Emerg Gth	13.1	-16.7																		
Universal World Equity	8.0	3.0	14.8	34.7	-2.1	4.1	-14.5	17.0	-12.1	35.5										
Universal World Gth RRSP	15.0	5.5																		
Universal World Inc RRSP	10.5	10.1																		
Universal World Prec Metal	44.1	3.0																		
Universal World Tactical Bd	7.5																			
University Avenue Bond	9.0	15.0	0.9																	
University Avenue Canadian	17.4	1.1	1.4	49.2	27.9	26.1														
University Avenue Growth	12.3	12.7	-3.3	-2.4	-1.7	16.8	-19.3	25.5	-25.9	49.6										
Vengrowth Investment	3.8																			
Vision Europe	15.9	16.4	6.5	3.1																
Westbury Cdn Life A	18.9	7.6	12.5	12.7	12.9	12.1	-2.6	18.5	-14.5	23.6	19.0	24.9	8.7	45.6	-3.0	-3.2	32.2	32.4	34.8	9.3
Westbury Cdn Life B	11.4	13.5	-0.5	14.0	9.2	18.2	5.1	8.9	6.6	1.9	13.6	23.1	6.4	30.8	20.9	-8.3	16.0	11.0	18.6	16.2
Westbury Cdn Life Bal	13.9	8.9	7.1	9.4	2.5															

Fund	1996	1995	1994	1993	1992	1991	1990	1989	1988	1987	1986	1985	1984	1983	1982	1981	1980	1979	1978	1977
Westbury Cdn Life Bond	8.8	10.8	-1.3	10.0	13.5															
Westbury Cdn Life C	5.1	6.5	5.2	4.7	5.4	8.9	11.5	10.7	7.4											
Westbury Cdn Life Eqty Gth	16.0	2.1	8.7	17.2	-0.3	5.9														
Working Opportunity	11.0	4.2	2.0	0.8																
Working Ventures Canadian	2.3	5.5	2.3	3.2	3.7	7.6														
Zweig Global Managed Asset	9.6																			
Zweig Strategic Growth	9.9	20.5	-0.2	33.8																

Survey of Fund Characteristics

THESE TABLES GO FAR BE-
yond the information that is normally available to the investor.
First, we have provided a risk-adjusted ranking, the PAL/SGK Rank.
[For those of you who are technically oriented, we have taken 12
month returns over 36 month end dates (to avoid single end date
month bias) and divided this by the standard deviation of those returns. The distribution of those returns was then quintiled after
eliminating the so-called outliers.] What does this really show? For
varying degrees of fund performance volatility, it highlights those
funds that have, on average, provided superior returns. Since volatility is an integral part of the ranking, we have provided a one to
five ranking of the volatility of the monthly returns (✈✈✈✈✈ =
high volatility, ✈ = low volatility) beside it.

We've included these figures for those readers who find comfort
in historical performance data. But as we show elsewhere in this
book, this is only one of many factors to consider.

Each of these tables also includes six performance columns. The
first three detail the average, highest and lowest 12-month returns
achieved by the fund over the three years ending Sept. 30, 1996. In
other words, if you took the 12 month return ending September
1996 and then the 12 month return ending August 1996, and so on
going back three years — these columns identify the highest, lowest
and average return values. The next three columns are basically the
same thing except they examine the average, highest and lowest 36
month returns (expressed as an annualized figure) over the five year
window ending Sept. 30, 1996.

Many of these tables include a column called 3 Year Tax
Efficiency. This is an estimate, expressed as a percentage, of the
fund's total return achieved over the past 36 months that is retained
by the taxable investor. A taxable investor in this context refers to
those who hold the mutual fund outside a tax-deferred plan (such

as an RRSP) or outside a tax-exempt plan. Mutual funds often distribute capital gains and interest income to unit holders at regular intervals. These distributions are often used to purchase additional units of the fund. Portfolio Analytics Limited calculates the Tax Efficiency Ratio by examining the amounts and types of distributions a fund has paid out over the past 36 months and estimates the taxes attracted using the following assumptions:

- Interest income is taxed at a marginal tax rate of 50 per cent.
- Capital gains distributions are taxed at a marginal tax rate of 37.5 per cent. Note: Dividend income generated by Canadian corporations is taxed at a more favourable rate than interest income. Unfortunately, comprehensive data on these are not available, and are assumed to be taxed at the 50 per cent rate. One can assume, therefore, that those funds distributing dividends from Canadian corporations will have an understated tax efficiency.
- Funds are held for at least the past 36 months and are still held. (Investors attract capital gains (or losses) on the disposal of fund assets based on current NAVP value and their adjusted cost base.)

By determining the tax payable by the investor, PAL then determined what percentage of the total return is actually retained by the investor. Remember, investors not participating in a tax deferred plan, must pay taxes on these distributions whether or not they sell their position.

For example, a money market fund that generates all of its total return with interest distributions, will have a tax efficiency of 50 per cent. An equity fund that had no distributions for the past 36 months will have a tax efficiency of 100 per cent.

Most of the other columns are self explanatory. The Canadian bond analysis columns and the Canadian equity analysis columns are expressed as a percentage of the Canadian bond sections and Canadian equity sections respectively. Currency exposure columns found in the Canadian bond fund tables detail the currency exposure of the Canadian bond sections only. Geographic allocation includes Canadian cash and does not account for exposure achieved through derivatives.

Tables © Portfolio Analytics Limited, 1996.

Portfolio Analysis: Canadian Stocks

Canadian Equity Funds (180)

Fund	PAL/SGK Rank	Volatility	Avg Ann Ret	Hi Ann Ret	Lo Ann Ret	Avg 3 Yr Ret	Hi 3 Yr Ret	Lo 3 Yr Ret	MER	% Foreign	% 3 Yr Tx Ef	Portfolio Date	% Cdn Eqty	% Resource	% Prec Metal	% Consumer	% Int Sens	% Industrial	Div Yield	Price/Eam	Price/Book	Avg Cap	Fund Size $mil
20/20 Canadian Growth	★★★	↑	6.6	20.3	-9.5	9.5	14.3	4.0	2.57	8	93	Sep96	81.0	37.0	11.0	13.4	16.1	22.4	Med	Med+	Med+	Med+	271.1
ABC Fundamental-Value	★★★	↑↑↑	10.1	25.7	-8.1	31.6	39.0	15.2	2.00	8	81	Sep96	86.8	27.5	2.4	27.7	19.2	23.2	High	Low	Low	Med-	152.4
ADMAX Cdn Performance	★★	↑↑↑	7.9	26.3	-12.9	8.4	12.4	3.8	2.61	1	98	Sep96	87.3	32.8	12.3	13.9	13.2	27.8	Med-	Med+	Med+	Med+	29.9
ADMAX Cdn Select Growth	★★★	↑	4.5	12.3	-4.3	3.9	6.3	0.3	2.63	1	73	Sep96	86.9	31.2	11.8	15.3	12.5	29.2	Med-	High	Med+	Med+	8.5
AGF Canadian Equity A	★★	↑↑↑↑	7.8	28.9	-14.8	9.1	13.2	4.2	2.81	17	100	Sep96	87.9	38.1	18.2	6.1	16.0	21.7	Med-	Med+	High	Med	153.1
AGF Canadian Equity B									3.30	17		Sep96	87.9	38.1	18.2	6.1	16.0	21.7	Med-	Med+	High	Med	533.4
AGF Canadian Equity C									3.17	17		Sep96	87.9	38.1	18.2	6.1	16.0	21.7	Med-	Med+	High	Med	23.1
AGF Growth Equity A	★	↑↑↑↑↑↑	6.6	32.1	-22.0	16.1	24.1	7.6	2.44	5	100	Sep96	90.1	33.2	9.9	16.5	7.1	33.4	Med-	High	High	Med-	212.8
AGF Growth Equity B									2.94	5		Sep96	90.1	33.2	9.9	16.5	7.1	33.4	Med-	High	High	Med-	453.9
AGF Growth Equity C									2.92	5		Sep96	90.1	33.2	9.9	16.5	7.1	33.4	Med-	High	High	Med-	11.9
AIC Advantage	★★★	↑↑↑↑↑↑	21.7	59.6	-19.4	21.2	27.6	10.1	2.55	13	100	Sep96	77.4		7.9	18.7	73.5	-	Med-	High	High	Med-	984.5
AIC Diversified Canada	★★★★★	↑	9.4	20.9	-1.9	13.4	17.5	9.8	2.75	15		Sep96	76.5		8.9	15.2	62.0	14.0	Med-	High	High	Med-	115.3
All-Canadian Capital	★★★★★	↑	9.0	20.7	-1.5	13.2	17.1	9.4	2.00	4	74	Sep96	53.2	3.1	31.6	35.1	7.3	20.2	Low	Low	Low	Low	14.7
All-Canadian Compound											68	Sep96							Med-	High	Low	Low	13.2
Altafund Investment Corp.	★★	↑↑↑↑↑↑	10.4	37.1	-12.7	15.4	24.2	8.1	2.38	8	94	Sep96	70.8	55.8	12.7	3.0	13.5	15.0	Med-	Low	Low	Med	194.7
Altamira Capital Gth	★★★	↑	7.1	18.1	-7.2	12.6	19.2	7.2	2.02	16	92	Sep96	77.6	50.5	19.6	6.0	2.9	20.9	Med-	High	Med+	Med	154.6
Altamira Equity	★★★★	↑↑	10.7	28.3	-7.6	18.7	31.9	8.8	2.31	5	62	Sep96	73.3	44.7	22.0	6.7	8.0	18.7	Med	Med	Med-	Med-	2,474.8
AMI Private Cap Equity	★★★	↑↑	9.0	23.5	-9.2	9.9	14.1	5.0	1.75	18	95	Sep96	79.7	21.8	4.7	14.1	41.8	17.6	High	Med+	Med	High	1.6
Apex Equity Growth									2.00	6		Sep96	94.2	39.4	17.9	5.7	16.0	21.0	Med-	Med+	High	Med	48.1
Associate Investors	★★★	↑↑	7.5	19.9	-9.7	7.9	11.5	3.2	2.01	1	76	Sep96	87.7	7.2	1.6		85.0	6.2	High	Low	Low	High	8.1
Atlas Cdn Large Cap Growth	★★★★	↑↑	10.0	21.9	-6.3	7.9	12.2	2.3	2.49	16	99	Sep96	74.9	25.6	3.7	16.1	28.1	26.5	Low	Med-	Med+	High	44.2
Atlas Cdn Large Cap Value									2.75			Sep96	95.5	27.4	9.7	15.5	28.7	18.7	Med+	Med-	Med-	Med+	9.5
Azura Growth RSP Pooled									2.18	-		Sep96	35.6	33.0	11.3	18.6	11.4	25.1	High	Med-	Med-	Med	8.7
Batirente Section Actions									1.54	16		Sep96	84.5	28.3	6.7	11.8	32.2	21.1	High	High	Med+	Med+	1.8
Beutel Goodman Cdn Equity	★★★★★	↑	8.8	20.4	-2.4	10.6	16.0	6.4	2.26	-	91	Jun96	94.6	35.2	5.6	19.6	16.7	22.9	High	Low	Low	Med	33.1
Bissett Canadian Equity	★★★	↑↑↑	12.0	26.5	-8.7	13.4	16.4	9.5	1.35	14	93	Sep96	81.1	28.7	1.1	15.3	23.0	31.9	Med	Low	High	Med	26.9
BNP (Canada) Equity	★★★	↑↑	9.2	22.6	-7.0	8.5	12.0	4.0	2.47	12	83	Sep96	80.5	29.4	8.0	14.1	27.3	21.3	Med+	Med	Med	High	5.3
BPI Canadian Equity Value	★★	↑↑↑↑↑↑	8.4	36.3	-15.4	8.5	12.0	4.1	2.74	14	95	Jun96	61.3	21.9	12.6	11.6	12.2	41.8	Med-	Med-	Med-	Med-	248.6
BPI Cdn Opportunities RSP									2.50			Sep96											84.6
C.I. Canadian Growth	★★★	↑	8.4	23.0	-7.5	14.4	20.0	8.8	2.40	4	79	Sep96	71.0	42.9	11.7	21.3	5.8	18.3	Med-	High	Med+	Med	1,079.1
C.I. Canadian Sector	★★★	↑	8.1	22.1	-7.4	9.2	12.7	4.3	2.42	5	100	Jul96	76.8		9.1	17.9	21.3	22.3	Med-	Med-	High	High	54.4
Canada Life Cdn Equity	★★★	↑↑	8.4	22.5	-10.0	10.3	13.7	5.5	2.25	18			55.3	29.4	8.6	11.9	18.3	21.5	Med+	Med-	Med-	High	436.8
Canada Life E-2	★★★	↑↑	9.0	23.1	-9.6	10.3	9.9	1.6	1.50										Med	Med	Med-	Med	114.4
Canadian Protected	★★★	↑	3.6	9.8	-3.7	6.9	9.9	4.4	2.40	13		Sep96		37.5					Med	Med	Med-	Med	2.3
CCPE Growth R	★★★★★	↑↑↑↑↑	9.6	20.0	-3.6	9.1	13.4	4.4	1.35										Med-	Med+	Med	Med	35.3
CDA Common Stock	★★	↑↑	6.1	19.5	-8.3	10.3	14.0	5.9	0.87	17		Sep96	74.8	52.1	20.1	4.4	3.5	20.0	Med-	Med+	Med	Med	57.1

Fund	PAL/SGK Rank	Volatility	Avg Ann Ret	Hi Ann Ret	Lo Ann Ret	Avg 3 Yr Ret	Hi 3 Yr Ret	Lo 3 Yr Ret	MER	% Foreign	% 3 Yr Tx Ef	Portfolio Date	% Cdn Eqty	% Re-source	% Prec Metal	% Con-sumer	% Int Sens	% Indus-trial	Div Yield	Price/ Earn	Price/ Book	Avg Cap	Fund Size $mill
Cdn Anaes Mutual Accum	★★★	↑↑↑	9.1	24.0	-10.2	8.6	12.6	4.1	1.62		86												35.5
Chou RRSP	★★	↑↑↑↑	6.9	24.5	-11.6	5.8	9.1	1.0	0.74		88												1.1
CIBC Canadian Equity	★★	↑↑↑	4.0	19.0	-14.1	5.9	10.0	1.8	2.05	—	97	Sep96	94.7	27.6	9.2	16.2	26.0	21.0	High	Med	Med	Med+	436.9
CIBC Canadian Index Fund									1.00			Sep96	97.2	25.3	10.3	13.5	28.7	22.1	High	High	Med+	High	49.2
Clean Environment Equity	★★	↑↑↑↑↑	8.9	28.0	-18.1				3.01	7	96	Aug96	80.8	5.5	6.2	40.6	14.7	33.1	Low	High	High	Med-	147.6
Co-Operators Canadian Eqty	★★★	↑	6.9	19.1	-7.0				2.07			Sep96	91.0	33.2	10.3	10.2	12.4	33.8	Med-	Med	Med	Med	11.9
Colonia Life Equity	★	↑↑↑	3.7	21.4	-15.1				2.14	—													12.5
Concorde Croissance	★★★★	↑↑↑	11.5	26.6	-7.5	9.6	12.4	6.1	2.14		97	Sep96	91.8	34.3	6.6	16.4	16.7	26.1	Med	Med	Med	Med+	25.1
Confed Equity	★★★	↑	8.2	21.9	-7.0	11.5	14.2	7.6	2.00	13		Mar96	96.0	32.3	6.7	18.6	25.2	17.2	Med	Low	Low	Med	32.0
Confed Life A	★★★★	↑	9.9	22.3	-5.9	10.6	13.3	7.1	0.48	17		Mar96	82.7	24.5	—	22.6	25.4	27.5	Med+	Low	Med-	Med+	24.5
Confed Life B	★★★★	↑↑↑	9.1	22.6	-6.6	10.8	15.7	4.8	0.96														32.0
Cornerstone Cdn Growth	★★★	↑↑↑↑	13.3	37.0	-9.4				2.06	—	78	Sep96	82.4	25.3	—	19.9	26.0	28.8	Med	Low	Med-	Med+	58.8
Cote 100 Amerique REER	★★	↑↑↑↑↑↑	10.7	36.6	-18.7				1.40	13	100	Jun96	96.5	41.0	6.1	6.4	15.8	30.7	Med	Low	Med-	Med	18.0
Cote 100 EXP									2.00	20		Jun96	80.3	2.4	—	37.9	23.6	36.1	Med+	Med-	Med+	Med+	14.8
CT Everest Stock	★★	↑	4.3	15.3	-12.2	9.9	13.7	4.4	1.82	26	93	Sep96	76.0	3.9	1.8	37.4	26.1	32.3	Med-	Med-	Med-	Med-	637.5
Desjardins Actions	★★★	↑	8.1	21.3	-9.4	9.0	13.5	4.2	1.93	1	91	Sep96	77.9	24.7	10.5	10.7	26.1	28.0	Med+	Med	Med+	High	76.1
Desjardins Environnement	★★★	↑	7.8	22.3	-11.4	7.9	12.1	0.9	2.14	—		Sep96	92.0	31.5	7.3	13.7	23.3	24.3	Med+	Med	Med	High	14.7
Desjardins Growth									1.80	6		Sep96	98.7	30.4	4.3	19.2	21.6	24.4	Med+	Med	Med	Med+	14.8
Desjardins Stock	★★★	↑↑↑	9.4	24.1	-8.6	11.2	15.0	6.9	1.99														47.0
Dolphin Growth	★★	↑	3.8	14.2	-7.9	8.8	11.5	4.0	2.00		16												0.6
Dynamic Cdn Growth	★	↑↑↑↑	4.5	21.4	-17.5	24.3	35.9	5.6	2.55	12	98	Sep96	83.5	44.4	8.4	17.6	2.0	27.7	Low	High	Low	Med-	581.2
Dynamic Fund of Canada	★	↑↑↑	1.3	16.1	-19.7	10.7	17.4	1.3	2.51	15	64	Sep96	82.1	52.2	9.2	8.2	10.3	18.7	Med-	High	Low	Med-	206.0
Elliott & Page Equity	★★★	↑↑↑↑	13.9	37.5	-9.0	13.7	19.2	7.9	2.04	3	70	Sep96	70.5	40.5	6.3	13.7	26.1	10.5	Med	Low	Low	Med+	472.6
Empire Elite Equity	★★	↑↑↑	7.6	25.8	-13.0	8.9	11.8	5.2	2.57	19		Sep96	91.4	39.1	10.9	6.5	16.7	31.5	Med	Low	Med	Med	345.1
Empire Group Equity	★★★	↑↑↑↑	8.7	26.2	-11.4	11.3	14.5	8.0	1.28	18		Sep96	78.7	23.5	9.3	16.5	27.0	22.1	Med+	Med+	Med	High	32.9
Empire Life 3	★★★	↑↑↑↑	8.7	27.8	-13.6	11.5	15.1	7.5	1.28	18		Sep96	77.9	23.6	9.7	16.2	28.8	22.2	Med+	Med+	Med	High	14.0
Empire Premier Equity	★★★	↑↑↑↑	8.4	27.1	-12.2	10.1	13.6	6.3	1.54	18		Sep96	80.5	23.5	10.2	17.6	27.6	21.6	High	Med+	Med	High	187.7
Equitable Life Cdn Stock	★★★★	↑	9.5	22.9	-5.7				2.25														35.1
Equitable Life Com Stock	★★★★★	↑↑↑	12.8	25.8	-2.8	12.7	16.9	7.7	1.04														19.1
Ethical Growth	★★★★	↑↑↑	11.4	27.0	-7.8	10.4	15.5	4.2	2.24	—	96	Sep96	80.4	23.4	8.4	16.4	27.8	22.2	Med+	Med+	Med	High	265.0
Ficadre Actions	★★★	↑↑↑↑↑	10.8	26.7	-9.4	10.1	14.5	4.5	2.14	20	96	Sep96	87.6	25.5	8.0	9.6	26.9	29.5	Med+	Low	Med	Med+	8.8
Fidelity Capital Builder	★★	↑↑↑↑	6.2	25.9	-16.1	8.3	11.8	3.9	2.53	156	99	Jun96	95.6	32.3	13.0	17.8	25.0	16.9	Med	Med-	Low	Med	627.1
First Canadian Eqty Index	★★★	↑↑↑↑	8.5	24.4	-11.4	9.9	14.9	4.7	1.49	0	96	Sep96	74.0	48.7	10.4	7.4	25.5	5.4	High	Med-	Med-	High	228.7
First Canadian Growth	★★★	↑↑↑	8.2	24.6	-12.2				2.26		99	Sep96	99.8	25.5	10.1	13.5	28.5	22.2	High	Med	Med+	High	248.5
Fonds Professionals Cdn Eqty	★★★	↑↑↑	8.3	23.4	-11.2	7.7	11.9	2.6	0.75	15	77	Sep96	94.4	37.2	14.8	12.5	19.8	20.4	Med+	Med	Med-	Med+	74.3
GBC Canadian Growth	★★	↑↑↑↑↑	10.5	33.7	-14.7	13.8	18.9	8.2	1.97	—	100	Aug96	78.9	17.3	4.2	28.5	10.5	28.9	Low	High	High	High	131.1
General Trust Cdn Equity	★★★	↑↑↑	8.8	22.1	-9.2	8.2	12.1	2.3	1.85			Sep96	94.2	33.8	10.3	17.2	23.2	21.7	Med+	Med-	Med-	Med+	29.5
Global Strategy Canada Gth	★★	↑↑↑↑	6.0	20.3	-12.1				2.65	4	90	Sep96	81.9	20.9		7.7	41.5	19.6	High	Low	Low	Med-	536.7

Portfolio Analysis: Canadian Stocks

Portfolio Analysis: Canadian Stocks

Fund	PAL/SGK Rank	Volatility	Avg Ann Ret	Hi Ann Ret	Lo Ann Ret	Avg 3 Yr Ret	Hi 3 Yr Ret	Lo 3 Yr Ret	MER	% Foreign	% 3 Yr Tx Ef	Port-folio Date	% Cdn Eqty	% Re-source	% Prec Metal	% Con-sumer	% Int Sens	% Indus-trial	Div Yield	Price/ Eam	Price/ Book	Avg Cap	Fund Size $mill
GWL Cdn Eqty (G) A	**	→→→	5.8	22.4	-14.3	9.2	13.4	4.5	2.64	-	-	Sep96	90.4	33.9	12.2	12.0	17.9	24.0	Med	Med	Med+	High	949.7
GWL Equity Index (G) A	***	→→	7.5	23.3	-12.0	9.5	14.5	4.2	2.64	-	-	Sep96	99.3	25.5	10.5	13.5	28.5	22.1	High	Med	Med	High	865.4
GWL Equity (M) A									2.82														29.8
GWL Equity (S) A									2.76														25.3
GWL Larger Company (M) A									2.82														10.3
Green Line Blue Chip Equity	**	→→	7.6	22.5	-12.5	6.8	10.7	1.8	2.30	18	87	Sep96	74.3	30.2	5.4	13.6	27.6	23.1	Med	Med-	Med+	Med	177.0
Green Line Canadian Equity	***	→→	6.3	19.0	-10.6	10.6	14.8	6.4	2.15	7	100	Sep96	90.2	28.6	6.2	13.0	20.2	22.0	Med	Med	High	Med+	402.4
Green Line Canadian Index	***	→→	9.1	25.4	-10.6	10.8	16.1	5.3	1.14		95	Sep96	99.9	25.5	10.5	13.5	28.4	22.1	High	Med	Med	High	198.1
Green Line Value									2.16	17		Sep96	68.1	20.5	6.7	30.9	27.4	14.5	Med-	Low	Med	Med-	75.3
GS Canadian Equity									2.90	3		Sep96	68.3	15.4	4.3	9.8	44.0	26.5	High	Low	Low	Med+	87.3
GT Global - Cda Growth Cl									2.95	25		Sep96	68.6	31.1	11.9	14.5	4.2	38.2	Low	High	High	Med-	262.5
Guardian Growth Equity A	**	→→→	6.2	26.0	-11.7	11.7	16.4	7.2	2.24		88	Sep96	85.7	32.7	3.2	14.1	24.7	25.3	Med	Med-	Med-	Med-	36.2
Guardian Growth Equity B									2.97			Sep96	85.7	32.7	3.2	14.1	24.7	25.3	Med	Med-	Med-	Med-	53.5
Hongkong Bank Equity	*	→→→→	4.2	22.2	-14.0	12.7	16.4	5.6	2.00	15	88	Sep96	80.4	28.0	8.6	18.8	21.0	23.6	Med	Med	High	High	80.5
HRL Canadian	*	→→→	-0.1	15.3	-20.1	4.4	8.2	0.5	1.85	2	92	Sep96	95.4	20.8	5.3	14.3	30.4	29.2	Med+	Med-	Med+	Med-	2.2
Ideal Equity	****	→→	13.1	28.0	-4.5	11.4	15.9	6.0	2.00			Sep96											49.6
IG Beutel Goodman Cdn Eqty									2.65			Sep96	96.0	35.4	6.6	19.8	18.5	19.7	High	Med-	Low	Med-	3.4
IG Sceptre Canadian Equity									2.65	18		Sep96	57.7	31.9	6.1	10.2	24.5	27.4	Med	Med-	Med+	Med	22.6
Imperial Growth Cdn Equity	***	↑	7.2	18.3	-6.4	9.3	12.8	6.1	1.95	7	88	Sep96	86.3	35.8	7.3	14.3	17.8	24.8	Med	Med-	Med	Med+	74.5
Ind. Alliance Ecoflex A	*****	↑	10.1	21.5	-5.2				2.14		96	Sep96	92.8	43.9	8.2	16.8	17.3	13.8	Med	Med-	Med-	Med+	59.4
Ind. Alliance Stocks	*****	↑	10.7	22.1	-4.7	14.4	17.7	10.1	1.61	-	99	Sep96	92.8	43.9	8.2	16.8	17.3	13.8	Med	Med-	Med-	Med+	31.0
Industrial Future	*****	↑	12.5	23.5	-2.1	17.6	24.9	10.8	2.38	18	95	Sep96	61.3	31.9	6.5	10.8	10.8	41.7	Med	Med+	Med+	Med	516.4
Industrial Growth	**	→→	5.5	19.5	-8.8	11.9	16.9	6.3	2.38	17	100	Sep96	79.6	48.2	14.3	9.2	6.3	21.9	Med	High	Low	Med	1,212.6
Industrial Horizon	**	→→	7.1	17.5	-5.8	12.1	17.2	8.0	2.38	7	87	Sep96	82.9	57.8	10.0	3.0	4.3	24.8	Med+	Med	Low	Med	1,070.8
Industrial Pension	****	↑	9.2	17.9	-4.0	15.3	20.5	11.1	2.44	10	91	Sep96	82.9	36.8	1.7	5.9	27.5	28.1	Med	Med	Med-	Med-	59.5
InvesNat Canadian Equity	****	→→→	9.4	22.8	-7.6	10.1	14.6	6.3	2.12		88	Sep96	88.9	33.8	4.1	17.0	23.2	21.9	Med	Med-	Med+	Med+	96.9
Investors Canadian Equity	***	→→→	7.7	21.7	-9.6	12.0	14.4	8.3	2.48	7	96	Sep96	89.0	33.5	8.9	12.9	20.4	24.3	Med+	Med-	Med-	Med+	2,737.7
Investors Retire Gth Port	***	↑	8.5	21.3	-6.5	10.4	13.8	6.6	0.21	24	99	Sep96	70.0	35.1	7.8	14.3	20.5	22.3	Med+	Med-	Med+	Med+	1,652.9
Investors Retirement	***	→→→	8.7	22.5	-7.7	10.5	14.7	5.8	2.40	8	100	Sep96	86.7	36.2	7.1	15.1	20.6	21.1	Med	Med+	Med+	Med+	2,362.0
Investors Summa	***	→→→	8.5	21.9	-9.1	8.6	11.4	3.8	2.52	17	86	Sep96	74.5	16.0	6.1	24.3	29.7	24.0	Med	Med+	Med+	Med	126.5
Ivy Canadian	*****	↑	12.4	22.4	0.1				2.37	14	96	Sep96	52.7	29.6	-	10.5	43.0	16.9	Low	Low	Med+	Med	1,799.7
Jones Heward	*	→→→→	2.3	16.9	-17.9	9.4	13.5	2.4	2.50	14	85	Sep96	76.2	36.7	6.7	9.9	30.7	30.7	High	Med-	Med	Med	71.2
Laurentian Canadian Equity	**	↑	5.9	19.1	-9.8	7.7	11.6	4.1	2.66	7	89	Sep96	88.1	35.8	7.3	14.2	17.8	24.9	Med+	Med+	High	Med	188.5
Leith Wheeler Cdn Equity									1.50	-		Sep96	94.1	22.2	3.8	18.7	38.8	16.5	High	Low	Low	Med-	2.7
London Life Cdn Equity									2.00														670.3
Mackenzie Sent Cda Equity	**	→→→→	7.4	24.6	-10.5	10.2	13.9	6.5	1.98	8	100	Sep96	65.2	50.0	-	13.9	31.9	4.2	Med	Med	Low	Med-	13.7
Manulife Cabot Blue Chip	**	→→	6.4	30.8	-8.2	17.2	21.9	7.4	2.50	14		Sep96	73.2	33.0	8.3	15.2	19.7	23.7	Med+	Med-	Low	Med+	9.4
Manulife Cabot Cdn Equity									2.50	-		Sep96	90.3	33.0	8.3	15.2	19.7	23.7	Med	Med	Med-	Med+	19.8

Portfolio Analysis: Canadian Stocks

Fund	PAL/SGK Rank	Volatility	Avg Ann Ret	Hi Ann Ret	Lo Ann Ret	Avg 3 Yr Ret	Hi 3 Yr Ret	Lo 3 Yr Ret	MER	% Foreign	% 3 Yr Tx Ef	Portfolio Date	% Cdn Eqty	% Resource	% Prec Metal	% Consumer	% Int Sens	% Industrial	Div Yield	Price/Earn	Price/Book	Avg Cap	Fund Size $mil
Manulife VistaFd 1 Cap Gns	★★	↑↑↑	7.5	26.1	-11.6	11.0	15.3	5.4	1.63	1		Sep96	88.4	41.3	22.6	7.5	7.4	21.2	Med-	Med+	Med	Med	78.3
Manulife VistaFd2 Cap Gns	★★	↑↑	6.7	25.1	-12.2	10.2	14.5	4.6	2.38	1		Sep96	88.4	41.3	22.6	7.5	7.4	21.2	Med-	Med+	Med	Med	355.6
Manulife VistaFd1 Equity	★★★	↑↑	8.6	24.3	-6.9	9.5	15.0	5.7	1.63	9		Sep96	76.0	49.0	19.1	7.3	2.9	21.7	Med-	High	Med	Med	52.7
Manulife VistaFd2 Equity	★★★	↑↑	7.8	23.4	-7.7	8.7	14.1	4.8	2.38	9		Sep96	76.0	49.0	19.1	7.3	2.9	21.7	Med-	High	Med	Med	278.1
Maritime Life Cdn Equity									2.05	–		Sep96	87.5	40.4	10.3	7.5	19.8	22.0	Med	Med-	Med-	High	57.2
Maritime Life Growth	★★	↑↑↑	7.0	23.4	-14.1	9.4	13.3	4.6	1.97	1		Sep96	96.7	28.2	8.4	14.4	24.1	24.8	Med+	Med-	Med-	Med+	295.4
Mawer Canadian Equity	★★	↑↑	6.4	21.5	-10.6				1.34			Sep96	92.7	28.2	6.9	14.8	27.5	22.6	High	Low	Med-	Med+	16.3
Maxxum Cdn Equity Growth	★★★	↑↑↑↑↑	14.1	39.0	-16.3	16.0	20.5	9.5	1.75	7	80	Sep96	85.3	34.7	14.8	11.9	19.1	19.4	Med	Med+	Med+	Med	150.4
Mclean Budden Equity Gth	★★	↑↑↑↑	9.0	29.3	-12.2	9.7	12.6	5.3	1.75	1	82	Sep96	91.8	24.6	3.5	12.6	30.6	28.8	Med	Med+	Med+	High	8.6
McLean Budden Pld Cdn Eq	★★★	↑	10.7	32.5	-11.5	11.8	15.2	7.2		1	89	Sep96	97.1	24.2	3.4	12.9	30.7	28.7	Med	Med+	Med+	Med+	175.0
MD Equity	★★	↑	4.3	15.6	-7.7	12.3	15.4	6.0	1.14	24	94	Sep96	62.3	25.7	9.1	12.7	28.4	24.1	Med	Low	Med-	Med+	1,441.3
MD Select									1.18	16	99	Sep96	72.0	34.5	3.2	12.9	23.8	25.6	Low	Med	Med	Med-	117.0
Merrill Lynch Cdn Equity									2.91	6		Sep96	79.6	24.9	8.8	20.4	12.0	33.9	Low	Med	Med	Med-	74.0
Metlife Mvp Equity	★★	↑	5.4	20.3	-12.5	6.7	10.8	1.4	2.00														27.9
Millennia III Cdn Eq 1	★★★	↑↑↑							2.75	8		Sep96	89.1	35.8	7.4	14.2	17.8	24.8	Med	Med	Med	Med+	42.1
Millennia III Cdn Eq 2	★★★	↑↑							2.93	8	85	Sep96	89.1	35.8	7.4	14.2	17.8	24.8	Med	Med	Med-	Med+	3.5
Mutual Equifund	★★★	↑↑↑	11.9	28.9	-8.6	9.7	15.1	3.2	1.79	13		Sep96	83.7	34.8	10.6	7.2	19.3	28.0	Med-	Med-	Med-	Med	96.7
Mutual Life A	★★★	↑↑↑	10.1	27.3	-11.1	9.2	13.7	3.1		16														113.2
Mutual Life B	★★★	↑↑↑↑	10.1	26.3	-10.3	8.7	13.5	3.0	2.29	16		Jul96											11.3
Mutual Premier Blue Chip	★★★	↑↑↑	13.8	38.6	-9.5	10.6	17.2	3.5	1.75	12	98	Sep96	85.4	36.3	9.5	9.5	21.4	23.4	Med+	Med-	Med	Med+	279.5
NAL-Canadian Equity	★★★	↑↑							2.00														75.8
NAL-Equity Growth									2.00														44.3
National Equities	★★★★	↑↑↑	9.6	22.6	-8.5	11.5	15.9	7.1	1.60			Sep96	89.6	31.6	4.0	12.3	35.7	16.4	High	Med	Med	High	70.6
National Trust Cdn Equity	★★	↑↑	4.5	14.1	-11.5	7.1	10.5	3.6	2.00		50	Sep96	99.5	33.6	7.1	10.5	28.2	20.6	High	Med	Med	High	144.6
NN Canadian 35 Index	★★★★★	↑	10.0	23.2	-3.8	9.2	14.3	3.7		15	80	Sep96	96.5	24.9	8.9	15.0	29.6	21.5	High	Med	Med	High	18.4
NN Canadian Growth	★★	↑↑↑	6.0	20.0	-10.2	7.2	11.2	2.9	2.25	10	82	Sep96	81.0	29.5	7.6	11.9	26.5	24.5	Med+	Med-	Med-	High	23.0
O.I.Q. Ferique Actions	★★★★	↑	10.4	21.5	-4.3	10.8	14.6	5.9	0.58			Jul96	88.1	27.5	9.1	3.1	25.7	21.6	Med+	Med-	Med-	Med+	95.0
O.I.Q. Ferique Croissance									0.63			Sep96	87.7	52.4	20.4	10.8	3.7	20.3	Med	Med+	Med-	Med	8.5
O'Donnell Growth									2.55	19		Sep96	62.9	33.2	10.2	13.6	12.0	33.8	Low	High	High	Low	169.4
OHA Canadian Equity	★	↑↑↑↑↑	5.6	25.4	-16.1	9.7	13.9	2.3	0.90			Sep96	84.4	25.6	16.8		26.0	18.1	Med+	Med+	Med	Med+	18.6
Optima Strat-Cdn Equity	★★★★★	↑	13.1	25.3	-0.8				0.42	16	100												137.1
Optimum Actions	★★★	↑↑							1.61			Sep96	90.3	28.6	6.6	12.5	31.4	20.9	Med+	Low	Med-	Med+	0.7
OTGIF Diversified	★★★	↑↑↑	8.8	24.4	-7.5	9.0	13.9	4.3	1.00	16	70	Sep96	77.5	30.6	8.7	14.9	28.1	17.8	Med+	Med-	Med-	High	32.7
PH & N Canadian Equity	★★★★★	↑	11.4	24.8	-5.2	12.5	17.5	7.9	1.13	15	94	Sep96	95.7	24.7	7.6	17.4	22.1	22.1	Med	Med-	Med+	Med+	365.2
PH & N Pooled Pension Tr	★★★★	↑↑↑	11.8	25.8	-4.6	12.2	16.3	7.8	0.58	15	86	Sep96	83.0	24.4	7.1	18.7	29.6	21.5	Med+	Med+	Med+	Med+	590.5
PH & N RSP/RIF Equity	★★★★★	↑	11.2	23.4	-4.5	12.7	16.7	8.4	1.21	15	89	Sep96	83.2	21.2	7.7	17.4	27.1	25.2	Med	Med	Med+	Med	114.8
PH & N Vintage	★★★★	↑↑↑	15.6	33.2	-5.4	15.3	18.1	11.1	1.75		86	Sep96	82.7	23.5	6.0		24.1	27.5	Med	Med	High	Med-	104.1
Pret et Revenu Canadien	★★★	↑↑	11.0	26.2	-8.8	11.4	15.3	6.1	1.79	–	98	Sep96	96.4	33.9	7.6		24.9	16.2	Med	Low	Low	Med	50.0

Portfolio Analysis: Canadian Stocks

Fund	PAL/SGK Rank	Volatility	Avg Ann Ret	Hi Ann Ret	Lo Ann Ret	Avg 3 Yr Ret	Hi 3 Yr Ret	Lo 3 Yr Ret	MER	% Foreign	% 3 Yr Tx Ef	Port-folio Date	% Cdn Eqty	% Re-source	% Prec Metal	% Con-sumer	% Int Sens	% Indus-trial	Div Yield	Price/Earn	Price/Book	Avg Cap	Fund Size $mil
Pursuit Canadian Equity	★★★	↑↑	8.9	22.0	-9.1	11.2	14.6	5.9	1.50		60	Sep96	99.0	8.6		49.5	17.4	24.5	Med	Med+	High	Med-	7.1
Royal Life Equity	★★★★	↑	8.8	20.0	-7.4	9.9	13.1	6.0	2.37	5	86	Sep96	87.5	27.6	6.0	24.7	20.4	21.2	High	Med-	Med-	Med	62.2
Royal Trust Cdn Stock	★★★	↑↑	8.7	23.7	-8.0	9.4	13.0	4.9	1.90	14	99	Sep96	73.9	26.9	15.2	11.4	21.6	24.9	Med+	Med	Med+	High	794.1
Royfund Canadian Equity	★★★	↑↑	8.9	24.0	-8.0	12.4	16.3	8.4	2.09	14	97	Sep96	76.2	27.7	14.8	11.4	21.4	24.6	Med+	Med	Med+	High	1,419.7
Saxon Stock	★★★★	↑↑↑↑	13.4	29.5	-7.4	17.6	22.8	10.8	1.87	5	97	Sep96	82.3	24.8	8.6	23.5	19.5	23.5	Med-	Med	Med-	Med+	10.4
Sceptre Equity Growth	★★★★	↑↑↑↑↑	26.6	53.6	-3.0	22.8	30.9	11.9	1.68	5	96	Sep96	79.5	33.7	7.6	17.0	10.5	31.2	Low	Low	Low	Med	152.8
Scotia Ex Canadian Growth	★★★★	↑↑↑	15.0	31.5	-8.5	14.4	19.5	7.2	2.11	3	80	Sep96	92.7	18.7	6.7	21.2	28.1	25.3	Med	Med+	Med+	Med	330.7
Scotia Ex Cdn Blue Chip	★★	↑↑	4.3	17.7	-13.5	6.3	9.2	2.9	2.05		97	Sep96	91.4	22.2	11.5	13.1	24.2	29.0	Med	Med+	Med+	High	254.2
Scudder Canadian Equity									1.25			Jun96	96.6	21.2	1.5	27.6	29.3	20.4	High	Low	Low	Med-	3.3
Spectrum United Cdn Eqty	★★★★	↑	8.6	20.2	-5.7	13.9	18.0	9.0	2.30	9	86	Sep96	74.0	37.5	8.6	9.9	24.3	19.8	Med	Low	Med-	Med	614.7
Spectrum United Cdn Inv	★★★★	↑↑↑	9.7	23.2	-7.0	7.7	12.4	2.1	2.28	12	94	Sep96	76.1	20.5	4.0	17.2	50.3	8.0	High	Low	High	High	48.3
Spectrum Utd Cdn Stock	★★★	↑	7.3	21.6	-8.3	8.6	12.8	3.8	2.28	10	89	Sep96	82.3	25.6	8.8	20.7	28.4	16.4	Med+	Med+	Med	High	92.7
SSQ - Actions Canadiennes	★★★	↑↑↑↑	9.6	28.7	-13.2	8.4	12.9	2.4		2		Sep96	96.1	43.1	8.5	13.4	11.7	23.3	Med-	Med-	Med-	Med-	40.5
Standard Life Equity	★★★★	↑	10.3	24.5	-6.4				2.00	15	83												11.4
Stone & Co Flagship Stock									2.85	5													26.3
Sunfund												Sep96	59.6	32.0	5.9	28.2	3.2	30.7	Low	High	Med-	Med-	36.2
Talvest Canadian Eqty Value	★★★★	↑	9.0	24.3	-8.6	9.8	14.3	4.7	1.53		81	Sep96	94.5	28.3	10.5	14.5	26.6	20.1	High	Med-	Low	Med	126.5
Talvest New Economy	★★★★	↑	8.7	20.5	-6.1	8.8	13.4	4.0	2.40			Sep96	79.6			26.9	8.6	64.6	Low	High	High	Med	121.3
Templeton Canadian Stock	★★★	↑	7.0	16.1	-8.4	10.8	16.0	6.3	2.44	21	97	Sep96	62.9	19.7		22.3	33.7	24.3	High	Med-	Low	Med	92.2
Top 50 Equity	★★	↑↑	5.2	19.3	-11.6	5.2	9.0	0.7	2.92		88	Sep96	98.1	30.4	6.7	5.1	34.8	22.9	High	Med-	Med-	High	3.6
Tradex Equity	★★★★	↑↑↑	13.7	31.6	-4.2	13.4	16.9	8.5	1.39	16	87	Sep96	77.5	26.0	5.3	20.8	24.2	23.7	Med-	Med	High	Med-	63.3
Trans-Canada Value	★	↑↑↑↑↑	0.7	30.5	-21.2	7.8	15.1	-1.9	3.00	22	92	Mar96	61.4	10.6		11.0	68.7	9.7	Low	Low	Med+	Med+	4.3
Transamerica Growsafe Eqty									2.25			Sep96	78.3	32.8	11.1	14.4	23.8	17.8	High	Low	Low	Med	16.3
Trimark Canadian	★★★★	↑	9.0	20.4	-7.1	14.4	18.0	11.3	1.53	22	84	Sep96	62.7	38.7	3.7	13.4	20.7	18.3	Med+	Med+	Low	Med	1,615.4
Trimark RSP Equity	★★★★	↑	8.6	19.5	-6.2	12.6	15.5	9.3	2.00	21	88	Sep96	64.8	35.1	4.2	12.5	22.6	22.1	Med	Med-	Low	Med	2,738.3
Trimark Select Cdn Growth	★★★★★	↑	9.3	19.8	-4.8				2.28	18	95	Sep96	60.5	34.5	4.4	10.5	29.2	16.2	Med	Low	Low	Med+	3,076.8
Universal Canadian Growth									2.41	16		Sep96	66.2	25.8	4.1	29.4	25.1	15.5	Med+	Med+	Med-	Med	549.3
University Avenue Canadian	★	↑↑↑↑↑	5.5	33.3	-18.6	14.1	24.6	5.3	2.48	13	89	Sep96	67.3	51.4	12.6	5.0	-	30.9	Low	Med+	Med+	Med	31.4
Westbury Cdn Life A	★★★	↑↑	10.3	23.1	-8.3	14.1	14.2	6.3	1.11			Sep96	99.3	22.9	12.4	11.7	31.4	21.7	High	Low	Med-	High	2.7
Westbury Cdn Life Eqty Gth	★★	↑↑	6.1	19.9	-11.0	8.2	12.4	4.0	2.42			Sep96	95.5	25.4	10.6	11.4	28.3	24.3	High	Med-	Med-	High	55.5
Median Canadian Equity Funds			8.7	23.2	-8.8	10.3	14.5	5.5	2.09	7.3	91		83.2	30.8	8.3	14.1	23.8	22.3					62.8
Average Canadian Equity Funds			8.7	24.3	-9.5	11.0	15.5	5.6	2.00	9.3	89		82.3	30.2	8.6	15.1	22.8	23.2					62.2

Portfolio Analysis: Canadian Stocks

Fund	PAL/SGK Rank	Volatility	Avg Ann Ret	High Ann Ret	Low Ann Ret	Avg 3 Yr Ret	High 3 Yr Ret	Low 3 Yr Ret	MER	% Foreign	% 3 Yr Tx Ef	Port-folio Date	% Cdn Eqty	% Re-source	% Prec Metal	% Con-sumer	% Int Sens	% Indus-trial	Div Yield	Price/ Earn	Price/ Book	Avg Cap	Fund Size $mil
Canadian Small to Medium Cap Equity Funds (55)																							
20/20 RSP Aggr Smaller Co	*****	↑	4.1	12.4	-2.3				2.51	6		Sep96	91.4	41.3	15.6	6.2	2.4	34.4	Low	High	High	Med-	188.3
20/20 RSP Aggressive Eqty		↑↑↑	4.5	35.3	-25.6				1.95	8	63	Sep96	86.9	46.2	19.3	8.0		26.5	Low	High	High	Med-	368.3
All-Canadian Consumer										3			51.2			98.0	2.1		High	High	Low	Low	1.1
Altamira Special Growth	★	↑↑↑				9.7	21.4	2.1	1.82	6	95	Sep96	82.9	26.9	9.9	23.4	9.2	30.6	Low	Med+	High	Low	323.8
Atlas Cdn Emerging Growth									2.41	1		Sep96	71.9	31.2	21.2	13.9	4.8	28.9	Low	High	High	Low	132.2
Atlas Cdn Emerging Value									2.75	1		Sep96	86.1	37.3	2.9	17.7	11.8	24.4	Med-	Med-	Med+	Low	11.0
Beutel Goodman Small Cap									2.50	1		Jun96	90.4	42.1	5.5	15.9	9.7	26.9	Low	Med-	Low	Low	4.2
Bissett Small Capital	★★★	↑↑↑↑	11.6	39.4	-16.4	18.5	27.2	11.6	2.00	5	95	Sep96	94.9	20.5	2.9	10.1	16.3	50.1	Med	Med-	Med	Low	18.7
BPI Canadian Small Comp	★★★★	↑↑↑↑↑	23.8	82.0	-10.5	7.9	14.7	0.9	2.74	11	99	Jun96	55.7	22.6	13.3	25.1	6.2	32.8	Low	Med+	High	Low	448.2
Cambridge Growth	★	↑↑↑	0.3	45.2	-26.9	17.1	36.6	2.4	3.00	2		Jun96	92.8	24.3	16.3	20.0	14.7	16.4	Low	High	Med-	Low	63.2
Cambridge Special Equity	★★	↑↑↑↑↑	16.0	118.8	-30.8				3.00		80	Jun96	95.8	21.7	9.8	14.5	5.1	14.8	Low	High	High	Low	20.4
CDA Aggressive Equity									1.00	7		Sep96	72.1	30.8	7.2	22.0	10.0	30.0	Low	Med	Med+	Low	6.6
CIBC Capital Appreciation	★	↑↑	1.9	16.3	-18.5	9.7	18.7	2.2	2.40	2	97	Sep96	85.0	29.4	10.1	20.8	20.6	19.1	Med-	Med+	Med+	Low	279.1
Colonia Life Special Gth	★★★★	↑↑↑	20.6	64.1	-9.4				2.14			Sep96	80.8	47.8	5.7	18.5		28.0	Med	Med	High	Low	14.4
Cote 100 REA - action												Jun96	91.9	13.2	3.0	70.0	3.4	10.4	Med-	Low	Low	Low	5.6
CT Everest Special Equity	★	↑↑	0.5	21.0	-22.8	8.0	15.7	1.4	2.14	12	100	Sep96	59.5	28.4	13.8	14.5	11.1	32.2	Low	High	High	Low	356.8
Cundill Security	★★★★★	↑↑	12.2	18.6	3.6	17.0	21.7	11.0	2.09	24	90	Jun96	58.5	5.2	2.6	63.4	18.0	10.7	Med+	High	Low	Low	17.2
Ethical Special Equity									2.68	12		Sep96	82.4	18.0	5.4	27.3	18.4	30.9	Med-	Med+	High	Low	22.0
Fidelity Cdn Gth Company									2.65	3		Jun96	69.6	6.2		44.2	7.5	42.1	Low	Med	Med	Med-	577.0
First Canadian Special Gth	★★	↑↑↑↑	6.0	31.9	-24.2				2.25	2	100	Sep96	80.3	19.0	9.8	23.0	7.0	41.3	Low	Med+	Med	Med-	109.0
Fonds D'Investissement REA	★	↑↑	1.2	14.1	-15.7				2.22			Sep96	86.4	9.0		52.1	8.1	30.8	Med-	Med+	Med	Low	44.6
General Trust Growth	★	↑↑	1.5	20.3	-16.9	9.6	19.6	3.3	2.16		81	Sep96	96.9	31.1	6.2	34.5	8.6	19.6	Low	Med+	Med	Low	12.4
Global Strategy Cdn Small									2.65			Sep96	86.5	24.9	0.5	23.6		50.9	Med-	Med-	Med	Low	98.4
Great-West Life Gth Eqty (A) A									3.18														26.8
Great-West Life Sm Co (M) A									2.82														17.5
Guardian Enterprise A	★★★★	↑↑↑↑↑	19.4	57.4	-14.3	12.6	19.5	5.2	2.13		88	Sep96	90.2	27.6	9.8	17.8	14.0	30.7	Low	High	High	Low	23.7
Guardian Enterprise B									2.80	5		Sep96	90.2	27.6	9.8	17.8	14.0	30.7	Low	High	High	Low	36.5
Hongkong Bank Sm Cap Gth									2.36			Sep96	86.3	29.5	11.5	16.0	9.7	33.3	Low	High	Med	Med-	21.6
Hyperion Small Cap Cdn Eqty									2.54			Sep96	92.2	22.9	4.4	40.8	13.8	18.1	Low	High	High	Low	48.0
IG BG Canadian Small Cap									2.65	10		Aug96	68.2	43.4	5.2	23.0	9.1	19.2	Med-	Med	Low	Low	12.7
Industrial Equity	★	↑↑↑	-1.5	16.8	-20.5	16.0	27.5	0.6	2.41	10	74	Sep96	73.0	47.6	2.4	17.5	4.1	28.3	Med-	Low	Low	Low	261.0
Investors Cdn Small Cap									2.65	12		Sep96	72.8	32.5	11.9	17.7	6.3	31.6	Med-	Med	Med-	Low	32.3
Ivy Enterprise									2.43	15		Sep96	66.2	4.3		30.3	31.5	33.9	Med-	Low	Med+	Med-	97.1
Laurentian Special Equity	★★★	↑↑	5.2	16.0	-11.9	12.1	15.7	6.9	2.66	9	80	Sep96	84.1	41.6	6.2	19.5	4.2	28.5	Low	High	High	Med-	143.9
Lotus Group Cdn Equity	★★	↑↑↑↑↑	8.1	55.9	-22.7				2.16	17	92	Sep96	78.5	27.1	11.0	11.9	13.7	36.4	Low	High	High	Med-	5.8
Manulife Cabot Cdn Growth									2.50			Sep96	81.4	30.5	7.2	22.9	10.3	29.2	Low	Med	Med-	Low	9.1

Portfolio Analysis: Canadian Stocks

Fund	PAL/SGK Rank	Volatility	Avg Ann Ret	High Ann Ret	Low Ann Ret	Avg 3 Yr Ret	High 3 Yr Ret	Low 3 Yr Ret	MER	% Foreign	% 3 Yr Tx Ef	Portfolio Date	% Cdn Eqty	% Resource	% Prec Metal	% Consumer	% Int Sens	% Industrial	% Div Yield	Price/Earn	Price/Book	Avg Cap	Fund Size $mil
Manulife Cabot Emerg Growth	★★★★★	↑↑↑↑↑	33.1	77.3	-16.9	38.1	45.9	28.2	2.50	17	94	Sep96	67.5	30.5	7.2	22.9	10.3	29.2	Low	Med	Med+	Low	5.2
Marathon Equity	★★★	↑↑	9.8	39.2	-10.5	19.2	24.1	13.7	2.50	3	77	Sep96	88.7	31.3	20.4	15.6	1.0	31.7	Low	High	High	Low	319.8
Mawer New Canada	★★★	↑↑	9.3	29.8	-13.7				1.29	1		Sep96	94.7	30.7	10.5	15.5	20.6	22.7	Med-	Low	Low	Low	78.6
Metlife Mvp Growth									2.00	10		Sep96	79.1	22.2	5.4	33.5	11.8	27.2	Med-	Med+	High	Low	41.6
Millennium Next Generation									2.50	9		Sep96	39.8	36.0	4.7	20.3	7.8	31.3	Med-	Med	High	Low	10.2
Multiple Opportunities	★★★★★	↑↑↑↑↑	35.6	90.1	-22.9	42.6	56.9	21.2	2.74	-	72	Jun96	36.4	18.3	49.4	12.3	-	20.0	Low	High	High	Low	14.3
Mutual Premier Growth	★★★★★	↑↑	14.2	31.3	-8.3				2.38	13	91	Sep96	83.8	26.7	9.4	12.4	10.4	41.1	Med-	High	High	Low	604.4
National TR Special Equity	★	↑↑	3.6	31.9	-22.6				2.50	6	99	Sep96	87.3	34.7	11.0	17.2	2.7	34.5	Low	High	High	Low	33.0
Navigator Value Inv Retire	★★★★★	↑↑↑	24.1	59.1	-11.9				2.71	1		Sep96	76.6	26.9	18.6	15.6	5.0	33.9	Low	High	High	Low	36.5
O'Donnell Cdn Emerging Gth									2.55	1		Sep96	64.6	29.6	22.0	16.8	2.8	28.7	Low	High	High	Med-	363.2
OTGIF Growth	★★★	↑	6.0	21.0	-10.6	7.6	11.4	3.2	1.00		66												17.4
Pacific Special Equity	★★★★★	↑↑↑↑↑	25.4	62.0	-11.9				2.80		88												14.3
Quebec Growth Fund Inc.	★	↑↑↑	3.1	21.3	-19.3	11.2	23.3	4.5	1.89		100												11.0
Resolute Growth									2.00	-													4.5
Royal Canadian Growth	★★	↑↑↑	6.0	29.4	-16.8				2.31	18	100	Sep96	71.9	25.4	7.2	16.1	12.2	39.1	Low	Med+	Med	Low	403.4
Royal Canadian Small Cap	★★	↑↑↑	5.9	30.6	-19.2				2.20	14	83	Sep96	89.1	14.6	4.2	18.1	13.8	49.4	Med-	Med	Low	Low	258.3
Royal Life Canadian Growth									2.35	-													31.3
Saxon Small Cap	★★	↑↑↑	4.7	22.0	-14.8	12.5	16.3	6.4	1.87		67												7.1
Spectrum United Cdn Gth	★★★★★	↑↑↑	18.7	42.9	-7.3	21.0	26.6	14.4	2.30	16	97	Sep96	67.7	32.8	7.7	20.4	1.6	37.6	Low	Med+	Med+	Low	706.5
Median Cdn Small to Medium Cap Equity Funds			6.0	31.9	-16.4	12.5	21.6	4.9	2.41	2.8	91		82.4	27.6	7.7	18.5	9.1	30.6					32.3
Average Cdn Small to Medium Cap Equity Funds			10.8	40.4	-15.9	16.1	24.6	7.7	2.35	5.9	87		78.3	27.1	9.4	24.2	9.1	29.3					124.0

Portfolio Analysis: Canadian Stocks

Fund	PAL/SGK Rank	Volatility	Avg Ann Ret	Hi Ann Ret	Lo Ann Ret	Avg 3 Yr Ret	Hi 3 Yr Ret	Lo 3 Yr Ret	MER	% Foreign	% 3 Yr Tx Ef	Portfolio Date	% Cdn Eqty	% Resource	% Prec Metal	% Consumer	% Int Sens	% Industrial	% Div Yield	Price/Earn	Price/Book	Avg Cap	Fund Size $mil
Canadian Resource Funds (21)																							
AGF Canadian Resources A	★★★	↑↑↑	9.2	46.4	-23.5	18.4	26.6	4.1	2.56	10	100	Sep96	76.3	63.2	22.1	1.2	4.7	8.8	Med+	Med-	Med-	Med-	107.8
AGF Canadian Resources B									3.06	10		Sep96	76.3	63.2	22.1	1.2	4.7	8.8	Med+	Med-	Med-	Med-	153.1
AGF Canadian Resources C									2.99	10		Sep96	76.3	63.2	22.1	1.2	4.7	8.8	Med+	Med	Med-	Med-	14.4
All-Canadian Resources Corp	★★★★★	↑	9.1	34.4	-3.5	21.3	33.2	5.3	2.01	12	80	Sep96	58.3	17.0	72.3		10.7	-	High	Med	Med-	Med+	4.9
Altamira Resource	★★	↑↑	2.0	29.5	-21.6	18.3	41.2	-1.4	2.31	6	80	Sep96	79.4	68.6	20.9		0.6	9.8	Med	Med+	Low	Med-	454.8
BPI Cdn Resource Fund Inc	★★	↑↑↑↑↑	8.7	67.7	-24.7	15.4	28.6	3.9	2.72	3	86	Jun96	57.8	54.0	30.2	2.8	4.7	8.3	Med	Med	Med-	Med-	64.9
Cambridge Resource	★★★	↑↑↑↑↑↑	25.3	149.4	-25.5	22.4	29.6	7.3	3.00	6	95	Jun96	83.2	34.3	32.6	1.2	2.8	17.3	Low	High	Med+	Low	40.9
CIBC Canadian Resources									2.25	0		Sep96	80.6	67.8	31.1		-	1.1	Med-	Med+	Med	Med-	81.4

Portfolio Analysis: Canadian Stocks

Fund	PAL/SGK Rank	Volatility	Avg Ann Ret	Hi Ann Ret	Lo Ann Ret	Avg 3 Yr Ret	Hi 3 Yr Ret	Lo 3 Yr Ret	MER	% Foreign	% 3 Yr Tx Ef	Portfolio Date	% Cdn Eqty	% Resource	% Prec Metal	% Consumer	% Int Sens	% Industrial	Div Yield	Price/ Earn	Price/ Book	Avg Cap	Fund Size $mil
CIBC Energy	★	→→	-3.9	33.3	-26.6	15.0	31.3	-9.7	2.00	-	-	Sep96	74.4	98.1	-	-	-	1.9	Low	Med-	Med	Med-	9.4
Dominion Equity Resource	★★★	→	6.2	28.4	-19.2				2.10	2	100	Sep96	94.6	100.0				-	Med-	Med+	Med-	Med	19.2
First Canadian Resource	★★★	→	5.3	30.3	-14.2	14.1	20.5	3.0	2.26	-	100	Sep96	85.1	67.7	28.3			4.0	Med+	Med	Med	High	52.0
First Heritage									4.24	11	65												4.4
Great-West Life Cdn Re (A) A									3.24														22.4
Green Line Energy									2.27	3		Sep96	66.7	82.5	1.3			16.2	Med-	Med-	Med+	Med	41.6
Green Line Resource									2.14	14		Sep96	73.0	64.2	27.9			7.9	Low	Low	Med+	Med	105.4
Investors Cdn Natural Res									2.65	8		Sep96	63.5	54.9	39.9		0.1	5.1	High	Low	Med-	High	21.0
Maxxum Natural Resource	★★★★★★	→→→→→	28.8	76.8	-13.2	30.9	37.1	17.4	1.76	5	82	Sep96	86.9	60.1	33.3		0.3	4.6	Med+	Med-	Med	Med+	97.5
Middlefield Growth	★★	→	2.5	23.1	-15.5	7.3	14.2	-1.9	3.08	2		Sep96	74.7	87.2	12.2	1.7		0.6	Med+	Med	Low	Med-	31.4
Royal Energy	★	→	-0.2	29.0	-19.1	14.5	26.9	-3.6	2.11	-													165.1
Standard Life Natural Res									2.00	8	5												6.9
Universal Canadian Resource	★★	→→→	4.3	39.1	-21.2	24.3	39.3	2.5	2.40	12	100	Sep96	80.5	85.8	10.3		0.7	3.2	Med-	Low	Low	Low	244.0
Median Canadian Resource Funds			5.7	33.8	-20.2	18.3	29.6	3.0	2.31	6.4	86		76.3	64.2	22.1		0.3	5.1					41.6
Average Canadian Resource Funds			8.1	48.9	-19.0	18.3	29.9	2.5	2.53	6.2	81		75.7	66.6	23.9	0.5	2.0	6.3					41.3

Portfolio Analysis: Canadian Stocks

Fund	PAL/SGK Rank	Volatility	Avg Ann Ret	Hi Ann Ret	Lo Ann Ret	Avg 3 Yr Ret	Hi 3 Yr Ret	Lo 3 Yr Ret	MER	% Foreign	% 3 Yr Tx Ef	Portfolio Date	% Cdn Eqty	% Resource	% Prec Metal	% Consumer	% Int Sens	% Industrial	Div Yield	Price/ Earn	Price/ Book	Avg Cap	Fund Size $mil
Precious Metals Funds (11)																							
Altamira Prec & Strat Metal									2.32	25		Sep96	61.4	30.3	63.8	2.3	3.2	0.4					125.9
Cambridge Precious Metals										-													11.6
CIBC Precious Metal									2.00			Sep96	87.4	13.4	86.6								11.2
Dynamic Precious Metals	★★★★	→→→	13.5	51.9	-11.5	26.7	37.3	11.8	2.57	22	100	Sep96	55.1	27.2	65.8	1.7	4.1	1.3	Med-	High	Med+	Med+	349.4
Friedberg Double Gold Plus	★	→	-0.7	23.0	-12.4	8.1	13.2	0.7			28													1.4
Global Strategy Gold Plus	★★★★★	→→→	27.6	94.9	-7.0	17.3	27.6	5.7	2.95	10	99	Sep96	72.3	30.2	62.8	0.8	5.3	0.9	Low	Low	Low	Low	148.4
Goldtrust	★	→	-0.5	24.8	-24.8				2.42	10	85	Sep96	26.7	3.9	89.9		6.2						14.7
Green Line Precious Metals									2.23	16		Sep96	75.9	18.5	78.9				Med	Med+	High	High	146.2
Maxxum Precious Metals	★★★★	→→→→→	30.0	102.7	-23.5	28.3	39.6	17.0	1.78	12	98	Sep96	67.1	28.5	64.2	2.0	2.7	5.3	Low	High	High	Med+	20.8
Royal Precious Metals	★★★★★	→→→→→	53.2	163.7	-13.7	28.5	47.0	8.4	2.21	16	100								Med-	Med+	Med+	Med	340.4
Scotia Ex Precious Metals									2.19	6		Sep96	69.5	21.5	78.5				Med	High	High	Med+	41.1
Median Precious Metals Funds			20.6	73.4	-13.0	26.7	37.3	8.4	2.21	10.4	99		68.3	24.4	72.1	0.4	2.9	0.2					41.1
Average Precious Metals Funds			20.5	76.8	-15.5	21.8	32.9	8.7	1.88	10.7	85		64.4	21.7	73.8	0.8	2.7	1.0					30.9

Portfolio Analysis: Canadian Stocks

Fund	PAL/SGK Rank	Volatility	Avg Ann Ret	Hi Ann Ret	Lo Ann Ret	Avg 3 Yr Ret	Hi 3 Yr Ret	Lo 3 Yr Ret	MER	% Fgn	Portfolio Date	% Pref Equity	% Cdn Equity	% Resource	% Prec Metal	% Consumer	% Interest Sens	% Industrial	Fund Size $ (mil)
Dividend Funds (36)																			
20/20 Dividend	★★★★★	↑↑↑	11.5	24.4	-6.6	11.7	15.9	6.7	1.98	1	Sep96	0.0	91.1	26.4	-	11.0	37.6	24.9	327.2
AGF High Income A	★★★★★	↑	7.8	16.3	-3.5	7.6	9.7	6.0	1.43	-	Sep96	17.5	12.1	13.3	-	-	86.7	-	91.2
AGF High Income B									1.94	-	Sep96	17.5	12.1	13.3	-	-	86.7	-	190.6
AGF High Income C									1.93	-	Sep96	17.5	12.1	13.3	-	-	86.7	-	20.2
Altamira Dividend									1.64	4	Sep96	26.3	43.4	14.4	-	10.6	59.9	15.2	97.3
Bissett Dividend Income	★★★★★	↑↑↑↑↑	13.8	28.5	-3.8	11.3	15.9	6.4	1.50	19	Sep96	10.0	55.2	26.8	-	8.9	53.4	10.8	11.0
BPI Income	★★★★★	↑↑↑	11.7	22.4	-2.6	8.6	12.6	3.8	1.08	-	Jun96	23.5	44.6	23.7	-	5.9	61.3	9.1	49.4
CIBC Dividend	★	↑↑↑↑↑	5.2	19.5	-13.7	7.4	11.0	3.0	1.80	5	Sep96	-	61.0	12.7	6.7	6.4	67.3	6.9	250.8
Concorde Dividendes									1.85	-	Sep96	-	81.7	25.4	-	8.4	66.2	-	4.8
CT Everest Dividend Income									1.87	-	Sep96	13.9	68.0	24.5	-	4.5	57.0	14.0	97.7
Desjardins Dividend									1.80	1	Sep96	14.6	63.0	9.5	-	15.1	58.9	16.5	23.3
Dynamic Dividend	★★★	↑↑↑↑↑	8.2	20.0	-6.6	8.6	10.8	6.2	1.61	4	Jun96	46.6	29.0	8.8	-	-	73.5	17.7	217.9
Dynamic Dividend Growth	★★★★	↑↑↑↑↑	10.5	22.9	-6.2	10.6	13.1	7.3	1.81	7	Jun96	21.4	47.1	22.4	-	10.3	51.1	16.2	59.2
First Canadian Dividend Income									1.71	-	Sep96	1.6	86.2	14.2	-	8.3	65.8	11.7	97.2
Green Line Dividend	★	↑↑	3.7	17.9	-7.8	6.7	10.4	4.9	2.06	-	Sep96	10.9	82.0	7.9	2.2	11.2	61.8	16.8	106.1
Guardian Monthly Dividend B									1.85	-	Aug96	39.0	23.4	21.7	-	-	75.0	3.3	354.3
Guardian Monthly Dividend A	★★★	↑↑	6.6	15.9	-5.0	6.8	8.1	5.1	1.25	-	Aug96	39.0	23.4	21.7	-	-	75.0	3.3	135.6
Hongkong Bank Dividend Inc									2.05	1	Sep96	1.6	69.4	15.4	-	6.6	69.6	8.3	33.6
Industrial Dividend	★★★★	↑↑	8.6	18.5	-4.8	16.1	22.4	10.0	2.39	11	Sep96	0.3	71.6	22.1	1.2	5.8	42.7	28.3	341.9
InvesNat Dividend	★★★★★	↑	8.2	18.5	-3.3	7.1	9.6	4.9	1.75	-	Sep96	55.7	21.4	14.9	-	-	85.1	-	10.7
Investors Dividend	★★★	↑	6.7	15.4	-6.1	7.0	9.4	4.2	2.34	-	Sep96	15.4	49.8	0.5	-	0.2	96.6	2.7	2,742.6
Laurentian Dividend	★★★	↑	6.4	15.1	-6.7				2.65	-	Sep96	19.3	53.5	8.4	-	12.4	62.6	16.6	317.0
Maritime Life Dividend Inc									2.05	-	Sep96	28.7	50.8	19.4	-	7.5	56.8	16.2	15.7
Maxxum Dividend	★★★★★	↑↑↑↑↑	12.1	26.8	-5.0	17.3	20.9	12.1	1.51	6	Jun96	3.8	76.0	19.6	7.2	20.0	42.8	10.5	84.4
MD Dividend	★★★★★	↑	8.3	17.0	-4.6				1.20	-	Sep96	42.6	31.6	2.9	-	-	97.1	-	71.7
National Trust Dividend	★	↑↑↑↑↑	5.7	18.4	-8.8				1.84	-	Jul96	1.9	68.3	3.8	-	4.5	75.4	16.4	28.0
NN Dividend									2.00	-	Jun96	24.4	35.4	14.8	-	18.0	59.3	8.0	45.5
PH & N Dividend Income	★★★★★	↑↑	10.4	21.1	-4.9	11.8	16.0	7.6	1.19	-	Jun96	6.1	72.7	8.9	-	5.8	81.2	4.1	88.9
Pret Et Revenu Dividendes									1.62	-	Sep96	-	73.9	21.2	-	7.7	68.6	2.5	5.6
Royal Trust Growth&Income	★★★	↑↑↑↑↑	8.0	22.7	-8.1	7.1	10.7	3.5	2.22	-	Jun96	2.8	81.4	7.4	1.2	6.5	75.1	9.8	66.4
Royfund Dividend	★★★★	↑↑↑	9.4	20.3	-6.9	7.9	10.7	4.1	1.86	-									345.5
Scotia Excelsior Dividend	★★★	↑↑↑↑↑	9.0	22.5	-6.1	7.9	10.7	4.1	1.07	-	Sep96	39.3	46.3	5.9	-	17.1	72.6	4.4	65.0
Spectrum United Dividend	★★	↑↑↑↑	6.8	18.3	-9.2	7.4	10.8	3.9	1.61	-	Sep96	25.3	37.0	-	-	-	100.0	-	57.2
Standard Life Canadian Dividend									1.50	-									4.3
Talvest Dividend	★★★★	↑↑	8.9	21.6	-7.4	8.3	12.6	2.4	1.99	3	Sep96	12.5	57.3	12.6	7.1	5.7	67.8	6.8	40.3
Trans-Canada Dividend									3.00	9	Jun96	-	47.3	9.6	9.4	10.8	45.2	24.9	6.7
Median Dividend Funds			8.3	19.8	-6.2	8.1	10.9	5.0	1.83			1503	52.2	13.8	-	6.4	67.6	8.7	69.0
Average Dividend Funds			8.5	20.2	-6.3	9.4	12.8	5.7	1.80	2.0		1703	52.3	14.3	1.0	6.7	68.3	9.6	66.4

United States Equity Funds (100)

Fund	PAL/SGK Rank	Volatility	Avg Ann Ret	Hi Ann Ret	Lo Ann Ret	Avg 3 Yr Ret	Hi 3 Yr Ret	Lo 3 Yr Ret	MER	% 3 Yr Tx Ef	Port-folio Date	% United States	% Canada	% Non North America	Fund Size $ mil
20/20 Aggressive Growth	★★★	↑↑↑↑↑↑	19.7	46.4	-7.1				2.54	93.1	Sep96	98.5	2.7	-	296.4
ABC American-Value	★★	↑↑↑							2.00		Sep96	56.3	16.7	-	5.6
ADMAX American Select Growth			5.5	25.1	-10.6	15.7	19.1	10.5	2.75	71.9	Sep96	86.8	-	9.7	1.9
AGF International Group American Gth A	★★★★	↑↑↑	17.3	31.9	0.3				2.37	96.9	Sep96	88.1	-	7.8	123.9
AGF International Group American Gth B									2.85		Sep96	88.1	-	7.8	50.0
AGF International Group American Gth C									2.84		Sep96	88.1	-	7.8	7.6
AGF International Group Special A	★★★	↑↑↑	11.3	30.8	-5.9	11.7	17.8	5.2	2.38	95.3	Sep96	88.7	0.4	-	119.4
AGF International Group Special B									2.87		Sep96	88.7	0.4	-	56.9
AGF International Group Special C									2.83		Sep96	88.7	0.4	-	2.4
AIC Value	★★★	↑↑↑↑↑↑	18.7	38.0	-7.2	17.7	21.2	10.5	2.60	100.0	Sep96	59.5	27.0	0.3	128.9
Altamira Select American	★★★★	↑↑↑	14.5	34.0	-0.3	20.7	28.2	14.7	2.32	91.6	Sep96	88.3	0.6	2.0	265.1
Altamira US Larger Company	★★★★	↑↑↑↑↑	20.4	39.7	-1.7	11.1	15.0	6.1	2.36	84.2	Sep96	86.5	-	-	92.9
Atlas American Large Cap Growth	★★★★	↑↑↑	17.4	31.3	0.1	15.1	19.2	11.0	2.69	100.0	Sep96	84.3	2.8	5.2	8.3
Beutel Goodman American Equity	★★★★	↑↑↑	11.1	25.8	-4.3	12.6	16.1	8.6	2.70	90.4	Jun96	93.8	-	-	5.0
Bissett American Equity	★★★★	↑↑↑	15.9	29.8	1.0	13.2	16.7	8.5	1.50	94.7	Sep96	100.4	-	2.4	8.2
BPI American Equity Value	★★★★	↑↑↑	15.4	34.0	-3.4	25.5	34.3	16.5	2.65	76.5	Jun96	93.1	-	3.5	56.5
BPI American Small Company	★★★★	↑↑↑	16.6	31.4	1.5				3.09	90.9	Jun96	94.0	-	-	85.3
C.I. American	★★★★★	↑↑↑	17.5	31.2	6.3				2.48	95.6	Sep96	87.4	2.2	4.9	170.3
C.I. American RSP									2.51		Jun96	102.1	0.9	-	14.3
C.I. American Sector	★★★★★	↑↑↑	17.1	30.6	6.4				2.50	100.0	Jun96				51.9
Cambridge American Growth	★	↑↑↑	-6.0	9.0	-19.4	8.5	15.4	-1.0	3.00		Jun96	70.7	17.6	-	0.8
Cassels Blaikie American	★★★	↑↑↑↑↑	19.2	39.2	-5.3				1.24	81.8	Sep96	100.5	-	-	12.2
CCPE US Equity									1.75						12.4
Century DJ	★★★★★	↑	3.9	6.3	1.8	4.1	5.8	3.1	1.80	100.0					0.3
Chou Associates	★★★	↑↑↑↑↑	14.6	32.2	-6.7	12.9	15.7	10.5	2.04	82.9					5.2
CIBC US Index RRSP									1.00		Sep96	9.1	-	-	11.0
CIBC US Equity	★★★★	↑↑↑	14.3	30.0	1.6	10.7	13.5	7.9	2.25	90.1	Sep96	94.1	-	-	64.6
CIBC US Opportunities									2.45		Sep96	92.0	-	-	11.7
Co-operators U.S. Equity									2.07		Aug96	97.6	-	-	3.9
Cornerstone US	★★★★★	↑↑↑	14.9	27.3	2.6	12.1	14.9	8.5	2.59	94.2	Aug96	98.1	-	-	24.7
CT Everest Amerigrowth	★★★★	↑↑↑	19.6	37.8	-0.7				1.41	64.9					246.0
CT Everest US Equity	★★★	↑↑↑	10.8	23.8	-4.7	9.9	12.7	7.3	2.25	79.3	Sep96	94.9	-	-	77.7
Desjardins Marche Amer															4.3
Dynamic Americas	★★	↑↑↑↑↑	13.0	43.0	-10.7	9.4	14.6	0.7	2.59	80.7	Sep96	76.9	-	-	45.2
Elliott & Page American Growth	★★★★	↑	12.7	26.6	1.1	11.3	14.1	7.1	1.35	79.6	Sep96	89.8	1.4	-	72.0
Fidelity Growth America	★★★★	↑↑↑	17.9	36.3	-1.2	17.7	22.7	13.0	2.33	75.8	Jun96	90.3	-	3.5	903.1

Fund	PAL/SGK Rank	Volatility	Avg Ann Ret	Hi Ann Ret	Lo Ann Ret	Avg 3 Yr Ret	Hi 3 Yr Ret	Lo 3 Yr Ret	MER	% 3 Yr Tx Ef	Port-folio Date	% United States	% Canada	% Non North America	Fund Size $ mil
Fidelity Small Cap America	★★★	↑↑	9.3	29.4	-9.4				2.60	80.2	Jun96	91.6	-	-	58.0
First Canadian US Growth	★★★★	↑↑↑↑↑	24.5	54.6	1.2	26.2	34.1	20.2	2.24	100.0					57.6
Formula Growth	★★	↑↑	6.9	23.0	-9.1	10.0	16.2	4.8	0.95	59.7	Sep96				263.4
General Trust US Equity									2.18		Sep96	95.8	0.2		5.6
Global Strategy US Equity									2.95		Jul96	78.6	0.8	0.6	5.8
Great-West Life US Equity (G) A									2.82		Aug96	85.0	0.8		92.2
Green Line US Index	★★★★	↑↑↑	19.3	36.5	-0.2	11.9	16.1	4.8	0.77	95.3	Sep96	96.6	0.8	1.9	66.7
GS American Equity									3.25		Sep96	99.2			8.1
GT Global America Growth									2.95		Sep96	89.5	4.8	2.9	17.5
Guardian American Equity A	★★★★	↑↑↑	15.4	31.3	1.0	16.5	21.0	11.6	2.40	72.6	Sep96	83.6	1.4	4.7	33.6
Guardian American Equity B									2.95		Sep96	83.6	1.4	4.7	14.5
Hyperion Value Line US Equity	★★★	↑↑↑↑↑↑	20.5	41.1	-6.8	15.9	21.1	9.6	3.01	82.5	Sep96	88.8	3.8		54.2
Industrial American	★★★★	↑	10.0	23.0	-4.0	13.0	15.9	9.1	2.38	92.4	Sep96	86.9	1.3		253.3
InvesNat Blue Chip American Equity	★★	↑↑	4.5	20.9	-10.1				2.42	97.9	Sep96	87.0			2.0
Investors US Growth	★★★★★	↑	14.8	26.4	4.1	15.0	17.9	12.6	2.40	98.6	Sep96	87.7			643.1
Investors US Opportunities									2.65		Sep96	89.2	2.2		23.4
Jones Heward American	★	↑↑↑	1.6	20.8	-17.1	6.5	10.6	1.6	2.50	76.8	Sep96	92.3			17.0
Laurentian American Equity	★★★★★	↑	14.0	25.7	4.0	13.1	15.9	8.7	2.65	89.0	Sep96	85.8	1.9		117.1
Leith Wheeler US Equity									1.34		Aug96	95.2			3.2
London Life US Equity	★★★	↑↑↑	9.1	26.4	-6.4	8.8	11.2	5.8	2.00						127.2
Manulife VistaFd1 American Stock									1.63						14.0
Manulife VistaFd2 American Stock									2.38						72.3
Margin of Safety	★★★★	↑↑	11.9	22.8	-1.4	10.2	13.6	7.7	2.04	79.2	Sep96	85.2			4.7
Maritime Life American Growth & Income									2.30						51.1
Maritime Life S&P 500									1.90						96.8
Mawer US Equity	★★★★	↑↑	16.2	30.0	1.2				1.33	89.9	Sep96	95.8			14.2
Maxxum American Equity									2.28		Jun96	77.4	1.0	8.3	14.6
McDonald New America									2.38						0.6
Mclean Budden American Growth	★★★★★	↑↑	16.9	29.8	2.1	11.9	17.2	5.9	1.75	87.1	Sep96	97.1			13.0
Mclean Budden Pooled American Equity	★★★★★	↑↑	19.4	32.6	5.0	14.4	19.8	8.1		98.8					117.3
MD US Equity	★★★★	↑↑↑↑↑	18.2	41.1	-0.8				1.17	100.0	Sep96	98.2			135.3
Metlife Mvp US Equity	★★★	↑↑↑↑	13.4	29.6	-4.1				2.00						12.7
Millennia III American Equity 1									2.80		Sep96	88.0	1.3		9.8
Millennia III Amerian Equity 2									2.98		Sep96	88.0	1.3		1.3
Mutual Amerifund	★★★★	↑↑	11.9	23.5	-1.0	11.0	13.9	8.4	2.10	62.1	Sep96	94.3	-		5.4
Mutual Premier American	★★★★	↑↑	11.1	22.0	-1.3				2.40	93.7	Sep96	91.6		1.1	21.7
NAL-US Equity									2.25					0.8	12.4
National Trust American Equity	★★★	↑↑↑	11.3	27.8	-7.4				2.59	83.3	Jul96	84.7		4.8	11.3

Fund	PAL/SGK Rank	Volatility	Avg Ann Ret	Hi Ann Ret	Lo Ann Ret	Avg 3 Yr Ret	Hi 3 Yr Ret	Lo 3 Yr Ret	MER	% 3 Yr Tx Ef	Portfolio Date	Geographic Allocation % United States	% Canada	% Non North America	Fund Size $ mil
Navigator American Value	****	↑↑↑	18.7	36.0	-0.5				2.72		Sep96	95.0	-	-	1.3
NN Can-Am									2.25	68.2	Aug96	19.6	-	-	132.8
O.I.Q. Ferique America									1.88		Sep96	10.7	-	-	1.8
O'Donnell American Sector Growth									2.65		Sep96	83.0	-	-	21.0
O'Donnell US Mid-Cap									2.65					1.4	7.6
Optima Strategy US Equity									0.43						50.5
PH & N Pooled US Pension	****	↑↑↑	17.4	36.2	2.2	16.9	19.5	13.9	0.05	100.0	Jun96	92.5		1.7	450.5
PH & N US Equity	****	↑↑↑	16.0	34.2	1.1	15.5	18.3	12.3	1.12	77.0	Aug96	93.0		1.7	353.1
Pret et Revenu Americain	***	↑↑↑↑↑	20.1	54.7	-2.8	11.9	21.9	5.5	2.15	87.3	Sep96	89.1	1.1	1.0	5.5
Prosperity American Performance	**	↑↑↑↑↑	6.0	25.5	-9.5				6.14	29.2	Sep96	5.2	44.1	59.9	0.0
Royal Life US Equity									-						4.2
Royal Trust American Stock	****	↑↑	14.4	28.6	-0.5	13.0	16.0	9.5	2.15	72.8	Sep96	89.1		1.4	146.8
Royfund US Equity	****	↑↑	15.9	31.5	0.3				2.09	86.4	Sep96	90.7		1.6	68.5
Scotia Canam Growth									1.34						70.3
Scotia Excelsior Amer Growth	****	↑↑	11.8	23.2	-3.1	12.7	17.3	8.9	2.19	68.6	Sep96	81.7			57.6
Scudder US Growth & Income									1.25						1.0
Spectrum United American Equity	***	↑↑↑↑↑	18.8	38.9	-4.1	10.9	17.8	5.5	2.30	74.9	Sep96	80.5		11.2	271.0
Spectrum United American Growth	****	↑↑↑↑↑↑	26.4	57.7	1.6	19.7	26.1	13.1	2.30	85.5	Sep96	83.7	1.3	5.9	75.9
Spectrum United Optimax USA									2.33		Sep96	95.4	2.1		6.5
SSQ - Actions Americaines	****	↑↑↑	21.6	40.1	1.3	12.2	20.2	4.1			Sep96	80.5			5.6
Standard Life US Equity									2.00						2.8
Top 50 US Equity	**	↑↑↑	7.4	21.6	-7.9				3.18		Sep96	67.2			0.7
Transamerica Growsafe US Equity									1.35						6.6
Universal US Emerging Growth	****	↑↑↑↑↑↑	29.6	66.8	3.9				2.40	98.8	Sep96	89.0	0.9	1.5	346.7
University Avenue Growth	***	↑↑↑	9.6	28.9	-7.7	3.1	11.3	-3.4	2.68	100.0	Sep96	49.5	5.6	4.6	0.6
Zweig Strategic Growth	****	↑↑	12.2	26.2	-0.2				2.62	95.5					156.1
Median U.S. Equity Funds			14.9	30.6	-1.0	12.6	16.7	8.5	2.33	88.2		88.7	-	-	19.3
Average U.S. Equity Funds			14.4	31.8	-2.5	13.2	17.8	8.2	2.17	85.6		83.8	2.0	2.4	17.5

North American Equity Funds (17)

Fund	PAL/SGK Rank	Volatility	Avg Ann Ret	Hi Ann Ret	Lo Ann Ret	Avg 3 Yr Ret	Hi 3 Yr Ret	Lo 3 Yr Ret	MER	% 3 Yr Tx Ef	Port-folio Date	% United States	% Canada	% Non North America	Fund Size $ mil
Altamira North American Recovery	★	↑	3.9	16.6	-11.3				2.31	90.8	Sep96	13.1	66.1	-	48.1
Champion Growth									2.50	100.0					3.2
Cote 100 Amerique	★★	↑↑↑↑	13.9	41.9	-17.7				1.40		Sep96	51.1	44.7		16.7
CT Everest North American	★	↑↑	3.1	17.5	-14.4	7.9	12.5	2.7	2.29	81.6	Sep96	98.1	-		27.2
Ethical North American Equity	★★★	↑↑↑	15.8	34.5	-4.4	12.8	17.2	7.5	2.55	81.0	Sep96				36.1
First American	★	↑	2.6	10.2	-7.1				2.80		Sep96				9.4
First Canadian NAFTA Advantage									2.25		Sep96	23.7	40.1	20.2	12.4
GBC North American Growth	★★	↑↑↑↑↑	13.6	38.8	-8.1	15.9	21.3	9.4	1.82	100.0	Aug96	75.3	10.7	3.0	119.0
Great-West Life North American Eqty (B) A									2.76			93.1	3.1	0.8	15.8
Green Line North American Growth A									2.39		Sep96	84.0		1.4	94.0
Green Line Science & Technology									2.63		Sep96	86.8	1.6		162.3
Imperial Growth North American Equity	★★★★★	↑	14.4	26.7	5.7	14.4	18.1	10.7	1.62		Sep96	44.6	43.8	0.5	3.2
Investors North Amerian Growth	★★★★	↑	11.0	25.1	-3.8	12.3	15.9	8.1	2.40	85.2	Sep96	41.9	50.7	0.4	1,326.4
Investors Special	★★	↑↑	8.3	24.8	-8.7	11.0	15.8	5.8	2.40	95.1	Sep96				405.8
Orbit North American Equity									2.50						1.1
PH & N North American Equity	★	↑↑↑↑↑	5.2	33.7	-19.7				1.12	88.9	Sep96	42.7	39.6	9.1	44.8
Special Opportunities	★	↑↑↑↑↑	10.7	45.2	-22.0	10.3	16.6	1.4	2.14	66.6	Apr96	14.0	46.5	-	4.5
Median North American Equity Funds			10.7	26.7	-8.7	12.3	16.6	7.5	2.39	88.9		44.6	39.6	0.4	27.2
Average North American Equity Funds			9.3	28.6	-10.1	12.1	16.8	6.5	2.23	87.7		51.4	26.7	2.7	22.0

International and Global Equity Funds (119)

Fund	PAL/SGK Rank	Volatility	Avg Ann Ret	Hi Ann Ret	Lo Ann Ret	Avg 3 Yr Ret	Hi 3 Yr Ret	Lo 3 Yr Ret	MER	% Foreign	% 3 Yr Tx Ef	Port-folio Date	% Can-ada	% U.S.	% Japan	% Pac Rim	% Eu-rope	% Asia	% Mex-ico	% Latin Amer	% Africa	% Mid East	Fund Size $mil
20/20 Aggr Global Stock	★★★	↑↑	8.1	18.0	-5.1	13.5	16.8	10.3	2.89	90		Sep96	9.7	19.6	1.9	11.5	47.6	1.2	2.8	3.0	-	1.4	40.4
20/20 International Value									2.52	96	68	Sep96	3.6	26.8	7.3	3.2	50.6	-	3.0	4.5	1.2	-	381.4
20/20 RSP Int'l Eqty Alloc										-		Jul96	100.1	2.7	-2.0	-	-0.8	-	-	-	-	-	238.2
ADMAX Global Health Sci	★★★	↑↑↑↑↑	4-	84.5	1.2				2.58	83	98	Sep96	16.6	79.1	-	-	3.4	0.3	1.1	1.0	-	0.9	128.6
ADMAX International	★	↑↑↑	2.1	21.7	-6.2	15.8	22.6	5.4	2.90	93	54	Sep96	6.6	27.3	11.1	14.4	38.3	-	1.3	2.6			20.5
AGF Int'l Grp World Eqty A										86		Sep96	13.8	31.0	10.2	5.5	33.0		1.3	2.6		2.6	4.6
AGF Int'l Grp World Eqty B										86		Sep96	13.8	31.0	10.2	5.5	33.0		1.3	2.6		2.6	67.4
AGF Int'l Grp World Eqty C										86		Sep96	13.8	31.0	10.2	5.5	33.0		1.3	2.6		2.6	5.1
AIC World Equity									2.75	89		Sep96	10.9	6.8	-	19.6	61.9			0.9			10.1

Portfolio Analysis: Geographic Allocation

Fund	PAL/SGK Rank	Volatility	Avg Ann Ret	Hi Ann Ret	Lo Ann Ret	Avg 3 Yr Ret	Hi 3 Yr Ret	Lo 3 Yr Ret	MER	% Foreign	% 3 Yr Tx Ef	Portfolio Date	% Canada	% U.S.	% Japan	% Pac Rim	% Europe	% Asia	% Mexico	% Latin Amer	% Africa	% Mid East	Fund Size $mil
Altamira Science & Tech	★★	↑	5.5	15.2	-4.0	13.6	17.3	7.2	2.37	89	73	Sep96	10.9	83.8			5.2			1.1	0.4	0.1	74.0
Atlas Global Value		↑							2.74	95		Sep96	4.7	34.2	14.4	10.9	33.3		1.1	6.1	0.5	0.3	14.8
Azura Growth Pooled	★	↑↑↑↑	3.3	17.3	-14.3	13.0	16.1	8.6	2.24	63	58	Aug96	36.6	23.3	4.8	8.0	17.1	1.3	1.6	4.4	0.9		18.7
Beutel Goodman Int'l Eq									2.60	88		Jun96	12.3	2.0	22.0	21.3	37.2						17.2
Bissett Multinational Gth									1.50	78		Sep96	22.2	64.3	14.8	3.6	10.6			2.9			6.8
BPI Global Equity	★★★	↑↑	8.9	19.9	-3.4	10.5	15.3	6.3	2.79	93	86	Jun96	7.3	36.5	4.5	9.8	34.8		0.9	2.1			91.6
BPI Global Small Companies	★	↑↑	4.8	31.6	-5.6	11.6	18.2	6.0	2.66	91	96	Jun96	8.8	29.5	9.8	5.3	45.7		0.9	1.6			87.2
BPI International Equity	★	↑↑↑	3.9	16.1	-9.2	11.4	12.0	5.7	2.69	94	72	Jun96	6.4	10.6	24.7	7.5	49.6		1.1	2.4			187.2
C.I. Global	★	↑↑↑	3.6	14.4	-11.6	6.9	14.3	3.4	2.54	92	84	Aug96	8.5	23.9	4.1	2.9	31.5	2.1	5.5	13.8	1.1	2.0	762.3
C.I. Global Equity RSP	★	↑↑↑	3.4	17.6	-12.4	8.3	18.2	-2.6	2.53	18	85	Feb96	82.2	7.1	0.4		0.6		0.3	6.5			278.6
C.I. Global Sector	★	↑↑	3.3	13.8	-11.5				2.56	99	100	Jun96		60.1	14.0	16.0							166.2
Cambridge Americas	★	↑↑↑↑↑↑	5.9	45.3	-7.7	15.6	16.8	9.0	3.00	60	79	Jun96	39.9	43.0						1.6			2.4
Cambridge Global		↑↑↑↑↑↑	-2.1	37.7	-2-	12.1	13.9	5.1	3.00	29	83	Jul96	71.1	4.5	18.0	4.2	3.9	4.6	3.9	2.7	0.9	1.0	4.8
Canada Life US & Int'l	★★★	↑↑	12.1	24.9	-3.1	9.4			2.40	88	88	Sep96	12.0	77.3	9.3	5.0	23.9					1.0	337.3
Capstone Int'l Invest Tr	★★	↑↑↑↑↑	8.8	34.5	-7.1				2.14	86	90	Sep96	13.6	10-	16.5	0.8	2.5						3.0
CDA International Equity									1.45	-		Sep96		25.1	16.3	1.9	25.9						5.1
CIBC Global Equity	★★	↑	4.3	13.4	-5.7				2.40	74	87	Sep96	25.8	37.8	11.2	5.5	20.4			0.2			125.5
CIBC Global Technology									2.25	85		Sep96	15.2	84.8									36.0
Clean Environment Int'l Eqty									3.01	39		Sep96	61.4				26.4						4.0
Concorde International									2.28	81		Sep96	19.2	46.3	4.0	6.3	20.4			1.1		1.7	2.8
Cornerstone Global	★★★	↑↑↑	11.5	24.7	-1.5	13.4	16.2	10.5	2.62	99	99	Sep96	0.9	47.9	3.9	4.2	26.4			3.1			10.1
CT Everest International	★	↑↑↑↑	2.1	16.3	-12.7	9.7	13.0	5.0	2.53	90	79	Sep96	9.9	17.3	4.9	4.0	46.7	0.4		2.2		0.2	106.5
Cundill Value	★★★★★	↑	11.4	15.8	7.3	18.9	21.8	12.7	2.06	61	92	Jun96	38.7	10.8	1.6	3.9	34.5			0.3			407.3
Desjardins International	★★★	↑↑	8.3	20.1	-2.6	14.0	18.6	9.1	2.37	28	100	Sep96	71.9	28.1	22.4	4.9	20.8						58.6
Dynamic Global Millennia									3.12	20		Sep96	79.7	13.2	5.3	8.7	23.8	2.3					6.2
Dynamic Global Resource	★	↑↑↑↑↑↑	4.8	39.0	-24.0				3.42	8		Sep96	91.8	2.4			6.7						61.7
Dynamic International	★★	↑↑↑↑↑	7.2	25.9	-9.5	12.3	16.6	6.3	2.79	75	100	Sep96	24.9	36.0	44.1	13.2	41.5	1.6		5.2	2.3		41.6
Elliott & Page Global Eqty									1.57	95		Sep96	4.7	37.3	5.2	10.3	42.7		0.4	2.5	0.6	2.7	33.8
Empire International Gth	★★	↑↑↑	7.3	22.6	-11.4	12.2	15.1	8.2	2.57	81	83	Sep96	18.9	51.8	25.4	1.1	48.6					3.6	60.2
Fidelity Int'l Portfolio	★★★	↑↑↑	9.7	24.3	-6.5	15.3	19.1	9.9	2.76	87	92	Sep96		23.0	23.7	20.3	29.0						1,053.6
First Canadian Int'l Gth	★★	↑↑	5.5	17.3	-5.6	5.1	8.7	-0.4	1.98	96	88	Sep96	4.1	2.4	2.9	9.8	41.5						147.7
Fonds Professional Intl Eqty	★★★	↑↑↑	9.0	19.2	0.2				0.75	72	100	Sep96	27.9	22.9	7.2	4.6	42.7		0.8	1.5			45.3
GBC International Growth	★	↑	-1.7	12.0	-17.8	4.7	8.6	0.6	1.78	99		Mar96	1.0	4.6	11.4	11.4	48.6		1.5	0.9		0.1	21.8
General Trust Int'l	★	↑	1.5	9.2	-5.6	10.5	15.6	4.2	2.15	88		Sep96	12.2	24.5	5.7	5.7	29.0						11.8
Global Strategy Diver World									2.50	17		Jun96	83.1		21.0		4.3	0.1	0.1	0.2		0.1	8.3
Global Strategy World Emerg									2.95	74		Jul96	25.8	32.0			25.8	0.4	0.7	2.1	0.2	1.5	97.7
Global Strategy World Eqty									2.95	90		Jul96	9.7	34.1			30.9		0.3	0.2		0.3	107.5
Green Line Global Select		↑							2.42	95		Sep96	5.2		15.7	13.8	30.7	0.5					71.6

Fund	PAL/SGK Rank	Volatility	Avg Ann Ret	Hi Ann Ret	Lo Ann Ret	Avg 3 Yr Ret	Hi 3 Yr Ret	Lo 3 Yr Ret	MER	% Foreign	% 3 Yr Tx Ef	Portfolio Date	Portfolio Analysis: Geographic Allocation										Fund Size $mil
													% Can ada	% U.S.	% Japan	% Pac Rim	% Eu rope	% Asia	% Mex ico	% Latin Amer	% Africa	% Mid East	
Green Line Int'l Equity	★	↑↑	3.7	16.3	-7.5				2.41	97	98	Sep96	3.2	0.2	32.4	16.7	44.1	0.4	0.3	2.8	-	-	106.7
Greystone Managed Global									2.45	92		Jun96	7.9	21.8	18.2	10.4	40.3	-	-	0.9	-	-	39.5
GS International Equity									3.25	79		Sep96	21.3	42.6	11.8	0.5	23.5	-	-	0.2	-	0.1	105.7
GT Global Gbl Infrastructure									2.95	82		Sep96	18.3	30.7	2.3	11.6	21.6	1.8	1.3	8.4	-	3.9	54.4
GT Global Gbl Nat Resours									2.95	71		Sep96	28.9	54.2	-	5.0	8.7	-	1.8	-	1.5	-	23.6
GT Global Gbl Telecomm									2.95	85		Sep96	14.6	44.5	5.9	10.9	18.0	-	1.5	3.1	-	1.5	382.2
GT Global Health Care									2.95	85		Sep96	15.1	76.2	-	0.9	6.5	-	0.8	-	-	-	225.1
Guardian Global Equity A	★★	↑↑↑↑	8.5	23.7	-9.0	13.0	16.1	8.9	1.98	86	100	Sep96	13.7	24.1	21.1	9.9	26.2	1.3	1.0	2.7	0.3	-	4.8
Guardian Global Equity B									2.86	86		Sep96	13.7	24.1	21.1	9.9	26.2	1.3	1.0	2.7	0.3	-	5.9
Hansberger Gbl Small Cap										86		Aug96	13.6	13.5	3.0	17.1	36.8	4.2	2.2	8.0	-	-	8.4
Hansberger International									2.61	76		Aug96	23.7	3.1	3.0	15.7	45.5	2.1	3.4	2.1	0.9	-	3-
Hansberger Value									2.61	73		Aug96	27.5	9.9	1.3	14.8	35.2	4.9	1.6	3.2	0.5	-	86.8
Hongkong Bank Americas									2.48	87		Sep96	12.5	74.8	-	-	0.2	-	5.2	7.3	-	-	12.5
HRL Overseas Growth	★	↑↑	3.9	14.3	-8.9	12.2	15.1	8.4	0.78	95	91	Sep96	4.7	2.2	23.9	17.7	43.8	1.2	2.1	4.4	-	-	74.6
Hyperion Gbl Sci & Tech	★★★★	↑↑↑↑	14.7	26.2	-0.1				2.25	94	92	Sep96	5.6	93.2	-	1.2	-	-	-	-	-	-	8.5
Ind. Alliance Ecoflex I									2.14	-		Sep96	10-	-	-	-	-	-	-	-	-	-	22.4
Ind. Alliance Int'l									1.61	-		Sep96	10-	-	-	-	-	-	-	-	-	-	1.7
Investors Global	★★★	↑↑	9.9	21.5	-1.1	12.6	16.5	9.4	2.46	90	86	Sep96	9.5	27.7	18.9	12.6	30.6	0.6	-	-	-	-	1,047.2
Investors Growth Portfolio	★★★	↑↑↑	10.5	22.1	-0.8	14.3	17.7	10.1	0.18	65	94	Sep96	34.7	38.8	7.6	5.9	12.6	0.3	0.1	-	-	-	379.0
Investors World Gth Port	★★★★★	↑	6.9	16.8	-4.0	10.9	13.5	5.8	0.22	80	99	Sep96	20.4	15.5	18.3	13.1	30.1	0.3	0.2	-	-	-	924.9
Ivy Foreign Equity	★★★★★	↑	13.4	18.0	6.8	12.3	15.7	6.4	2.40	67	93	Sep96	33.0	58.6	-	-	8.4	-	-	-	-	-	210.6
Laurentian Commonwealth	★★★	↑	6.0	14.5	-3.0	10.9	13.5	5.8	2.70	73	80	Sep96	27.3	20.6	21.6	9.5	20.9	-	-	-	-	-	317.1
Laurentian International	★★★	↑	6.6	14.9	-1.0	12.3	15.7	6.4	2.70	91	86	Sep96	9.4	26.3	26.7	11.9	25.7	-	-	-	-	-	180.7
London Life Int'l Equity									2.50	100		Aug96	0.5	0.8	42.0	7.7	49.1	-	-	-	-	-	104.1
Lotus International Equity									2.21	91		Sep96	9.2	0.8	27.7	13.1	41.7	-	-	-	-	-	9.2
Mackenzie Sentinel Global	★★	↑↑↑	5.8	16.4	-6.1	13.8	18.1	7.2	0.51	97	100	Sep96	9.2	2.0	33.2	8.5	47.9	0.4	2.0	3.0	0.9	0.2	7.8
Manulife Cabot Global Eqty									2.50	80		Sep96	2.7	2.0	14.6	10.4	28.3	0.8	0.6	0.9	-	-	17.5
Manulife VistaFd1 Gbl Eqty									1.63	89		Sep96	19.8	27.0	-	-	-	-	-	-	-	-	13.7
Maritime Life Gbl Equities									2.30	100		Sep96	-	-	-	-	-	-	-	-	-	-	7.7
Mawer World Investment	★★	↑↑↑	7.0	18.5	-4.1	13.6	17.9	9.6	1.33	98	90	Sep96	2.5	21.2	20.9	27.7	28.6	0.7	0.4	1.3	-	-	33.3
Maxxum Global Equity	★	↑↑↑↑↑	3.6	19.5	-13.5				2.54	97		Sep96	3.5	6.7	12.5	15.1	49.1	-	1.5	8.7	3.1	-	12.6
McLean Budden Pld Off Eqty							12.5	17.1	7.0		97	97	Sep96	9.0	34.3	20.5	14.9	24.9	-	-	-	-	-	151.1
MD Growth Investments	★★★	↑↑↑↑	9.5	23.6	-5.5	17.0	21.0	11.9	1.15	91	96	Sep96	-	31.4	2.2	10.1	40.6	0.1	1.7	3.7	1.2	-	2,205.1
Middlefield Glo Technology									2.50	100		Sep96	-	10-	-	-	-	-	-	-	-	-	0.3
Millennia III Int'l Eqty 1									2.90	90		Sep96	9.6	27.0	26.6	11.9	24.9	-	-	-	-	-	27.0
Millennia III Int'l Eqty 2									3.08	90		Sep96	9.6	27.0	26.6	11.9	24.9	-	-	-	-	-	2.0
Mutual Premier Int'l	★★	↑↑	6.7	15.2	-6.2				2.38	90		Sep96											44.1
NAL-Global Equity	★★	↑↑	7.4	19.8	-2.5				2.50	92	98	Sep96	8.3	2.3	21.2	12.1	56.2	-	-	-	-	-	55.1

Fund	PAL/SGK Rank	Volatility	Avg Ann Ret	Hi Ann Ret	Lo Ann Ret	Avg 3 Yr Ret	Hi 3 Yr Ret	Lo 3 Yr Ret	MER	% Foreign	% 3 Yr Tx Ef	Portfolio Date	% Canada	% U.S.	% Japan	% Pac Rim	% Europe	% Asia	% Mexico	% Latin Amer	% Africa	% Mid East	Fund Size $mil
												Portfolio Analysis: Geographic Allocation											
National Global Equities	★★	→→	**7.8**	22.8	-6.6	14.2	17.9	8.8	2.40	100		Sep96	0.4	-	-	-	99.6	-	-	-	-	-	33.9
National Trust Int'l Equity									2.79	86		Sep96	13.6	0.7	34.9	12.5	38.3	-	-	-	-	-	17.6
O.I.Q. Ferique Internation									1.19	8		Aug96	91.8	-	5.1	0.6	2.5	-	-	-	-	-	18.6
OHA Foreign Equity	★★★★★	→	**12.3**	21.8	0.6				1.70	60	71	Sep96	39.8	60.2	-	-	-	-	-	-	-	-	1.3
Optima Strat Int'l Equity									0.48	89													48.2
Optimum International									1.97	172		Sep96	-71.8	89.7	19.5	4.3	58.4	-	-	-	-	-	3.1
Orbit World	★	→→	**-1.7**	16.5	-11.6	7.4	14.2	0.2	2.50	53	11												4.6
OTGIF Global	★★★	→→	**8.4**	21.4	-3.7	10.2	12.2	7.8	1.00		73												7.3
PH & N Int'l Equity									1.49	97		Sep96	3.1	0.8	26.3	19.9	5-	-	-	-	-	-	272.9
Pret et Revenu Int'l									2.06	76		Aug96	24.0	29.7	7.0	6.2	31.4	0.1	0.4	0.6	0.1	0.4	12.1
Pursuit Global Equity									1.75	91		Sep96	8.6	3.8	4.4	17.0	62.3	0.8	1.7	-	1.3	-	5.3
Royal International Equity	★★★	→	**6.8**	16.5	-3.7				2.50	85	95												83.0
Royal Life Int'l Equity									2.60	99		Sep96	1.2	29.6	6.3	3.1	59.8	-	-	-	-	-	8.9
Royal Life Science & Tech									2.53	95													73.4
Saxon World Growth	★★★★★	→→	**17.1**	33.2	4.6	22.9	29.4	15.2	1.87	85	73	Sep96	15.3	68.0	-	-	16.7	-	-	-	-	-	34.7
Sceptre International	★	→→→	**5.1**	22.4	-9.3	18.2	28.1	10.6	2.10	98	89	Sep96	1.6	23.8	15.0	28.2	24.9	1.5	0.3	3.3	0.6	0.8	141.9
Scotia Ex International	★★	→→	**5.2**	16.7	-9.3	12.3	16.9	6.0	2.24	96	87	Sep96	4.1	32.9	27.8	8.2	24.9	-	-	2.1	-	-	132.4
Scudder Global									1.75	99		Jun96	0.7	25.8	12.4	8.4	47.6	-	-	2.8	2.3	-	8.2
Spectrum United Gbl Telecom									2.55	83		Sep96	17.1	33.0	13.6	13.2	14.2	-	0.2	8.4	-	0.4	92.2
Spectrum United Global Eqty	★	→→→→	**5.3**	21.3	-10.8	9.2	12.1	5.6	2.30	82	85	Sep96	17.5	28.4	6.6	12.4	31.6	-	1.6	1.8	-	-	16.2
Spectrum United Global Gth	★	→→	**-0.1**	12.8	-11.4	11.7	19.8	-0.1	2.30	98		Sep96	2.1	23.8	36.5	10.5	20.6	0.6	3.6	2.3	-	-	19.5
Standard Life Int'l Equity									2.00	93													6.0
Talvest Global RRSP	★	→→→	**3.3**	14.8	-10.6				2.50	6	44	Sep96	94.4	-	-	5.6	-	-	-	-	-	-	15.0
Templeton Global Small Co	★★★	→→→	**11.6**	25.5	-6.2	16.4	21.0	11.9	2.55	70	84	Jun96	30.1	19.9	0.6	11.1	33.0	1.0	1.4	2.7	-	-	249.5
Templeton Growth	★★★★	→	**9.8**	19.3	-2.2	17.1	21.6	11.4	2.01	82	86	Sep96	18.3	31.1	1.9	8.6	33.2	0.2	2.1	4.0	0.5	-	5,550.0
Templeton Int'l Stock	★★★	→→	**1-**	2-	-4.8	2-	25.9	13.3	2.51	87	98	Sep96	12.9	1.8	3.2	14.9	62.5	0.4	2.1	2.1	-	-	1,822.3
Trimark Americas	★	→→→→→→	**6.2**	26.1	-11.5				2.52	87	97	Sep96	13.2	52.5	-	-	1.1	-	10.9	22.3	-	-	325.8
Trimark Discovery									2.50	33		Sep96	66.8	33.2	-	-	-	-	-	-	-	-	134.2
Trimark Fund	★★★★★	→	**15.7**	24.4	5.3	22.1	27.9	15.9	1.52	87	87	Sep96	12.9	66.5	7.1	1.6	11.9	-	-	-	-	-	2,182.7
Trimark Select Growth	★★★★★	→	**14.0**	22.0	3.8	19.7	25.5	14.1	2.25	88	92	Sep96	12.0	65.8	6.9	1.9	13.3	-	0.1	-	-	-	4,069.9
Universal Americas	★	→→→→→→	**2.7**	22.0	-19.1	10.3	20.3	5.3	2.53	86	47	Sep96	13.6	58.7	-	-	4.2	-	2.8	20.2	0.5	-	63.1
Universal Growth									2.39	70		Sep96	30.3	63.8	3.6	-	2.4	-	-	-	-	-	224.0
Universal World Equity	★★	→→	**6.4**	17.2	-5.7	14.9	19.4	8.0	2.45	98	100	Sep96	2.4	2.0	33.3	8.6	48.0	0.8	0.6	0.9	-	-	292.8
Universal World Gth RRSP									2.44	15		Sep96	84.8	0.7	-	9.0	0.9	0.5	0.1	3.4	0.6	-	190.3
Median Int'l and Global Equity Funds			6.7	19.8	-5.7	12.6	17.1	8.0	2.44	86.6	88		13.6	26.9	6.9	7.6	25.9	-	-	0.9	-	-	44.1
Average Int'l and Global Equity Funds			7.3	21.8	-6.3	13.1	17.7	7.7	2.17	77.9	85		22.7	29.3	10.7	7.7	25.7	0.4	0.8	2.1	0.2	0.3	44.7

Fund	Avg Ann Ret	Hi Ann Ret	Lo Ann Ret	Avg 3 Yr Ret	Hi 3 Yr Ret	Lo 3 Yr Ret	MER	% Fgn	% 3 Yr Tx Ef	Portfolio Date	% Canada	% United States	% Japan	% Pac Rim	% Europe	% Asia	% Mexico	% Latin Amer	% Africa	% Mid East	Fund Size $ mil
Emerging Markets Funds (26)																					
20/20 Emerging Markets Value							3.50	90		Sep96	10.2	3.2	-	33.2	16.7	6.5	4.4	24.7	1.1	-	14.4
AIC Emerging Markets							2.75	93		Sep96	6.9	5.1	-	62.6	11.9		5.3	8.1	-	-	2.8
Altamira Global Discovery							3.13	98		Sep96	1.7	6.0	-	20.7	19.0	4.1	7.4	31.4	8.6	0.7	24.8
BPI Emerging Markets							2.97	93		Jun96	6.6	12.6	-	31.6	13.7	2.7	7.4	15.8	8.6	0.9	4.4
C.I. Emerging Markets	-6.0	35.7	-28.8				2.96	99	51	Aug96	1.1	10.8	-	29.6	3.6	4.7	9.4	25.8	12.2	2.7	376.5
C.I. Emerging Markets Sector	-6.2	35.5	-28.9				2.98		100												65.3
CDA Emerging Markets*							1.45			n/a*											0.5
CIBC Emerging Economies							2.70	91		Sep96	8.5	4.3	-	39.5	9.3	4.9	11.1	18.0	4.4	-	12.7
CT Everest Emerging Market							3.34	94		Sep96	6.3	6.6	-	43.0	7.2	4.1	6.6	19.3	6.2	0.2	33.3
Elliott & Page Emerging Market							1.76	100		Sep96	0.0	4.2	-	29.4	22.4	10.8	7.7	20.2	4.7	0.1	20.7
First Canadian Emerging Market							2.13	95		Sep96	4.9	2.2	-	31.8	13.5	5.2	10.6	21.0	9.3	1.5	22.2
Green Line Emerging Markets	-2.4	37.9	-24.2	10.1	27.0	1.0	2.75	98	91	Sep96	1.6	9.4	0.2	34.5	7.7	11.5	10.0	16.0	4.1	4.9	154.0
Guardian Emerging Market A							2.01	89		Sep96	10.8	8.8	-	28.7	14.5	7.2	4.8	21.0	2.1	2.1	1.7
Guardian Emerging Markets B							2.97	89		Sep96	10.8	8.8	-	28.7	14.5	7.2	4.8	21.0	2.1	2.1	4.5
Hansberger Developing Markets								59		Aug96	41.0	-	2.5	31.9	4.9	12.5	-	2.7			5.1
Hongkong Bank Emerging Market							2.89	92		Sep96	7.7	2.8	0.4	34.4	7.5	5.6	12.9	19.5	6.2	2.6	9.3
Laurentian Emerging Market							2.95	90		Sep96	9.8	3.7	-	37.9	14.0	8.3	5.7	14.2	6.4	-	4.1
MD Emerging Markets							2.47	94		Sep96	6.1	0.9	0.3	30.0	11.7	10.1	12.7	23.0	4.2	0.9	46.1
Merrill Lynch Emerging Markets							3.25	86		Aug96	14.4	4.1	-	25.5	8.4	8.0	12.6	19.9	4.4	2.6	57.0
Mutual Premier Emerging Market							3.73	93		Sep96	6.8	3.8	-	40.2	5.2	3.8	10.1	18.1	10.0	1.9	21.0
National Trust Emerging Markets							3.08	100		Sep96	-0.1	4.6	-	55.0	2.2	7.7	3.3	22.3	5.0	-	11.2
Scudder Emerging Markets							2.00	95		Jun96	4.6	6.0	-	30.7	17.2	-	1.5	27.9	9.0	1.7	2.8
Spectrum United Emerging Markets							2.58	96		Sep96	3.6	8.6	-	29.3	18.8	3.9	5.9	21.8	3.5	1.6	17.2
Templeton Emerging Markets	1.9	21.9	-16.1	16.2	22.9	6.7	3.30	89	89	Sep96	11.0	1.0	0.1	25.0	27.3	4.0	7.9	20.2	2.1	1.1	943.9
Tradex Emerging Markets Country							3.58	101		Sep96	-1.3	38.2	-	25.2	33.5	2.5		1.9			2.6
Universal World Emerging Growth							2.56	93		Sep96	6.5	5.1	7.0	22.1	30.5	6.4	4.6	11.1	3.9	1.5	129.9
*Fund of funds																					
Median Emerging Markets Funds	-4.2	35.6	-26.5	13.2	25.0	3.8	2.95	93.5	90		6.5	4.8	-	31.2	13.6	5.4	7.0	20.0	4.4	1.0	15.8
Average Emerging Markets Funds	-3.2	32.8	-24.5	13.2	25.0	3.8	2.79	92.5	83		7.5	6.7	0.4	33.4	14.0	5.9	7.0	18.5	4.9	1.2	15.8

Portfolio Analysis: Geographic Allocation

Fund	PAL/SGK Rank	Volatility	Avg Ann Ret	Hi Ann Ret	Lo Ann Ret	Avg 3 Yr Ret	Hi 3 Yr Ret	Lo 3 Yr Ret	MER	% 3 Yr Tx Ef	Port-folio Date	% Can-ada	% United States	% Asia	% Japan	% Pac Rim	% Europe	Fund Size $ mil
Asia and Pacific Rim Funds (48)																		
20/20 Asia Pacific	**	↑	-2.6	19.6	-17.8				2.67	100.0	Sep96	-1.0	-	1.0	0.0	92.9	7.0	97.1
20/20 India		↑							3.49		Sep96	-0.3	3.5	95.5	-	-	1.2	18.9
ADMAX Dragon 888									2.94		Sep96	12.4	-	-	-	81.9	5.7	3.0
ADMAX Korea	***	↑↑↑↑↑	-1.4	41.4	-29.2	10.5	18.4	-2.0	3.20		Sep96	12.6	2.5	-	-	84.8		39.9
ADMAX Tiger	*	↑↑↑	-7.6	27.7	-19.0	12.4	26.7	-2.3	3.20		Sep96	0.7	4.6	4.4	1.0	83.0	3.5	57.1
AGF International Group Asian Growth A	*****	↑↑	7.8	37.4	-10.8				2.41	100.0	Sep96	4.3	0.6	0.4	-	89.6	5.2	106.9
AGF International Group Asian Growth B									2.87		Sep96	4.3	0.6	0.4	-	89.6	5.2	485.3
AGF International Group Asian Growth C									2.83		Sep96	4.3	0.6	0.4	-	89.6	5.2	13.6
AGF International Group China Focus A									2.99		Sep96	18.8	1.0	7.2	13.4	53.8	5.9	1.9
AGF International Group China Focus B									3.50		Sep96	18.8	1.0	7.2	13.4	53.8	5.9	13.5
AGF International Group China Focus C									3.48		Sep96	18.8	1.0	7.2	13.4	53.8	5.9	1.4
Altamira Asia Pacific	*	↑↑↑	-6.4	26.6	-17.4				2.38		Sep96	25.9	5.7	2.9	-0.2	61.1	1.1	250.2
Apex Asian Pacific									2.00		Aug96	3.4	5.3	1.1	16.9	69.6	3.7	20.9
Atlas Pacific Basin Value									2.90		Sep96	1.6	-	3.1	58.9	36.5		14.8
C.I. Pacific	***	↑	-0.2	25.8	-17.9	17.5	28.9	6.4	2.60	100.0	Sep96	1.4	0.7	4.1	4.9	87.8	0.8	971.1
C.I. Pacific Sector	***	↑	-0.5	25.6	-17.8	17.1	28.5	6.1	2.62	100.0	Sep96							179.7
Cambridge China									3.00		Jun96	74.5	4.8	3.7	-	-	17.1	2.8
Cambridge Pacific	*	↑	-8.2	10.7	-25.6	6.4	15.8	-1.8	3.00		Jun96	34.1	0.2	6.8	1.3	46.7	11.0	5.9
CDA Pacific Basin									1.45		Sep96	100.0	-	-	-	-	-	1.7
CIBC Far East Prosperity	****	↑↑↑	2.1	26.4	-18.9				2.85	100.0	Sep96	7.2	0.4	0.6	16.4	71.3	3.9	259.2
CT Everest Asiagrowth									2.32		Sep96	48.9	-	-	21.3	29.8		207.3
Dynamic Far East									3.50		Sep96	35.9	3.1	2.5	9.0	38.5	5.4	4.1
Elliott & Page Asian Growth									1.49		Sep96	1.5	1.2	1.5	38.6	55.2	1.9	27.6
Ethical Pacific Rim									2.60		Sep96	7.8	-	-	-	86.5	5.7	12.1
Fidelity Far East	******	↑↑↑↑↑	9.5	42.5	-21.5	22.0	33.8	13.7	2.82	99.5	Sep96	1.6	0.1	1.6	-	93.8	2.9	1,626.0
First Canadian FarEast Growth	****	↑↑↑↑	1.9	27.8	-24.3				2.14		Jun96	1.8	0.2	0.4	-	94.5	3.1	51.9
Global Strategy Asia									2.95	98.8	Jun96	97.1	-	-	-	2.9		28.2
Global Strategy Diversified Asia									2.70		Jun96	5.0	2.7	-	-	87.2	5.1	64.9
Green Line Asian Growth									2.82		Sep96	0.8	0.0	3.8	-	91.2	4.1	13.6
GT Global Pacific Growth									2.95		Sep96	1.5	1.4	7.2	34.4	52.3	1.8	5.1
Guardian Asia Pacific A									1.86		Sep96	1.5	1.4	7.2	34.4	52.3	1.8	2.7
Guardian Asia Pacific B									2.99		Sep96							
Hansberger Asian	*	↑	-4.3	17.8	-21.7				2.98	100.0	Aug96	18.7	0.2	9.9	1.2	67.7	0.7	105.6
Hongkong Bank Asian Growth									2.34		Sep96	18.8	-	1.0	-	77.1	3.1	51.2
Hyperion Asian	***	↑↑↑↑	0.9	28.8	-21.0	20.4	37.3	8.0	3.26	98.5	Sep96	4.9	1.6	0.3	15.1	74.1	3.9	186.8
InvesNat Far East Equity									2.49		Sep96	1.4	3.7	-	-	92.7	2.3	22.2

Fund	PAL/SGK Rank	Volatility	Avg Ann Ret	Hi Ann Ret	Lo Ann Ret	Avg 3 Yr Ret	Hi 3 Yr Ret	Lo 3 Yr Ret	MER	% 3 Yr Tx Ef	Port-folio Date	Portfolio Analysis: Geographic Allocation						Fund Size $ mil
												% Can-ada	% United States	% Asia	% Japan	% Pac Rim	% Europe	
Investors Pacific International	★★★★★	↑	4.3	31.7	-12.9	21.5	32.9	9.8	2.58	99.8	Sep96	0.2	1.4	2.3		86.6	7.1	1,229.5
Laurentian Asia Pacific									2.70		Sep96	8.4	2.5	0.9	32.0	53.3	2.8	12.4
Maritime Life Pacific Basin									2.30		Sep96	-	11.3	-	39.0	47.4	2.3	14.9
Navigator Asia Pacific									2.99		Sep96	18.6	1.3	5.8	-	74.2	-	2.4
NN Can-Asian	★★★★	↑↑↑↑↑	5.5	31.9	-22.9				2.25	75.0	Sep96	92.6	5.1	-	0.1	2.3	-	118.0
Royal Asian Growth	★★★★	↑↑↑	1.9	24.5	-19.3				2.64	96.2	Sep96							163.4
Sceptre Asian Growth	★★★	↑↑↑↑↑	-0.3	37.7	-19.9				2.40	79.7	Sep96	4.1	8.3	4.3	7.7	68.2	4.2	24.2
Scotia Excelsior Pacific Rim									2.18		Sep96	17.4	20.9	-	35.3	24.2	2.2	27.9
Scudder Pacific									1.75		Jun96	9.2	7.6	3.8	28.4	49.4	1.7	1.3
Spectrum United Asian Dynasty									2.58		Sep96	1.1	0.8	1.1	20.2	75.1	1.6	13.2
Trimark Indo-Pacific									2.74		Sep96	4.9	0.9	5.3	10.8	72.9	5.2	217.6
Universal Far East									2.60		Sep96	1.7	0.5	1.6	0.6	90.3	5.4	106.1
Median Asia and Pacific Rim Funds			-0.2	27.7	-19.3	17.3	28.7	6.2	2.7	99.8		5.2	1.0	1.1	0.3	70.4	3.3	25.9
Average Asia and Pacific Rim Funds			0.1	28.5	-19.9	16.0	27.8	4.7	2.7	96.0		17.9	2.3	4.3	9.7	61.5	3.8	143.8

Fund	Avg Ann Ret	Hi Ann Ret	Lo Ann Ret	Avg 3 Yr Ret	Hi 3 Yr Ret	Lo 3 Yr Ret	MER	Port-folio Date	Geographic Allocation			Fund Size $ mil
									% Canada	% Japan	% United States	
Japanese Equity Funds (16)												
ADMAX Nippon	2.1	40.3	-29.1				3.08	Sep96	11.2	88.8	-	30.6
AGF International Group Japan A	-4.3	17.0	-22.3	5.9	12.6	-4.1	2.55	Sep96	1.6	97.0	-	55.2
AGF International Group Japan B							3.05	Sep96	1.6	97.0	-	101.8
AGF International Group Japan C							3.06	Sep96	1.6	97.0	-	7.6
Altamira Japanese Opportunity							2.38	Sep96	48.6	49.4	1.2	30.1
CIBC Japanese Equity							2.60	Sep96	5.0	95.0	-	28.4
Fidelity Japanese Growth	-3.7	22.7	-24.4				2.99					264.4
First Canadian Japan Growth							2.05	Sep96	3.0	97.0	-	18.2
Global Strategy Diversified Japan							2.62	Jun96	79.6	2.7	17.6	20.3
Global Strategy Japan							2.95	Jul96	9.7	89.3	1.0	35.8
Green Line Japanese Growth							2.66	Sep96	1.4	98.6	-	34.0
InvesNat Japanese Equity							2.43	Sep96	0.5	99.5	-	22.7
Investors Japanese Growth	-1.8	21.2	-16.1	12.0	20.7	-2.1	2.47	Sep96	5.7	91.6	-	684.6
McDonald New Japan							2.47	Sep96	3.7	88.2	8.1	0.8
Royal Japanese Stock	-4.9	21.1	-25.0	8.0	16.8	-4.9	2.64	Sep96				72.0
Universal Japan							2.54	Sep96	2.9	94.1	-	34.6
Median Japanese Equity Funds	-3.7	21.2	-24.4	8.0	16.8	-4.1	2.6		3.3	93.1	-	32.3
Average Japanese Equity Funds	-2.5	24.5	-23.4	8.6	16.7	-3.7	2.7		11.6	85.4	1.9	90.1

Fund	Avg Ann Ret	Hi Ann Ret	Lo Ann Ret	Avg 3 Yr Ret	Hi 3 Yr Ret	Lo 3 Yr Ret	MER	% 3 Yr Tax Efficiency	Port-folio Date	% Canada	% United States	% Europe	Fund Size $ mil
European Equity Funds (32)													
ADMAX Europa Performance	4.0	10.2	-4.98				3.48	87.5	Sep96	15.4	4.1	80.5	1.7
AGF International Group Germany A							2.36		Sep96	4.2	-	95.8	1.3
AGF International Group Germany B							2.83		Sep96	4.2	-	95.8	9.4
AGF International Group Germany C							2.83		Sep96	4.2	-	95.8	1.1
AGF International Group Germany M							1.36		Sep96	4.2	-	95.8	36.1
AGF International Group European Growth A							2.79		Sep96	14.2	1.6	84.2	8.1
AGF International Group European Growth B							3.33		Sep96	14.2	1.6	84.2	61.5
AGF International Group European Growth C							3.31		Sep96	14.2	1.6	84.2	10.3
Altamira European Equity	11.0	19.4	0.98				2.41	91.0	Sep96	4.2	0.8	93.8	140.6
Atlas European Value							2.85		Sep96	0.9	1.0	96.1	13.6
CDA European							1.45		Sep96	100.0	-	-	1.6
CIBC European Equity							2.50		Sep96	9.9	1.8	85.7	12.3
CT Everest Eurogrowth							2.18		Sep96	0.4	-	99.6	82.8
Dynamic Europe	8.4	19.8	-4.42	11.9	16.0	8.4	2.70	100.0	Sep96	9.7	4.7	72.7	59.9
Fidelity European Growth	12.8	19.8	2.28				2.81	99.1	Sep96	5.7	-	93.1	8.4
First Canadian Europe Growth							2.19		Jun96	95.0	-	4.9	65.4
Global Strategy Diversified European	6.7	18.0	-8.06	5.9	9.3	2.9	2.68	78.9	Jun96	3.8	0.3	93.7	76.2
Global Strategy Euro Plus							2.95		Jun96	3.6	-	96.4	38.3
Green Line European Growth							2.66		Sep96	2.8	-	89.9	51.3
Hansberger European	2.6	11.4	-9.34				2.60	100.0	Aug96	12.5	-	83.0	22.0
Hansberger European Sector	2.4	10.9	-8.95				2.62	100.0	Sep96	1.3	-	93.6	18.5
Hongkong Bank European Growth	8.2	13.9	-0.78	11.8	14.7	9.3	2.42	89.3	Sep96	4.4	4.5	95.6	26.4
Hyperion European	8.7	15.4	-0.04				3.03	85.8	Aug96	0.7	5.0	93.6	13.5
InvesNat European Equity							2.25		Sep96	4.5	-	95.5	874.8
Investors European Growth	10.8	17.4	0.43	12.2	15.7	8.1	2.46	97.2	Sep96	0.7	0.2	93.6	11.9
Laurentian Europe							2.70		Sep96	4.5	-	95.5	31.9
NN Can-Euro							2.25			97.7	-	2.3	155.1
Royal European Growth	9.7	16.2	2.35	15.3	18.6	10.5	2.68	100.0	Jun96	5.1	0.9	93.1	1.7
Scudder Greater Europe							1.75		Sep96	13.2	0.5	84.7	23.9
Spectrum United European Gth							2.56		Sep96	7.1	5.9	84.9	159.7
Universal Euro Opportunity							2.48			0.9	0.5	98.6	24.5
Vision Europe	11.7	21.3	0.65				3.24	85.1	Jul96				
Median European Equity Funds	8.6	16.8	-0.41	11.9	15.7	8.4	2.6	94.1		4.4	0.5	93.1	24.2
Average European Equity Funds	8.1	16.1	-2.49	11.4	14.9	7.9	2.6	92.8		14.7	1.3	82.5	90.2

Portfolio Analysis: Geographic Allocation

Fund	Avg Ann Ret	Hi Ann Ret	Lo Ann Ret	MER	% 3 Yr Tax Efficiency	Port-folio Date	% Canada	% United States	% Mexico	% South & Central America	Fund Size $ mil
Latin American Equity Funds (12)											
20/20 Latin America				3.22		Sep96	0.34	1.1	10.8	87.7	196.1
Atlas Latin American Value				2.94		Sep96	-0.90	10.7	35.8	54.5	18.7
C.I. Latin American			-6.04	32.90	-37.07	3.01	100.0	Aug96	1.83	6.7	26.3	62.3	345.9
Fidelity Latin Amer Growth				3.38							149.5
Global Strategy Diversified Latin				2.70		Jun96	82.69	1.9	1.6	11.4	19.4
Global Strategy Latin American				2.95		Jul96	10.66	3.8	14.1	63.9	9.4
Green Line Latin American Growth				2.72		Sep96	1.48	11.6	29.8	55.4	26.1
GT Global Latin American Growth				2.95		Sep96	8.65	12.8	28.3	48.7	11.0
Investors Latin American Growth				2.75		Sep96	0.90	10.1	28.4	57.0	10.2
Navigator Latin America				2.88		Sep96	12.02	4.0	16.4	67.6	1.6
Royal Latin American				3.86							15.6
Scotia Excelsior Latin American				2.17		Sep96	12.50	6.0	29.1	52.5	16.9
Median Latin American Equity Funds	-6.04	32.90	-37.07	2.9	100.0		7.18	6.5	26.4	56.2	17.8
Average Latin American Equity Funds	-6.04	32.90	-37.07	3.0	100.0	Sep96	12.31	12.1	21.1	52.7	68.4

Portfolio Analysis: Canadian Bonds

Fund	PAL/SGK Rank	Volatility	Avg Ann Ret	Hi Ann Ret	Lo Ann Ret	Avg 3 Yr Ret	Hi 3 Yr Ret	Lo 3 Yr Ret	MER	% 3 Yr Tx Ef	Port-folio Date	% Cdn Bonds	Avg Matur (Years)	% Short Bonds	% Med Bonds	% Long Bonds	% Cdn Curr	% US Curr	% Other Curr	Fund Size $ mil
Canadian Bond Funds (115)																				
20/20 Income	★	↑↑↑	6.6	17.5	-10.4	6.5	8.4	4.5	1.98	42	Sep96	80.4	3.7	67.7	32.3	-	100.0	-	-	65.0
Acadia Bond									1.97		Sep96	22.1	0.3	100.0	-	-	100.0	-	-	1.4
AGF Canadian Bond A	★★	↑↑↑↑↑	8.3	21.8	-11.3	7.9	10.1	5.7	1.40	48	Sep96	97.2	11.1	22.5	50.0	27.5	100.0	-	-	174.4
AGF Canadian Bond B									1.90		Sep96	97.2	11.1	22.5	50.0	27.5	100.0	-	-	610.3
AGF Canadian Bond C									1.90		Sep96	97.2	11.1	22.5	50.0	27.5	100.0	-	-	8.2
Altamira Bond	★★	↑↑↑↑↑↑	10.6	28.5	-10.3	9.6	12.8	6.8	1.31	63	Sep96	70.5	11.8	15.4		84.6	100.0	-	-	113.2
Altamira Income	★★	↑↑↑↑↑↑	9.4	23.0	-9.1	9.5	12.3	6.0	1.00	50	Sep96	75.1	13.2	10.2	24.2	65.6	43.1	56.9	-	605.0
AMI Private Capital Income	★★★	↑↑	7.9	17.9	-7.4	7.5	9.3	5.7	1.25	44	Sep96	80.9	7.9	48.1	26.3	25.7	100.0	-	-	2.0
Apex Fixed Income									1.75		Sep96	91.4	10.4	27.4	38.7	33.8	100.0	-	-	22.2
Atlas Canadian Bond	★★★	↑↑	7.9	19.9	-6.9	7.2	9.0	5.4	1.98	57	Sep96	81.5	7.4	14.0	77.6	8.4	100.0	-	-	15.1
Atlas Canadian High Yield Bond									1.90		Sep96	81.5	5.5	42.2	40.4	17.4	88.7	11.3	-	60.3
Batirente Sec Obligations	★★★★	↑↑↑↑	10.6	23.8	-6.2	9.3	11.8	7.3	1.50	100	Sep96	87.3	10.6	5.9	43.1	51.0	100.0	-	-	25.9
Beutel Goodman Income	★★	↑↑↑↑↑	8.7	22.1	-10.0	7.6	9.8	5.5	1.32	45	Jun96	97.1	8.7	26.9	37.5	35.6	100.0	-	-	44.6

Fund	PAL/SGK Rank	Volatility	Avg Ann Ret	Hi Ann Ret	Lo Ann Ret	Avg 3 Yr Ret	Hi 3 Yr Ret	Lo 3 Yr Ret	MER	% 3 Yr Tx Ef	Port-folio Date	% Cdn Bonds	Avg Matur (Years)	% Short Bonds	% Med Bonds	% Long Bonds	% Cdn Curr	% US Curr	% Other Curr	Fund Size $ mil
Bissett Bond	****	↑↑↑	9.7	22.1	-6.3	8.2	10.5	6.0	0.75	64	Sep96	88.7	7.2	14.5	72.3	13.2	100.0			19.0
BNP (Canada) Bond	***	↑↑↑	8.0	20.5	-8.7	7.1	9.3	5.3	1.67	51	Sep96	93.7	8.4	39.7	33.0	27.3	100.0			5.0
BPI Canadian Bond	**	↑	3.9	15.6	-9.4	5.1	7.5	2.2	1.50		Jun96	88.9	24.0	17.1	2.7	80.2	100.0			36.4
C.I. Canadian Bond	****	↑↑↑	9.1	20.2	-4.9				1.65	62	Sep96	68.2	4.6	38.1	-	61.9	100.0			28.3
Canada Life Fixed Income	**	↑↑↑	7.5	19.2	-9.3	6.7	8.7	5.1	2.00		Jul96	97.0	8.6	48.1	27.0	24.9	100.0			127.3
CCPE Fixed Income	****	↑↑↑	8.8	19.2	-5.6	8.3	10.1	6.7	1.35	43										18.8
CIBC Canadian Bond	*	↑↑↑↑↑	7.7	21.1	-11.6	6.2	8.6	4.2	1.50		Sep96	96.3	9.5	29.6	43.3	27.1	100.0			331.3
Clean Environment Income									1.99											2.8
Co-Operators Fixed Income	***	↑↑↑↑↑	9.4	22.3	-8.2				2.07		Aug96	83.7	8.8	28.5	38.1	33.4	100.0			9.8
Colonia Life Bond	****	↑↑↑	8.5	20.1	-5.9				1.60		Sep96	67.3	3.0	84.9	-	15.1	100.0			10.2
Concorde Revenu	***	↑↑↑	7.3	18.3	-8.1				2.09	52	Sep96	82.0	8.7	35.6	36.2	28.2	100.0			8.0
Confed Fixed Income	***	↑↑↑	7.6	18.6	-7.2	6.8	8.6	5.1	2.00											25.0
Confed Life C	****	↑↑↑	8.0	19.1	-7.1	7.2	9.0	5.5	1.44	51	Mar96	99.5	8.9	33.8	42.6	23.6	100.0			25.0
Cornerstone Bond	****	↑↑↑↑	8.7	20.0	-7.0	7.5	9.7	5.6	1.25		Sep96	77.8	5.9	30.7	41.0	28.2	100.0			38.0
CT Everest Bond	**	↑↑	8.1	20.6	-8.7	6.9	9.0	4.9	1.34		Sep96	103.8	5.0	47.4	50.0	2.6	100.0			551.5
Desjardins Bond	****	↑↑↑↑	9.8	22.1	-6.8	8.5	10.8	6.5	1.66	56										59.2
Desjardins Obligations	***	↑↑↑↑	8.2	20.2	-8.8	7.4	9.5	5.7	1.62	57	Sep96	81.5	7.8	33.1	34.6	32.3	100.0			56.1
Dynamic Income	*****	↑	9.0	14.5	4.6	9.4	11.4	8.0	1.68	25	Sep96	35.6	0.9	93.7	6.3	-	33.1	45.3	21.6	353.3
Elliott & Page Bond	*	↑↑↑	5.5	16.7	-9.4	4.9	6.6	3.1	1.69		Sep96	86.1	10.1	52.8	12.6	34.5	100.0			31.7
Empire Bond	***	↑↑↑	7.5	18.1	-6.8	6.5	8.5	4.7	2.18		Sep96	88.5	6.4	28.3	50.0	21.7	100.0			59.4
Empire Group Bond	*****	↑↑↑	10.3	20.8	-3.7	9.6	11.9	7.6	1.28		Sep96	87.4	6.9	29.6	33.7	36.7	100.0			26.0
Equitable Life Accum	****	↑↑↑↑↑	9.3	21.1	-6.6	8.1	9.9	6.0	1.56	58										17.0
Ethical Income	***	↑↑↑↑↑	9.1	22.6	-9.1	7.4	10.3	4.7	1.66	53	Sep96	94.5	8.7	24.1	47.4	28.5	98.5	1.5		74.9
Ficadre Obligations	***	↑↑↑↑	8.1	19.8	-8.0	6.4	8.3	4.8	1.67	42	Jun96	83.9	7.6	36.4	37.6	26.0	100.0			11.2
Fidelity Canadian Bond	*	↑↑↑↑	5.4	18.0	-12.5	6.7	8.6	4.5	1.55	60	Jun96	95.6	7.9	37.1	40.9	21.9	100.0			64.7
First Canadian Bond	***	↑↑↑↑	8.7	22.1	-8.7	7.4	9.7	5.3	1.51	61	Sep96	83.1	6.1	5.8	76.1	18.0	100.0			413.6
Fonds Professionnels Bond	*****	↑	8.4	16.4	-3.6	7.2	8.2	6.1	0.75	49	Aug96	40.3	2.2	7.0	81.9	11.2	100.0			73.3
GBC Canadian Bond	****	↑↑↑↑	9.2	21.3	-7.6	8.2	10.4	6.3	1.18		Sep96	97.7	7.0	21.2	78.8	-	100.0			32.2
General Trust Bond	**	↑↑↑↑	7.3	19.4	-9.0	6.9	8.5	5.3	1.59		Sep96	95.0	8.1	36.5	32.0	31.6	100.0			47.7
Great-West Life Cdn Bond (G) A	**	↑↑↑	7.0	18.2	-8.8	6.3	8.1	4.4	2.16		Sep96	92.4	8.4	43.6	29.0	27.3	98.8	1.2		546.1
Great-West Life Gov't Bond (G) A									2.16		Sep96	98.6	3.7	74.7	25.3	-	100.0			16.4
Great-West Life Income (G) A									2.16		Sep96	76.8	5.0	45.4	54.6	-	100.0			20.8
Green Line Canadian Bond	****	↑↑↑↑	10.0	22.2	-8.0	8.3	10.2	6.1	1.00	62	Sep96	95.4	9.2	43.4	35.2	21.4	96.7	3.3		322.4
Green Line Cdn Gov't Bond	****	↑↑↑↑	9.1	20.9	-7.2	7.7	9.8	5.5	1.01	55	Sep96	95.0	8.5	45.8	27.2	27.1	100.0			130.4
Green Line Real Return Bond									1.74		Sep96	96.9	23.7	3.1	-	96.9	100.0			10.3
Hongkong Bank Canadian Bond									1.32		Sep96	91.6	8.9	28.0	42.0	29.9	100.0			22.8
HRL Bond	***	↑↑↑	8.1	19.3	-7.6	6.9	9.1	5.2	1.63	55	Sep96	93.5	11.2	26.8	45.8	27.5	86.1	13.9		5.2
Hyperion High Yield Bond	*	↑↑↑↑↑	8.2	23.4	-12.0	6.3	9.3	3.9	2.10	33	Sep96	98.4	17.8	-	44.5	55.5	100.0			8.6

Portfolio Analysis: Canadian Bonds

Portfolio Analysis: Canadian Bonds

Fund	PAL/SGK Rank	Volatility	Avg Ann Ret	Hi Ann Ret	Lo Ann Ret	Avg 3 Yr Ret	Hi 3 Yr Ret	Lo 3 Yr Ret	MER	% 3 Yr Tx Ef	Portfolio Date	% Cdn Bonds	Avg Matur (Years)	% Short Bonds	% Med Bonds	% Long Bonds	% Cdn Curr	% US Curr	% Other Curr	Fund Size $ mil
Ideal Bond	★★★	↑↑↑	7.9	19.9	-8.2	7.3	9.2	5.4	2.00			86.0	8.5	36.8	39.1	24.0	100.0			20.0
IG Sceptre Canadian Bond									1.98		Sep96	85.3	4.3	57.0	30.7	12.3	100.0			1.0
Industrial-Alliance Bonds	★★★	↑↑	8.2	19.1	-7.3	6.9	8.9	5.3	1.61		Sep96	85.3	4.3	57.0	30.7	12.3	100.0			21.1
Industrial-Alliance Ecoflex B	★★★	↑↑	7.6	18.4	-7.8				2.14		Sep96	85.9	12.0	-	-	100.0	100.0			27.2
Industrial Bond	★	↑↑↑↑↑	8.0	22.2	-11.6	6.8	9.6	4.5	1.98		Sep96	85.9	8.8	27.4	42.8	29.9	100.0			409.2
InvesNat Canadian Bond	★★★	↑	7.1	17.3	-5.6				1.47	56	Sep96	96.1	7.1	28.5	49.3	22.2	100.0			15.2
Investors Corporate Bond									1.89	52	Sep96	86.2	9.7	11.3	49.9	38.8	91.3	8.7		761.7
Investors Government Bond	★★★	↑↑↑	8.6	20.3	-7.5	7.3	9.4	5.4	1.91	58	Sep96	57.4	8.3	20.0	49.6	30.5	100.0			1,582.5
Investors Income Portfolio	★★★★	↑	7.8	17.3	-5.4	6.6	8.2	5.1	0.18	56	Sep96	92.9	7.8	27.6	38.0	34.5	95.6	4.4		917.1
Jones Heward Bond	★★	↑↑↑	7.3	19.1	-9.6	6.3	8.5	4.3	1.75	45	Sep96	77.8	7.9	35.6	31.3	33.1	100.0			3.6
Laurentian Income	★★★	↑↑	7.7	18.7	-7.1	6.8	9.0	5.0	2.14	53	Sep96	96.1	10.5	47.6	16.3	36.1	100.0			158.1
Leith Wheeler Fixed Income									0.80											3.4
London Life Bond	★★★	↑↑↑↑↑	8.3	20.7	-9.3	7.0	9.0	5.2	2.00		Sep96	88.2	10.6	32.6	39.7	27.7	95.4	4.6		540.3
Lotus Group Bond									0.98											1.4
Manulife Cabot Divers Bond	★	↑↑↑↑↑↑	6.0	19.1	-11.4	6.2	8.6	3.1	2.00		Sep96	55.3	6.2	45.2	31.0	23.8	75.6	24.4		4.4
Manulife VistaFund1 Bond	★	↑↑↑↑	5.3	18.2	-12.1	5.4	7.8	2.4	1.63		Sep96	73.7	22.1	10.6	24.7	64.7	43.5	56.5		18.4
Manulife VistaFund2 Bond	★★★	↑↑↑	7.4	18.3	-8.4	6.9	8.8	5.3	2.38		Sep96	73.7	22.1	10.6	24.7	64.7	43.5	56.5		131.7
Maritime Life Bond	★★★	↑↑↑	8.7	20.3	-7.8				1.99		Sep96	81.1	8.8	38.6	26.2	35.2	100.0			72.4
Mawer Canadian Bond									0.92	53	Sep96	84.0	6.6	52.1	28.0	19.9	99.3	0.7		25.7
Mawer Canadian High Yield Bond											Sep96	89.3	6.1	26.4	55.3	18.4	99.8	0.2		4.0
Maxxum Income	★★	↑↑↑↑↑	8.9	22.5	-9.4	7.6	10.9	5.0	1.51	52	Sep96	93.2	13.7	1.1	56.0	42.9	84.6	15.4		76.0
McDonald Enhanced Bond	★★★	↑↑↑↑	9.0	21.0	-8.3	7.9	10.2	6.0	2.74	50	Sep96	95.1	6.0	55.3	29.9	14.8	94.6	2.1	3.2	0.2
Mclean Budden Fixed Income	★★★★	↑↑↑↑↑	10.5	23.0	-7.0	9.3	11.5	7.3	1.00	70	Sep96	89.6	10.1	28.0	40.6	31.4	97.9	2.1		10.7
McLean Budden Pooled Fixed-Income	★★★★	↑↑↑	9.0	20.7	-7.8	8.4	10.3	6.6		96	Sep96	92.1	10.1	27.7	36.5	35.7	98.1	1.9		208.4
MD Bond	★★	↑↑	6.6	17.4	-8.3	5.6	7.4	4.1	1.03		Sep96	97.7	8.8	36.2	41.7	22.2	100.0			356.4
Metlife Mvp Bond									2.00											23.5
Millennia III Income 1									2.23											11.3
Millennia III Income 2									2.41											0.9
Mutual Bond	★★	↑↑	7.1	18.4	-8.7	6.6	8.7	5.0	1.85	47	Sep96	79.9	7.2	36.1	36.6	27.3	100.0			19.5
Mutual Life 2	★★★★★	↑	9.3	18.9	-4.0	8.5	10.8	6.5			Sep96	79.9	7.2	36.1	36.6	27.3	100.0			5.4
Mutual Premier Bond	★★★	↑↑	7.4	19.0	-8.7	7.6	9.7	5.6	1.90	55	Sep96	74.7	6.4	43.6	32.5	24.0	100.0			83.2
NAL-Canadian Bond	★★★★	↑↑	8.6	20.3	-6.4	7.5	9.7	5.6	1.75		Sep96	90.3	8.8	33.7	37.0	29.2	100.0			24.5
National Fixed Income	★★★	↑↑↑↑	8.1	19.6	-8.5	7.5	9.7	5.4	2.00		Sep96	84.6	7.8	15.8	51.3	32.9	100.0			44.2
National Trust Canadian Bond	★★★	↑↑↑↑↑	9.2	22.1	-7.9				1.34	55	Sep96	98.7	8.9	12.8	65.6	21.7	100.0			86.0
Navigator Canadian Income									2.45		Sep96	85.2	4.8	54.1	34.9	11.0	80.2	19.8		8.5
NN Bond	★★★★	↑↑↑↑	9.1	21.6	-6.4	7.6	10.3	5.5	2.00	47	Sep96	98.7	9.5	49.9	19.4	30.8	100.0			18.8
O.I.Q. Ferique Obligations	★★★★	↑↑↑	8.9	20.2	-6.4	8.2	10.0	6.6	0.59	53	Sep96	77.7	7.7	30.9	36.1	33.0	100.0			48.9
O'Donnell High Income									2.00		Sep96	82.9	5.3	42.3	36.9	20.9	78.4	21.6		47.4

Fund	PAL/SGK Rank	Volatility	Avg Ann Ret	Hi Ann Ret	Lo Ann Ret	Avg 3 Yr Ret	Hi 3 Yr Ret	Lo 3 Yr Ret	MER	% 3 Yr Tx Ef	Portfolio Date	% Cdn Bonds	Avg Matur (Years)	% Short Bonds	% Med Bonds	% Long Bonds	% Cdn Curr	% US Curr	% Other Curr	Fund Size $ mil
OHA Bond	★★★	↗↗↗	8.9	19.6	-7.7	7.6	9.2	5.4	0.90	45	Sep96	78.2	4.3	38.0	51.8	10.3	100.0	-	-	32.1
Optima Strategy Cdn Fixed Income	★★★	↗↗↗↗	9.3	22.9	-7.7				0.41	100										88.6
Optimum Obligations	★★★★	↗↗↗↗↗	10.1	22.7	-7.0	9.0	11.1	7.0	1.38	45	Sep96	83.0	9.9	5.4	49.3	45.3	100.0	-	-	2.9
PH & N Bond	★★★★★	↗↗↗	9.8	21.1	-6.1	9.0	11.2	7.2	0.60	53	Sep96	84.5	7.5	47.0	22.3	30.7	100.0	-	-	982.0
Pret Et Revenu Obligations	★★★	↗↗↗	8.3	19.7	-7.9	7.5	9.5	5.5	1.50	54	Sep96	84.3	8.6	34.8	37.5	27.7	100.0	-	-	47.2
Pursuit Canadian Bond	★	↗	4.2	13.5	-6.0	6.1	8.2	3.3	0.80	30	Sep96	98.0	12.4	-	76.3	23.7	100.0	-	-	15.6
Royal Life Income	★★	↗↗↗	7.6	19.4	-8.7	6.5	8.5	4.9	1.88	49	Sep96	95.9	8.1	20.0	64.8	15.2	100.0	-	-	28.7
Royal Trust Bond	★★★	↗↗↗	8.2	20.7	-8.8	7.4	9.9	5.2	1.39	56	Sep96	95.9	13.1	24.2	40.2	35.6	100.0	-	-	701.6
Royfund Bond	★★★	↗↗↗	8.3	20.0	-7.4	7.3	9.6	5.2	1.52	53	Sep96	96.4	13.0	26.8	38.5	34.7	100.0	-	-	705.2
Sceptre Bond	★★★★	↗↗↗	8.4	19.2	-6.2	7.5	9.3	5.8	1.25	44	Sep96	94.3	9.5	41.3	34.4	24.4	94.7	-	5.3	6.1
Scotia Excelsior Income	★★★★	↗↗↗	9.3	22.2	-6.8	7.7	10.0	5.7	1.37	59	Sep96	69.3	3.8	37.2	56.5	6.3	100.0	-	-	279.8
Spectrum United Long-Term Bond	★	↗↗↗↗↗	7.6	21.5	-12.7	6.9	9.7	4.6	1.76	49	Sep96	91.4	20.1	-	-	100.0	100.0	-	-	79.7
Spectrum United Mid-Term Bond	★★	↗↗↗↗↗	7.7	20.1	-10.6	6.8	9.0	4.8	1.59	38	Sep96	98.0	7.7	15.5	58.6	25.9	100.0	-	-	413.2
SSQ - Obligations	★★★★★	↗↗	10.3	21.8	-5.4	8.9	10.9	7.0	-	51	Sep96	90.3	6.9	26.8	60.3	12.9	100.0	-	-	43.6
Standard Life Bond	★★★	↗↗↗↗	8.7	21.0	-7.2				1.50											6.9
Talvest Bond	★★★	↗↗↗↗	8.3	19.9	-8.0	7.4	9.6	5.5	1.99	54	Sep96	93.0	8.8	32.8	42.3	24.9	100.0	-	-	80.7
Templeton Canadian Bond	★★★	↗	4.9	11.4	-5.6	5.6	7.2	4.3	1.65	47	Sep96	61.2	5.0	68.7	8.6	22.7	100.0	-	-	19.2
Top 50 T-Bill Bond	★	↗↗↗	2.1	9.5	-10.0	0.8	1.9	(1.0)	2.62		Sep96	89.3	6.4	-	100.0	-	100.0	-	-	1.1
Tradex Bond	★	↗↗↗↗	6.6	18.5	-10.0	5.3	7.1	3.7	1.59	32	Jun96	100.0	7.1	15.9	80.6	3.5	100.0	-	-	10.3
Trans-Canada Bond	★★★★	↗	5.8	14.9	-3.6	4.8	6.5	3.3	2.49	34	Jun96	62.0	6.8	7.8	51.2	41.0	100.0	-	-	1.8
Transamerica Growsafe Bond									2.00		Sep96	57.2	7.5	20.5	56.6	22.9	100.0	-	-	5.6
Trimark Advantage Bond									1.25		Sep96	82.1	8.4	27.0	42.0	30.9	87.2	12.8	-	49.8
Trimark Canadian Bond									1.25		Sep96	93.7	8.7	42.6	34.3	23.1	96.6	3.4	-	44.4
University Avenue Bond	★★★★★	↗	9.7	19.6	-3.1				1.99	66	Sep96	98.0	6.5	44.1	19.3	36.6	100.0	-	-	1.9
Westbury Canadian Life B	★★★★	↗↗	8.8	19.4	-7.3	8.0	10.5	6.0	1.02		Sep96	83.2	8.6	15.8	44.5	39.6	100.0	-	-	1.6
Westbury Canadian Life Bond	★★	↗↗	6.7	17.2	-8.3	6.5	8.0	4.7	2.50		Sep96	81.9	9.0	43.2	28.9	28.0	97.6	2.4	-	12.9
Median Canadian Bond Funds			8.3	19.9	-7.8	7.3	9.4	5.4	1.63	53		87.8	8.4	30.2	37.8	27.3	100.0	-	-	27.2
Average Canadian Bond Funds			8.1	19.8	-7.8	7.2	9.3	5.3	1.57	53		84.5	8.6	31.7	38.4	29.0	95.2	3.6	0.3	26.6

Portfolio Analysis: Canadian Bonds

Canadian Short Term Bond Funds (19)

Fund	Avg Ann Ret	High Ann Ret	Low Ann Ret	Avg 3 Yr Ret	High 3 Yr Ret	Low 3 Yr Ret	MER	% Fgn	% 3 Yr Tx Ef	Port-folio Date	Avg Matur (Years)	% Short Bonds	% Med Bonds	% Long Bonds	% Cdn Curr	% U.S. Curr	% Other Curr	Fund Size $ mil
Altamira Short-Term Government Bond							1.33	8		Sep96	0.7	53.2	46.8	-	100.0	-	-	67.7
CIBC Canadian Short-Term Bond	8.1	17.9	-4.3	5.4	6.4	4.3	1.25		59	Sep96	3.7	97.9	2.1	-	100.0	-	-	108.1
Dynamic Government Income							0.83			Sep96	3.3	100.0	-	-	100.0	-	-	12.7
Empire Foreign Currency Canadian Bond							2.18			Sep96	3.3	-	100.0	-	-	100.0	-	4.3
Fidelity Canadian Income							1.25			Jun96	3.6	67.1	32.9	-	100.0	-	-	33.9
Global Strategy Bond							1.50			Sep96	3.0	89.6	10.4	-	100.0	-	-	15.4
Green Line Short-Term Income	7.1	12.6	-1.3				1.20	6	50	Sep96	1.4	100.0	-	-	100.0	-	-	164.2
Guardian Canadian Income A							1.24	12		Sep96	1.5	77.6	22.4	-	100.0	-	-	17.3
Guardian Canadian Income B							1.91	12		Sep96	1.5	77.6	22.4	-	100.0	-	-	5.6
InvesNat Short-Term Government Bond	6.9	14.7	-2.6	6.3	7.6	5.0	1.35		54	Sep96	2.3	100.0	-	-	100.0	-	-	86.0
Laurentian Government Bond	6.8	14.0	-2.3	6.0	7.1	4.7	2.14		49	Sep96	1.7	72.0	28.0	-	100.0	-	-	79.4
Mawer Canadian Income	8.1	18.2	-6.5				0.96	2	64	Sep96	3.8	46.2	42.8	10.9	100.0	-	-	18.8
MD Bond & Mortgage	6.6	10.9	-0.4				1.14	9		Sep96	2.4	98.2	1.8	-	100.0	-	-	71.8
Optima Strategy Short Term							0.34			Sep96	-	100.0	-	-	-	-	-	59.8
PH & N Short-Term Bond & Mortgage	7.6	16.1	-3.6	6.9	8.4	5.6	0.67		57	Sep96	3.0	100.0	-	-	99.5	0.5	-	128.0
Scotia Excelsior Defensive Inc							1.37	12		Sep96	1.8	100.0	-	-	100.0	-	-	128.9
Scudder Canadian Short-Term Bond							0.50	1		Jun96	2.4	100.0	-	-	100.0	-	-	3.8
Talvest Income	7.6	15.7	-3.8	7.0	8.4	5.7	1.50		53	Sep96	3.5	93.8	3.9	2.3	100.0	-	-	102.9
Trimark Government Income							1.25			Sep96	2.7	84.0	16.0	-	100.0	-	-	155.3
Median Canadian Short-Term Bond Funds	7.4	15.2	-3.1	6.3	7.6	5.0	1.25		54		2.6	91.7	7.2	-	100.0	-	-	67.7
Average Canadian Short-Term Bond Funds	7.4	15.0	-3.1	6.3	7.6	5.1	1.26	3.5	55		2.5	81.0	18.3	0.7	94.4	5.6	-	65.8

Canadian Mortgage Funds (32)

Fund	PAL/SGK Rank	Volatility	Avg Ann Ret	High Ann Ret	Low Ann Ret	Avg 3 Yr Ret	High 3 Yr Ret	Low 3 Yr Ret	MER	% 3 Yr Tx Ef	Port-folio Date	% Cash	% MBS	% Cdn Bonds	Canadian Bonds % Short Bonds	Canadian Bonds % Med Bonds	Canadian Bonds % Long Bonds	Fund Size $ mil
Acadia Mortgage									2.03		Sep96	100.0	-	-	-	-	-	0.2
Apex Mortgage	★★	↑↑↑	7.8	14.7	-1.4	7.2	8.4	5.8	1.75	54	Aug96	2.2	19.6	77.0	100.0	-	-	1.0
CIBC Mortgage	★★★	↑↑							1.60		Sep96	5.1	94.8	-	-	-	-	1,392.1
Colonia Life Mortgage	★	↑↑	7.6	13.2	-0.1	6.5	7.8	5.6	1.87	52	Sep96	29.0	71.0	-	-	-	-	4.2
Concorde Hypotheques	★★★★	↑	5.9	11.5	-3.3	7.3	8.1	6.5	1.87	54	Sep96	-0.2	79.1	21.1	100.0	-	-	5.2
CT Everest Mortgage			7.3	12.9	0.0				1.58		Sep96	12.8	65.2	27.3	65.7	34.3	-	667.6
Desjardins Hypotheque	★★★	↑↑	7.4	13.1	-0.7	6.9	7.7	5.9	1.63	55	Aug96	15.3	0.4	84.3	97.3	2.6	0.1	237.2

Fund	PAL/SGK Rank	Volatility	Avg Ann Ret	High Ann Ret	Low Ann Ret	Avg 3 Yr Ret	High 3 Yr Ret	Low 3 Yr Ret	MER	% 3 Yr Tx Ef	Port-folio Date	% Cash	% MBS	% Cdn Bonds	Canadian Bonds % Short Bonds	% Med Bonds	% Long Bonds	Fund Size $ mil
Desjardins Mortgage	★★★★	↑	8.3	12.8	2.1	7.3	8.3	6.3	1.66		Sep96	14.7	85.3					22.2
Equitable Life of Canada Mortgage									2.25									1.3
Ficadre Hypotheques									1.50		Sep96	7.7		90.0	100.0			0.3
First Canadian Mortgage	★★	↑↑↑↑↑	8.1	15.5	-2.1	7.4	8.5	6.1	1.23	56	Sep96	4.0	95.3					2,031.1
General Trust Mortgage	★★★★★	↑	6.3	10.1	1.1	6.7	7.9	5.8	1.57		Sep96	23.7	75.9					58.4
Great-West Life Mortgage (G) A	★	↑↑↑↑↑	7.0	15.4	-4.4	6.4	7.7	5.2	2.40		Sep96	0.3	71.6	21.3	100.0			638.6
Green Line Mortgage-Backed	★★	↑↑↑	6.8	12.5	-1.8	6.3	7.0	5.3	1.58	53	Sep96	4.0	73.6					82.7
Green Line Mortgage	★★	↑↑↑	7.1	13.1	-2.0	7.0	8.0	6.0	1.71	51	Sep96	6.7	88.2	2.9	100.0			911.9
Hongkong Bank Mortgage	★★★★★	↑	9.0	16.1	1.1				1.76	68	Sep96	12.1		2.3		100.0		172.5
Ind. Alliance Ecoflex H	★★	↑	6.4	11.8	-1.2				2.14		Sep96	7.6	92.4					11.6
Ind. Alliance Mortgages	★★★	↑↑↑	6.9	12.4	-0.7	6.5	7.2	5.5	1.61		Sep96	7.6	92.4					5.5
Industrial Mtge Securities	★	↑↑↑↑↑↑	6.3	19.9	-9.9	7.5	9.9	5.2	1.86	60	Sep96	12.4	50.4	17.6	1.0	10.5	88.5	750.2
InvesNat Mortgage	★★★★	↑	7.8	12.9	0.5	7.5	8.5	6.6	1.55		Sep96	12.2	87.5	0.2	100.0			350.7
Investors Mortgage	★	↑↑↑↑↑	6.8	13.5	-3.1	6.0	7.0	4.8	1.90	49	Sep96	0.7						2,968.8
Ivy Mortgage									1.90		Sep96	8.9	83.8	6.7	100.0			141.1
London Life Mortgage	★★	↑↑	7.2	13.2	-0.2	7.0	8.4	6.3	2.00									410.9
Mutual Premier Mortgage	★★★	↑↑	7.3	13.1	-1.1				1.58	52	Sep96	10.4	74.9	14.8	100.0			151.7
National Trust Mortgage	★★	↑↑↑	7.5	14.1	-1.5				1.52	52	Sep96	11.5	88.2					64.3
OTGIF Mortgage Income	★★★★★	↑	8.3	13.9	1.7	8.2	9.0	7.6	0.75	42	Sep96	0.8	67.4	31.8	40.0	36.1	23.9	105.8
Pret et Revenu Hypotheque	★	↑↑↑	7.0	13.7	-3.2	6.6	7.5	5.6	1.65	43	Jun96	1.3	85.5	13.0	100.0			94.3
Royal Trust Mortgage	★★	↑↑	6.5	11.9	-1.6	5.7	6.4	4.9	1.74		Sep96	5.2	91.5	3.0	100.0			877.2
Royfund Mortgage	★★★	↑↑↑↑↑	7.4	13.6	-0.7				1.81	55								1,022.5
Scotia Excelsior Mortgage	★★	↑↑↑↑↑	8.2	15.3	-2.3	6.0	7.3	4.5	1.56	61	Sep96	10.8	82.1	9.6	100.0			524.5
Spectrum United Short-Term Bond	★	↑↑↑↑↑	7.2	15.2	-4.3	8.4	9.1	7.4	1.80	52	Sep96	7.1						14.7
SSQ - Hypotheques	★★★★★	↑	8.9	13.3	2.1						Sep96	5.8	94.2					2.7
Median Canadian Mortgage Funds			7.3	13.2	-1.2	6.9	8.0	5.8	1.69	53		7.6	74.9	0.2	40.1			123.4
Average Canadian Mortgage Funds			7.3	13.7	-1.4	6.9	8.0	5.8	1.67	53		11.0	58.4	13.6	40.1	6.1	3.7	251.2

U.S. & International Bond Funds (70)

Fund	PAL/SGK Rank	Volatility	Avg Ann Ret	High Ann Ret	Low Ann Ret	Avg 3 Yr Ret	High 3 Yr Ret	Low 3 Yr Ret	MER	% Fgn	% 3 Yr Tx Ef	Port-folio Date	% Cash	% Fgn Bonds	% Cdn Bonds	Canadian Bonds % Shorts Bonds	% Med Bonds	% Long Bonds	Fund Size $ mil
20/20 Foreign RSP Bond	★	↑↑↑	4.3	14.1	-7.1				2.02	30	24	Sep96	2.7	29.3	65.6	54.8	45.2		77.6
20/20 US S-T High Yield	★	↑↑↑↑↑↑	4.7	17.0	-9.7				2.49	102	17	Sep96	3.4	84.9					23.1
20/20 World Bond			6.5	12.6	1.3				1.99	48	64	Sep96		48.2	34.2	34.1	65.9		53.9
ADMAX World Income	★★★★★	↑	6.6	13.9	-3.0	7.5	9.4	4.7	2.33	7	39	Sep96	8.2	7.4	70.1	26.4	55.1	18.6	14.0
AGF Global Government Bond A	★★★★	↑							1.28	64		Sep96	11.1	64.5	8.0	27.3	72.7		36.8
AGF Global Government Bond B									1.78	64		Sep96	11.1	64.5	8.0	27.3	72.7		123.1
AGF Global Government Bond C									1.76	64		Sep96	11.1	64.5	8.0	27.3	72.7		1.5
AGF RSP Global Income A	★★★	↑	4.6	12.5	-2.4				1.79	46	42	Jun96	4.2	46.5	47.7	29.5	70.5		6.8
AGF RSP Global Income B									2.30	46		Jun96	4.2	46.5	47.7	29.5	70.5		30.5
AGF RSP Global Income C									2.29	46		Jun96	4.2	46.5	47.7	29.5	70.5		0.7
AGF US Income A	★	↑	2.6	9.7	-8.4				1.92	58		Sep96	41.7	57.9					3.6
AGF US Income B									2.44	58		Sep96	41.7	57.9					13.3
AGF US Income C									2.38	58		Sep96	41.7	57.9					0.3
Altamira Global Bond	★★★	↑↑	6.2	13.8	-5.6				1.83	9	56	Sep96	11.0	33.5	54.1	42.2	19.2	38.6	59.5
Altamira Spec High Yield B									1.91	-31		Sep96	23.5	24.4	44.2	31.5	51.8	16.8	3.1
Atlas World Bond									2.02	21		Sep96	32.6	20.3	44.4	31.6	68.4		47.9
BPI Global RSP Bond									1.50	26		Jun96	3.9	26.0	63.8	23.8	15.3	60.9	3.0
C.I. Global Bond RSP	★★★	↑↑↑↑↑↑	8.3	19.9	-3.6				2.09	67	58	Mar96	18.4	22.3	27.1	21.0	79.0		108.3
C.I. New World Income									2.23	83		Aug96	15.5	83.1	1.5		100.0		7.4
C.I. World Bond	★★	↑↑↑↑↑↑	6.8	19.6	-5.7				2.07	77	49	Sep96	5.8	76.7	17.5	1.3	98.7		119.8
Canada Life International Bond									2.00										59.7
CIBC Global Bond									1.90	51		Sep96	10.0	51.2	36.0	25.6	74.4		48.0
CT Everest International Bond									2.00	53		Sep96	8.2	45.6	37.2	56.3	43.7		67.0
Dynamic Global Bond	★★★★★	↑↑↑↑	9.8	19.8	-1.7	11.0	13.5	8.0	1.94	29	61	Sep96	10.2	28.6	60.3	60.4	39.6		471.2
Elliott & Page Global Bond									1.69	94		Sep96	4.4	87.6	2.5		100.0		14.9
Ethical Global Bond									1.97	8		Sep96	18.2	7.7	71.1	14.5	47.5	37.9	7.6
Fidelity Emerging Markets Bond									2.33										41.4
Fidelity North American Income	★	↑↑↑↑↑↑	-1.0	9.2	-15.0				1.75	37		Jun96	28.4	12.3	56.6	95.7	4.3		164.0
Fidelity RSP Global Bond		↑↑↑↑							2.37	41		Jun96	3.4	41.1	53.2	11.5	80.9	7.6	79.7
First Canadian International Bond	★★★★★	↑↑↑↑	10.0	17.6	0.0				1.99		63	Sep96	100.0						90.6
Friedberg Foreign Bond									0.93										5.0
Global Strategy Diversified Bond	★	↑↑↑↑↑↑	4.5	11.8	-7.9	5.4	8.1	3.2	2.29	21	29	Jun96	69.0	20.5	9.9	76.7	23.3		550.2
Global Strategy Diversified ForeignBond									2.29	28		Jun96	47.1	26.5					3.6
Global Strategy World Bond	★	↑↑↑↑↑↑	4.2	11.9	-8.8	5.6	8.6	2.8	2.27	73	25	Jul96	26.1	72.4	1.4			100.0	394.3
Great-West Life Global Income (A)									2.70										6.7
Great-West Life International Bond(H) A									3.02										17.3

Fund	PAL/SGK Rank	Volatility	Avg Ann Ret	High Ann Ret	Low Ann Ret	Avg 3 Yr Ret	High 3 Yr Ret	Low 3 Yr Ret	MER	% Fgn	% 3 Yr Tx Ef	Portfolio Date	% Cash	% Fgn Bonds	% Cdn Bonds	% Shorts Bonds	% Med Bonds	% Long Bonds	Fund Size $ mil
															Canadian Bonds				
Green Line Global Government Bnd	★★★	↑↑	6.6	14.3	-1.0				2.14	86	51	Sep96	8.4	84.9	3.2	100.0			105.9
Green Line Global RSP Bond									2.07	35		Sep96	4.0	34.6	59.7	26.0	68.4	5.6	77.4
GS International Bond									2.70	34		Sep96	37.7	24.8	35.9	43.2	53.7	3.1	7.6
GT World Bond									2.45	95		Sep96	6.9	89.6	3.6	38.9	61.1		3.1
Guardian Foreign Income A									2.09	68		Sep96	50.5	48.0					2.8
Guardian Foreign Income B									2.82	68		Sep96	50.5	48.0					2.2
Guardian International Income B									2.09	-9		Aug96	-77.1	33.6	44.8	30.8	69.2		185.7
Guardian International Income A	★★	↑↑↑↑↑	6.8	17.9	-6.3	8.3	10.0	5.4	2.17	-9	49	Aug96	-77.1	33.6	44.8	30.8	69.2		61.6
Hongkong Bank Global Bond									2.18	89		Sep96	7.7	83.9	6.8		100.0		10.2
InvesNat International RSP Bond									2.19	79		Sep96	9.8	78.6	8.5		100.0		4.2
Investors Global Bond	★★	↑↑↑	5.1	12.5	-2.9				2.23	88	40	Sep96	1.9	88.3	7.8	47.3	52.7		266.4
Investors North American High Yield									1.10	68		Sep96	32.2	42.6	29.9	13.3	56.7	30.0	4.4
Lotus Group International Bond									1.63	-			4.5		95.5	26.0	74.0		3.6
Manulife Vistafund1 Global Bond									2.38										2.5
Manulife Vistafund2 Global Bond										46		Jun95	52.2	45.7					28.0
McLean Budden Pooled International Income										27	30	Sep96	2.0	26.7	71.1	28.4	50.9	20.8	11.8
MD Global Bond									1.13	85	41	Sep96	5.8	84.6	7.1	75.4		24.6	56.7
Merrill Lynch World Bond									2.33	45		Sep96	7.1	44.3	47.3	23.9	39.3	36.8	28.0
National Trust International RSP Bond									2.15	33		Jul96	0.2	33.1	65.1		61.8	38.2	10.3
NN Can-Global Bond									2.00	2		Sep96	100.0						4.4
Optima Strategy Global Fixed Income									0.49										76.4
Pret Et Revenu Mond Oblig									1.93	38		Sep96	13.7	37.6	48.3	26.7	73.3		1.0
Pursuit Global Bond									1.75	46		Jun96	58.8	30.9	9.0		100.0		5.3
Royal Trust International Bond	★★★★	↑↑↑	6.8	15.9	-4.1				1.86	33	30	Jun96	10.7	33.0	51.8	46.9	45.4	7.8	228.8
Royfund International Income	★★★★★	↑	7.3	15.9	-1.5				1.97	10	41			9.9		45.7			151.4
Scotia Canam Income	★★	↑↑↑↑↑	5.8	17.2	-5.3				1.60	25	26	Sep96	20.3	9.9	68.2	45.7	54.3		25.7
Scotia Excelsior Global Bond									1.86	84		Sep96	6.6	24.7	5.9		100.0		12.1
Spectrum United Global Bond	★★★	↑↑↑	7.2	16.1	-3.1				2.03	32	42	Sep96	1.8	83.8	12.7	76.1	23.9		10.7
Spectrum United RSP International Bond									1.97			Sep96	3.6	28.7	65.8	53.4	46.6		107.7
Standard Life International Bond									2.00										5.5
Talvest Foreign Pay Canadian Bond	★★★	↑↑↑	5.7	13.6	-4.7	7.1	8.9	5.1	2.15	69	42	Sep96	-1.5	68.5	28.6	40.9	59.1		127.0
Templeton Global Bond	★★★	↑	5.8	12.4	-3.6				2.25	66	41	Sep96	2.6	66.0	28.9	80.4	19.6		54.8
Universal World Income RRSP									2.16	16		Sep96	73.9	15.8	9.6		19.5	80.5	295.5
Universal Wrld Tactical Bond									2.62	79		Sep96	24.9	71.8					28.6
Median U.S. and International Bond Funds			6.2	14.1	-4.1	7.3	9.2	4.9	2.05	46.5	42		10.0	44.3	28.6	26.4	52.7		26.8
Average U.S. and International Bond Funds			5.9	14.8	-4.8	7.5	9.7	4.8	2.02	46.0	42		10.1	45.0	27.9	26.8	46.6	8.6	28.6

Canadian Balanced Funds (122)

Fund	PAL/SGK Rank	Volatility	Avg Ann Ret	High Ann Ret	Low Ann Ret	Avg 3 Yr Ret	High 3 Yr Ret	Low 3 Yr Ret	MER	% Fgn	% 3 Yr Tx Ef	Portfolio Date	% Cash	% Cdn Equity	% Fgn Equity	% Cdn Bonds	% Fgn Bonds	Fund Size $ mil
ABC Fully-Managed	★★★	↑↑↑↑↑↑	12.8	32.2	-6.5	20.8	28.2	14.4	2.00	6	69	Sep96	15.5	51.5	6.5	26.0	-	40.1
Acadia Balanced									2.27	-		Sep96	37.4	47.3	-	15.3	-	3.1
AGF Growth & Income A	★★	↑↑↑↑↑↑	13.1	36.5	-6.7	12.1	17.7	7.1	2.00	4	93	Sep96	24.7	43.2	4.0	24.5	-	48.1
AGF Growth & Income B									2.50	4		Sep96	24.7	43.2	4.0	24.5	-	288.6
AGF Growth & Income C									2.50	4		Sep96	24.7	43.2	4.0	24.5	-	25.0
Altamira Balanced	★	↑↑↑	5.6	20.7	-11.3	9.9	13.0	3.5	2.00	-	79	Sep96	4.2	45.1	9.7	38.9	0.1	98.6
Altamira Growth & Income	★	↑↑↑↑	5.3	19.3	-9.0	10.9	16.5	6.4	1.41	9	76	Sep96	7.2	56.6	6.2	17.7	-	288.5
AMI Private Capital Optimix	★★★	↑↑↑↑	8.7	21.6	-8.4	8.7	11.7	5.7	1.75	17	79	Sep96	6.8	39.6	14.7	27.1	-	4.0
Asset Builder I									2.25	16		Sep96	11.3	34.2	15.6	39.0	-	17.2
Asset Builder II									2.26	16		Sep96	12.9	50.3	15.6	21.3	-	18.1
Asset Builder III									2.25	15		Sep96	14.9	59.9	15.4	9.7	-	15.4
Asset Builder IV									2.25			Sep96	15.1	63.5	15.4	6.0	-	8.7
Asset Builder V									2.26	15		Sep96	16.9	63.2	15.0	4.8	-	3.8
Atlas Canadian Balanced	★★★★★	↑↑	9.9	19.9	-3.1	8.4	11.5	5.4	2.27	20	89	Sep96	8.7	31.2	19.6	39.0	-	31.4
Azura Balanced RSP Pooled									2.20	15		Sep96	13.4	29.4	5.3	8.4	0.9	11.4
Azura Conservative Pooled									2.06	25		Aug96	32.1	3.4	18.6	17.3	5.7	2.6
Batirente Sec Diversifee	★★★	↑↑↑↑	9.5	22.4	-6.5	8.5	11.3	6.0	1.50		100	Sep96	10.0	17.3	-	57.2	-	42.8
Beutel Goodman Balanced	★★★★	↑	8.0	19.1	-6.4	9.7	13.2	7.2	2.20	19	73	Jun96	4.6	38.0	18.4	37.8	-	152.8
Bissett Retirement	★★★★	↑↑↑↑↑	11.6	24.4	-5.3	11.1	13.6	7.9	0.36	22	85	Sep96	5.3	36.3	22.4	33.1	-	10.0
BPI Canadian Balanced	★	↑↑↑↑↑	5.5	20.8	-12.3	7.2	10.1	4.0	2.57	11	43	Jun96	20.6	44.4	10.7	17.0	-	76.8
C.I. Canadian Balanced	★★★★★	↑	9.4	23.1	-4.7				2.35		79	Sep96	34.5	43.0	-	22.5	-	428.9
C.I. Canadian Income									1.89	-		Sep96	29.6	29.8	-	40.6	-	58.9
Caldwell Securities Assoc	★★★★★	↑	12.0	26.6	-0.7	13.9	19.0	9.0	2.46	16	82	Sep96	17.9	47.9	18.0	16.0	-	60.5
Cambridge Balanced	★	↑↑↑↑↑↑	(0.7)	22.0	-19.5	7.5	14.1	0.2	3.00	10	52	Jun96	7.3	71.9	6.7	13.5	-	33.3
Canada Life Managed	★★★	↑↑↑↑	8.5	21.3	-8.5	8.7	11.3	5.7	2.25	7		Jul96	7.7	35.5	17.6	37.9	-	836.6
Capstone Investment Trust	★★	↑↑↑↑↑	7.7	19.8	-9.8	8.2	10.2	5.4	2.14	19	79	Sep96	19.0	29.0	18.9	30.7	2.1	8.1
Cassels Blaikie Canadian	★★★★★	↑	9.3	19.6	-4.4	8.9	11.2	6.6	1.16	21	72	Sep96	3.9	35.1	21.3	39.0	-	13.7
CCPE Diversified	★★★★	↑↑↑	9.2	20.5	-4.9	8.3	11.0	5.3	1.35	100		Sep96						31.3
CDA Balanced	★★★	↑↑↑	8.9	19.5	-5.8	8.6	10.7	5.5	0.92	16	82	Sep96	3.7	34.1	10.1	28.3	2.6	37.9
CIBC Balanced	★★	↑↑↑	6.6	18.9	-9.7	6.8	10.5	3.9	2.05	10	94	Sep96	4.2	55.4	4.7	30.2	-	677.7
Clean Environment Balanced	★	↑↑↑↑	4.7	14.1	-11.5				2.99	5		Sep96	33.3	61.9	-	-	-	18.5
Colonia Strategic Balanced									0.25	-		Sep96	19.2	54.1	-	26.7	-	7.6
Concorde Equilibre									2.08	11		Sep96	16.2	39.6	7.4	31.4	-	14.1
Cornerstone Balanced	★★	↑↑↑↑↑↑	10.2	29.4	-10.5	7.8	11.8	3.2	2.59		61	Sep96	8.2	50.7	-	40.6	2.9	40.3
CT Everest Balanced	★★	↑↑↑	7.1	20.3	-10.6	8.3	10.7	5.6	2.09	32	80	Sep96	21.1	36.1	9.9	38.9	2.9	994.0
Desjardins Diversified	★★★★	↑↑↑	9.0	21.3	-7.0	9.8	12.3	7.4	1.80	5		Sep96	19.4	47.9	5.5	26.9	-	54.8

Portfolio Analysis

Columns under "Portfolio Analysis" are: % Cash, % Cdn Equity, % Fgn Equity, % Cdn Bonds, % Fgn Bonds.

Fund	PAL/SGK Rank	Volatility	Avg Ann Ret	High Ann Ret	Low Ann Ret	Avg 3 Yr Ret	High 3 Yr Ret	Low 3 Yr Ret	MER	% Fgn	% 3 Yr Tx Ef	Portfolio Date	% Cash	% Cdn Equity	% Fgn Equity	% Cdn Bonds	% Fgn Bonds	Fund Size $ mil
Desjardins Equilibre	★★★	↑↑	8.1	20.8	-8.0	9.5	12.3	6.7	1.96	4	87	Sep96	13.0	53.9	3.4	27.2	0.9	331.2
Dolphin Income	★★★★★	↑	6.9	17.3	-0.9	6.8	9.3	5.7	1.80	100								0.2
Elliott & Page Balanced	★★★	↑↑↑↑↑	10.1	27.6	-8.4	12.7	16.5	8.5	2.02	8	74	Sep96	7.6	50.5	7.0	33.7	0.7	197.1
Empire Balanced	★★★	↑↑↑	8.0	21.3	-7.4	8.1	11.2	5.6	2.57	11		Sep96	6.0	43.2	10.6	39.0		145.5
Ethical Balanced	★★	↑↑↑↑↑	9.1	22.9	-9.1	8.3	10.8	4.5	2.21	19	82	Sep96	11.7	33.3	19.3	35.3		178.1
Ficadre Equilibre	★★★	↑↑↑	10.1	22.9	-6.7	8.2	11.5	4.1	2.20	8	86	Sep96	6.4	49.1	5.2	32.1	2.9	27.0
Fonds Professional Growth Income									0.75	7		Sep96	18.1	40.0	·	20.5	7.3	33.9
Fonds Professionals Balananced	★★★★★	↑	8.4	16.5	-3.3	7.6	9.0	5.9	2.13	12	71	Sep96	41.5	15.1	6.6	26.5	5.1	380.5
General Trust Balanced	★★★	↑↑↑	7.9	18.2	-5.9	7.5	9.6	4.7	2.64	16		Sep96	7.9	40.6	15.6	34.4		49.3
Global Strategy Income Plus	★★★★	↑↑↑	9.1	21.8	-4.9				2.64	2	76	Sep96	0.5	66.5	1.5	21.5		389.1
Great-West Life Diversified (G) A	★★	↑↑	6.4	18.2	-8.8	7.1	9.3	4.7	2.64	12		Sep96	9.6	35.1	11.9	23.2		431.8
Great-West Life Equity Bond (G) A	★	↑↑↑↑↑	6.6	21.1	-11.3	7.8	10.3	5.0	2.64			Sep96	4.6	58.9	0.0	34.7		301.4
Green Line Balanced Growth	★★★	↑↑↑↑↑	9.5	23.0	-8.9	6.6	9.7	3.4	2.27	19	87	Sep96	18.2	38.0	16.0	27.4		154.2
Green Line Balanced Income	★★	↑↑↑↑	7.4	20.5	-9.9	6.4	9.1	3.0	2.28	20	84	Jun96	7.2	37.0	15.3	34.3	1.1	117.6
Greystone Managed Wealth									2.85	3		Sep96	23.2	53.8	3.2	19.3		2.6
GS Canadian Balanced									2.99	1		Sep96	16.3	62.7	0.9	18.9		70.4
GT Canada Income									2.45	16		Sep96	11.3	72.4	16.4			86.1
Guardian Canadian Balanced A	★★★★★	↑	7.9	15.2	-1.2	8.8	10.6	7.4	1.92	17	72	Sep96	30.4	31.8	6.3	19.9	7.0	57.7
Guardian Canadian Balanced B									2.76	17		Sep96	30.4	31.8	6.3	19.9	7.0	189.1
Hongkong Bank Balanced	★★	↑↑↑↑↑	7.4	20.8	-10.1	9.7	12.7	7.0	1.94	9	81	Sep96	7.0	38.3	8.6	45.3		133.5
HRL Balanced	★	↑↑↑	5.1	16.3	-10.5	6.4	10.1	2.8	1.24	23	66	Sep96	15.1	29.4	20.5	32.0	1.9	35.3
ICM Balanced	★★★	↑↑↑	8.8	20.5	-7.0	9.8	12.1	7.5	1.83	13	67	Jun96	8.0	42.0	12.8	36.8	0.2	62.6
Ideal Balanced	★★★★★	↑↑↑	9.8	21.7	-4.6	9.0	11.7	6.6	2.00	100		Sep96	15.4	53.6		39.1		146.9
IG Beutel Goodman Canadian Balanced									2.65			Sep96	30.5	27.5	16.1	25.0		7.4
IG Sceptre Canadian Balanced									2.65	21		Sep96	12.6	56.7	4.5	25.0		9.8
Imperial Growth Diversified	★★★★	↑	8.0	18.0	-4.8	7.8	10.1	5.4	2.00	4		Sep96						11.2
Industrial Alliance Diversified	★★★★★	↑	9.3	19.9	-4.9	10.6	13.4	7.8	1.61			Sep96	3.7	45.7	4.4	38.6		210.6
Industrial Alliance Ecoflex D	★★★★★	↑	8.7	19.3	-5.4				2.14			Sep96	3.7	45.7	4.4	38.6		247.5
Industrial Balanced	★★★	↑↑↑	6.7	19.3	-8.5	9.0	12.1	5.8	2.37	4	74	Sep96	6.4	46.9	4.4	38.5	0.1	391.0
Industrial Income	★★	↑↑↑↑↑	8.0	21.2	-8.9	7.8	10.3	5.9	1.87	2	34	Sep96	11.0	17.9	1.7	64.7		2,681.7
InvesNat Retirement Balanced	★★★★	↑↑↑	8.1	18.7	-5.6	7.5	9.9	5.5	2.10	16	81	Sep96	6.5	42.6	15.4	34.1	0.4	260.8
Investors Income Plus Port	★★★★	↑	6.9	16.1	-5.5	6.2	8.2	4.4	0.17	2	63	Sep96	9.9	20.3	1.6	39.8		1,255.8
Investors Mutual	★★★	↑↑	7.3	20.4	-8.2	10.5	13.4	7.3	2.34	11	87	Sep96	6.1	52.1	10.5	30.2	0.3	772.5
Investors Ret. Plus Port	★★★★	↑↑↑↑↑	7.3	16.8	-5.1	8.6	10.9	6.3	0.18	21	83	Sep96	8.3	35.2	11.5	17.9	9.0	1,562.3
Ivy Growth & Income	★★★★★	↑↑↑↑↑	12.4	23.3	-1.6	8.0	10.6	4.0	2.13	15	93	Sep96	38.7	46.0	9.2	9.1		340.6
Jones Heward Canadian Balanced	★	↑↑↑↑	5.5	19.6	-11.2	6.6	9.2	4.0	2.40	15	80	Sep96	1.5	43.2	15.3	36.2		53.2
Laurentian Canadian Balanced	★★★	↑	7.1	17.9	-6.3				2.65	5	80	Sep96	10.2	58.3	4.5	26.6		139.6
Leith Wheeler Balanced	★★★★	↑	7.6	15.3	-4.3	9.8	11.6	7.4	1.18	16	72	Sep96	0.9	37.6	16.1	45.3		36.6

Fund	PAL/SGK Rank	Volatility	Avg Ann Ret	High Ann Ret	Low Ann Ret	Avg 3 Yr Ret	High 3 Yr Ret	Low 3 Yr Ret	MER	% Fgn	% 3 Yr Tx Ef	Port-folio Date	% Cash	% Cdn Equity	% Fgn Equity	% Cdn Bonds	% Fgn Bonds	Fund Size $ mil
London Life Diversified	**	↑↑↑	7.5	19.8	-7.9	8.6	10.6	6.4	2.00	100	59	Sep96	6.0	35.6	13.5	44.6	0.0	1,190.5
Lotus Group Balanced	*	↑↑↑↑↑	5.5	19.0	-12.5	8.5	10.5	4.7	2.14	14		Sep96	4.5	40.7	-	28.7		64.0
Manulife Vistafd1 Diversified	**	↑↑↑	7.9	22.5	-8.2	8.4	12.2	5.6	1.63	9		Sep96	4.5	40.7	-	28.7	9.3	60.1
Manulife Vistafd2 Diversified	**	↑↑↑	7.1	21.6	-8.9	7.5	11.3	4.8	2.38	9		Sep96	4.5	40.7	-	28.7	9.3	446.5
Maritime Life Balanced	****	↑↑	9.1	21.3	-5.5	8.3	11.3	4.9	1.97	15		Sep96	16.4	31.7	14.7	35.8	-	312.0
Mawer Canadian Diversified Investment	****	↑↑	8.8	20.0	-6.3	8.6	11.2	6.0	1.01	20	68	Sep96	13.0	37.5	15.9	28.1	-	19.7
Mawer Cdn Balanced RSP	****	↑↑	8.8	20.3	-6.1	9.0	11.5	6.6	0.90	20	67	Sep96	10.8	37.5	16.5	32.2	0.4	52.3
Maxxum Canadian Balanced	*	↑↑↑↑↑↑	8.0	25.7	-14.4	9.7	12.6	6.1	1.50	2	72	Sep96	4.4	57.8	2.0	35.0	-	90.3
McDonald Canada Plus									2.24	19		Sep96	3.3	58.1	18.0	19.2	-	2.0
Mclean Budden Balanced	***	↑↑↑↑↑	9.6	23.0	-8.8	9.0	11.5	5.9	1.75	14	71	Sep96	11.4	36.2	14.0	36.5	-	11.9
McLean Budden Pooled Bal	****	↑↑↑↑↑	10.7	23.8	-7.5	10.8	13.0	7.9	-	1	85	Sep96	10.1	34.2	0.3	38.9	-	163.6
MD Balanced	****	↑↑↑	9.5	21.5	-6.4				1.15	18	98	Sep96	7.9	53.9	17.9	18.3	0.0	497.0
Metlife Mvp Balanced	**	↑↑	6.1	19.5	-10.1	6.2	8.7	2.9	2.00	-								32.0
Millennia III Canadian Balanced 1									2.74	5		Sep96	6.7	58.8	4.9	29.4	-	25.5
Millennia III Canadian Balanced 2									2.92	5		Sep96	6.7	58.8	4.9	29.4	-	2.2
Millennium Diversified									2.50	15		Sep96	50.8	22.7		26.3	-	4.0
Mutual Diversifund 40	***	↑↑↑↑↑	9.7	23.3	-7.5	8.3	11.5	4.7	1.77	13	72	Sep96	13.1	36.3	13.5	35.0	-	264.2
Mutual Premier Diversified									2.33	13		Sep96	10.2	57.5	11.7	20.1	-	138.3
NAL-Canadian Diversified	***	↑↑↑↑↑↑↑	11.9	31.1	-7.7	9.3	14.1	4.7	1.75	12		Sep96	11.5	44.4	8.7	28.4	-	98.7
National Balanced	***	↑↑↑↑	8.3	20.9	-9.0	8.1	10.7	4.7	2.00	100	82	Sep96	2.7	44.6	13.0	39.2	-	64.1
National Trust Balanced	***	↑↑↑↑	8.5	22.9	-9.3	8.9	11.7	6.3	1.81	13	82	Sep96	5.2	39.2	11.8	43.8	-	140.0
NN Balanced	****	↑↑↑↑	9.1	22.1	-7.0	9.8	12.7	6.5	2.25	12	71	Sep96	2.8	50.8	5.0	34.8	-	69.6
O.I.Q. Ferique Equilibre	*****	↑↑↑↑	9.8	20.2	-4.5	9.0	11.6	6.7	0.44	8	74	Sep96	14.7	43.5		40.8	-	198.3
OHA Balanced	***	↑↑↑↑	9.7	20.8	-5.4	9.3	11.7	6.6	0.90	-	92	Sep96	13.6	14.4	0.6	59.7	-	2.2
Optimum Equilibre	***	↑↑↑↑	9.4	21.6	-6.8	10.9	13.2	8.3	1.38	23	66	Sep96	12.7	37.4	11.9	34.5	-	18.1
OTGIF Balanced	*****	↑↑↑↑	8.7	22.5	-6.9	10.6	13.2	8.1	1.00	14	70	Sep96	8.9	34.0	13.1	36.6	-	42.9
PH & N Balance Pension Trust	*****	↑↑↑↑↑	10.7	22.8	-4.5	9.8		6.9	-	15	70	Sep96	5.7	35.0	13.1	41.9	-	1,038.2
PH & N Balanced	***	↑↑↑	10.2	21.9	-4.4	9.8		6.6	0.92	18	89	Sep96	9.8	40.8	14.2	34.4	-	209.4
Royal Balanced	**	↑↑↑	7.7	20.7	-7.7	9.8	12.1	8.3	2.31	15	76	Sep96	1.5	47.9	14.1	46.6	0.1	3,008.3
Royal Life Balanced	***	↑↑↑	7.6	19.6	-9.2	7.9	10.4	5.5	2.34	3	82	Sep96	11.0	29.2	3.0	32.6	-	113.0
Royal Trust Advantage Balanced	***	↑↑↑	7.6	19.9	-7.1	8.4	12.4	5.8	1.83	7	89	Jun96	12.4	30.3	7.3	23.1	0.7	429.1
Royal Trust Advantage Growth	***	↑	7.5	20.2	-7.5	8.5	10.9	5.7	1.99	8	73	Jun96	11.8	19.6	7.5	36.1	0.7	166.6
Royal Trust Advantage Income	*	↑	7.5	18.4	-6.0	7.7	9.5	5.8	1.69	6		Jun96	15.8		5.6	34.2	0.4	151.7
Saxon Balanced	*****	↑↑↑↑↑↑	12.3	26.7	-5.7	15.0	19.0	9.9	1.87	3	90	Sep96	5.2	59.1	2.0	21.4	-	5.9
Sceptre Balanced Growth	*****	↑↑↑	12.1	27.6	-8.7	11.0	14.0	6.6	1.57	15	82	Sep96	9.0	37.7	11.4	34.2	2.1	78.4
Scotia Excelsior Balanced	***	↑↑↑↑↑	8.4	21.2	-7.9	9.3	12.6	6.4	2.01	18	85	Sep96	14.4	42.2	16.4	40.3	-	324.5
Spectrum United Canadian Portfolio	***	↑↑↑↑	10.0	24.0	-8.0	10.9	14.0	8.2	2.08	19	86	Sep96	9.0	31.5	18.1	33.0	0.0	156.4
Spectrum United Diversified	**	↑↑↑↑	7.0	20.5	-10.5	7.1	10.1	4.4	2.28	14	75	Sep96	2.8	42.3	12.3	40.1	0.9	139.6

Fund	PAL/SGK Rank	Volatility	Avg Ann Ret	High Ann Ret	Low Ann Ret	Avg 3 Yr Ret	High 3 Yr Ret	Low 3 Yr Ret	MER	% Fgn	% 3 Yr Tx Ef	Portfolio Date	% Cash	% Cdn Equity	% Fgn Equity	% Cdn Bonds	% Fgn Bonds	Fund Size $ mil
SSQ - Equilibre	★★★	↑↑↑↑↑	10.2	24.1	-7.6				2.00	11	76	Sep96	11.5	45.7	5.0	30.7	-	19.1
Standard Life Balanced	★★★	↑↑↑↑	9.1	21.5	-7.2				2.15	15	89	Jun95	8.2	34.8	14.5	42.4	-	12.9
Templeton Balanced	★★★	↑↑	7.7	21.0	-10.0	10.3	14.7	5.8	3.00	23	74	Sep96	1.8	41.1	22.9	31.7	-	32.7
Trans-Canada Pension	★	↑↑	(0.5)	19.2	-13.0	9.9	17.4	1.4	2.00	8		Jun96	20.8	71.6	7.6	-	-	0.8
Transamerica B.I.G.	★★★★★★	↑	8.6	16.0	-0.5	9.2	11.1	7.8		21		Sep96	29.0	32.6	0.6	19.9	10.4	81.4
Transamerica Growsafe Balanced		↑↑	10.6	24.1	-6.2	13.1	16.1	9.9	2.00	10	80	Sep96	36.4	28.7	-	24.7	9.6	20.1
Trimark Income Growth	★★★★★	↑↑	10.0	20.9	-5.0	12.1	14.4	9.6	1.69	18	85	Sep96	12.4	37.6	15.9	32.6	-	361.4
Trimark Select Balanced	★★★★★	↑	10.9	24.2	-7.1	9.6	12.3	6.1	2.21	21	75	Sep96	11.8	39.4	20.4	27.3	-	2,496.7
Trust Pret et Revenu retra	★★★★	↑↑↑↑↑	8.6	20.6	-6.2	8.0	11.7	4.9	1.81	10		Sep96	2.5	51.3	6.7	28.7	2.9	56.4
Westbury Canadian Life Balanced	★★★★	↑↑							2.41	0		Sep96	52.0	22.3	-	23.7	-	22.7
Median Canadian Balanced Funds			8.6	20.8	-7.2	8.7	11.5	5.8	2.04	11.9	79		11.0	41.0	8.6	30.7	-	64.1
Average Canadian Balanced Funds			8.4	21.3	-7.4	9.1	12.1	5.9	1.92	14.9	77		10.1	39.3	11.4	29.8	0.9	56.4

Fund	PAL/SGK Rank	Volatility	Avg Ann Ret	High Ann Ret	Low Ann Ret	Avg 3 Yr Ret	High 3 Yr Ret	Low 3 Yr Ret	MER	% Fgn	% 3 Yr Tx Ef	Portfolio Date	% Cash	% Cdn Equity	% Fgn Equity	% Cdn Bonds	% Fgn Bonds	Fund Size $ mil
International Balanced Funds (24)																		
Atlas American Advan Value									2.70	82		Sep96	20.7	-	81.9	-	-	7.0
Azura Balanced Pooled									2.29	47		Aug96	15.0	9.0	38.7	8.6	4.7	14.5
Beutel Goodman Private Bal	★★★★★	↑↑↑	10.1	21.4	-3.0	11.2	12.7	9.4	1.10	28	74	Jun96	3.9	40.4	15.9	21.3	11.7	36.4
BPI Global Balanced RSP	★★★★	↑	5.7	15.4	-2.3	13.3	16.4	6.3	2.52	9	99	Jun96	20.0	44.1	1.9	24.3	7.5	195.6
BPI North American Balanced RSP	★★	↑↑↑↑↑↑	8.2	23.8	-11.6				2.75	92	85	Apr96	14.4	0.4	42.1	7.2	33.2	16.8
C.I. International Balanced									2.63	17		Feb96	21.0	0.3	9.8	6.0	4.1	77.5
C.I. International Balanced RSP									2.53	97		Aug96	44.9	0.3	52.6	-	-	116.0
Caldwell Securities International	★★★	↑↑↑	7.6	19.7	-6.7				2.60	93	81	Sep96	5.7	2.9	49.0	2.7	38.4	4.1
Elliott & Page Global Balananced									2.22	83	91			1.4	52.6	1.9	30.1	10.2
Fidelity Asset Manager	★	↑↑↑↑↑	5.3	16.4	-7.3				2.77	81		Jun96		0.3	49.8	0.9	23.1	235.0
Global Strategy World Balanced									2.58	81		Sep96	2.3	-	56.8	9.6	28.1	12.8
GT Global Growth & Income									2.95	34		Aug96	19.2	-	13.3	9.6	28.1	8.6
Guardian International Balanced B									2.96	34		Aug96	12.5	-	13.3	9.6	28.1	80.5
Guardian International Balanced A	★	↑↑↑↑↑↑	4.9	19.3	-10.5				2.36	43		Aug96	12.5	-	49.8	-	-	8.0
Horizons I Multi-Asset									3.60									21.5
Investors Growth Plus Portfolio	★★★★★	↑↑	9.2	18.9	-1.6	10.6	13.2	8.2	0.18	43	81	Sep96	10.7	13.4	40.0	25.8	0.3	260.1
Laurentian Global Balanced	★★★★★	↑	6.4	15.7	-1.6	9.2	11.9	5.2	2.70	84	78	Sep96	7.8	-	54.9	8.0	28.7	27.8

Fund	PAL/SGK Rank	Volatility	Avg Ann Ret	High Ann Ret	Low Ann Ret	Avg 3 Yr Ret	High 3 Yr Ret	Low 3 Yr Ret	MER	% Fgn	% 3 Yr Tx Ef	Port-folio Date	% Cash	% Cdn Equity	% Fgn Equity	% Cdn Bonds	% Fgn Bonds	Fund Size $ mil
Merrill Lynch Capital Asset									3.25	92		Sep96	8.0		47.3		42.4	16.6
Merrill Lynch World Allocation	★★	↑↑↑↑↑	8.8	22.1	-8.6	9.5	11.4	7.0	3.08	89	75	Sep96	4.3	3.2	67.8	7.2	9.9	50.8
Spectrum United Global Diversified									2.30	43		Sep96	15.7	18.0	35.7	20.4	5.6	30.0
Templeton Global Balanced									2.55	77		Sep96	7.1	0.9	50.9	13.1	21.4	11.3
Templeton International Balanced									2.55	85		Aug96	12.2		48.6		32.1	9.4
Transamerica Growsafe Intl									2.45	66		Sep96	55.8			12.8	29.1	14.8
Universal World Balanced RRSP									2.43			Sep96	81.1		10.1	2.0	3.3	198.6
Median International Balanced Funds			7.6	19.3	-6.7	10.6	12.7	7.0	2.57	80.6	81		12.5	0.3	41.1	7.2	16.5	19.1
Average International Balanced Funds			7.4	19.2	-5.9	10.8	13.1	7.2	2.50	64.6	81		18.0	6.1	35.5	8.2	17.4	61.0

Fund	PAL/SGK Rank	Volatility	Avg Ann Ret	High Ann Ret	Low Ann Ret	Avg 3 Yr Ret	High 3 Yr Ret	Low 3 Yr Ret	MER	% Fgn	% 3 Yr Tx Ef	Port-folio Date	% Cash	% Cdn Equity	% Fgn Equity	% Cdn Bonds	% Fgn Bonds	Fund Size $ mil
Asset Allocation Funds																		
20/20 American Tactical Asset Allocation	★★★★★	↑↑↑↑↑	11.2	24.3	-5.1	12.3	14.9	7.3	2.64	99	68	Aug96	8.3	0.5	39.9		51.2	290.3
20/20 Canadian Tactical Asset Allocation	★★★	↑↑↑	6.6	19.1	-9.7	8.3	11.4	5.4	2.50	19	72	Sep96	0.3	60.0	18.7	19.7	0.0	689.4
20/20 European Asset Allocation	★★★★	↑↑	5.5	14.4	-5.5				2.62	102	100	Sep96			102.1			37.0
20/20 World	★	↑↑↑↑↑	0.5	16.0	-16.2	11.0	17.5	4.1	2.60	94	63	Sep96		1.3	47.2	7.4	45.2	154.1
ADMAX Asset Allocation	★★★★	↑	5.1	12.9	-4.3				2.65	0	89	Sep96	18.0	44.2		36.5		6.6
Altamira Global Diversified	★★★	↑↑↑↑↑	8.5	24.4	-4.5	10.4	14.2	6.6	2.00	81	100	Sep96	10.0		80.8		7.8	51.9
Apex Balanced Allocation									2.00	2		Sep96	36.5	18.9	1.7	42.2		105.9
Co-Operators Balanced	★★★★★	↑↑↑↑↑	11.4	26.6	-7.0				2.07									
Desjardins Divers Audaciou									1.75	10		Sep96	11.3	30.6	9.9	4.1		59.2
Desjardins Divers Moderate									1.65	7		Sep96	12.7	15.1	6.6	8.2		77.9
Desjardins Divers Secure									1.55	1		Sep96	54.4	7.4	1.2	7.9		58.5
Dynamic Global Partners									2.68	62		Sep96	11.7	4.7	42.9	21.3	17.4	53.8
Dynamic Partners	★★★★★	↑↑	6.8	17.5	-5.2	15.0	19.3	7.4	2.45	23	83	Sep96	22.4	34.4	12.9	19.8	10.1	1,767.1
Dynamic Team	★★★	↑↑↑↑↑	6.9	17.8	-9.4	12.7	15.6	7.4	0.98	20	78	Sep96	16.0	30.5	9.0	29.3	10.8	122.7
Empire Asset Allocation									2.57	11		Jun96	11.4	48.2	11.3	28.6		75.5
Fidelity Canadian Asset Allocation	★★★	↑↑↑↑↑	7.8	23.2	-10.8	6.6	10.2	3.2	2.58	14		Sep96	5.7	47.0	13.7	32.8		277.6
First Canadian Asset Allocation									1.97	10	82	Jun96	2.8	46.3	9.2	40.0		272.6
Investors Asset Allocation									2.75	1		Sep96	24.7	39.2	0.1	30.9		931.2
Protected American	★★★	↑	3.0	8.7	-3.4	8.4	11.6	1.1	2.30	18		Sep96	94.1					2.3
Scotia Excelsior Total Return	★★★	↑↑↑↑↑	7.3	19.5	-11.1	11.6	13.6	8.3	2.32	20	81	Sep96	14.0	49.5	19.0	17.9		331.7
Spectrum United Asset Allocation	★★★★	↑↑↑	6.9	19.5	-8.6				2.25	20	86	Sep96	24.5	32.6	16.2	20.7	1.9	388.1

| Fund | PAL/SGK Rank | Volatility | Avg Ann Ret | High Ann Ret | Low Ann Ret | Avg 3 Yr Ret | High 3 Yr Ret | Low 3 Yr Ret | MER | % Fgn | % 3 Yr Tx Ef | Port-folio Date | % Cash | Portfolio Analysis | | | | Fund Size $ mil |
														% Cdn Equity	% Fgn Equity	% Cdn Bonds	% Fgn Bonds	
Talvest Canadian Asset Allocation	★★★★	↗↗	7.4	16.8	-4.3	8.1	11.7	5.6	2.42	11	69	Sep96	3.6	59.7	10.6	24.7	-	197.3
Talvest Global Asset Allocation	★★	↗	3.7	11.9	-5.5	11.1	15.7	4.8	2.75	87	61	Sep96	9.7	0.7	64.5	1.9	19.9	75.1
Templeton Canadian Asset Allocation									2.15	19		Sep96	12.8	36.0	17.5	31.0	0.7	23.9
Universal World Asst Allocation									2.45	95		Sep96	9.8	-	61.6	-	25.0	235.5
Median Asset Allocation Funds			6.9	17.8	-5.5	11.0	14.2	5.6	2.42	19.0	81		11.5	30.6	13.3	19.7	-	114.3
Average Asset Allocation Funds			6.6	18.2	-7.4	10.5	14.2	5.6	2.27	34.4	79		17.3	25.3	24.9	17.7	7.9	261.9

APPENDIX 4

Survey of Standard Performance

THIS IS A LIST OF OVER 1,200 mutual funds that have at least one year's worth of performance data to Sept. 30, 1996. These are the annualized compound rates that you normally see published in the financial press and in advertisign copy. These tables include the manager tenure columns, which detail the number of years the current manager has been managing the fund (as of Sept. 30, 1996). Please note that some fund companies equate manager with management team/committee.

Fund	1 Year	2 Year	3 Year	5 Year	10 Year	Manager Tenure (Years)
Canadian Equity Funds						
20/20 Canadian Growth	7.8	7.6	8.6	8.3	-	0.3
ABC Fundamental-Value	18.9	10.3	15.2	25.7	-	7.6
ADMAX Cdn Performance	17.2	11.6	8.7	9.7	-	0.8
ADMAX Cdn Select Growth	4.3	6.7	3.9	3.4	-	0.6
AGF Canadian Equity A	20.0	11.4	9.2	10.4	5.4	-
AGF Canadian Equity B	19.4	-	-	-	-	-
AGF Canadian Equity C	19.1	-	-	-	-	-
AGF Growth Equity A	24.1	13.2	9.0	19.6	9.9	32.0
AGF Growth Equity B	23.6	-	-	-	-	2.0
AGF Growth Equity C	23.2	-	-	-	-	2.0
AIC Advantage	59.6	37.7	26.3	27.9	15.5	
AIC Diversified Canada	50.6	-	-	-	-	
All-Canadian Capital	5.1	6.5	11.1	10.8	7.4	
All-Canadian Compound	4.5	6.0	10.7	10.5	7.2	
Altafund Investment Corp	34.9	15.5	13.1	20.7	-	1.6
Altamira Capital Growth	3.5	3.5	8.2	12.6	9.4	2.3
Altamira Equity	14.1	9.6	9.8	22.5	-	9.0
AMI Private Cap Equity	22.2	13.2	11.6	10.6	-	8.8
Apex Equity Growth	19.1	12.6	-	-	-	
Associate Investors	19.9	13.6	9.8	9.4	7.7	46.5
Atlas Cdn Large Cap Growth	21.1	14.9	12.0	8.5	6.6	11.0
Atlas Cdn Large Cap Value	7.0	-	-	-	-	2.0
Batirente Section Actions	16.6	11.3	-	-	-	2.6
Beutel Goodman Cdn Equity	13.5	7.3	11.5	8.4	-	5.6

Table © Portfolio Analytics Limited, 1996

Fund	1 Year	2 Year	3 Year	5 Year	10 Year	Manager Tenure (Years)
Bissett Canadian Equity	26.5	19.4	13.9	15.9	11.0	10.5
BNP (Canada) Equity	17.4	11.8	10.3	9.7	-	
BPI Canadian Equity Value	21.9	14.0	8.5	11.9	-	2.3
BPI Cdn Opportunities RSP	87.9	-	-	-	-	1.2
C.I. Canadian Growth	11.0	7.4	9.6	-	-	3.8
C.I. Canadian Sector	10.7	7.0	9.4	11.5	-	8.9
Canada Life Cdn Equity	16.1	12.8	9.7	10.8	8.4	
Canada Life E-2	17.3	13.5	10.4	11.9	9.1	
Canadian Protected	4.4	5.1	2.7	6.9	7.5	11.8
CCPE Growth R	15.2	11.1	11.4	8.5	7.6	
CDA Common Stock	6.3	4.5	6.3	9.2	8.5	2.6
Cdn Anaes Mutual Accum	19.1	13.0	10.7	9.1	7.2	
Chou RRSP	10.9	10.4	6.7	7.6	-	10.0
CIBC Canadian Equity	12.3	6.9	4.9	6.3	-	
Clean Environment Equity	19.5	17.3	10.1	-	-	
Co-Operators Canadian Eq	12.0	8.1	8.8	-	-	4.8
Colonia Life Equity	16.5	9.5	5.7	-	-	
Concorde Croissance	19.7	15.1	12.0	-	-	1.8
Confed Equity	21.9	12.3	11.5	11.5	8.0	
Confed Life A	22.3	13.2	13.2	12.9	9.3	
Confed Life B	22.6	13.2	12.4	12.5	9.1	
Cornerstone Cdn Growth	20.7	13.4	12.1	12.6	-	2.8
Cote 100 Amerique REER	27.3	19.5	10.9	-	-	4.0
Cote 100 EXP	29.6	23.3	-	-	-	2.5
CT Everest Stock	11.8	8.1	6.2	11.4	-	
Desjardins Actions	14.9	9.8	9.4	9.5	6.0	1.8
Desjardins Environnement	12.1	9.3	9.8	8.5	-	1.8
Desjardins Growth	13.9	10.3	-	-	-	1.8
Desjardins Stock	16.8	11.8	10.9	11.8	8.5	1.8
Dolphin Growth	2.8	3.2	5.8	8.1	6.1	
Dynamic Cdn Growth	16.4	7.0	7.0	23.5	10.8	
Dynamic Fund of Canada	9.8	3.4	3.9	11.6	9.4	1.8
Elliott & Page Equity	21.2	14.2	12.7	16.3	-	2.8
Empire Elite Equity	17.4	12.3	9.3	11.3	7.0	3.8
Empire Group Equity	20.2	13.5	11.0	12.7	9.5	3.8
Empire Life 3	19.6	13.8	11.3	12.8	9.6	3.8
Empire Premier Equity	18.6	12.8	10.8	12.1	9.5	3.8
Equitable Life Cdn Stock	20.8	12.3	12.0	-	-	
Equitable Life Common Stock	24.3	16.5	15.3	13.3	8.2	
Ethical Growth	17.4	15.0	11.7	10.4	10.0	
Ficadre Actions	19.2	15.0	11.7	11.2	-	
Fidelity Capital Builder	16.0	9.9	7.8	10.0	-	0.6
First Canadian Eqty Index	17.5	11.0	10.4	10.2	-	
First Canadian Growth	19.8	13.6	8.6	-	-	
Fonds Professionals Cdn Eqty	14.9	11.3	8.7	8.2	-	
GBC Canadian Growth	30.1	19.8	12.6	19.3	-	
General Trust Cdn Equity	17.0	11.4	10.7	8.6	5.8	3.2
Global Strategy Canada Gth	18.2	12.1	7.6	-	-	4.5

Fund	1 Year	2 Year	3 Year	5 Year	10 Year	Manager Tenure (Years)
Great-West Life Cdn Eq (G) A	16.3	8.8	6.8	11.5	-	5.8
Great-West Life Eqty Idx (G) A	16.1	9.7	9.5	9.6	6.9	9.8
Green Line Blue Chip Eqty	18.3	11.6	9.7	8.7	-	9.1
Green Line Canadian Equity	16.5	10.9	8.8	10.6	-	8.7
Green Line Canadian Index	17.8	11.5	11.1	10.9	7.8	4.8
Green Line Value	34.0	19.9	-	-	-	2.8
GT Global Canada Growth Cl	47.7	-	-	-	-	1.8
Guardian Growth Equity A	26.0	12.5	9.2	14.8	-	7.8
Hongkong Bank Equity	22.2	8.7	8.1	13.2	-	4.0
HRL Canadian	15.3	7.4	3.9	5.4	-	0.3
Ideal Equity	24.8	16.6	14.4	12.4	-	9.7
Imperial Growth Cdn Equity	13.9	8.6	8.7	10.0	12.6	
Industrial Alliance Ecoflex A	13.2	10.9	11.8	-	-	3.8
Industrial Alliance Stocks	13.8	11.5	12.2	13.3	9.7	27.4
Industrial Future	7.7	12.1	12.6	14.0	-	6.8
Industrial Growth	9.7	4.2	7.0	9.7	7.8	28.8
Industrial Horizon	10.0	5.3	9.2	9.8	-	9.5
Industrial Pension	15.2	10.1	12.5	13.3	6.9	2.1
InvesNat Canadian Equity	16.7	12.2	10.3	11.3	-	7.9
Investors Canadian Equity	18.6	10.2	10.0	12.7	8.7	11.8
Investors Retire Gth Port	16.7	10.3	10.0	10.3	-	7.7
Investors Retirement	17.7	10.1	10.5	9.9	8.7	3.8
Investors Summa	19.6	14.7	10.4	10.5	-	7.8
Ivy Canadian	17.1	14.8	12.5	-	-	4.0
Jones Heward	15.2	10.3	4.1	12.1	8.1	
Laurentian Canadian Equity	13.0	7.3	7.0	8.4	5.8	1.8
Leith Wheeler Cdn Equity	16.4	8.3	-	-	-	
London Life Cdn Equity	18.8	10.4	9.9	11.9	8.9	15.8
Mackenzie Sent Cdn Equity	14.9	3.6	11.9	14.2	8.1	
Manulife Cabot Blue Chip	15.2	12.1	-	-	-	
Manulife Cabot Cdn Equity	17.1	12.5	-	-	-	
Manulife VistaFd 1 Cap Gns	9.2	6.0	5.9	11.5	9.0	
Manulife VistaFd 2 Cap Gns	8.4	5.2	5.1	10.7	8.2	
Manulife VistaFd 1 Equity	7.9	6.1	7.3	9.0	7.6	
Manulife VistaFd 2 Equity	7.1	5.4	6.5	8.1	6.8	
Maritime Life Cdn Equity	17.7	-	-	-	-	
Maritime Life Growth	19.4	11.7	8.5	10.7	6.6	1.8
Mawer Canadian Equity	8.5	7.4	6.7	-	-	2.6
Maxxum Cdn Equity Growth	20.1	19.0	11.8	17.8	10.6	0.9
Mclean Budden Equity Gth	29.3	17.3	11.4	12.6	-	
McLean Budden Pool Cdn Eqty	32.5	19.8	13.3	15.0	11.2	
MD Equity	13.1	5.7	8.0	11.4	9.3	
MD Select	24.5	13.1	-	-	-	2.9
Metlife Mvp Equity	12.1	6.8	6.8	6.9	-	
Mutual Equifund	19.6	13.9	12.1	9.8	6.5	3.8
Mutual Life A	17.3	13.2	10.7	10.0	6.6	3.8
Mutual Life B	17.5	13.5	10.4	9.6	6.8	3.8
Mutual Premier Blue Chip	16.9	11.6	10.9	-	-	3.8

Fund	1 Year	2 Year	3 Year	5 Year	10 Year	Manager Tenure (Years)
NAL-Canadian Equity	22.0	14.1	12.1	11.5	-	
NAL-Equity Growth	23.3	-	-	-	-	
National Equities	18.3	13.9	12.2	12.2	9.0	3.0
National Trust Cdn Equity	13.5	8.7	6.4	8.6	7.4	8.8
NN Canadian 35 Index	17.4	10.7	12.3	8.7	-	7.5
NN Canadian Growth	15.8	8.8	8.3	7.7	4.4	3.9
O.I.Q. Ferique Actions	17.4	12.5	12.3	10.9	9.6	
OHA Canadian Equity	22.9	12.2	3.9	13.2	-	2.8
Optima Strategy Cdn Equity	18.2	16.7	13.7	-	-	3.3
Optimum Actions	16.8	11.0	-	-	-	2.7
OTGIF Diversified	17.9	11.3	10.3	9.4	7.5	21.7
PH & N Canadian Equity	22.0	14.1	14.3	12.4	9.8	25.3
PH & N Pooled Pension Tr	23.6	15.2	14.3	12.8	10.0	15.1
PH & N RSP/RIF Equity	20.4	14.4	13.6	12.7	9.8	24.9
PH & N Vintage	33.2	22.6	18.0	17.9	14.6	10.5
Pret et Revenu Canadien	18.0	15.0	11.3	13.0	8.4	1.4
Pursuit Canadian Equity	22.0	15.9	9.8	13.4	5.6	13.6
Royal Life Equity	16.4	11.3	11.2	10.6	-	6.8
Royal Trust Cdn Stock	14.8	10.4	9.7	10.1	7.5	
Royfund Canadian Equity	15.0	10.5	10.3	12.0	6.8	
Saxon Stock	22.3	18.8	13.4	18.3	7.4	
Sceptre Equity Growth	38.5	30.7	29.0	21.2	-	3.4
Scotia Excelsior Cdn Growth	25.6	20.0	16.3	14.4	10.4	
Scotia Excelsior Cdn Blue Chip	16.7	8.2	6.4	8.5	-	
Spectrum United Cdn Equity	18.6	10.8	10.9	14.5	10.0	
Spectrum United Cdn Inv	20.2	13.6	10.9	8.6	6.2	
Spectrum United Cdn Stock	14.5	9.8	9.2	8.2	-	
SSQ - Actions Canadiennes	18.7	14.3	9.6	10.3	8.3	2.1
Standard Life Equity	18.8	13.4	12.5	-	-	
Sunfund	17.8	11.8	10.9	9.6	8.1	
Talvest Canadian Eqty Value	8.0	8.9	8.3	7.9	8.3	12.8
Talvest New Economy	16.7	15.3	-	-	-	1.8
Templeton Canadian Stock	15.8	9.4	10.8	9.7	-	5.8
Top 50 Equity	16.2	8.1	6.9	6.7	-	
Tradex Equity	31.6	20.1	16.9	14.1	10.0	
Trans-Canada Value	19.1	7.3	3.6	8.4	7.1	
Transamerica Growsafe Eqty	15.5	11.0	-	-	-	
Trimark Canadian	14.7	9.1	11.7	14.4	11.8	1.8
Trimark RSP Equity	12.2	7.8	10.7	11.9	-	1.8
Trimark Select Cdn Growth	11.9	8.6	11.4	-	-	1.8
Universal Canadian Growth	13.2	-	-	-	-	1.2
University Avenue Canadian	17.4	8.9	6.4	18.1	-	1.0
Westbury Cdn Life A	18.9	13.2	12.9	12.9	9.6	6.8
Westbury Cdn Life Eq Gth	16.0	8.8	8.8	8.5	-	6.8

Canadian Small to Mid Cap Equity Funds

Fund	1 Year	2 Year	3 Year	5 Year	10 Year	Manager Tenure (Years)
20/20 RSP Aggressive Eqty	60.4	41.1	-	-	-	2.8
All-Canadian Consumer	2.8	2.5	5.7	-	-	

Fund	1 Year	2 Year	3 Year	5 Year	10 Year	Manager Tenure (Years)
Altamira Special Growth	27.2	13.6	4.9	18.2	11.6	3.8
Atlas Cdn Emerging Gth	43.0	-	-	-	-	2.0
Atlas Cdn Emerging Value	26.7	-	-	-	-	2.0
Beutel Goodman Small Cap	40.4	-	-	-	-	
Bissett Small Capital	34.9	20.7	15.9	-	-	4.8
BPI Canadian Small Comp	49.7	32.9	21.2	23.9	-	2.3
Cambridge Growth	19.9	4.9	1.2	10.7	10.4	10.1
Cambridge Special Equity	42.5	20.2	8.1	15.9	-	
CDA Aggressive Equity	23.0	11.3	-	-	-	
CIBC Capital Appreciation	9.6	6.6	3.0	13.7	-	
Colonia Life Special Gth	64.1	34.4	24.2	-	-	3.3
CT Everest Special Equity	14.7	6.9	2.6	12.1	-	
Cundill Security	12.4	13.8	15.2	12.1	8.0	15.8
Ethical Special Equity	13.1	-	-	-	-	
Fidelity Cdn Gth Company	22.0	23.0	-	-	-	1.3
First Canadian Special Gth	27.8	17.6	6.5	-	-	
Fonds D'Investissement REA	11.4	6.7	2.7	-	-	
General Trust Growth	20.0	7.1	4.3	14.5	-	8.7
Global Strategy Cdn Small	22.7	-	-	-	-	1.8
Guardian Enterprise A	50.7	29.5	18.6	16.7	10.5	1.8
Hongkong Bank Sm Cap Gth	38.8	-	-	-	-	1.8
Hyperion Small Cap Cdn Eqty	23.2	17.9	-	-	-	
Industrial Equity	16.8	2.1	2.9	16.7	7.4	14.8
Ivy Enterprise	20.5	-	-	-	-	15.3
Laurentian Special Equity	8.1	7.7	8.2	11.2	-	1.8
Lotus Group Cdn Equity	43.4	15.8	13.0	-	-	3.2
Manulife Cabot Cdn Growth	37.9	17.7	-	-	-	
Manulife Cabot Emerg Gth	33.5	16.5	-	-	-	
Marathon Equity	52.1	48.2	33.2	43.3	18.0	2.0
Mawer New Canada	37.2	17.2	15.4	21.3	-	8.8
Metlife Mvp Growth	24.0	16.5	12.3	-	-	
Millennium Next Generation	42.0	31.9	-	-	-	2.8
Multiple Opportunities	49.5	48.8	34.3	38.4	16.7	
Mutual Premier Growth	20.3	18.3	14.3	-	-	3.8
National Trust Special Equity	27.6	13.5	6.7	-	-	3.8
Navigator Value Inv Retire	47.1	31.8	26.6	-	-	
OTGIF Growth	14.0	9.8	8.0	8.0	7.1	
Pacific Special Equity	27.9	33.5	18.0	-	-	
Quebec Growth Fund Inc.	18.5	12.3	5.3	18.8	-	
Resolute Growth	40.4	20.0	-	-	-	
Royal Canadian Growth	17.4	10.8	7.2	-	-	3.8
Royal Canadian Small Cap	15.3	9.5	6.3	-	-	
Royal Life Canadian Growth	17.8	-	-	-	-	2.0
Saxon Small Cap	13.3	9.8	7.2	13.7	6.6	10.8
Spectrum United Cdn Gth	24.3	21.9	17.7	21.6	11.3	

Canadian Resource Funds

Fund	1 Year	2 Year	3 Year	5 Year	10 Year	Manager Tenure (Years)
AGF Canadian Resources A	41.4	17.0	9.5	22.7	13.2	36.6

Fund	1 Year	2 Year	3 Year	5 Year	10 Year	Manager Tenure (Years)
AGF Canadian Resources B	40.9	-	-	-	-	1.8
AGF Canadian Resources C	40.5	-	-	-	-	1.8
All-Canadian Resources Corp.	-2.1	0.7	10.9	14.1	4.9	
Altamira Resource	25.5	6.3	4.1	26.0	-	1.8
BPI Cdn Resource Fund Inc	39.6	13.1	6.6	22.2	12.4	2.3
Cambridge Resource	91.1	32.9	16.5	30.9	12.3	10.1
CIBC Canadian Resources	8.9	-	-	-	-	
Dominion Equity Resource	33.3	3.2	-2.6	19.2	2.9	8.3
First Canadian Resource	23.5	11.2	7.1	-	-	
First Heritage	12.8	2.2	4.8	12.8	4.3	10.2
Green Line Energy	34.7	-	-	-	-	1.9
Green Line Resource	38.4	15.6	-	-	-	2.8
Maxxum Natural Resource	49.3	35.5	22.5	35.7	-	0.9
Middlefield Growth	23.1	7.7	3.1	11.1	-	5.8
Royal Energy	29.0	5.7	1.6	17.9	13.0	16.1
Standard Life Natural Res	28.6	-	-	-	-	
Universal Cdn Resource	39.1	9.3	8.2	26.4	12.4	14.8

Precious Metals Funds

Fund	1 Year	2 Year	3 Year	5 Year	10 Year	Manager Tenure (Years)
Altamira Prec & Strat Metals	39.8	27.2	-	-	-	
Dynamic Precious Metals	36.6	11.5	17.4	24.6	12.2	6.8
Friedberg Double Gold Plus	-0.7	-5.2	3.4	4.5	-	8.8
Global Strategy Gold Plus	71.9	35.4	33.1	-	-	3.1
Goldtrust	17.6	0.4	5.7	15.9	4.5	
Green Line Precious Metals	82.8	-	-	-	-	1.9
Maxxum Precious Metals	80.9	37.3	33.2	32.1	-	
Royal Precious Metals	71.9	50.7	39.1	30.6	-	
Scotia Excelsior Precious Metals	49.6	18.4	-	-	-	0.2

Canadian Labour-Sponsored Funds

Fund	1 Year	2 Year	3 Year	5 Year	10 Year	Manager Tenure (Years)
Integrated Growth	-12.6	-16.1	-	-	-	0.9
C.I. Covington	8.4	-	-	-	-	1.8
Canadian Medical Discov.	6.8	-	-	-	-	1.6
Capital Alliance Ventures	8.8	-	-	-	-	
DGC Entertainment Ventures	9.8	5.2	-	-	-	
First Ontario	1.6	-	-	-	-	
Retrocomm Growth	0.8	-	-	-	-	1.5
Sportfund	17.6	-	-	-	-	
Trillium Gth Cap Inc.	0.2	-	-	-	-	
Vengrowth Investment	3.8	-	-	-	-	1.8
Working Opportunity (EVCC)	11.0	7.5	5.7	-	-	
Working Ventures Canadian	2.3	3.9	3.4	3.4	-	6.7

Dividend Funds

Fund	1 Year	2 Year	3 Year	5 Year	10 Year	Manager Tenure (Years)
20/20 Dividend	17.0	15.2	13.1	12.2	9.9	5.8
AGF High Income A	11.9	10.4	8.2	9.1	-	12.8
AGF High Income B	11.2	-	-	-	-	2.0
AGF High Income C	11.3	-	-	-	-	2.0
Altamira Dividend	16.0	14.5	-	-	-	2.2

Fund	1 Year	2 Year	3 Year	5 Year	10 Year	Manager Tenure (Years)
Bissett Dividend Income	22.0	19.1	14.0	12.5	-	4.8
BPI Income	17.6	16.1	12.4	9.1	7.7	2.3
CIBC Dividend	15.0	10.0	6.9	8.3	-	
Concorde Dividendes	25.7	-	-	-	-	1.8
CT Everest Dividend Income	19.6	-	-	-	-	
Desjardins Dividend	15.1	13.0	-	-	-	1.8
Dynamic Dividend	14.1	12.4	8.7	10.0	8.7	6.8
Dynamic Dividend Growth	19.9	14.9	11.8	12.2	7.5	6.8
First Canadian Div Income	21.3	-	-	-	-	
Green Line Dividend	17.9	8.2	7.4	9.5	-	9.1
Guardian Monthly Dividend A	11.5	10.5	6.7	8.5	7.1	6.3
Hongkong Bank Dividend Inc	21.9	-	-	-	-	1.8
Industrial Dividend	17.1	10.7	11.6	14.5	8.1	2.1
InvesNat Dividend	12.5	11.1	8.2	-	-	4.2
Investors Dividend	14.9	10.6	8.2	8.9	8.6	11.3
Laurentian Dividend	13.2	10.2	7.9	8.2	8.1	1.8
Maritime Life Dividend Inc	12.8	-	-	-	-	1.8
Maxxum Dividend	20.3	15.4	13.6	17.2	-	0.9
MD Dividend	13.4	11.5	9.2	-	-	4.1
National Trust Dividend	18.4	9.9	8.2	-	-	3.8
NN Dividend	16.3	13.8	-	-	-	2.4
PH & N Dividend Income	21.1	15.4	13.1	12.8	10.5	19.3
Pret Et Revenu Dividendes	26.2	-	-	-	-	1.4
Royal Trust Growth & Income	22.7	14.1	10.5	9.1	6.8	
Royfund Dividend	19.8	15.0	11.7	-	-	
Scotia Excelsior Dividend	18.4	13.6	9.7	9.3	-	
Spectrum United Dividend	13.9	11.0	8.2	8.3	-	
Standard Life Cdn Dividend	24.0	-	-	-	-	
Talvest Dividend	14.4	-	-	-	-	
Trans-Canada Dividend	14.5	11.1	11.9	7.6	6.8	7.6

United States Equity Funds

Fund	1 Year	2 Year	3 Year	5 Year	10 Year	Manager Tenure (Years)
20/20 Aggressive Growth	14.5	22.9	15.3	-	-	3.3
ADMAX American Select Grth	2.3	9.1	5.9	-	-	4.9
AGF Int'l Group Amer Gth A	20.0	24.3	16.1	17.4	11.3	3.6
AGF Int'l Group Amer Gth B	19.6	-	-	-	-	3.6
AGF Int'l Group Amer Gth C	19.1	-	-	-	-	3.6
AGF Int'l Group Special A	3.8	14.8	9.4	12.8	10.9	6.8
AGF Int'l Group Special B	3.1	-	-	-	-	2.0
AGF Int'l Group Special C	3.3	-	-	-	-	2.0
AIC Value	33.8	30.7	20.2	21.8	-	
Altamira Select American	14.7	16.4	14.8	22.0	-	5.4
Altamira US Larger Company	10.9	21.7	16.4	-	-	3.2
Atlas Amer Large Cap Growth	19.5	22.1	14.7	13.2	8.7	11.0
Beutel Goodman Amer Eqty	12.8	14.1	11.4	15.6	-	1.6
Bissett American Equity	13.3	18.8	13.7	14.1	9.7	4.8
BPI American Equity Value	13.2	17.1	13.0	13.5	-	
BPI American Small Comp	15.6	21.3	16.5	23.4	-	5.4

Fund	1 Year	2 Year	3 Year	5 Year	10 Year	Manager Tenure (Years)
C.I. American	18.0	19.7	15.7	-	-	4.2
C.I. American Sector	17.5	19.1	15.4	-	-	3.9
Cambridge American Growth	-4.6	-2.4	-8.3	-	-	
Cassels Blaikie American	19.0	24.6	14.7	10.9	12.5	14.9
CCPE US Equity	12.4	15.3	-	-	-	
Century DJ	6.3	4.6	3.8	4.6	4.1	
Chou Associates	19.2	22.4	12.1	15.5	-	10.0
CIBC US Equity	20.9	17.0	12.3	13.6	-	
Co-operators US Equity	20.7	37.9	-	-	-	
Cornerstone US	18.1	18.7	13.8	14.0	7.8	
CT Everest Amerigrowth	17.5	23.3	15.9	-	-	3.8
CT Everest US Equity	10.3	14.3	7.6	10.8	-	
Dynamic Americas	32.0	20.4	12.2	13.4	10.2	1.8
Elliott & Page Amer Gth	12.8	14.9	12.8	12.9	8.7	3.5
Fidelity Growth America	8.8	21.8	13.6	20.0	-	6.1
Fidelity Small Cap America	4.3	18.5	-	-	-	2.5
First Canadian US Growth	-2.9	12.1	7.3	-	-	
Formula Growth	25.7	30.8	20.2	29.2	16.0	
General Trust US Equity	13.2	14.2	6.5	14.4	11.6	1.1
Global Strategy US Equity	15.7	-	-	-	-	1.8
Great-West Life US Eqty (G) A	11.7	-	-	-	-	
Green Line US Index	19.1	23.4	16.1	13.6	-	4.8
GT Global America Growth	7.9	-	-	-	-	2.0
Guardian American Equity A	8.4	18.3	12.8	17.0	12.1	
Hyperion Value Line US Eqty	14.8	25.7	13.8	18.7	-	
Industrial American	11.4	11.2	10.5	13.0	9.6	5.8
InvesNat Blue Chip Amer Eqty	15.0	10.9	5.4	-	-	1.1
Investors US Growth	16.1	18.2	13.3	16.8	13.0	8.9
Jones Heward American	7.5	8.0	2.7	9.5	8.7	1.4
Laurentian American Equity	13.2	14.1	11.9	13.7	9.2	
Leith Wheeler US Equity	12.7	17.1	-	-	-	2.4
London Life US Equity	16.8	13.6	9.7	11.9	-	
Manulife Vistafd 1 Amer Stock	9.2	-	-	-	-	
Manulife Vistafd 2 Amer Stock	8.4	-	-	-	-	
Margin of Safety	18.6	17.1	11.3	11.4	-	8.2
Maritime Life Amer Gth & Inc	19.3	18.5	-	-	-	2.8
Maritime Life S&P 500	17.1	-	-	-	-	1.8
Mawer US Equity	21.1	21.4	14.2	-	-	1.9
Maxxum American Equity	26.1	-	-	-	-	1.8
Mclean Budden American Gth	16.8	21.5	15.6	13.7	-	
McLean Budden Pld Amer Eqty	18.8	23.6	18.1	16.1	13.6	
MD US Equity	15.4	23.4	14.7	-	-	4.1
Metlife Mvp US Equity	20.1	20.2	11.6	-	-	
Mutual Amerifund	14.6	16.4	10.3	12.3	9.0	3.8
Mutual Premier American	13.8	15.7	9.7	-	-	3.4
NAL U.S. Equity	11.8	14.7	-	-	-	
National Trust American Eqty	16.6	16.5	9.4	-	-	
Navigator American Value	18.5	-	-	-	-	

Fund	1 Year	2 Year	3 Year	5 Year	10 Year	Manager Tenure (Years)
NN Can-Am	16.0	22.0	14.8	-	-	4.0
Optima Strategy US Equity	28.2	25.4	-	-	-	2.4
PH & N Pooled US Pension	27.2	22.0	16.8	18.8	15.0	2.8
PH & N US Equity	25.5	20.6	15.4	17.7	13.9	2.8
Pret et Revenu Americain	16.7	24.5	14.9	15.3	11.0	1.8
Prosperity American Perf	-9.5	3.2	2.4	-	-	
Royal Trust American Stock	11.6	17.4	12.8	14.5	11.8	
Royfund US Equity	12.1	18.9	13.4	-	-	
Scotia Canam Growth	17.4	23.1	-	-	-	
Scotia Excelsior Amer Gth	8.1	13.5	11.5	12.9	-	
Spectrum United Amer Eqty	25.1	26.4	16.1	14.3	11.2	0.8
Spectrum United Amer Gth	30.2	32.5	21.3	22.3	14.0	0.8
Spectrum United Optimax USA	13.7	15.9	-	-	-	
SSQ - Actions Americaines	28.5	27.5	18.7	13.4	-	2.1
Standard Life US Equity	15.0	-	-	-	-	
Top 50 US Equity	0.3	9.2	3.2	-	-	
Universal US Emerg Growth	24.1	33.9	23.1	-	-	4.8
University Avenue Growth	12.3	12.5	7.0	3.3	4.4	3.8
Zweig Strategic Growth	9.9	15.1	9.8	-	-	4.6

Specialty Funds

Fund	1 Year	2 Year	3 Year	5 Year	10 Year	Manager Tenure (Years)
20/20 Managed Futures Value	13.5	-	-	-	-	1.4
Atlas Managed Futures	-3.3	-	-	-	-	1.9
Contrarian Strategy FUT LP	-11.8	-1.9	6.7	11.1	-	
Friedberg Currency	26.2	-	-	-	-	
Goldfund Limited	10.3	-2.9	5.4	16.4	4.9	
Universal World Precious Metal	44.1	21.8	-	-	-	2.7

North American Equity Funds

Fund	1 Year	2 Year	3 Year	5 Year	10 Year	Manager Tenure (Years)
Altamira North Amer Recovery	14.5	4.6	8.5	-	-	3.2
Champion Growth	14.6	12.1	-	-	-	
Cote 100 Amerique	31.6	22.6	12.7	-	-	4.0
CT Everest North American	11.7	6.2	4.5	10.0	6.9	
Ethical North Amer Equity	12.5	21.5	12.8	13.6	8.2	
First American	-0.3	2.8	-0.1	-	-	4.8
First Canadian NAFTA Adv	15.7	-	-	-	-	2.0
GBC North American Growth	10.6	18.3	9.6	17.8	12.0	
Green Line North Amer Gth A	23.0	25.9	-	-	-	2.8
Green Line Science & Tech	16.9	40.9	-	-	-	2.8
Imperial Gth North Amer Eqty	14.2	14.6	13.2	14.8	8.9	24.8
Investors North Amer Gth	12.3	12.2	10.3	13.1	12.3	1.8
Investors Special	11.3	10.9	7.2	12.5	12.1	2.8
PH & N North American Equity	31.9	8.5	8.4	-	-	4.1
Special Opportunities	15.4	10.6	7.9	10.5	-	
Standard Life Gth Equity	17.9	-	-	-	-	

International and Global Equity Funds

Fund	1 Year	2 Year	3 Year	5 Year	10 Year	Manager Tenure (Years)
20/20 International Value	11.9	10.5	10.3	13.3	-	1.9
20/20 RSP Int'l Eqty Alloc	14.5	10.5	-	-	-	3.0

Fund	1 Year	2 Year	3 Year	5 Year	10 Year	Manager Tenure (Years)
ADMAX Global Health Science	31.7	44.6	29.9	-	-	4.8
ADMAX International	-5.2	-0.8	5.7	11.9	-	8.8
AGF Int'l Group World Eq A	7.8	-	-	-	-	1.4
AGF Int'l Group World Eq B	7.2	-	-	-	-	1.4
AGF Int'l Group World Eq C	7.2	-	-	-	-	1.4
AIC World Equity	7.7	5.2	-	-	-	
Altamira Science & Tech	26.7	-	-	-	-	1.2
Atlas Global Value	9.5	6.8	9.0	12.6	-	6.6
Azura Growth Pooled	12.2	-	-	-	-	1.3
Beutel Goodman Int'l Eqty	11.6	3.8	8.1	-	-	
Bissett Multinational Gth	23.8	21.2	-	-	-	2.2
BPI Global Equity	12.4	9.1	10.9	12.3	-	5.4
BPI Global Opportunities	13.5	-	-	-	-	1.4
BPI Global Small Companies	8.6	4.4	12.8	-	-	2.8
BPI International Equity	10.8	4.2	6.8	10.2	-	2.3
C.I. Global	11.4	5.1	6.9	12.8	9.0	6.0
C.I. Global Equity RSP	10.4	5.6	5.1	-	-	3.2
C.I. Global sector	10.9	4.6	6.6	12.5	-	6.0
Cambridge Americas	45.3	20.3	11.2	14.4	-	2.5
Cambridge Global	37.7	10.7	7.4	12.4	8.5	10.1
Canada Life US & Int'l	15.6	15.0	13.7	16.4	13.3	
Capstone Int'l Invest Trust	21.2	10.6	10.9	13.7	-	
CCPE Global Equity	6.2	-	-	-	-	
CDA International Equity	10.6	-	-	-	-	1.8
CIBC Global Equity	10.2	6.3	5.9	10.5	-	
Clean Environment Int'l Eq	13.6	8.5	-	-	-	
Concorde International	9.6	-	-	-	-	1.4
Cornerstone Global	14.6	12.5	11.7	13.7	11.3	
CT Everest International	12.6	3.3	5.1	8.0	-	
Cundill Value	11.9	11.7	12.7	15.9	11.8	21.8
Desjardins International	10.8	8.6	9.1	13.7	10.5	1.8
Dynamic Global Millennia	37.4	16.2	6.9	9.7	-	6.8
Dynamic Global Resource	66.4	-	-	-	-	1.4
Dynamic International	18.3	10.6	9.9	13.3	6.1	10.8
Elliott & Page Global Eqty	12.1	10.0	-	-	-	2.3
Empire International Gth	11.8	9.2	9.6	12.5	-	3.8
Equitable Life Int'l	14.8	-	-	-	-	
Fidelity Int'l Portfolio	12.7	11.9	10.2	14.4	-	2.6
First Canadian Int'l Gth	9.8	5.6	7.5	-	-	4.2
Fonds Professional Int'l Eqty	14.6	11.5	9.1	-	-	
GBC International Growth	4.7	-1.6	-0.4	3.6	-	
General Trust Int'l	7.3	3.4	5.3	9.5	-	1.1
Global Strategy Divers World	10.5	-	-	-	-	1.8
Global Strategy World Emerg	24.3	-	-	-	-	1.8
Global Strategy World Eqty	12.2	-	-	-	-	
Great-West Life Int'l Eqty (P) A	11.0	-	-	-	-	1.9
Green Line Global Select	15.9	11.1	-	-	-	2.8
Green Line Int'l Equity	11.1	4.5	6.9	-	-	3.8

Fund	1 Year	2 Year	3 Year	5 Year	10 Year	Manager Tenure (Years)
Greystone Managed Global	15.8	13.3	-	-	-	
GT Global Gbl Infrastructure	20.4	-	-	-	-	2.0
GT Global Gbl Nat Resourcs	45.0	-	-	-	-	2.0
GT Global Gbl Telecomm	9.3	-	-	-	-	2.0
Guardian Global Equity A	13.5	10.1	11.4	10.3	5.4	6.8
Hongkong Bank Americas	18.4	-	-	-	-	1.9
HRL Overseas Growth	11.0	4.9	6.8	-	-	0.3
Hyperion Global Sci & Tech	18.7	19.1	13.6	14.3	12.0	4.8
Investors Global	12.2	11.5	10.5	11.7	-	1.8
Investors Growth Portfolio	14.1	12.6	10.8	13.6	-	7.7
Investors World Gth Port	8.7	7.1	7.8	-	-	3.8
Ivy Foreign Equity	10.0	13.9	11.5	-	-	4.0
Laurentian Commonwealth	6.9	5.5	6.3	10.2	8.9	2.0
Laurentian International	7.2	5.7	6.7	11.0	8.1	2.0
London Life Int'l Equity	7.9	-	-	-	-	
Lotus International Equity	2.6	-	-	-	-	1.3
Mackenzie Sentinel Global	7.3	5.0	7.7	10.1	-	
Manulife Cabot Global Eqty	7.8	10.0	-	-	-	
Manulife Vistafd 1 Global Eqty	10.0	-	-	-	-	
Manulife Vistafd 2 Global Eqty	9.2	-	-	-	-	
Maritime Life Gbl Equities	6.0	-	-	-	-	1.8
Mawer World Investment	13.0	6.5	10.4	12.5	-	8.9
Maxxum Global Equity	7.1	-	-	-	-	1.8
McLean Budden Pld Offsh Eqty	12.1	3.8	7.3	11.1	-	
MD Growth Investments	13.8	11.7	12.8	16.6	11.7	
Mutual Premier Int'l	11.4	8.2	9.4	-	-	3.4
NAL-Global Equity	5.6	5.3	8.3	-	-	
National Global Equities	14.2	9.1	9.1	13.6	-	3.0
National Trust Int'l Equity	10.7	6.3	-	-	-	2.3
O.I.Q. Ferique International	11.2	5.5	-	-	-	2.8
OHA Foreign Equity	8.9	14.5	14.8	-	-	2.8
Optima Strategy Int'l Equity	20.6	13.8	-	-	-	2.4
Optimum International	6.2	11.6	-	-	-	2.1
Orbit World	0.8	-4.5	2.0	5.7	-	1.0
OTGIF Global	12.1	10.9	9.5	10.9	-	5.8
PH & N Int'l Equity	11.2	8.1	-	-	-	2.6
Pret Et Revenu Int'l	12.0	-	-	-	-	1.8
Pursuit Global Equity	14.2	-	-	-	-	1.2
Royal International Equity	10.4	8.1	9.2	-	-	
Royal Life Int'l Equity	10.8	-	-	-	-	2.0
Royal Life Science & Tech	17.2	-	-	-	-	1.3
Saxon World Growth	9.5	16.7	15.6	19.2	12.9	
Sceptre International	11.8	5.3	10.7	18.1	-	9.9
Scotia Excelsior International	7.8	6.8	7.2	11.9	8.2	
Spectrum United Gbl Telecom	3.0	16.2	-	-	-	
Spectrum United Gbl Eqty	15.1	7.7	6.9	9.7	-	
Spectrum United Global Gth	-1.3	-2.7	-0.1	9.8	3.3	
Standard Life Int'l Equity	10.5	-	-	-	-	

Fund	1 Year	2 Year	3 Year	5 Year	10 Year	Manager Tenure (Years)
Talvest Global RRSP	12.2	4.5	5.6	-	-	1.8
Templeton Global Small Cos	9.4	13.0	12.0	16.0	-	1.8
Templeton Growth	9.3	10.6	11.9	17.0	12.4	9.8
Templeton Int'l Stock	14.1	10.8	13.7	19.1	-	7.8
Trimark Americas	16.4	5.9	9.4		-	2.8
Trimark Fund	9.5	14.4	15.9	21.1	15.0	2.8
Trimark Select Growth	8.8	12.9	14.2	19.2	-	2.8
Universal Americas	14.4	1.7	7.1	11.8	9.3	4.8
Universal Growth	5.2	-	-	-	-	1.5
Universal World Equity	8.0	5.5	8.5	11.0	7.6	1.8
Universal World Gth RRSP	15.0	10.1	-	-	-	2.1

Emerging Markets Funds

Fund	1 Year	2 Year	3 Year	5 Year	10 Year	Manager Tenure (Years)
20/20 Emerging Mkts Value	-2.0	-13.5	-	-	-	0.5
AIC Emerging Markets	8.8	-6.9	-	-	-	
Altamira Global Discovery	6.0	-6.0	-	-	-	2.2
C.I. Emerging Markets	3.2	-12.9	1.0	9.2	-	5.1
C.I. Emerging Mkts Sector	2.8	-13.1	0.8	-	-	3.8
CDA Emerging Markets	2.5	-	-	-	-	1.8
CT Everest Emerging Market	6.4	-	-	-	-	
Elliott & Page Emerg Mkt	-1.0	-9.1	-	-	-	2.3
Fidelity Emerg Mkts Ptl	20.3	-	-	-	-	0.4
First Canadian Emerg Mkt	2.0	-	-	-	-	2.0
GFM Emerging Mkts Country	2.3	-	-	-	-	1.4
Globeinvest Emerg Mkt Ctry	4.8	-	-	-	-	1.3
Green Line Emerging Mkts	4.0	-9.1	4.5	-	-	3.9
Guardian Emerging Mkt A	11.9	6.9	-	-	-	2.3
Hongkong Bank Emerging Mkt	1.9	-	-	-	-	1.8
Laurentian Emerging Market	2.7	-	-	-	-	1.8
MD Emerging Markets	6.0	-	-	-	-	1.9
Mutual Premier Emerging Mk	3.8	-	-	-	-	
National Trust Emerg Mkts.	6.3	-13.1	-	-	-	2.3
Spectrum United Emerg Mkts	23.0	2.4	-	-	-	
Templeton Emerging Markets	11.1	-0.2	6.7	13.1	-	5.1
Tradex Emerg Mkts Country	4.9	-	-	-	-	1.8
Universal World Emerg Gth	13.1	-2.9	-	-	-	2.9

Asia and Pacific Rim Funds

Fund	1 Year	2 Year	3 Year	5 Year	10 Year	Manager Tenure (Years)
20/20 Asia Pacific	5.6	-4.0	3.3	-	-	0.3
20/20 India	-33.8	-	-	-	-	
ADMAX Dragon 888	-4.9	-8.3	-	-	-	2.5
ADMAX Korea	-29.2	-15.9	-2.0	0.2	-	
ADMAX Tiger	-16.4	-14.6	-2.3	7.6	-	6.3
AGF Int'l Group Asian Gth A	4.5	2.1	12.7	-	-	2.8
AGF Int'l Group Asian Gth B	4.0	-	-	-	-	2.0
AGF Int'l Group Asian Gth C	4.0	-	-	-	-	2.0
AGF Int'l Group China Focus A	-1.1	-5.2	-	-	-	2.5
AGF Int'l Group China Focus B	-1.6	-5.7	-	-	-	2.5
AGF Int'l Group China Focus C	-1.5	-5.7	-	-	-	2.5

Fund	1 Year	2 Year	3 Year	5 Year	10 Year	Manager Tenure (Years)
Altamira Asia Pacific	-16.8	-15.7	-3.4	-	-	4.3
Apex Asian Pacific	5.1	2.4	-	-	-	
Atlas Pacific Basin Value	-3.4	-6.8	-	-	-	2.8
C.I. Pacific	8.3	-2.1	6.4	14.8	10.3	6.0
C.I. Pacific Sector	7.9	-2.5	6.1	14.3	-	6.0
Cambridge China	-3.5	-0.6	-	-	-	2.4
Cambridge Pacific	10.7	-4.5	-	7.1	-3.5	7.4
CDA Pacific Basin	10.0	-	-	-	-	1.8
CIBC Far East Prosperity	11.0	-1.1	6.1	-	-	
CT Everest Asiagrowth	9.3	1.8	-	-	-	2.8
Dynamic Far East	10.5	6.9	-	-	-	2.4
Elliott & Page Asian Gth	4.6	3.7	-	-	-	
Ethical Pacific Rim	10.6	-	-	-	-	
Fidelity Far East	18.8	10.1	14.2	23.8	-	5.1
First Canadian FarEast Gth	10.7	-	-	-	-	2.0
Global Strategy Asia	9.6	-0.3	7.7	-	-	3.1
Global Strategy Divers Asia	5.5	-3.2	-	-	-	2.7
Green Line Asian Growth	6.6	0.5	-	-	-	2.8
GT Global Pacific Growth	18.7	-	-	-	-	2.0
Guardian Asia Pacific A	3.9	3.7	-	-	-	2.3
Hansberger Asian	2.9	-5.8	-0.3	-	-	0.4
Hansberger Asian Sector	2.4	-6.0	-	-	-	0.4
Hongkong Bank Asian Growth	7.8	3.3	-	-	-	2.9
Hyperion Asian	13.6	-1.1	8.0	19.2	-	8.4
InvesNat Far East Equity	16.8	9.1	-	-	-	2.2
Investors Pacific Int'l	5.0	0.3	9.8	18.3	-	5.9
Laurentian Asia Pacific	2.5	-	-	-	-	1.8
Maritime Life Pacific Basin	8.1	-1.2	-	-	-	2.8
Navigator Asia Pacific	9.2	-	-	-	-	
NN Can-Asian	19.6	7.6	8.1	-	-	3.1
Royal Asian Growth	10.4	1.1	7.1	-	-	
Sceptre Asian Growth	6.3	-3.1	8.9	-	-	1.3
Scotia Excelsior Pacific Rim	2.9	-	-	-	-	
Spectrum United Asian Dyn	5.6	-0.5	-	-	-	18.8
Trimark Indo-Pacific	13.4	7.3	-	-	-	2.1
Universal Far East	9.1	-1.1	-	-	-	2.9

Japanese Equity Funds

Fund	1 Year	2 Year	3 Year	5 Year	10 Year	Manager Tenure (Years)
ADMAX Nippon	12.8	4.1	1.6	-	-	4.3
AGF Int'l Group Japan A	4.0	-5.3	-3.3	2.4	2.7	2.8
AGF Int'l Group Japan B	3.7	-	-	-	-	2.0
AGF Int'l Group Japan C	3.4	-	-	-	-	2.0
Altamira Japanese Opp	7.1	-4.7	-	-	-	2.2
CIBC Japanese Equity	3.0	-	-	-	-	
Fidelity Japanese Growth	-1.7	-7.0	-3.8	-	-	3.3
First Canadian Japan Gth	-1.1	-	-	-	-	2.0
Global Strategy Divers Jap	-1.6	-6.0	-	-	-	2.5
Global Strategy Japan	-3.6	-	-	-	-	1.8

Fund	1 Year	2 Year	3 Year	5 Year	10 Year	Manager Tenure (Years)
Green Line Japanese Growth	2.9	-	-	-	-	1.9
InvesNat Japanese Equity	0.8	-5.0	-	-	-	0.5
Investors Japanese Growth	-1.4	-5.1	-2.1	6.2	4.0	2.8
Royal Japanese Stock	-4.8	-9.9	-4.8	2.2	0.7	
Universal Japan	-1.8	-5.4	-	-	-	2.5

European Equity Funds

Fund	1 Year	2 Year	3 Year	5 Year	10 Year	Manager Tenure (Years)
ADMAX Europa Performance	9.3	7.8	6.3	-	-	4.8
AGF Int'l Group Germany A	18.1	-	-	-	-	1.8
AGF Int'l Group Germany B	17.2	-	-	-	-	1.8
AGF Int'l Group Germany C	17.2	-	-	-	-	1.8
AGF Int'l group Germany M	18.9	-	-	-	-	1.8
AGF Int'l Group Euro Gth A	16.7	12.5	-	-	-	2.5
AGF Int'l Group Euro Gth B	16.5	12.0	-	-	-	2.5
AGF Int'l Group Euro Gth C	16.4	12.1	-	-	-	2.5
Altamira European Equity	14.2	13.6	12.6	-	-	3.2
Atlas European Value	16.6	14.6	-	-	-	2.8
CDA European	14.2	-	-	-	-	1.8
CT Everest Eurogrowth	17.5	12.5	-	-	-	
Dynamic Europe	15.6	14.7	13.3	11.0	-	
Fidelity European Growth	14.7	16.0	14.7	-	-	4.3
First Canadian Europe Gth	13.2	-	-	-	-	2.0
Global Strategy Divers Euro	14.9	12.4	8.0	-	-	3.8
Global Strategy Euro Plus	16.7	-	-	-	-	1.8
Green Line European Growth	22.4	-	-	-	-	1.9
Hansberger European	11.4	7.5	5.5	5.9	-	0.4
Hansberger European Sector	10.9	7.1	5.4	-	-	0.4
Hongkong Bank European Gth	15.7	-	-	-	-	1.9
Hyperion European	12.0	12.1	10.1	12.1	-	
InvesNat European Equity	13.4	12.1	11.9	-	-	0.9
Investors European Growth	14.2	13.9	11.8	11.7	-	6.1
Laurentian Europe	12.1	-	-	-	-	1.8
NN Can-Euro	17.9	-	-	-	-	1.3
Royal European Growth	13.7	12.1	12.8	13.1	-	
Spectrum United European Gth	21.8	-	-	-	-	
Universal Euro Opportunity	29.9	27.6	-	-	-	2.1
Vision Europe	15.9	16.1	12.8	-	-	4.8

Latin American Equity Funds

Fund	1 Year	2 Year	3 Year	5 Year	10 Year	Manager Tenure (Years)
20/20 Latin America	8.2	-8.1	-	-	-	2.7
Atlas Latin American Value	24.7	-13.2	-	-	-	2.8
C.I. Latin American	14.5	-11.8	1.1	-	-	3.1
C.I. Latin American Sector	14.3	-11.7	-	-	-	2.3
Fidelity Latin Amer Growth	21.2	-14.1	-	-	-	2.8
Global Strategy Divers Latin	16.3	-9.5	-	-	-	2.5
Global Strategy Latin Amer	10.6	-5.1	-	-	-	2.5
Green Line Latin Amer Gth	12.0	-	-	-	-	1.9
GT Global Latin Amer Gth	26.2	-	-	-	-	2.0
Navigator Latin America	35.6	-	-	-	-	

Fund	1 Year	2 Year	3 Year	5 Year	10 Year	Manager Tenure (Years)
Royal Latin American	11.2	-	-	-	-	
Scotia Excelsior Latin American	32.2	-	-	-	-	

Canadian Bond Funds

Fund	1 Year	2 Year	3 Year	5 Year	10 Year	Manager Tenure (Years)
20/20 Income	8.3	9.7	5.5	8.2	7.9	0.3
Acadia Bond	6.8	-	-	-	-	1.8
AGF Canadian Bond A	11.4	12.9	7.1	10.4	9.6	34.2
AGF Canadian Bond B	10.8	-	-	-	-	2.0
AGF Canadian Bond C	10.8	-	-	-	-	2.0
Altamira Bond	11.1	16.2	8.0	11.6	-	5.8
Altamira Income	8.0	12.6	7.3	11.2	11.5	9.1
AMI Private Capital Income	10.9	11.5	7.2	9.6	-	8.8
Apex Fixed Income	9.8	10.5	-	-	-	
Atlas Canadian Bond	10.5	11.4	6.8	9.2	8.8	11.8
Atlas Cdn High Yield Bond	12.4	-	-	-	-	2.0
Batirente Sec Obligations	12.8	14.3	9.1	11.5	-	8.8
Beutel Goodman Income	11.4	13.1	7.5	10.0	-	1.8
Bissett Bond	12.7	13.4	8.8	9.9	9.9	10.1
BNP (Canada) Bond	10.8	11.8	7.3	9.3	-	
BPI Canadian Bond	4.4	5.9	3.3	6.6	-	2.3
BPI Income	17.6	16.1	12.4	9.1	7.7	2.3
C.I. Canadian Bond	13.7	13.5	8.3	-	-	3.8
Canada Life Fixed Income	9.9	11.1	6.5	8.8	8.7	
CCPE Fixed Income	11.0	12.0	7.5	10.1	9.1	2.0
CIBC Canadian Bond	10.8	12.2	6.2	8.9	-	
Clean Environment Income	6.8	5.2	-	-	-	
Co-operators Fixed Income	11.2	13.1	7.9	-	-	4.8
Colonia Life Bond	8.5	10.2	7.0	-	-	
Concorde Revenu	9.0	10.4	6.5	-	-	1.8
Confed Fixed Income	9.5	11.1	6.8	8.8	9.5	
Confed Life C	9.8	11.5	7.1	9.3	10.0	7.2
Cornerstone Bond	9.8	11.5	7.3	9.1	-	
CT Everest Bond	9.6	11.5	6.8	9.1	-	
Desjardins Bond	12.6	13.4	8.5	10.8	11.1	12.8
Desjardins Obligations	10.5	11.8	7.2	9.2	8.8	7.8
Dynamic Income	8.1	10.4	8.4	10.0	10.1	17.2
Elliott & Page Bond	8.5	8.9	4.5	7.1	-	
Empire Bond	9.3	10.6	6.5	8.3	8.5	4.8
Empire Group Bond	12.2	13.2	9.4	11.3	10.9	4.8
Equitable Life Cdn Bond	10.6	10.7	6.6	-	-	
Equitable Life Accum	12.3	12.8	8.2	10.4	10.5	
Ethical Income	10.9	12.9	7.5	8.6	8.6	
Ficadre Obligations	9.8	11.3	7.0	8.4	-	
Fidelity Canadian Bond	10.6	9.3	5.4	8.6	-	4.1
First Canadian Bond	11.1	12.4	7.6	9.6	-	
Fonds Professionals Bond	10.0	11.1	7.2	9.1	9.4	
GBC Canadian Bond	11.7	12.8	8.1	10.3	10.2	
General Trust Bond	11.6	11.8	6.6	9.4	9.0	1.9

Fund	1 Year	2 Year	3 Year	5 Year	10 Year	Manager Tenure (Years)
Great-West Life Cdn Bd (G) A	9.5	10.4	6.1	8.4	8.5	5.8
Great-West Life Gov't Bd (G) A	9.1	-	-	-	-	1.9
Great-West Life Income (G) A	13.2	-	-	-	-	1.9
Green Line Canadian Bond	13.1	14.1	9.0	10.5	-	8.7
Green Line Cdn Gov't Bond	11.2	12.4	8.0	9.1	-	3.8
Green Line Real Return Bond	8.0	-	-	-	-	1.9
Hongkong Bank Cdn Bond	11.0	-	-	-	-	1.8
HRL Bond	11.1	11.6	7.0	8.9	-	0.3
Hyperion High Yield Bond	10.9	13.1	6.5	9.1	-	1.8
Ideal Bond	9.8	11.4	6.9	9.4	-	9.7
Industrial Alliance Bonds	10.5	11.5	7.0	8.8	9.5	19.4
Industrial Alliance Ecoflex B	9.9	10.9	6.4	-	-	3.8
Industrial Bond	11.6	12.9	6.7	9.4	-	7.8
InvesNat Canadian Bond	10.9	10.7	6.8	-	-	1.9
Investors Corporate Bond	11.2	11.0	-	-	-	1.8
Investors Government Bond	10.8	12.2	7.6	9.2	9.4	12.6
Investors Income Portfolio	9.9	10.8	7.0	8.2	-	7.7
Jones Heward Bond	10.1	11.3	6.4	8.4	-	0.3
Laurentian Income	9.7	10.7	6.7	8.4	8.8	7.8
Leith Wheeler Fixed Income	10.8	11.7	-	-	-	
London Life Bond	11.0	12.2	7.1	9.1	8.1	5.2
Lotus Group Bond	12.1	12.3	-	-	-	2.7
Manulife Cabot Divers Bond	7.5	8.7	-	-	-	
Manulife Vistafnd 1 Bond	6.9	9.6	4.4	8.5	9.2	
Manulife Vistafnd 2 Bond	6.1	8.8	3.6	7.6	8.4	
Maritime Life Bond	9.8	10.7	6.5	8.8	-	2.8
Mawer Canadian Bond	11.8	12.4	7.9	-	-	3.6
Maxxum Income	9.5	12.6	7.4	9.0	9.5	9.1
Mclean Budden Fixed Income	11.7	13.0	7.8	9.9	-	
McLean Budden Pld Fxd Inc	13.2	14.5	9.3	11.3	11.1	
MD Bond	11.8	12.6	8.3	10.4	-	8.8
Metlife Mvp Bond	6.3	9.3	5.0	7.4	-	
Mutual Bond	9.2	10.4	6.3	8.6	-	3.8
Mutual Life 2	12.4	12.3	8.8	9.8	10.1	3.8
Mutual Premier Bond	9.6	10.8	6.5	-	-	3.8
NAL Canadian Bond	9.5	11.5	7.4	9.2	-	
National Fixed Income	10.5	11.5	7.3	9.4	9.3	
National Trust Cdn Bond	11.2	12.7	7.9	9.6	9.3	8.8
Navigator Canadian Income	12.6	11.8	-	-	-	
NN Bond	11.8	12.8	7.9	9.5	-	4.3
O.I.Q. Ferique Obligations	11.5	12.4	8.1	10.4	10.0	
OHA Bond	11.7	12.8	7.6	9.9	-	5.8
Optima Strategy Cdn Fxd Inc	11.3	13.0	8.0	-	-	3.3
Optimum Obligations	12.4	14.1	8.7	11.4	10.3	10.4
PH & N Bond	12.2	13.2	8.9	10.9	11.1	6.2
Pret Et Revenu Obligations	9.7	11.4	7.4	9.5	-	1.4
Pursuit Canadian Bond	5.6	5.9	4.3	7.2	-	10.0
Royal Life Income	10.5	11.9	6.7	8.7	-	6.8

Fund	1 Year	2 Year	3 Year	5 Year	10 Year	Manager Tenure (Years)
Royal Trust Bond	9.9	11.6	7.0	9.4	9.3	
Royfund Bond	9.6	11.3	7.1	9.3	9.3	
Sceptre Bond	10.6	11.6	7.5	9.4	9.8	0.6
Scotia Excelsior Income	10.2	12.3	8.1	9.0	-	
Spectrum United L-T Bond	10.0	12.3	6.4	9.6	-	
Spectrum United M-T Bond	10.1	11.7	6.6	9.1	-	
SSQ - Obligations	13.3	13.6	9.4	11.1	11.4	1.8
Standard Life Bond	10.7	12.0	7.5	-	-	
Talvest Bond	10.4	11.6	7.3	9.3	9.7	11.8
Templeton Canadian Bond	8.9	8.1	5.0	7.5	-	6.8
Top 50 T-Bill Bond	9.0	7.0	1.3	3.8	-	
Tradex Bond	10.7	11.0	5.7	7.7	-	1.4
Trans-Canada Bond	5.5	7.7	5.3	6.2	-	1.5
Transamerica Growsafe Bond	7.3	8.2	-	-	-	
Trimark Advantage Bond	13.7	-	-	-	-	1.8
Trimark Canadian Bond	12.4	-	-	-	-	1.8
University Avenue Bond	9.0	12.0	8.2	-	-	3.6
Westbury Cdn Life B	11.4	12.5	7.9	9.4	8.7	6.8
Westbury Cdn Life Bond	8.8	9.8	5.9	8.2	-	2.8

Canadian Short Term Bond Funds

Fund	1 Year	2 Year	3 Year	5 Year	10 Year	Manager Tenure (Years)
Altamira S-T Gov't Bond	8.1	10.9	-	-	-	2.2
CIBC Cdn Short-Term Bond	9.8	10.6	7.0	-	-	
Dynamic Government Income	11.1	10.6	-	-	-	2.8
Empire Fgn Curr Cdn Bond	2.4	2.0	-	-	-	2.3
Fidelity Canadian Income	10.0	-	-	-	-	1.8
Global Strategy Bond	9.1	8.9	-	-	-	2.7
Green Line Short Term Inc	8.8	8.6	6.4	6.5	-	7.8
Guardian Canadian Income A	8.0	8.6	-	-	-	2.3
InvesNat S-T Gov't Bond	10.3	9.7	6.7	8.1	-	1.9
Laurentian Government Bond	8.4	8.5	6.1	7.4	-	7.8
Mawer Canadian Income	13.7	12.2	8.2	-	-	3.6
MD Bond & Mortgage	8.5	-	-	-	-	1.1
Optima Strategy Short Term	8.4	8.1	6.3	-	-	3.5
PH & N S-T Bond & Mortgage	10.8	11.0	-	-	-	2.8
Scotia Excelsior Defensive Inc	9.0	9.4	6.8	8.0	-	
Talvest Income	10.5	9.9	7.2	8.4	9.0	11.8
Trimark Government Income	9.2	9.6	-	-	-	2.9

Canadian Mortgage Funds

Fund	1 Year	2 Year	3 Year	5 Year	10 Year	Manager Tenure (Years)
Acadia Mortgage	3.7	-	-	-	-	1.8
Apex Mortgage	7.4	-	-	-	-	
CIBC Mortgage	9.9	9.6	7.6	8.9	9.6	
Colonia Life Mortgage	8.3	9.0	6.8	-	-	4.3
Concorde Hypotheques	7.0	7.4	5.9	7.7	-	1.8
CT Everest Mortgage	7.4	8.2	7.1	8.1	9.1	
Desjardins Hypotheque	7.9	8.6	6.9	7.7	9.0	7.8
Desjardins Mortgage	9.4	9.7	7.5	8.2	9.7	7.8
Equit Life Mortgage	7.3	-	-	-	-	

Fund	1 Year	2 Year	3 Year	5 Year	10 Year	Manager Tenure (Years)
Ficadre Hypotheques	6.7	-	-	-	-	
First Canadian Mortgage	9.7	9.8	7.6	8.9	9.9	
General Trust Mortgage	6.5	6.8	6.2	7.5	8.7	1.9
Great-West Life Mtg (G) A	9.1	9.6	6.2	8.1	8.7	9.8
Green Line Mortgage-Backed	8.2	8.5	6.4	7.5	-	7.8
Green Line Mortgage	7.9	8.5	6.6	8.2	9.5	9.8
Hongkong Bank Mortgage	10.4	10.2	9.6	-	-	3.8
Industrial Alliance Ecoflex H	7.3	7.5	5.9	-	-	3.8
Industrial Alliance Mortgages	7.9	8.0	6.5	7.5	9.1	19.4
Industrial Mtge Securities	11.6	9.4	6.4	9.2	9.8	14.5
InvesNat Mortgage	8.8	8.9	7.5	8.7	-	5.2
Investors Mortgage	8.3	8.9	6.2	7.2	8.5	10.0
Ivy Mortgage	9.9	9.4	-	-	-	2.7
London Life Mortgage	8.3	8.8	6.8	8.6	9.3	
Mutual Premier Mortgage	8.5	8.9	6.8	-	-	3.4
National Trust Mortgage	9.2	9.2	6.9	-	-	3.8
OTGIF Mortgage Income	9.9	9.7	8.1	9.0	9.4	21.8
Pret et Revenu Hypotheque	8.0	8.2	6.2	7.8	8.8	1.4
Royal Trust Mortgage	8.0	8.3	5.9	7.0	8.6	
Royfund Mortgage	9.1	8.8	7.4	-	-	
Scotia Excelsior Mortgage	9.6	10.0	7.9	-	-	
Spectrum United S-T Bd	8.8	9.3	6.3	7.0	7.8	0.8
SSQ - Hypotheques	10.0	10.0	8.5	9.3	-	5.6

U.S. & International Bond Funds

Fund	1 Year	2 Year	3 Year	5 Year	10 Year	Manager Tenure (Years)
20/20 Foreign RSP Bond	5.4	8.4	2.9	-	-	0.3
20/20 US S-T High Yield	8.4	7.2	-	-	-	2.3
20/20 World Bond	6.4	9.9	3.0	-	-	0.3
ADMAX World Income	11.9	9.1	6.7	-	-	4.8
AGF Global Gov't Bond A	9.2	9.7	5.3	9.5	-	10.0
AGF Global Gov't Bond B	8.6	-	-	-	-	2.0
AGF Global Gov't Bond C	8.4	-	-	-	-	2.0
AGF RSP Global Income A	5.9	7.1	4.3	-	-	3.1
AGF RSP Global Income B	5.1	-	-	-	-	2.0
AGF RSP Global Income C	5.4	-	-	-	-	2.0
AGF US Income A	3.8	6.1	1.0	-	-	3.8
AGF US Income B	3.3	-	-	-	-	2.0
AGF US Income C	3.3	-	-	-	-	2.0
Altamira Global Bond	7.5	10.2	4.6	-	-	2.8
Altamira Spec High Yield B	14.8	-	-	-	-	1.2
Atlas World Bond	11.3	11.9	-	-	-	2.5
BPI Global RSP Bond	11.0	-	-	-	-	1.4
C.I. Global Bond RSP	10.4	12.1	6.6	-	-	
C.I. New World Income	23.7	12.0	-	-	-	
C.I. World Bond	10.0	10.7	6.3	-	-	
Canada Life Int'l Bond	6.4	9.9	-	-	-	
CIBC Global Bond	6.7	-	-	-	-	
CT Everest Int'l Bond	6.0	-	-	-	-	

Fund	1 Year	2 Year	3 Year	5 Year	10 Year	Manager Tenure (Years)
Dynamic Global Bond	7.1	13.1	8.0	12.0	-	8.3
Elliott & Page Global Bond	5.5	9.6	-	-	-	2.3
Ethical Global Bond	6.8	-	-	-	-	
Fidelity Emerging Mkts Bnd	37.3	14.0	-	-	-	1.3
Fidelity North Amer Income	6.8	-0.3	0.6	-	-	3.8
Fidelity RSP Global Bond	3.5	6.9	-	-	-	2.6
First Canadian Int'l Bond	6.8	11.4	7.5	-	-	3.2
Global Strategy Divers Bond	9.7	9.9	3.9	8.5	-	4.8
Global Strategy Divers Fgn Bnd	9.1	8.2	-	-	-	2.1
Global Strategy World Bond	9.5	9.7	3.5	8.6	-	4.8
Great-West Life Int'l Bnd (P) A	6.9	-	-	-	-	0.8
Green Line Global Gov't Bnd	5.3	8.8	5.4	-	-	3.9
Green Line Global RSP Bond	7.9	10.5	-	-	-	2.8
GT World Bond	16.2	-	-	-	-	2.0
Guardian Foreign Income A	10.4	10.8	-	-	-	2.3
Guardian Int'l Income A	10.3	11.6	5.4	10.6	-	3.1
Hongkong Bank Global Bond	5.4	-	-	-	-	1.9
InvesNat Int'l RSP Bond	6.3	-	-	-	-	1.8
Investors Global Bond	4.1	7.2	3.7	-	-	4.1
Lotus Group Int'l Bond	-1.6	7.1	-	-	-	2.6
Manulife Vistafd 1 Gbl Bond	5.5	-	-	-	-	
Manulife Vistafd 2 Gbl Bond	4.7	-	-	-	-	
MD Global Bond	5.2	-	-	-	-	1.9
National Trust Int'l RSP Bo	9.5	11.2	-	-	-	2.3
Optima Strategy Gbl Fxd Inc	8.5	10.2	-	-	-	2.4
Pret Et Revenu Mond Oblig	0.8	-	-	-	-	1.4
Pursuit Global Bond	4.8	-	-	-	-	1.2
Royal Trust Int'l Bond	5.3	9.2	4.6	-	-	
Royfund Int'l Income	5.2	8.8	5.2	-	-	
Scotia Canam Income	2.8	7.4	3.3	-	-	
Scotia Excelsior Global Bond	4.2	-	-	-	-	
Spectrum United Global Bond	5.4	10.2	-	-	-	
Spectrum United RSP Int'l Bnd	3.4	9.1	4.9	-	-	
Standard Life Int'l Bond	2.2	-	-	-	-	
Talvest Fgn Pay Cdn Bond	6.2	9.8	4.7	-	-	3.8
Templeton Global Bond	9.8	9.7	5.5	9.2	-	6.8
Universal World Inc RRSP	10.5	10.1	-	-	-	2.1
Universal World Tactical Bnd	7.5	-	-	-	-	1.9

Canadian Balanced Funds

Fund	1 Year	2 Year	3 Year	5 Year	10 Year	Manager Tenure (Years)
Acadia Balanced	6.4	-	-	-	-	1.8
ABC Fully-Managed	20.4	13.4	14.4	18.1	-	8.7
AGF Growth & Income A	30.8	17.8	14.7	13.9	9.8	12.8
AGF Growth & Income B	30.2	-	-	-	-	2.0
AGF Growth & Income C	30.3	-	-	-	-	2.0
Altamira Balanced	7.2	6.4	4.5	10.3	5.5	2.3
Altamira Growth & Income	9.5	1.4	7.1	10.2	10.3	8.8
AMI Private Cap Optimix	16.8	12.7	9.6	10.1	-	8.8

Fund	1 Year	2 Year	3 Year	5 Year	10 Year	Manager Tenure (Years)
Asset Builder I	11.9	12.0	-	-	-	
Asset Builder II	12.2	11.9	-	-	-	
Asset Builder III	13.1	11.7	-	-	-	
Asset Builder IV	12.7	11.2	-	-	-	
Asset Builder V	12.9	11.4	-	-	-	
Atlas Canadian Balanced	14.2	13.6	9.7	9.3	-	7.2
Azura Conservative Pooled	8.2	-	-	-	-	1.3
Batirente Sec Diversifee	13.2	13.3	8.7	10.1	-	
Beutel Goodman Balanced	12.0	9.4	9.5	9.8	-	5.6
Bissett Retirement	18.7	16.7	11.8	13.0	-	5.2
BPI Canadian Balanced	11.2	8.2	5.4	9.3	-	2.3
C.I. Canadian Balanced	10.0	8.8	9.9	-	-	3.8
C.I. Canadian Income	13.8	-	-	-	-	2.0
Caldwell Securities Assoc	15.9	11.6	16.4	11.5	-	6.0
Cambridge Balanced	15.6	4.4	1.9	10.1	9.1	10.1
Canada Life Managed	13.6	12.4	8.8	10.5	9.0	
Capstone Invest. Trust	18.8	12.1	9.3	9.7	7.6	
Cassels Blaikie Canadian	14.3	12.8	10.0	10.4	9.3	12.3
CCPE Diversified	15.5	12.3	9.5	9.6	8.7	2.0
CDA Balanced	14.8	12.4	9.5	10.1	9.2	2.6
CIBC Balanced	11.5	9.8	6.5	7.6	-	
Clean Environment Balanced	14.1	11.8	7.4	-	-	
Concorde Equilibre	14.9	-	-	-	-	1.4
Cornerstone Balanced	17.2	11.9	9.1	9.3	6.3	
CT Everest Balanced	11.9	10.6	7.0	10.0	-	
Desjardins Diversified	13.8	11.8	9.3	11.1	-	1.8
Desjardins Equilibre	12.0	10.3	8.3	10.3	7.9	1.8
Dolphin Income	17.3	12.4	9.3	10.5	10.4	
Elliott & Page Balanced	15.3	11.3	9.7	13.5	-	8.3
Empire Balanced	12.9	11.4	8.3	9.4	-	3.8
Ethical Balanced	10.3	12.2	8.4	8.7	-	
Ficadre Equilibre	14.4	13.4	10.2	9.6	7.2	
Fonds Professional Gth Inc	9.7	-	-	-	-	
Fonds Professionals Bal	11.3	10.9	7.7	9.1	9.0	
General Trust Balanced	12.9	11.1	8.0	9.0	-	1.1
Global Strategy Income Pls	21.8	14.9	11.0	-	-	4.5
Great-West Life Divers (G) A	11.4	9.2	6.5	8.6	-	8.5
Great-West Life Eqty Bnd (G) A	13.6	9.7	6.9	10.0	-	8.5
Green Line Balanced Growth	19.7	15.2	9.5	9.1	-	4.8
Green Line Balanced Income	13.9	11.0	7.8	8.1	-	8.7
Greystone Managed Wealth	7.2	7.1	-	-	-	
Guardian Canadian Bal A	10.8	9.4	7.9	9.6	9.9	10.3
Hongkong Bank Balanced	17.2	11.5	8.8	12.2	-	4.0
HRL Balanced	11.9	8.4	6.7	6.6	7.5	0.3
ICM Balanced	13.4	11.4	8.8	11.3	-	8.8
Ideal Balanced	12.4	12.5	9.6	10.4	-	9.7
Imperial Gth Diversified	12.2	10.3	8.2	9.1	-	1.8
Industrial Alliance Diversified	11.7	11.1	9.7	10.8	-	9.8

Fund	1 Year	2 Year	3 Year	5 Year	10 Year	Manager Tenure (Years)
Industrial Alliance Ecoflex D	11.1	10.5,	9.1	-	-	3.8
Industrial Balanced	10.6	8.8	7.4	9.6	-	5.8
Industrial Income	11.1	11.7	7.3	9.7	9.7	7.8
InvesNat Retirement Bal	12.4	11.3	8.0	9.3	-	1.4
Investors Income Plus Port	11.1	10.0	7.0	7.8	-	7.7
Investors Mutual	14.2	9.2	9.0	10.9	9.3	0.8
Investors Retire Plus Port	12.2	9.3	8.0	9.0	-	7.7
Ivy Growth & Income	19.3	16.8	11.1	-	-	4.0
Jones Heward Cdn Balanced	9.5	8.8	5.2	9.9	7.7	
Laurentian Cdn Balanced	11.2	9.2	7.1	7.8	-	2.0
Leith Wheeler Balanced	12.3	10.5	8.8	11.1	-	
London Life Diversified	14.3	10.6	8.4	10.5	-	3.1
Lotus Group Balanced	15.0	10.3	6.4	10.4	7.8	7.8
Manulife Vistafd 1 Divers	8.3	8.3	6.6	8.7	8.2	
Manulife Vistafd 2 Divers	7.5	7.5	5.8	7.9	7.4	
Maritime Life Balanced	14.0	11.8	9.1	9.3	8.3	1.8
Mawer Canadian Div Invest	12.7	11.7	8.5	9.7	-	8.8
Mawer Cdn Balanced RSP	12.5	11.7	8.6	10.0	-	8.7
Maxxum Canadian Balanced	15.2	13.6	8.3	12.1	-	4.4
McDonald Canada Plus	11.9	7.9	-	-	-	
Mclean Budden Balanced	18.6	15.2	9.8	11.2	-	
McLean Budden Pooled Bal	19.5	16.0	11.3	-	-	
MD Balanced	13.5	12.2	10.1	-	-	4.1
Metlife Mvp Balanced	9.4	8.3	6.1	7.3	-	
Millennium Diversified	16.5	12.1	-	-	-	2.8
Mutual Diversifund 40	14.5	12.4	9.2	9.4	7.7	3.8
Mutual Premier Diversified	15.8	12.2	-	-	-	3.8
NAL Balanced Growth	16.5	-	-	-	-	
NAL Canadian Diversified	17.6	13.5	10.4	10.8	-	
National Balanced	14.8	12.3	9.1	-	-	3.0
National Trust Balanced	13.8	12.0	8.4	10.0	-	6.4
NN Balanced	15.7	12.7	9.7	10.4	-	3.9
O.I.Q. Ferique Equilibre	13.2	12.1	10.2	10.5	10.2	
OHA Balanced	18.1	13.4	9.2	-	-	2.3
Optimum Equilibre	11.4	13.0	8.6	10.3	8.7	10.4
OTGIF Balanced	14.4	11.6	9.0	10.4	9.3	10.8
PH & N Balance Pension Tr	17.5	14.1	11.4	12.2	-	8.1
PH & N Balanced	16.2	13.2	11.0	11.7	-	5.2
Royal Balanced	12.2	9.9	8.1	11.1	-	
Royal Life Balanced	12.8	11.2	8.4	9.5	-	6.8
Royal Trust Adv Balanced	11.5	10.1	7.7	9.5	-	
Royal Trust Adv Growth	12.8	10.1	7.8	9.6	-	
Royal Trust Adv Income	11.0	10.2	7.4	9.1	-	
Saxon Balanced	17.8	16.6	11.9	15.7	6.7	5.8
Sceptre Balanced Growth	25.4	17.6	13.8	13.1	10.8	3.6
Scotia Excelsior Balanced	13.2	11.3	8.7	9.9	-	
Spectrum United Cdn Port	15.6	13.7	10.0	12.4	-	
Spectrum United Diversified	12.7	10.5	7.1	8.5	-	

Fund	1 Year	2 Year	3 Year	5 Year	10 Year	Manager Tenure (Years)
SSQ - Equilibre	15.9	13.9	9.7	-	-	1.4
Standard Life Balanced	14.9	13.2	9.2	-	-	
Templeton Balanced	11.9	9.4	9.5	10.1	-	0.8
Trans-Canada Pension	19.2	5.8	4.5	8.7	7.0	7.4
Transamerica B.I.G.	11.2	10.3	8.5	9.9	9.0	
Transamerica Growsafe Bal	11.8	9.6	-	-	-	
Trimark Income Growth	11.7	11.8	10.5	13.1	-	
Trimark Select Balanced	12.1	11.0	10.3	12.3	-	1.8
Trust Pret et Revenu retra	15.3	14.5	10.3	11.6	9.5	1.4
Westbury Cdn Life Balanced	13.9	11.3	9.9	8.3	-	5.4

International Balanced Funds

Fund	1 Year	2 Year	3 Year	5 Year	10 Year	Manager Tenure (Years)
Atlas American Advan Value	17.6	-	-	-	-	2.0
Azura Balanced Pooled	9.5	-	-	-	-	1.3
Beutel Goodman Private Bal	14.1	13.0	10.5	12.6	-	7.0
BPI Global Balanced RSP	5.4	4.8	6.6	11.5	-	0.3
BPI North American Bal RSP	6.1	8.6	6.9	-	-	2.5
C.I. International Bal	10.6	-	-	-	-	2.0
C.I. Intl. Balanced RSP	9.4	-	-	-	-	2.0
Caldwell Securities Int'l	11.8	8.4	12.1	-	-	4.8
Elliott & Page Global Bal	7.6	8.7	-	-	-	2.3
Fidelity Asset Manager	12.8	8.5	6.3	-	-	0.6
Global Strategy World Bal	7.8	-	-	-	-	1.8
GT Global Growth & Income	11.6	-	-	-	-	2.0
Guardian Intl. Balanced A	13.1	8.6	4.7	-	-	3.1
Horizons I Multi-Asset	6.7	5.5	-	-	-	
Investors Growth Plus Port	12.5	11.6	8.9	11.0	-	7.7
Laurentian Global Balanced	7.8	8.0	5.3	9.0	-	2.8
Spectrum Utd Global Divers	10.6	11.9	7.8	10.7	-	
Templeton Global Balanced	11.9	-	-	-	-	0.8
Templeton Int'l Balanced	12.1	-	-	-	-	2.0
Transamerica Growsafe Int'l	12.2	9.1	-	-	-	
Universal World Bal RRSP	14.1	10.5	-	-	-	2.7
Zweig Global Managed Asset	9.6	-	-	-	-	1.3

Asset Allocation Funds

Fund	1 Year	2 Year	3 Year	5 Year	10 Year	Manager Tenure (Years)
20/20 Amer Tac Asset Alloc	9.7	15.6	8.3	13.4	-	0.3
20/20 Cdn Tac Asset Alloc	11.7	9.1	7.9	8.7	-	0.3
20/20 European Asset Alloc	9.7	8.6	6.3	-	-	0.7
20/20 World	6.6	0.4	4.1	10.1	-	0.3
ADMAX Asset Allocation	10.9	7.1	6.7	-	-	4.3
Altamira Global Diversifie	17.0	10.1	9.4	10.5	3.0	
Apex Balanced Allocation	10.3	9.4	-	-	-	1.3
Desjardins Divers Audaciou	11.8	-	-	-	-	1.8
Desjardins Divers Moderate	10.7	-	-	-	-	1.8
Desjardins Divers Secure	7.6	-	-	-	-	1.8
Dynamic Global Partners	12.3	10.2	-	-	-	2.4
Dynamic Partners	9.8	8.4	8.4	14.8	-	1.8
Dynamic Team	16.1	10.4	8.5	13.5	9.7	5.8

Fund	1 Year	2 Year	3 Year	5 Year	10 Year	Manager Tenure (Years)
Empire Asset Allocation	12.4	9.5	-	-	-	2.4
Equitable Life Asset Alloc	12.2	-	-	-	-	
Fidelity Cdn Asset Alloc	18.5	-	-	-	-	1.8
First Canadian Asset Alloc	13.3	11.6	7.2	8.2	-	
Investors Asset Allocation	15.3	12.8	-	-	-	2.8
Protected American	3.0	3.7	2.2	7.9	-	10.8
Scotia Excelsior Total Return	11.0	10.6	9.4	12.0	-	
Spectrum United Asset Alloc	12.0	9.6	7.1	-	-	
Talvest Canadian Asset All	10.0	10.3	7.6	8.4	8.7	10.8
Talvest Global Asset Alloc	6.5	4.1	5.1	10.2	-	
Templeton Cdn Asset Alloc	12.6	-	-	-	-	0.8
Universal World Asst Alloc	2.4	3.3	-	-	-	2.9

Canadian Money Market Funds

Fund	1 Year	2 Year	3 Year	5 Year	10 Year	Manager Tenure (Years)
C.I. Short-Term Sector	2.6	3.0	2.8	3.1	-	
20/20 Money Market	5.3	5.6	5.2	5.6	-	
Acadia Money Market	4.5	-	-	-	-	1.8
ADMAX Cash Performance	4.3	4.8	4.4	-	-	4.0
AGF Money Market Acct A	4.5	5.2	4.8	5.1	7.6	12.8
AGF Money Market Acct B	3.9	-	-	-	-	2.0
AGF Money Market Acct C	4.5	-	-	-	-	2.0
AIC Money Market	4.3	5.0	-	-	-	
AMI Private Cap Money Mkt.	5.3	5.8	5.3	5.7	-	8.8
Apex Money Market	4.5	5.3	-	-	-	
Atlas Canadian Money Mkt	4.6	5.3	4.9	5.2	7.5	11.8
Atlas Canadian T-Bill	4.4	5.0	4.6	4.9	-	
Batirente Sec Marche Monet	4.3	5.1	4.8	5.4	-	8.8
Beutel Goodman Money Mkt	5.3	5.9	5.5	6.1	-	1.8
Bissett Money Market	5.8	6.2	5.7	5.9	-	3.2
BNP (Canada) Cdn Money Mkt	4.7	5.2	4.8	5.0	-	
BPI T-Bill	5.4	5.8	5.2	5.5	7.8	2.3
C.I. Money Market	5.0	5.7	5.3	5.6	-	6.0
Canada Life Money Market	4.6	5.1	4.7	5.0	7.1	
Capstone Cash Management	5.0	5.9	5.5	5.9	-	
CCPE Money Market	5.3	-	-	-	-	
CDA Money Market	5.4	6.0	5.6	5.9	7.9	23.9
CIBC Canadian T-Bill	4.4	5.0	4.5	4.7	-	
CIBC Money Market	4.4	5.1	4.6	4.8	-	
CIBC Premium Cdn T-Bill	4.9	5.6	5.2	5.4	-	
Colonia Life Money Market	4.7	5.6	4.9	-	-	
Concorde Monetaire	4.6	5.3	5.0	-	-	1.8
Cornerstone Gov't Money	4.4	5.2	4.9	5.1	-	4.8
CT Everest Money Market	4.4	5.0	4.6	4.9	-	
Desjardins Marche Monetaire	4.3	5.0	4.6	5.0	-	7.8
Dynamic Money Market	4.2	5.3	4.9	5.2	7.4	5.8
Elliott & Page Money	4.9	5.6	5.3	5.7	8.1	12.3
Elliott & Page T-Bill	3.6	4.0	-	-	-	2.5
Empire Money Market	4.0	4.7	4.3	4.7	-	7.7

Fund	1 Year	2 Year	3 Year	5 Year	10 Year	Manager Tenure (Years)
Equitable Life Money Mkt	4.0	-	-	-	-	
Ethical Money Market	4.6	5.1	4.7	5.1	7.6	
Ficadre Monetaire	4.9	5.2	4.8	5.3	-	
Fidelity Cdn Short-Term Asset	4.2	4.9	4.5	4.8	-	5.8
First Canadian Money Mkt	4.6	5.2	4.8	5.2	-	
First Canadian T-Bill	4.6	5.2	4.8	-	-	
Fonds Professionals S-Trem	6.2	6.6	6.0	6.4	-	
GBC Money Market	4.6	5.3	5.0	5.4	-	
General Trust Money Market	4.6	5.3	4.9	5.4	-	1.9
Global Strategy Money Mkt	4.4	5.2	4.9	5.3	-	
Great-West Life M Mkt (G) A	3.7	4.5	4.1	4.5	7.0	5.8
Green Line Canadian T-Bill	4.9	5.5	5.0	-	-	8.7
Green Line Cdn Money Mkt	5.0	5.6	5.2	5.6	-	8.7
Guardian Cdn Money Mkt A	4.5	5.2	4.9	5.2	7.8	9.7
Hongkong Bank Money Market	4.9	5.5	4.9	5.0	-	7.8
HRL Instant $$	5.3	5.9	5.4	5.6	-	0.3
ICM Short Term Investment	6.0	6.6	6.2	-	-	4.1
Ideal Money Market	5.6	6.3	-	-	-	3.0
Imperial Gth Money Market	3.8	4.6	4.2	4.6	-	7.8
Industrial Alliance Ecoflex M	4.2	4.7	-	-	-	5.2
Industrial Alliance Money Mkt	4.2	4.7	4.2	4.5	-	5.1
Industrial Cash Management	4.9	5.7	5.3	5.6	7.8	12.1
Industrial Short-Term	4.2	4.9	4.4	4.6	-	5.8
InvesNat Corp Cash Mgmt	5.3	-	-	-	-	1.8
InvesNat Money Market	4.7	5.3	4.8	5.2	-	1.9
InvesNat T-Bill Plus	5.0	5.6	5.1	5.4	-	1.9
Investors Money Market	4.5	5.3	4.9	5.1	7.4	11.4
Jones Heward Money Market	4.9	5.4	-	-	-	0.3
Laurentian Money Market	4.4	5.1	4.7	5.0	7.5	7.8
Leith Wheeler Money Market	4.9	5.5	-	-	-	
London Life Money Market	5.1	5.6	5.1	5.8	-	
Lotus Group Income	5.1	5.6	5.2	5.5	-	13.8
Manulife Cabot Money Mkt	4.1	5.1	-	-	-	
Manulife Vistafd 1 S-T Sec	5.2	5.7	5.2	5.3	7.6	
Manulife Vistafd 2 S-T Sec	4.4	5.0	4.4	4.5	6.8	
Maritime Life Money Market	3.9	4.2	3.7	4.6	6.8	14.8
Mawer Canadian Money Mkt	5.0	5.5	5.0	5.3	-	3.1
Maxxum Money Market	5.3	5.8	5.4	5.8	-	3.8
Mclean Budden Money Mkt	5.0	5.6	5.1	5.3	-	
MD Money	5.3	5.9	5.4	5.6	7.5	4.8
Metlife Mvp Money Market	4.6	5.0	4.4	4.5	-	
Mutual Money Market	4.5	5.3	4.9	5.2	7.2	3.8
NAL-Canadian Money Market	4.6	5.0	4.4	5.0	-	
National Money Market	3.9	4.7	4.2	-	-	
National Trust Money Mkt	4.7	5.2	4.7	5.0	-	6.4
NN Money Market	5.1	5.8	5.3	5.6	-	6.4
NN T-Bill	4.6	4.9	4.3	4.9	-	9.8

Fund	1 Year	2 Year	3 Year	5 Year	10 Year	Manager Tenure (Years)
O.I.Q. Ferique Revenu	5.6	6.2	5.8	6.2	8.1	
OHA Short Term	4.9	5.5	5.1	5.6	-	5.8
Optimum Epargne	4.3	5.3	5.0	5.6	7.8	10.3
OTGIF Fixed Value	5.6	6.1	5.6	6.6	8.1	21.8
PH & N Canadian Money Mkt	4.9	5.7	5.3	5.7	7.9	9.4
Pret Et Revenu Money Mkt	4.7	5.3	4.9	5.3	-	1.4
Pursuit Money Market	5.5	5.9	5.5	6.0	-	8.7
Royal Life Money Market	5.9	6.1	5.7	-	-	
Royal Trust Cdn Money Mkt	4.3	5.0	4.5	4.9	-	
Royal Trust Cdn T-Bill	4.5	4.9	4.3	-	-	
Royfund Canadian Money Mkt	4.3	5.0	4.5	5.0	-	
Royfund Canadian T-Bill	4.6	5.3	4.8	5.3	-	5.6
Sceptre Money Market	5.3	5.7	5.3	5.5	-	0.8
Scotia Excelsior Money Market	4.6	5.3	4.8	5.1	-	
Scotia Excelsior Premium T-Bill	5.0	5.7	5.2	-	-	
Scotia Excelsior T-Bill	4.5	5.3	4.9	-	-	
Spectrum United Cdn T-Bill	4.6	5.2	4.8	5.1	-	0.8
Spectrum United Savings	4.6	5.3	4.9	5.2	-	
SSQ - Marche Monetaire	6.1	6.5	-	-	-	2.7
Standard Life Money Market	5.5	5.8	5.2	-	-	
Talvest Money	5.3	5.9	5.5	5.8	7.7	10.6
Templeton T-Bill	4.6	5.3	4.9	5.2	-	7.8
Trans-Canada Money Market	5.3	5.7	5.5	5.6	6.4	6.8
Transamerica Growsafe MMF	4.2	4.1	-	-	-	
Trimark Interest	4.7	5.5	5.0	5.4	-	3.8
Westbury Cdn Life C	5.1	5.8	5.6	5.4	-	9.8

U.S. & International Money Market Funds

Fund	1 Year	2 Year	3 Year	5 Year	10 Year	Manager Tenure (Years)
AGF Int'l Group S-T Income A	3.4	-	-	-	-	2.0
AGF Int'l Group S-T Income B	2.8	-	-	-	-	2.0
AGF Int'l Group S-T Income C	2.9	-	-	-	-	2.0
AGF US$ Money Mkt Acct	4.6	4.7	4.1	3.8	-	5.8
Altamira S-T Global Income	4.7	2.5	3.5	7.6	-	2.8
Atlas Amer Money Market	4.5	4.6	4.0	3.5	-	
C.I. US Money Market	4.9	-	-	-	-	1.7
CIBC US$ Money Market	4.3	4.5	3.9	3.5	-	
Fidelity US Money Market	4.3	-	-	-	-	1.9
Green Line US Money Market	4.4	4.5	3.9	3.5	-	8.7
Guardian US Money Market A	4.5	4.7	4.1	3.7	5.8	9.7
InvesNat US Money Market	4.4	4.4	3.8	3.4	-	1.9
PH & N $US Money Market	5.1	5.2	4.6	4.1	-	6.0
Royal Trust $US Money Mkt	4.4	4.6	3.9	3.4	-	
Royfund US Money Market	4.4	4.5	3.9	3.4	-	
Spectrum Utd US$ Money Mkt	4.2	4.6	4.2	3.4	-	0.8
Universal US Money Market	3.8	3.9	-	-	-	2.1

Fund	1 Year	2 Year	3 Year	5 Year	10 Year	Manager Tenure (Years)
Real Estate Funds						
Dynamic Real Estate Equity	43.4	-	-	-	-	1.4
Investors Real Property	4.3	4.4	3.0	1.4	4.9	1.8
Royal Lepage Commercial	-0.9	0.8	2.5	0.3	-	

Index